Roman Cities

Les villes romaines
by Pierre Grimal
Translated and Edited by
G. Michael Woloch

Together with a
Descriptive Catalogue
of Roman Cities
by G. Michael Woloch

The University of Wisconsin Press

Published 1983

The University of Wisconsin Press
114 North Murray Street
Madison, Wisconsin 53715

The University of Wisconsin Press, Ltd.
1 Gower Street
London WC1E 6HA, England

Les villes romaines by Pierre Grimal copyright © 1954
Presses Universitaires de France

First Printing

Printed in the United States of America

For LC CIP information see the colophon

ISBN 0-299-08930-4 cloth
ISBN 0-299-08934-7 paper

Contents

Part II

Figures and Maps

Figures

Maps

Preface

"Roman cities" can be defined in several different ways, but perhaps the most useful is "cities which existed within the boundaries of the Roman Empire." Needing a limit in time as well as in area, we might add "and which were founded before the beginning of the Late Roman period, A.D. 284." This definition includes many cities besides Rome itself and those founded by people with Roman citizenship. It even includes cities which had been abandoned (or nearly so) by the time the Roman Empire, as a system of government, began, a date which we might set at 31 B.C. The importance of these abandoned cities arises from the fact that many of the cities founded by Roman citizens (or by Italic peoples related to the original Romans) were influenced in their urban planning by the Greeks and the Etruscans. But the sites of Roman cities were so well chosen that most of them survive, and some indeed flourish, at the present time.

Interested in the historical and archaeological study of these cities, I devised and, in 1973, began teaching a course on Roman cities at McGill University. I soon discovered that courses on this subject or similar ones were taught at other universities but that the only book available was *Les villes romaines* by Pierre Grimal, professor of Latin literature at the Sorbonne in Paris. It is number 657 in the "Que sais-je" series; the fourth edition was published in 1971 and the fifth in 1977.

In 1974, I decided to translate this book into English for use in my course and was generously granted permission to do so by the publisher, Presses Universitaires de France (Paris). It occurred to me that his book would, for several reasons, also be of interest to a much larger public: the subject matter attracts a varied group of readers. *Les villes romaines* is an excellent brief introduction to the topic, characteristic of the "Que sais-je" series (which now contains nearly 2,000 volumes by recognized scholars in various branches of human knowledge). And I found Grimal's style exceptionally readable and informative. Speaking of a much longer book which has been translated into English, Grimal's *The Civilization of Rome* (New York 1963), Raymond Bloch said in its preface, "What strikes me personally is the ease with which Pierre Grimal has been able to make use of an immense store of information (of whose underlying presence one is constantly aware while reading the text) to create a general picture that is at once just, exact, and rich in nuances." I think that the same holds true for his book on Roman cities.

It must be indicated that with so many cities to choose from, Grimal limited his book to the western half of the Roman Empire, including Tripolitania, Italy, and the Rhine Valley. This would have been a practical decision in any case, but it was made necessary because of the restricted size of books in the "Que sais-je" series.

Having completed the translation, I obtained a sabbatical leave for the academic year 1977-1978. I had already felt that Grimal's short book would be made still more useful if I were to keep it as a base and to add my own work to it. The first draft of the various sections of this volume was written during that sabbatical year.

The first section of my part is the notes, in which I search out Grimal's many sources and supplement them. The reader, I believe, will find something of value in these notes, which amplify Grimal's discussions and sometimes bring them up to date. My notes, which follow Grimal's text, are numbered serially within his introduction and each of his four chapters. His own notes are indicated by asterisks and come at the bottom of the pages in his text; I recommend them to researchers and do not repeat their contents later. If the reader desires more information on a city mentioned by Grimal, he should also look it up in my next section, the *Descriptive Catalogue*. I must emphasize that I wrote all my notes, and indeed my entire addition to his book, in a spirit of esteem for M. Grimal's views and conclusions.

Next in this volume comes my *Descriptive Catalogue of Roman Cities*. This began as an index to my translation of *Les villes romaines* and still retains Grimal's geographical limits. We find that if we omit a small number of cities in France that occur only in lists, he mentioned seventy-eight cities. They constitute a judicious selection from the many that could have been chosen, and I have written an article on each of them. These seventy-eight cities, however, seemed to call for the addition of a limited number of cities related to them in various but close ways. These related cities are not described separately but are included in one of the seventy-eight articles. Where they are in fact discussed is indicated by an alphabetical entry. I have designated them with the sign +, and the result is that there are about one hundred cities in the *Catalogue*.

I have used the modern name in English for cities, if there is one. If not, the name in the official local language is employed. For North Africa, transliterations from the Arabic are controversial, and I have followed the spellings now used by the National Geographic Society (Washington, D.C.).

Cities which have a modern name and head articles are written in small capital letters throughout this volume (e.g. LONDON, PARIS). Rome is an exception. Ancient names of cities and Greek and Latin words in general are italicized. Sometimes ancient city-names head articles *(Pompeii, Volubilis)*. Contrary to scholarly practice, the catalogue is arranged by the modern names to make it easier to use for the majority of readers, but I have included reference-entries for those ancient names which differ very much from the present ones. At the top of the article on each city, the full ancient name is stated, just after the modern name. My index to Grimal's text remains, and it follows the city names at the top of each article. Normally, what Grimal has said is not repeated; these points can be found where he wrote them, as indicated by the index.

In the articles, I have endeavored to supplement with social,

economic, and historical background what is in my notes and
what Grimal has said about each city. Furthermore,
architecture, archaeology, planning, and geography all play their
roles. Although the emphasis is up to A.D. 565, the end of the
Late Roman period, as a rule I outline what happened up to
the present. (I recommend that *The Princeton Encyclopedia
of Classical Sites [PECS]* also be consulted for the dates of
individual ancient structures, as well as for other archaeological
questions.)

Each article in the present work is provided with good
working bibliographies for the cities mentioned. I have also
added bibliographies for the appropriate frontier regions under
WROXETER, MAINZ, *Lambaesis* and *Volubilis* (for Britain, the
Rhine Valley, Algeria and Morocco); two Alpine districts which
had troops in them are treated under FREJUS and TURIN. In
addition, there are bibliographies for some ancient documents
which seem to be of historical interest for particular cities.
The reader should not be daunted by the bibliographies; they
can be disregarded. But if one wishes to use the catalogue as
a research tool, one will look at the bibliography for the city
being studied, bibliographies for cities geographically near it
and the Master Bibliography below, as well as the pertinent
notes and glossary entries. One will find publications in English
about our cities, even those not in Britain. When a work was
originally not in English but was translated, I have usually
cited the English version instead or, as a second choice, the
French. This was also done to make the catalogue easier to
use. As a further aid, the most useful or definitive works on
particular cities are indicated with an asterisk, but this has
been done sparingly.

Frequently cited titles of books and a few articles are
abbreviated or shortened, and these formulations are explained
in the Master Bibliography. Sometimes, however, a book title
or the name of a periodical is abbreviated in just one article,
but then the full name can easily be found above it in the
article's bibliographies. I have usually written out the names
of journals. A few quite important works containing articles by
different authors are abbreviated and cited in the text without
the names of the editors (e.g. *PECS* and *ESAR*), but the

abbreviations and the full references are listed in the Master Bibliography. The volume number of *ESAR* is not given in the text but is mentioned in the article's bibliographies. In individual bibliographies, works by the same author are listed in alphabetical order, with the exception that articles by one author in the same journal are listed chronologically.

In this volume, after my *Descriptive Catalogue* come two bibliographies, which I assembled: the Master Bibliography and a List of Ancient Sources. The latter contains a short list of ancient authors' names and recent compilations of ancient sources; all of these are explained. In the Master Bibliography, we find books recommended for the topics discussed and explanations of the titles abbreviated in this volume. My systems for choosing English versions of books and for using asterisks are the same in the Master Bibliography as in the individual bibliographies.

The final section of this volume is the Glossary. Every technical, historical, or Latin term mentioned above it is explained. There are also a number of ethnological terms (such as Samnites and Ostrogoths), as well as some comparative groupings (e.g., cities [Roman], comparison in area). The Glossary contains bibliographical references for further study. I have included the List of Ancient Sources and the Glossary with the intention that the present volume may be read with profit by the nonspecialist as well as the scholar.

One will perceive that this is a book for readers on all levels, from the beginner to the researcher in a number of fields. Although it is essentially a synthesis of archaeology and history, it will also be of use for reference and study in geography, urban studies, and the social sciences. Besides students in university and college courses (and scholars), I have in mind as readers members of the general public, be they educated travelers, armchair archaeologists or history buffs.

I hope that this joining of Pierre Grimal's clear and felicitous survey of Roman cities with my development of his work will prove to be a coherent and useful whole. Together the two parts should compose a successful guide to the Roman city and a testimony to its continuing vitality.

Acknowledgments

Permission to reproduce figures in this volume was granted by Thames and Hudson, Ltd. (London), J. Burdy (Lyons), Holle Bild-Archiv (Baden-Baden), A. Mondadori, S.p.A. (Milan), and Encyclopaedia Britannica, Inc. (Chicago). I should like to thank Professor E. T. Salmon (Hamilton, Ontario) for his help in negotiating with Thames and Hudson. The Columbia University Press allowed me to reproduce the Roman Charter of *Urso*, included below under OSUNA. Permission to translate *Les villes romaines* by Pierre Grimal and to use my translation in this volume was granted by Presses Universitaires de France. Mr. Thompson Webb, director of the University of Wisconsin Press, was kind enough to represent me in the later stage of the negotiations with P.U.F. I am indebted to Professor Grimal for his encouragement after he saw my translation and my part of this book.

A number of people at McGill University helped to make this book possible. Unfortunately, it is not possible to mention all of them here. The McGill University Book Store published the small experimental edition. During several years, the text was typed at the university's Computing Centre, which provided a subsidy. The Faculty of Graduate Studies and Research awarded me a grant for proofreading. For help in obtaining financial assistance for a sabbatical leave in 1977-1978, I should like to thank the then Dean of the Faculty of Arts, Robert Vogel, and the Chairman of the Department of Classics at that time, G. L. Snider, Jr. Colleagues in the Department of Classics gave useful advice, and the students

who took my courses on Roman cities and Roman history offered
many good suggestions.

I should like to thank J. Launay and G. M. de Durand (both
of Montreal) for aid with a few questions about the translation.
Those whose names follow answered questions about my work:
H. Thompson (Princeton, New Jersey), P. MacKendrick
(Madison, Wisconsin), E. M. Wightman (Hamilton, Ontario),
R. Calvert (Sackville, New Brunswick), A. T. Hodge (Ottawa),
C. W. Dearden (Wellington, New Zealand), K.-V. Decker
(Mainz), A. Hurst and B. Grange (Geneva), P. Roesch and R.
Lauxerois (Lyons), R. Chevallier, M. Fleury, F. Brun, and L.
Kahil (all of Paris). I am most grateful to J. E. Stambaugh
(Williamstown, Massachusetts) for sending me a copy of his as
yet unpublished source-book on Greek and Roman cities and
to M. Leglay (Paris), who has sent me offprints over the years.

The following were kind enough to read through the
manuscript and to offer suggestions and criticisms: the late J.
H. Oliver (Baltimore), L. Richardson, Jr. (Rome), E. W. Gray
(Oxford), P. MacKendrick, E. T. Salmon, M. Leglay, and M.
Hammond (Cambridge, Massachusetts), as well as the
reviewers for the University of Wisconsin Press. Of course
those listed are in no way responsible for any of my mistakes.

Three of those mentioned in the preceding paragraph taught
me, and I should like to add that the inspiration of my teachers
at Western Reserve Academy, where my interest in classics
was first wakened, and at Yale, Oxford, and Johns Hopkins
Universities has not been forgotten.

The Fondation Hardt made it possible for me to spend two
weeks of study at its villa near Geneva in March 1978, and
Professor Paul Roesch arranged for my wife and me to spend
the six previous weeks in Lyons. My wife, Mary C. Moffat,
has helped me in countless ways to work on this book, and I
should like to dedicate my part of it to her. To those named
above, and more, my sincere thanks are due.

G. Michael Woloch
Montreal
September 27, 1981

Part I
Les villes romaines
by Pierre Grimal

Introduction

It was the Romans who, in the western provinces of their Empire, founded the first cities. While in the East flourishing or famous cities had existed for a long time before the Roman conquest, such was not the case in Gaul, in Britain, on the banks of the Rhine, in Spain, and in most of North Africa. To be sure, the Celtic or Iberian inhabitants had many centers of settlement, and the remains have been found and studied in our day. These were places of refuge, usually located on high sites and protected by walls, most often made of unmortared stone. Inside the enclosure, as is today seen at *Alesia* (ALISE-STE.-REINE, not far from Dijon), huts, grouped in neighborhoods, bordered large open areas, where markets and perhaps political assemblies were held; but these clusters, where homes seem to have been for the most part located according to no plan, did not constitute cities worthy of that name. The Romans introduced and imposed new forms, which were to be characteristic of human settlements for centuries.

This evolution has become evident, for example, with discoveries made during the exploration of the Plateau of ENSERUNE, half-way between NARBONNE and MONTPELLIER. There, above the well-cultivated plain, lay a native city, whose slow development we may follow. It took place under the distant influence of Hellenic models, brought in by merchants from Greek colonies located along the coast from MARSEILLES to AMPURIAS, and these results occurred elsewhere, for example at *Glanum* (just south of ST.-REMY-DE-PROVENCE). But when, at the end of the second century B.C., the city of NARBONNE

3

(Narbo Martius) was founded by the Romans, the old *oppidum* or town was abandoned and the new city benefited.[1] It is possible that this abandonment had been ordered by the Romans, who were unwilling to allow, near the road which secured communications with a restive Spain, the menace of a lofty city to exist in the hands of an insufficiently pacified populace. It is certain, in any case, that the attraction of Narbonne played a role in this matter. The Roman city offered not only a new habitat but also ideas which were destined to overturn the old-fashioned way of life, as well as the political and social organization of the entire area.

The military strength of the peoples conquered by the Romans was indeed broken by the legions, while it was the Roman city which—at least in the western provinces—assured the Romanization of the vanquished territory. The Romans were not mistaken about this point, and they used their city planning as a powerful political tool. Tacitus wrote for the Caledonian chieftain Calgacus (A.D. 83/84) a violent attack on the urban life which profoundly changed the customs of his fellow Britons and, he said, gradually accustomed them to slavery. But it was not only the attractions of luxury, of baths, of a better life, and of idleness in the shadow of the conquerors which could have had that power.[2] The Roman city represented not only a certain number of material conveniences; it was above all the stronghold of a cultural, religious, social, and political system which formed the very structure of Roman civilization.

For a Roman indeed, as it was elsewhere for a Greek, every human cluster of settlement was not a city. This was not formed by the simple juxtaposition of dwellings for individuals or for families. It truly came about only to the extent that its inhabitants succeeded in creating there the means for a collective life: temples, meeting-halls, official buildings of all kinds, and public fountains where one comes to draw the water necessary for life and for family worship. Finally, the very ground of the city was consecrated to the gods and formed a sacred place, irreplaceable and unchangeable.

In this respect, Roman cities—and, especially, those which were founded by citizens taken from Rome and which are called colonies—were reflections of Rome. They reproduced as precisely as possible the institutions, monuments, and cults of the mother city, which remained the *Urbs*, the City *par excellence*, and throughout the Empire, deep in the farthest provinces, were found the essential elements of the capital.

The City of Rome was bounded by a sacred frontier—which was called the *pomerium* (q.v.)—and its territory was protected by its own divinities and rites. Even at the time when the continual increase of the population had extended the actual settlement well beyond the ancient *pomerium*, the City did not have the same religious and administrative status as the surrounding countryside. It kept an unchallenged first place, and from it came all legal authority. Every year, for example, the consuls, when entering office, had to climb to the Capitol (q.v.), where they swore an oath to Jupiter, the ruling god of the City. If that ceremony did not take place, they did not formally hold their authority. And that authority was different, depending on whether they used it inside or outside the city. Consular power was in principle absolute inside the urban boundary, while, outside of it, this power was limited by very exact constitutional rules. Returning from his wars, a victorious general was forbidden to cross the *pomerium* as long as he wanted to remain an *imperator*, and he waited, for example, for the Senate to vote him the honors of a triumph. If, even by mistake, he placed a foot inside the *pomerium*, he lost his rank and could no longer aspire to a triumph.

These prescripts, and others like them, show that the concept of a city was by nature essentially religious and spiritual. Other considerations—material, architectural, strategic, and economic—only followed. Before being a place of refuge or pleasure, the Roman city was a religious center and, something quite similar, a judicial center. The reason for planting colonies in the conquered provinces was to create footholds inside the annexed territory, and this aim was realized. The *pagani* (q.v.), the villagers, the peasants, and all who were dispersed and neither lived nor thought according to Roman ways—these were ignored.

Not all the cities planted in the Empire were colonies; that

is to say not all of them were originally settled by Roman
citizens. Many, especially in the East and in Italy itself, existed
before the conquest, and Rome had only to impose its authority
on the previous political structure. Each of the conquered cities
was tied to Rome by a treaty which gave it a certain status.
Most often, the vanquished cities kept a great autonomy for
all their local affairs and continued to have their traditional
political assemblies. The same held true for native cities which,
in the West, were founded even after the conquest, without
importing Roman citizens. But, very rapidly, these cities tended
to model themselves on the colonies and to borrow their
institutions. There was soon in the Empire no city which did
not have its Senate (which was called the *ordo* of the decurions
[q.v.]), its body for popular elections and its magistrates, who
were divided into colleges and who corresponded to the consuls
and aediles (q.v.) of Rome. Thus, each province was gradually
composed of a mosaic of cities, which were its political units.
Each city was composed of both the city proper, which was
the administrative center, and around that a rather large
territorium (q.v.), which was under its control. The city's
inhabitants had a rank greater than those in the country, and
it was comparable to that which Roman citizens held, in
comparison with the inhabitants of the provinces. It is this
rigid parallelism between Rome and the provincial cities which
is the basis for the entire history of the Roman cities. Urban
planning was not, then, a theoretical or purely technical art.
Its aim was to give a material body to that essentially abstract
and spiritual reality which was the City.

During the past hundred years—and a bit more—scientific
archaeology has come into being. With its aid, our knowledge
of Roman cities has increased and become exact to a degree
which had never been expected. No year passes without new
discoveries adding brush-strokes to the painting: ruins are
brought to light by excavations, and monuments are disengaged
from extraneous constructions which hid or disfigured them.

We thus learn gradually what ancient cities really looked like. One notices then that everywhere are found buildings, which, if not always similar in form, were at least analogous in purpose and in function. In the center is the *forum* (q.v.), which was the public square, with its subsidiary buildings: the Capitol, temple of the state religion, the *curia* (q.v.), where the decurions' meetings were held, and the *basilica* (q.v.) or courthouse. Next, we find a theater or amphitheater (sometimes both) for performances and contests respectively; temples built for various divinities; baths, enormous bathing establishments, which played, we shall see, an important role in social life; aqueducts, fountains, and all the sanitary installations necessary for a large human settlement; and finally, prestige constructions, triumphal arches, votive columns, and statues. By means of the last, objects of ambition and mutual rivalry, the spirit of the city was expressed.

The city, founded during a time of conquest and inside a still turbulent province, was often surrounded with walls. And even if, later, all kinds of inroads had been made on this barrier by private builders, the moment came when it was necessary to restore it, when the Roman peace was threatened and the barbarian invasions brought back instability to the Empire.

Such are the basic elements of city life. There is only a small number of them, and their repetition in each city must give rise to a certain monotony. Let us not, however, imagine that all Roman cities are entirely the same. North African cities looked different from the cities of Great Britain. Local variations occurred and caused a certain diversity. Mixed types of architecture were created, and native traditions modified the classical models which the Roman builders brought in. This can be noticed, especially, in religious buildings. We notice it to an equal extent in houses, which are less subject to official rules than are public monuments. The fact remains that the essential city tends to conform to an almost unchangeable norm, to the essential prototypes of the capital.

The apogee of the Roman cities occurred in the first and second centuries of our era. It was then that they attained a

magnificence which is difficult for us to imagine. But these
happy centuries were followed by periods of instability and
wars which forced the cities to turn inwards and to cut the
most vulnerable limbs from their bodies. In Gaul, for example,
in the last third of the third century, we see them close
themselves in behind hastily constructed walls, shored up by
previous monuments. Amphitheaters with strong walls, tombs,
and terraces of temples furnished with little expense the basic
materials for defense. Haphazard building materials were
borrowed from buildings left outside the new barrier and
relegated to destruction. At the beginning of the Middle Ages,
a new city was formed in this way, in fear and in confusion, on
a limited part of the Roman city. Still later, the medieval city
gave birth to a modern city. Thus, continuity is unbroken
between the ancient cluster of settlement and the city which
we know today. It still frequently happens that the modern
plan lets us recognize the general outlines of Roman city
planning. This is the case with cities such as PARIS, LYONS,
BORDEAUX, TOULOUSE, TURIN, FLORENCE, VERONA and many
others which owe their general orientation and the plan of one
of their parts to the ancient Roman center. An additional reason
for seeking out and comparing the plans of such Roman cities
is the attempt to discover their previous history, the evidence
for which lies beneath the streets of our day.[3] And, wherever
one places the Roman city, one finds the origin of that
phenomenon which is considered one of the most important
in western history: the formation of powerful urban centers.
This is especially true of the Latin-speaking provinces, to the
west of the Adriatic Sea (in Europe) and the Gulf of Sidra (off
North Africa), where Roman urban planning was not
superimposed on a Greek or eastern city planning.[4] That is
why we shall limit our study to this territory, inside of which
there still exist large areas more or less obscure, depending
on the level of the advancement of archaeological research. In
North Africa, for example, it is easier to disengage ancient
cities, for nothing disturbs the excavator in a country whose
urban tradition was not carried on with the same continuity as
in Europe. The secrets of *Lutetia*, on the other hand, remain

deeply hidden under the various Parises which have succeeded each other across the ages. But what we can now learn about the Roman cities, wherever they are found, is enough to make clear the deep impression left by Rome on the territories which formed its Empire and to show the continually active reality of Roman civilization.

Chapter One

The General Principles of Roman City Planning

In order to impose pacification after their conquests, the Romans had to develop already existing cities or to found new ones, and they were forced to work out in detail a thorough body of principles in city planning so as to have uniform *a priori* solutions for all the practical problems. This seemed to be all the more necessary because the first groups usually sent as colonists were veteran soldiers, not very capable of originality but disciplined and tenacious. The native working force was large but without training in trades or professions. This led to the adoption of simple techniques, such as the widespread use of concrete (q.v.), for it was quicker and easier than construction in dressed stone, which was mainly used for architectural facings (see building methods, Roman, in the glossary below). But before building the monuments, it was necessary to lay out the city, while foreseeing its general groupings, the links between its sections and the locations of its essential organs. Like modern city planners, were the founders going to study minutely the geographic, demographic, and economic conditions? Would they be inspired by the climate, the orientation, and the general characteristics of the site or its surrounding areas? So many precautions were usually impossible. It was necessary to move quickly and, once the site of the future city had been chosen, to begin building without delay. Thus the Roman founders were content to use a simple plan, always the same, which had the advantage of being easy to understand.

A normal city, in the eyes of the Romans, was laid out in a

10

square or a rectangle crossed by two perpendicular roads which met the middles of the four outside lines. One of these two axes was oriented from north to south. It was called the *cardo* (q.v., which means pivot or door hinge, because it followed the ideal line on which the sky seemed to swing). The east-west axis was the *decumanus* (q.v.), a term whose meaning is obscure. It certainly refers to the number ten, but we cannot clearly discern the reason for this fact. During the foundation, the founder, who was a magistrate officially entrusted with that duty (or, more usually and in practice, a surveyor who was his assistant), determined first of all the location of the center-point of the future city. At this spot, where the *decumanus* and the *cardo* crossed, he put the *groma*, an instrument for locating by observation the line of the *decumanus*. To do this, he began by marking the sun when it rose, and this gave the true East at the date of the founding.[1] It was easy to trace the *cardo* next, by finding the perpendicular at the place where the *groma* rested. Equal distances were measured along the two axes by starting at their intersection, depending on the surface area which was intended for the colony. At those outer points were the main gates. The outline of the enclosure brought into being the square (or rectangle) of which the *cardo* and the *decumanus* were the medians. Thus the city would have four gates, one at each cardinal point of the compass. It would then be possible to lay out the secondary roads in the manner of a chessboard. One thus obtained secondary *decumani* and *cardines,* parallel respectively to the two principal axes.[2] The units outlined in this way (the squares of the chessboard) were assigned to the inhabitants according to their ranks and offices.

Such a procedure is obviously very artificial. It is applicable only to unoccupied land, without too large irregularities. This was how, each evening, the officers in charge of setting up camp enclosed their troops while on campaign. In this way, colonies seem to be simply a development of the camp system, a part of the military discipline in which the veterans were trained. The advantages are obvious: comparable shares were assigned to each, and this satisfied the Roman spirit of equality.

Furthermore, such a settlement, because of its regular shape, was easy to defend.[3] It was in fact the shape of military colonies, established in badly pacified lands, and that is why we find the most characteristic examples in North Africa, especially at TIMGAD (fig. 1). There vast plains spread out near the Aurès Mountains. In that nomadic country, no native village existed beforehand. The Roman foundation was the only city for miles around. The principles could be rigorously applied. TIMGAD was, at least in its origin, nothing but a huge camp of stone and concrete, permanently planted at one of the outposts of the Empire.

One would be wrong, however, to think that the chessboard pattern and the geometric rigidity of this kind of founding are entirely explained by military influence. The reality is much more complicated. There was, in the founding of the city, an element for which military training cannot account: no practical consideration would explain the *orientation* of the *decumanus*. That can be ascribed only to a religious motive, and it is very certain that the foundation of a city was a sacred act. Ancient authors have copiously described the ritual performed at those times. They tell us that the founder himself, dressed in a toga draped in an ancient fashion, began by taking the auspices (q.v.), in order to assure himself by visible signs that the gods were not opposed to the establishment of a city in the chosen place. Then he took the handles of a plow with a bronze share, drawn by a white heifer and a white bull, and traced a furrow around the future city, at the place where the walls should be built. He took plenty of care to make sure that the earth raised up by the plowshare fell inside the boundary, and, behind him, helpers picked up the clods which sometimes fell outside and threw them back where the ritual prescribed. At the sites designated for the gates, the founder raised the plowshare, in order to leave entries devoid of any consecration. Once the celebrant returned to his point of departure, the city was essentially founded.

This rite was supposed to have been enacted by Romulus himself around the primitive Rome, and it was said that Remus

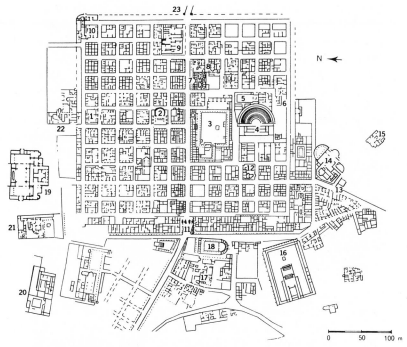

Figure 1. Plan of Timgad

Following C. Courtois, *Timgad, antique Thamugadi* (Algiers 1951), and M. I.
Finley (ed.), *Atlas of Classical Archaeology* (New York 1977) p. 74

1. Small North Baths
2. Public Library
3. Forum (v. Figure 9)
4. Theater
5. Basilica
6. Temple of Mercury (?)
7. East Market
8. Small East Baths
9. Large East Baths
10. Northeast Temple
11. Arch (called Trajan's)
12. Small Central Baths

13. Industrial section
14. Large South Baths
15. Small South Baths
16. Capitol
17. Baths of the Market of Sertius
18. Market of Sertius
19. Large North Baths
20. Temple of the Genius Coloniae
21. Baths
22. North Gate
23. East Gate

had been killed by his brother because, in order to deride the ceremony, he had crossed with a leap the ditch and miniature embankment which the plow had just formed.[4] The rite is easy enough to understand. Its purpose was to outline the future city, around which the bronze plow (the exclusive choice of that metal brings us back to a time when iron was not yet regularly used) drew a line of magical protection. From the earth cut by the plowshare rose infernal divinities, who took possession of the ditch and made it *religiously* uncrossable. Whoever did not take the precaution of entering the urban territory by the gates, where the ground, having remained intact, formed an effective protection against the nether gods, became by that very act *sacer;* consecrated yet cursed, he was pledged to the subterranean divinities and had to be put to death at once, for the defilement with which he was thus stained became a danger for the whole city. Only this belief explains the old legend, which, not without scandal, places the murder of a brother at the very origins of a city.

This ritual of designating the urban territory was completed by two others, which were both rituals of consecration. One was done for the infernal gods. At a central point in the future city, a circular pit was dug, called the *mundus* (perhaps because it was thought to reproduce the design of the sky, which had that name), where offerings were put for Those Below. Three times each year, the slab which ordinarily covered this hole was ceremoniously removed. On those days, all official business came to a halt in the city. The *mundus* (q.v.) was open, and since communication had been established with the spirits of the underworld, any project would have been doomed to failure.

The purpose of the last ritual was to place the future city under the protection of the gods from Above and especially under that of a triad composed of Jupiter, Juno, and Minerva. These three divinities received a common temple with three chapels, which was the Capitol (that is to say the Head) of the city. Ideally, this sanctuary ought to have been placed on a high point, so that the divine guests could see the greatest

possible surface of the city. It was an old and deeply rooted belief that the protection of a god only worked effectively over the land which he could *see*. So when the Capitol could not be placed on the top of the hill, it was put on a high *podium*, an artificial terrace which was used instead. Usually, this Capitol was built next to the main square, in the very center of the colony.

We see therefore that the old-fashioned teachings on the founding of cities included two distinct series of rules: one part was technical, consisting of geometry alone, while the other was an archaic ritual. But nothing assures us that these two elements were originally joined. They were, indeed, in the foundings which took place during the classical era, but had they always been? The consecration of the ground and the plowing of a magic furrow do not imply by themselves that the city had to take the shape of a square and that all of its land had to be divided in the manner of a chessboard by a network of streets. Only one feature is common, the aligning of the two axes to follow the "lines of force" of the universe, as they were imagined then. It is possible that this characteristic allowed the integration in a more ancient ritual a technique which in itself was not at all sacred.

However that may have been, the ancient authors are unanimous in affirming that the ritual of founding, in its two aspects, practical and religious, had been taught to the Romans by the Etruscans (q.v.).[5] And nothing puts that affirmation in doubt. The Capitoline triad is Etruscan, as are the temples with a triple *cella* (with three chapels), where Jupiter, Juno, and Minerva dwell. Similarly, the importance of the underworld divinities, the precautions taken against them, the endeavor to control and use their evil powers—all this makes us think of the Etruscan demonology, such as we see it depicted in the cemetery paintings of TARQUINIA, for example. The name of *groma*, used for the surveying instrument, is very probably an Etruscan term, and if the ritual kept some Latin elements, earlier than the Etruscan influence, these elements have been obscured by it to the extent of being unrecognizable.

MARZABOTTO, CAPUA VETERE, and *Volsinii*

Two cities, undeniably Etruscan and which go back to the sixth century B.C., already present the general characteristics of Roman colonies. The first is the city called MARZABOTTO, after the place where the excavations took place, and whose ancient name is unknown to us. It was placed on a gently sloping plateau, on the banks of the Reno, twenty-five kilometers southwest of BOLOGNA. Its streets formed a perfect checkerboard with straight lines. The units bordered by the *decumani* and the *cardines* all have a length of 165 meters, and their breadth varies from 40 meters to 60. The two main streets are 15 meters wide; the secondary streets are about a third the width. The Capitol was set on a height dominating the city, and there, among various religious monuments, a cone-shaped pit has been discovered. It was filled with sacrificial remains and was undoubtedly the *mundus*. The city of MARZABOTTO was certainly Etruscan. It was doubtless founded by colonists who came from BOLOGNA, a powerful Etruscan city and its neighbor, and they guarded the valley of the Reno and the pass through the Apennines. It was brutally destroyed by the Gauls early in the fourth century B.C.,[6] with the result that we have certain proof of what must have been an Etruscan foundation at the time when that people had attained the apogee of their civilization and power.

The other city is *Capua*. Ancient *Capua* was not located on the modern site of CAPUA, which occupied, after A.D. 856, the site of Roman *Casilinum*, but it was rather where the present-day Santa Maria CAPUA VETERE is, in the middle of a large plain. It was founded by the Etruscans when they penetrated into southern Italy, and it kept the outline which its founders had made for it. This may still be seen in the arteries of the modern village, whose main street, the Corso Umberto I, follows the ancient *decumanus maximus* (fig. 2), which crossed the city from west to east from the Gate of Rome (or Porta Romana) to the Porta Albana. The main *cardo* may be found on a perpendicular road, at an equal distance from the east and west walls. The *cardo* and the *decumanus* crossed near

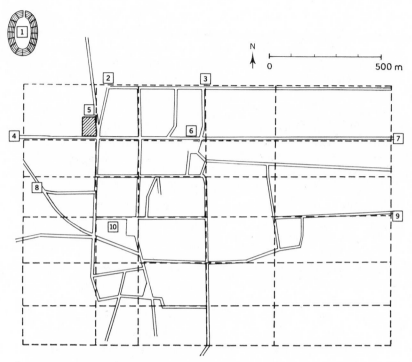

Figure 2. Plan of Ancient Capua
Dotted lines = ancient streets; solid lines = modern streets. Following J.
Heurgon, *Recherches sur . . . Capoue préromaine* (Paris 1942)

1. Amphitheater
2. Gate of the Volturnus River
3. Gate of Jupiter
4. Gate of Rome
5. Baths
6. Aedes Alba
7. Porta Albana
8. Capitol
9. Gate of Juno
10. Seplasia

the present-day Piazza San Pietro, and it is there where in ancient times the White House *(Aedes Alba)*, the building of the city's Senate, stood. Another important place was the *Seplasia,* the business center, where were located the makers of perfumes, so numerous at *Capua.* This area was next to the Capitol, whose high building dominated the western part of the city.*

But, even if it is certain that the Etruscans sometimes used, at least in founding their colonies, the principles which would become those of Roman city planning, one would be wrong to imagine that *all* the Etruscan cities were built according to a chessboard plan. Some recent excavations† show, for example, that the Etruscan *Volsinii* (q.v.), whose site overlooks present-day BOLSENA, in no way reproduces the geometric pattern of *Capua* and MARZABOTTO. It was built on rough ground, with a total difference in level of 200 meters, and covered four separate hills. On one of them, a temple has been found, undoubtedly from the third century B.C., and it seems to have harbored a divine triad, but we cannot yet know whether it was the only "Capitol" of the city. It is difficult to imagine that under such circumstances and on such a site, the pattern of the streets (which, moreover, still escapes us) could have conformed to the theoretical chessboard. In any case, the enclosure is not rectangular but follows an irregular outline with numerous angles, which improved defense. So it is likely that the pattern of the roads was in accordance with the levels of the land, as is the case at Vetulonia, another Etruscan city which does not correspond to the principles of the ritual.

For Etruscan cities as for Roman cities, it is obviously advisable to distinguish between foundations set on a plain and those placed on an acropolis (q.v.). Only on the former could a rigid chessboard pattern be imposed. The others used

---

*J. Heurgon, *Recherches sur l'histoire, la religion et la civilisation de Capoue préromaine*, Bibliothèque des Ecoles françaises d'Athènes et de Rome 154 (Paris 1942), pp. 124-130.

†R. Bloch, "Volsinies étrusque et romaine," *Mélanges de l'Ecole française de Rome* 62 (1950): 53-120.

the chosen site as well as possible, especially with regard to defense. Even in the eyes of the Etruscans, the square city, with its two perpendicular axes, its checkerboard network of streets and its four gates, was only an ideal, which one approached as close as possible, insofar as practical conditions permitted.

Within central Italy, regular cities were exceptions. Except for the areas under Etruscan or, later, Roman influence, such planning did not exist at all. Before the arrival of the Romans, the mountaineers' cities on the plateaus and in the inner regions of the Apennines were only villages of moderate size, above some escarpment. Some crags or a cliff formed a natural defense, and these refuges barely deserved to be called cities. Until a period as late as the beginning of our era, immense regions at the very gates of Rome, the lands of the Paeligni, the Vestini, the Marsi, and the Marrucini did not have a real city.[7] Even today, many large villages in those regions preserve the same character. They are visible from afar, packed on the top of a peak. Their space is very restricted, and their streets, narrow and winding, make one think of a labyrinth rather than the order of a chessboard.

Nevertheless, these Italian villages are generally the direct heirs of a Roman city. But the Roman settlement in these places only followed an original native agglomeration, whose capricious plan it kept. This often happened in the Latin colonies (see *colonia*), which were established at a relatively early date (between the fourth and the third centuries B.C.); their inhabitants, without being made Roman citizens, had certain judicial rights. Roman garrisons were placed there and remained for a long time, sheltered from surprise attack, and it was only at the end of the Second Punic (Carthaginian) War (at the beginning of the second century B.C.) that the Romans occupied the flat lands and founded geometrically shaped cities there. The ancient villages then lost their importance to their more accessible rivals, which were located closer to the main commercial routes. This Etrusco-Roman type of city, the regular colony,* was entirely different from the fortress-city with an acropolis. In the latter case, the classical forms of Roman urban planning had to be modified, somehow or other, according to local conditions, and these hill-towns have lasted down to the present day. Compromises were made, which gave to the Roman cities of central Italy their special character: ASSISI, in Umbria, remains perched on its hill; *Tusculum* (q.v., now Frascati),[8] *Tibur* and *Praeneste* (now TIVOLI and PALESTRINA), within sight from Rome, still keep today irregular plans, which bear witness to their distant origins.

The very concept of a square city is obviously in contrast with the special inclinations of a large number of Italian cities, and it had to be imported into the major part of the peninsula and imposed by conquest. We should certainly like to know how it originated. But, with regard to this point, we are reduced to conjectures.

About eighty years ago, archaeologists were attracted by some discoveries which appeared, at the time, to have brought a solution to the problem. There was a series of human settlements, which extended from the end of the second millennium to, roughly, the eighth century B.C.† These "cities," generally of modest size, were scattered in the southern part of the plain of the Po. They were found to be numerous in the regions of MANTUA, PARMA, and MODENA, where their remains formed layers of earth especially rich in organic matter,

---

*For example *Norba* (q.v.), cf. G. Schmiedt and F. Castagnoli, "L'antica città di Norba," *L'universo* 37 (1957): 125-148; also see on *Alba Fucens*, F. De Visscher et al., *Les fouilles d'Alba Fucens* (Brussels 1955). The editor would like to add the following. These cities were Latin colonies of Rome. In 273 B.C., thirty years after *Alba Fucens* (q.v.), came the Latin colony at *Cosa, Etruria*, which like the other two, provides an example of an orthogonal city not set on a plain but, ingeniously, on a hilltop. Note that their axes have to deviate from the cardinal points of the compass because of the terrain (Castagnoli, *Orthogonal Town Planning* 121). Contrast nonorthogonal DJEMILA. Ward-Perkins compares *Norba, Alba Fucens* and *Cosa* to *Priene* (see pp. 22-23 below) and calls these plans in difficult terrain "something of a tour de force" *(Cities* 27). In the case of *Cosa* (q.v.), the literature is mainly in English.

†G. Saeflund, *Le Terremare* (Lund/Leipzig 1939), pp. 233 ff.

which the peasants used for fertilizer and which they called
"terramara" (that is to say "marl"). This name remains attached
to these prehistoric villages, where for a long time people tried
to see cities founded by the ancestors of the Latins during the
slow migration which took place from Central Europe to
Latium. It was believed that the huts of which they consisted
were placed according to the traditional rules of cities with
decumani and *cardines*.

In reality, the facts are much less clear and convincing than
people supposed. The archaeologists' imaginations, in the en-
thusiasm of their first discoveries, often led them to hasty conclusions, and these poor outposts, limited to a well-defined
region of northern Italy, were far from having all the characteristics of an Etruscan or Roman city. We do not know at all
if the inhabitants of the terramara settlements were the ancestors of the Latins. Everything suggests on the contrary that
such was not the case, and, anyway, it was on a baseless hypothesis that the complicated Etruscan ritual for founding cities was assigned to these unknown people. The Etruscan ritual was obviously linked to their particular concept of the
universe.

It is certainly not in Italy that we must look for the origin of
the square city but elsewhere inside the Mediterranean world.
We know that geometric cities, rather similar in their general
outline to the Etruscan colonies, were built in the East well
before the time when MARZABOTTO and CAPUA were founded.
Towards the end of the sixth century B.C., at the latest, the
same urban plan was used in Ionia (q.v.) and spread from there.
When the city of Miletus was rebuilt in 479 B.C., after its total
destruction by the Persians in 494, the inhabitants gave it an
entirely new plan like a chessboard, without taking account of
the older city. And before that, the same Milesians had used
the same design for their colony of Olbia, on the Black Sea,
which had been demolished by a fire and which they had to
rebuild completely. Nothing is opposed to the theory that the
Etruscan architects had undergone Ionian influence: what is
true of sculpture, of ceramics, of painting, and of myths can

be equally true of city planning. The relations between Etruria and the eastern lands were close enough that the hypothesis, taken alone, presents no problems.

Tradition, helped by a brief passage in Aristotle, usually honored the architect Hippodamus of Miletus, who flourished around the middle of the fifth century, as the originator and popularizer of the geometric plan in the Greek world. But the dates do not jibe. We can at least admit that he was the chief publicizer and that he introduced it in Greece proper (notably in Piraeus), as well as in the colonies founded during that period, such as *Thurii* (q.v.), an Athenian colony in southern Italy (founded in 443), and perhaps at Olynthus (in Chalcidice, about a hundred kilometers southeast of present-day Salonica). From that time, the Hippodamian plan, as it was called, became usual for the foundation and modification of cities. It triumphed during the Hellenistic period. The Italian excavations at the site of Camiros, on the island of Rhodes, show us a city of this type: dominated by an archaic acropolis, where the sanctuaries are clustered, the city flows down a slightly concave slope to the sea. The longitudinal streets follow the lines of the largest slope, the transversal streets run along the contour lines. Viewing the whole, we have the impression of a huge theater, whose stage would be the port and the sea. The same general plan is found at *Priene* in Asia Minor (fig. 3), which was completely rebuilt at the end of the fourth century, as well as at Halicarnassus (also on the west coast of Turkey). It is a fact that at *Priene* the rectangular plan, applied very strictly for the outline of the streets, had no influence on the overall shape of the city wall, which was not rigid and made use of the movements of the ground, as at *Volsinii*. The temple of Athena Polias (the guardian of the city) was built on a terrace dominating the central square (the *agora*), somewhat as the Capitol of MARZABOTTO overlooks the rest of the city.

These examples of regular cities founded by the Greeks are not at all limited to the East. Without even speaking of *Thurii*, founded rather late, we observe that the Greek colonies of Campania, *Posidonia (Paestum,* to the south of Salerno) and

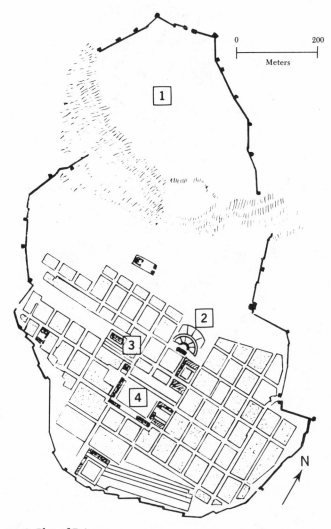

Figure 3. Plan of Priene
Following A. von Gerkan, *Griechische Staedteanlagen* (Berlin and Leipzig 1924) pl. 9

1. Acropolis   3. Temple of Athena Polias
2. Theater   4. Agora

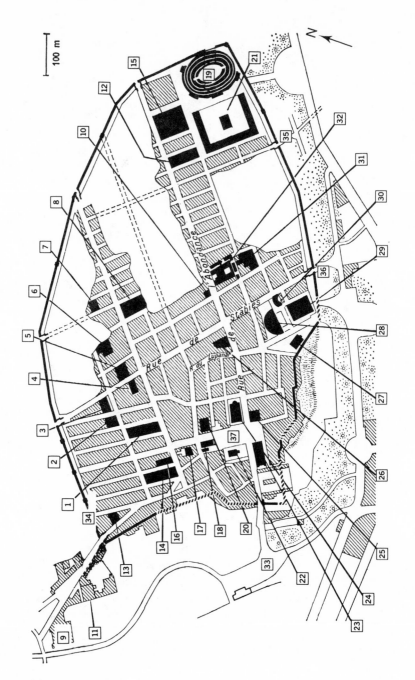

24

NAPLES itself were laid out according to an analogous plan. It has been shown that the Greek Neapolis (Naples) was divided by three main streets oriented from east to west, which crossed perpendicular streets, like *cardines* at intervals. Similarly, the wall of *Paestum* has four main gates where four streets ended, obviously in the shape of a cross. Neither NAPLES nor *Paestum* (q.v.) could have undergone, at the time of their founding (towards the end of the sixth century), the least Etruscan influence.[9] The same is true of the city of *Selinus*, in Sicily, which was completely rebuilt during the last years of the fifth century.

When the Etruscans invaded Campania, they found geometric cities, a fashion which was spreading. We have an example of this at *Pompeii*, the Campanian city which the eruption of Vesuvius in A.D. 79 so-to-speak fossilized and handed over to us almost intact. *Pompeii* (q.v.) also has a checkerboard pattern (fig. 4), which was not oriented in accordance with the rules of the Etruscan teachings but whose relationship with the Etrusco-Roman cities is evident. It is now av-

Figure 4. Plan of Pompeii

1. House of the Faun
2. House of the Vettii
3. House of the Golden Cupids
4. House of Orpheus
5. House of L. Jucundus
6. House of the Silver Wedding Anniversary
7. House of M. Fronto
8. House of the Centenarian
9. House of Diomedes
10. House of Verecundus
11. House of Cicero
12. House of Loreius Tiburtinus
13. House of the Surgeon
14. House of Pansa
15. House of Julia Felix
16. House of the Tragic Poet
17. Forum Baths
18. Temple of Jupiter (Capitol)
19. Amphitheater
20. Market
21. Palaestra
22. Temple of Apollo
23. Basilica
24. Building of Eumachia
25. Comitium (Assembly)
26. Stabian Baths
27. Triangular Forum
28. Large theater
29. Gladiators' barracks
30. Small theater
31. House of Menander
32. House of the Cryptoporticus
33. Gate of the Sea
34. Gate of Herculaneum
35. Gate of Nocera
36. Gate of Stabiae
37. Forum (v. Figure 11)

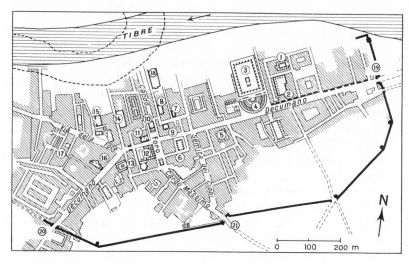

Figure 5. Schematic Map of the Ruins of Ostia

1. Barracks of the fire department (Vigiles)
2. Baths and palaestra
3. Square of the shipping companies (Piazzale delle Corporazioni)
4. Theater
5. College of the Augustales
6. Forum Baths
7. House of Diana
8. House of the Paintings
9. Restaurant (Thermopolium)
10. Capitol
11. Curia
12. Basilica
13. Market
14. Grain depot of Epagathus
15. House of Amor and Psyche
16. Christian basilica
17. Baths of the Seven Wise Men
18. Museum
19. Gate of Rome
20. Gate of the Sea
21. Gate of Laurentum

erred, whatever may have been said, that *Pompeii* never knew
the least "Etruscan phase." It was founded at the end of the
sixth century B.C. by a native people, the Oscans, and was
directly influenced by the nearby Greek colonies. Faithful to
the practice of Greek engineers, the founders began by surrounding their city with a wall of dressed stone, strictly a Hellenic practice.[*10] The gates, which were set in at that time,

---

*A. Maiuri, "Studi e Ricerche sulla Fortificazione di Pompei," *Monumenti
Antichi* ... 23 (1929): 113-286; idem, "Greci ed Etruschi a Pompei," *Atti della
Reale Accademia d'Italia* (1944): 121-149.

show that the network of city roads was already in outline what it would remain until the end.

The examination of these various facts doubtlessly allows us to glimpse the beginnings of the plan of the Etrusco-Roman colonies. It seems very certain that models offered in Italy itself by the Greek colonies contributed greatly to its success. We should even think that the traditional form, such as we find it in the Roman colonies founded at the edge of the sea beginning in the fourth century B.C. (notably at *Ostia*, see fig. 5),* was the result of a compromise between the demands of ritual and the innovations of the Greek architects. The preeminence accorded to the main *cardo* and *decumanus* is explained by the ritual, but all the rest is derived from a technique which is not particularly Italian. The cultural and commercial exchanges between the two halves of the Mediterranean world were much more important than we are inclined to believe today, after centuries have passed. Like all its civilization, Roman city planning was the result of a fertile synthesis and not an autonomous development from some mythical and completely formed entity.[11]

*G. Calza et al., *Scavi di Ostia* I (Rome 1953); (general topography).

Chapter Two

The Urban Development of Ancient Rome

If it is true that Roman colonies were, in the eyes of their founders, nothing but images of the mother-city (see pp. 4-5 above), we must investigate the principles which were used during the creation and the urban development of Rome.

The archaeological evidence and the historical facts here are still far from being clear. There exists a tradition according to which Rome was founded towards the middle of the eighth century (in 753 B.C., according to the most generally used chronology)[1] by Latin colonists from the city of *Alba Longa* (q.v., about twenty-five kilometers southeast of Rome), led by two brothers, Romulus and Remus, who located a village of shepherds on the Palatine Hill. It is also said that Romulus, after having taken the auspices, traced the ritual ditch around the hill, the area which was the cradle of Rome. Then, when other settlements were also placed on the neighboring hills, these various villages gradually formed a federation, which had as its center "neutral" ground in the little plain, or rather the bottom of the valley, where today the Forum lies. A wall built around these different inhabitants and enclosing them all brought unity to the new city. Thus, the Palatine was thought of as the first Rome, the square Rome, and only this conformed to the ritual and the rules for founding cities.*

But there are many difficulties with this tradition. The

---

*On these problems see R. Bloch, *Les origines de Rome*, "Que sais-je?" no. 216 (Paris 1959) and, same author and title, Club français du livre (Paris 1960).

shepherds' village on the Palatine certainly existed. The remains of their huts have recently been found. On the other hand, there is no trace of the primitive wall which these inhabitants would have built, if not the legendary Romulus himself. One searches in vain for the outer gates which ought to have marked the *decumanus* and the *cardo*. It is very likely that the Palatine City is a legend, which took form late, for reasons of political opportunism. One cannot see, moreover, at the core of the tradition which we have just related, how Latin peoples could have employed rites whose Etruscan character is undeniable. We know today—what, out of patriotism, the Roman historians were forced to hide somehow or other—that Rome had an Etruscan period when the Tarquins ruled, that is to say a century and a half after the traditional date assigned to the first founding. And the Etruscan hill *par excellence* is not the Palatine but the Capitol (officially called *Mons Tarpeius* or Hill of the Tarquins), and the oriented and regular city is still recognizable at the foot of that hill. It is in the Forum, on the plain, that Rome was founded.

The memory of four very ancient gates has been preserved for us there. There was no longer any need for them during the classical period, but they bear witness to a previous state of affairs. One of them opened on the north of the Forum. This was the Gate of Janus. On the south was the Porta Romana. The one to the east was called, in the classical era, the Sister's Beam (an allusion to the legend of the Horatii. It was there that the young Horatius, who had murdered his sister, entered the City and was purified, after his acquittal by the people).[2] To the west was a cursed gate, of bad omen, perched on an inaccessible rock, on the bottom slope of the Capitol, and it always remained open, although no one could go through it—whence its name of *Porta Pandana*, the Open Gate. The *decumanus* was formed by the street which later became *Via Sacra*, and the *cardo* was a transverse road, which in the classical period was extended, to the north by the *Argiletum* and to the south by the Street of the Etruscans, the *Vicus Tuscus*.[3]

Such was most likely the beginning of Rome: an Etruscan

colony, a simple market dominated and watched by a garrison placed on top of the Capitol. There the inhabitants of the villages scattered on the neighboring heights first gathered, to meet with merchants from central and southern Italy. Salt was undoubtedly one of the main commodities, as well as products imported from the south and Etruria. When, towards the end of the sixth century B.C., the Etruscans, shaken, ended their power by retreating north of the Tiber, the Roman people gained their independence, and Rome became an autonomous city.

It was towards the end of that period that one of these kings built the large wall which is attributed to one of them, Servius, and it outlined in a general way the limits of settlement. This Servian Wall enclosed the seven traditional hills: that is, besides the three *montes* (isolated heights) of the Capitol, the Palatine, and the Aventine, four elongated hillocks, which are really extensions of the Esquiline Plateau and which were called the Quirinal, the Viminal, the Oppian, and the Caelian (fig. 6).[4] The general outline of these fortifications reminds us of those which we saw at *Volsinii*. In both cases, it was necessary to defend undulating land, with a view only to military needs. There was, therefore, a dichotomy between the religious city, enclosed inside its *pomerium* (see p. 5 above), and the military city, bounded by a wall of considerable size. Between the two was the actual settlement, located on the slopes and crowded along the roads which led from the center to the gates.

Soon we recognize neighborhoods being formed: the patricians wished to live on the Palatine or the heights of the Quirinal. The common people massed in the narrow valley of the Subura, between the Viminal and the Oppian. It was especially the plebeians who lived on the Aventine, for a long time destined, because of its outlying position, to receive only a scattered population. In the depression between the Capitol and the Palatine, two commercial streets, the *Vicus Iugarius* and the *Vicus Tuscus*, were lined with stores and artisans' workshops. On the banks of the Tiber were the markets, where cowherds set up camp and bargemen went ashore. There stood the cattle market (Forum Boarium), the vegetable market

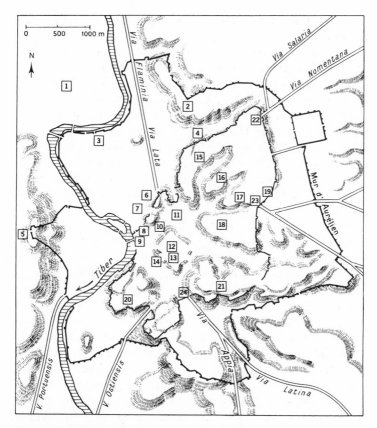

Figure 6. Plan of Ancient Rome

1. Plain of the Vatican
2. Hill of Gardens
3. Campus Martius
4. Servian Wall
5. Janiculum
6. Arx
7. Capitolium
8. Vegetable market
9. Cattle market
10. Velabrum
11. Forum
12. Palatine Hill
13. Germalus
14. Circus Maximus
15. Quirinal
16. Viminal
17. Cispian Hill
18. Oppian Hill
19. Esquiline Plateau
20. Aventine Hill
21. Caelian Hill
22. Porta Collina
23. Porta Esquilina
24. Porta Capena

(Forum Holitorium) and, soon, the port of Rome, the
Emporium.[5]

The old "oriented" city, overflowing on all sides, remained
the center of Rome. There stands the Forum, which means
public square, where popular assemblies were periodically held
in the enclosure of the *Comitium*, especially consecrated for
that purpose. Not far away is the *Curia*, the usual meeting-
place of the Senate. The rest of the square was bordered with
shops: one row, on the north, was the *Tabernae Novae* (or
New Shops), another, on the south, the *Tabernae Veteres* (the
Old Shops).[6] Originally, the main market—for meat and fish—
was held in the Forum. Gradually, other businesses were
located there, and in the classical period, we see there only
money-changers, goldsmiths, and jewelers. The markets for
livestock retreated and clustered immediately to the north of
the old Forum.

The Forum was not the only part of the site of Rome which
remained free of buildings. Even inside the walls, the long
valley which lies between the Palatine and the Aventine and
which was called the Valley of the Great Circus *(Circus
Maximus)* was reserved for the celebration of certain games,
especially horse races, one of the oldest rites of Roman religion.
Just outside the walls and close to the north side of the Capitol
was the largest plain on the site, which a religious law excluded
from the city. It was called the *Campus Martius* (Field or Plain
of Mars). Outlined on the south by the steep cliff of the Capitol
and then that of the Quirinal, it ended on the west at the bank
of the river and on the north and northeast at the bottom slopes
of the Hill of Gardens *(Collis Hortulorum*, today the Pincio).
According to legend, it had belonged to the last kings of Rome,
and after the expulsion of the tyrants, it was nationalized, that
is, consecrated exclusively to the service of the community.
There the men mustered when under arms, and youths took
part in their military training. When republican institutions
evolved and the Romans came to regard the popular assembly
which grouped the citizens according to centuries (their military
units) as the most important and the only vital one, the *Comitia
Centuriata* were held on the Field of Mars for elections and

making laws. So the old *Comitium* was abandoned at the very moment when it became too small to hold the endlessly growing mass of citizens.[7]

The republican city was linked together and set around the Forum. The oriented plan is no longer evident. The *cardo* and *decumanus* were lost under the pavement of the square, and a star-shaped plan was gradually formed. The streets went in different directions from the four primitive gates towards those of the Servian Wall, and this radiating system would become from then on the framework of the city. At the Gate of Janus began two main roads, the *Vicus Longus* (Long Street), which reached the Porta Collina (or Quirinal Gate) after following the slopes of the Quirinal and, from there, headed towards the Sabine (q.v.) country; also there was the Street of the Subura, which climbed the Esquiline and, at the Esquiline Gate allowed passage towards the Latins.[8] The eastern end of the *decumanus*, as one might have expected, was linked with the road leading, through the Porta Capena, to the ancient federal sanctuary in the Alban Hills, where a procession led by the chief Roman magistrates went every year during the *Feriae Latinae* to offer a solemn sacrifice to Jupiter.

New routes were soon added to these primitive ones, as relations between Rome and the neighboring lands became more frequent. Towards the north was the *Via Lata* (Wide Street), which crossed the Campus Martius and was the urban part of the road (called the *Via Flaminia* after its builder), which put Rome in communication with its first northern conquests. On the south, the Ostia Road *(Via Ostiensis)* went past the Aventine and led towards the port of Rome on the sea. Built rather late were the roads which crossed the river at the foot of the Capitol and entered the territory on the right bank of the Tiber. Although Rome today is a river city, the Tiber seems originally to have slowed rather than helped its development. The only purpose of the first bridge was to provide an easy access to the fort placed on the heights of the Janiculum; built entirely of wood and without any metal, it could easily be destroyed. During the centuries when the Etruscans were the masters of the right bank, Rome remained obstinately confident

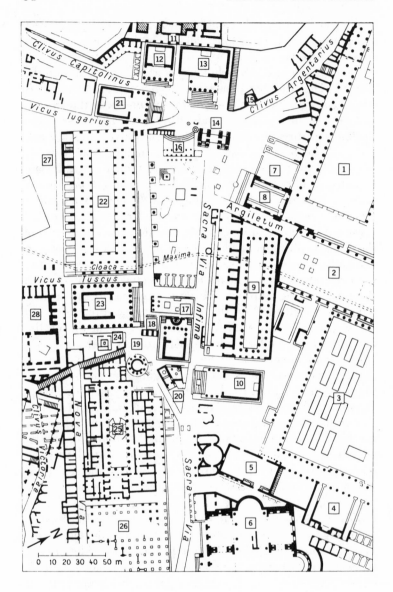

in the protection which the river provided, and it cannot be considered, at least at its origin, a bridge city. The heart of the City was the Forum and not on the river.

Inside the network of the roads, public and private buildings were put up long before one could discern a definite plan. It does not seem that Rome, in the fifth or fourth century B.C., was divided into regular blocks. Nevertheless, from the beginning of this period, attempts to regulate the center of the City may be discerned.

The first concerned the drainage of the Forum. At the bottom of this valley flowed all the water from the hills, and floods of the Tiber sometimes added to the swamp. In order to dry out this area, a canal was dug, at first open and later, perhaps at the beginning of the second century B.C., covered by a solid vault. This was the *Cloaca Maxima*, the great sewer of Rome, whose ruins still exist (see p. 75 above—ed.). Pavement covered the ground of the square, and an attempt was made to give it a regular form. After the fifth century B.C., the old *decumanus*, which did not follow a natural line of the landscape, was given up, and the foot of the Capitol was taken as the starting point (fig. 7). The construction of the Temple of Saturn and of the

Figure 7. Plan of the Roman Forum

1. Forum Iulium
2. Forum of Nerva
3. Forum of Peace (Vespasian)
4. Temple of Peace
5. Library of Peace
6. Basilica of Constantine
7. Porticoed annex to the Curia
8. Curia
9. Basilica Aemilia
10. Temple of Antoninus and Faustina
11. Tabularium (archives)
12. Temple of Vespasian
13. Temple of Concord
14. Arch of Septimius Severus
15. Tullianum (prison)
16. Rostra
17. Temple of Julius Caesar
18. Arch of Augustus
19. Temple of Vesta
20. Regia
21. Temple of Saturn
22. Basilica Iulia
23. Temple of Castor
24. Fountain of Juturna
25. House of the Vestals
26. Pearl Dealers' Portico
27. Graecostadium (shops)
28. Vestibule of the Imperial Palace

Temple of Castor provided the outline of the unit and served as the first markers. But it was only at the beginning of the second century B.C. that the north side of the square was modified, when the Romans began to build the great basilicas. With the Basilica Aemilia, the Forum became as we see it now, a vast, monumental unit (but no longer oriented, and the new alignment made a significant angle with the older Via Sacra), dominated by the two summits of the Capitol. On the south of the hill was the *Capitolium* (q.v.), crowned by the Temple of Jupiter Optimus Maximus (the Best and the Greatest), the center and symbol of Roman power; on the north was the Citadel (the *Arx*), with the Temple of Juno *Moneta*. At the beginning of the first century B.C., the dictator Sulla joined the *Capitolium* and the *Arx* with an imposing monument which served as a façade for the buildings on the hill and a "backdrop" for the Forum. This monument, called the *Tabularium*—for it held the official archives (the *tabulae*)—has survived to our day. On its enormous substructure, Michelangelo built his palaces.[9]

The last step in the development of the square was the building by Caesar of the immense Basilica Iulia, destined to be a counterpart, on the south, for the Basilica Aemilia. From that time on, until the end of the Empire, the Forum remained unchangeable.

We see how slowly the center of the City evolved. Until the end of the Republic, urban planning in Rome remained far behind not only that of the eastern cities but also that of southern Italy. Only in 54 B.C. was the first theater built of stone opened in Rome. For almost two hundred years, certainly, several theatrical performances were on the schedule for the games each year, but because of an old custom, comedies and tragedies took place in wooden theaters, which were taken down after the festival. Pompey was the first to feel himself strong enough to overcome the opposition of the Senate, mindful of ancestral usages, and to build on the Campus Martius a theater like those which the cities of southern Italy had already had for a long time. Less than ten years later, Caesar planned to build a second theater, but he was prevented by his death.

His adopted son, Augustus, took up the project and finished it. In 13 B.C., he dedicated the building (fig. 17) to the memory of his nephew, the young Marcellus.[10]

The main problem at that time was not so much putting up new public buildings as finding open space. Rome had remained a small city while becoming the capital of an immense Empire. After two centuries, the number of its citizens had increased well out of proportion to its facilities for public life. The old Forum was overcrowded; an ever-increasing number of cases was brought before the courts, which met out-of-doors in the public square. The two basilicas could no longer hold visitors and businessmen. So when he came to power, Caesar eagerly prepared a new urban plan. Knowing that the problem could easily be solved by disregarding the old prohibition and building on the Campus Martius, the dictator decided to change the course of the Tiber and to move it to the foot of the Vatican hills. He would have thus annexed a large plain, where a new Campus Martius might have been put. The old one would have been built over and used by private citizens. Moreover, the old Forum would have been doubled by adding another, more modern one, designed on the model of a Greek *agora* (public square).

His last battles, in North Africa and Spain, had not yet taken place when this project was started. Caesar arranged the purchase, at very high prices, of privately owned land near the Forum, and the new artificial bed for the river was begun. But after the Ides of March, the most original part of this plan, the annexation of the Vatican Plain and the "replacement" of the Campus Martius were abandoned under the pretext of a religious scruple. Only the new Forum was built; Augustus completed it and dedicated it to the memory of his adoptive father. But the main problem had not been solved: Rome always lacked space.

Augustus, in response, tried to find building sites on the distant Esquiline Plateau and, for that reason, put an end to the old cemetery which lay outside the Servian Wall. But this was only a makeshift. Some notable landowners, for whom Maecenas, the friend of Augustus, had provided the example, built magnificent mansions there, but the Esquiline was too far from the center, and it remained mainly a neighborhood of gardens and parks. Most of the Romans continued to crowd into apartment blocks which tried to offset the lack of ground area by their height. These *insulae* were put in any possible place: on the steep slopes of the Capitol or the Quirinal, on the parts of the Campus Martius which were abandoned or ceded to private citizens. The old Servian Wall was destroyed to make room for housing. Nevertheless, in spite of everything, Rome remained too small up to the end.

With the Empire and a strong government, the city could be run more effectively. So the emperors kept trying to adorn the city in order to provide a setting for public life worthy of Roman greatness. Their activity was focused on the center. There, the Forum Iulium or Forum of Caesar served as a model. It was the first of a series of monumental precincts, joined together, which are called the Imperial Fora (fig. 8). These differently shaped enclosures were built by Augustus, Vespasian, Domitian, Nerva, and Trajan, one after the other. At the center of each was a temple dedicated to a divinity especially honored by the Princeps (emperor). The surrounding colonnades of each unit provided shade or protection from the weather for pedestrians, the unemployed and merchants. Annexed to the fora were rooms for lectures or public readings, libraries, and various government offices. The Forum built for Trajan by the architect Apollodorus of Damascus was the last of these.[11] It was finished off by a hemicycle, for which the lowest slopes of the Quirinal were cut away and a market installed.[12]

With the Imperial Fora and the building of a gigantic amphitheater, the Colosseum (see pp. 64-65 below), a city plan was completed whose outlines remained, whatever one may have said, remarkably clear and coherent. By A.D. 113, the center of Rome was opened and vast spaces were made available for walking, business, and pleasure. Rome had in large measure caught up with the East and had truly become the "Queen of Cities." She could serve as a model for innumerable provincial cities which prospered in the West under the shelter of the Roman Peace.

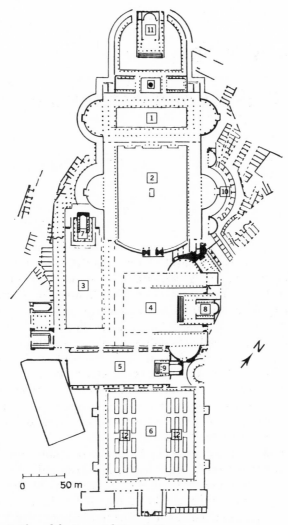

Figure 8. Plan of the Imperial Fora in Rome

1. Basilica Ulpia
2. Forum of Trajan
3. Forum Iulium
4. Forum of Augustus
5. Forum of Nerva (started by Domitian)
6. Forum of Peace (Vespasian)
7. Temple of Venus Genetrix
8. Temple of Mars the Avenger
9. Temple of Minerva
10. Trajan's Market
11. Temple of Trajan
12. Gardens

39

Chapter Three

Typical Urban Structures

Fora

Rome was born around its Forum. In the same way, every provincial city had in its center a public square around which all the activities of business and public life were concentrated.[1] Strictly speaking, a *forum* was enough to make a city. Along the highways which crossed the provinces, there were a number of small villages which had only such names as: Forum Appii, Forum Clodii, Forum Popilii,[2] etc., as well as "markets" scattered throughout Italy, points of contact where the natives encountered Roman civilization and ended up by settling. Thus, FREJUS, in Provence, was first a Forum of Caesar (Forum Iulii),[3] where Octavian, the dictator's adopted son, settled veterans of the Eighth Legion.

In certain respects, these provincial fora resembled the *souks* which are still found today in North Africa and which are temporary fairgrounds where the nomads come to get their supplies and to sell the yield of their herds. Similarly, some Roman merchants imported manufactured articles, which they exchanged for the products of local industry or agriculture.[4] Grouped in *conventus* (associations), they provided themselves with institutions comparable to those of Rome, and they had their political meetings in the fora. Gradually, the most outstanding of the native heads of family were allowed to take part in public life. A provincial city was born, where it soon became impossible to distinguish between the local people and the families of Roman origin.

At first, a forum consisted of a public square, an empty area around which the merchants placed their shops. Afterwards, people began to build more long-lasting stores. From the end of the third century B.C., the cities of southern Italy borrowed from the Greek colonies the use of colonnades (porticoes) which enclosed Hellenic *agorai*. Even before the Roman occupation, *Pompeii* (q.v.) had a forum surrounded by a colonnade dating from the Samnite period (doubtless built a little before 200 B.C.). At Rome itself, the first porticoes in the Forum only appeared with the construction of the basilicas, about thirty years later.

The Roman architect Vitruvius explains to us that there is an appreciable difference between the porticoes of the fora and those of the Hellenic *agorai:* the forum of a Roman city was used for shows.[5] It was there, for example, that gladiatorial combats took place during the funerals of important men. The colonnades had to allow a large number of spectators to cluster in the shade, while making it still possible to see. So the columns had to be placed as far apart as possible, and projecting balconies *(maeniana)* were placed along the upper floor of the portico and rented out by the town.[6] While the *agorai* were noticeably square, the fora (ideally) were rectangular, one-and-a-half times longer than wide. The shops were set back in the portico so as to provide free space. They opened under the colonnade, sometimes towards the forum and sometimes away from it. For example in the Forum of TIMGAD (fig. 9), the south wing of the portico held a row of shops, which faced the forum, while another row, on the north side, faced the *decumanus maximus* (q.v.).

In rectangularly planned cities, the forum was usually located in the center, at the point where the *decumanus* and the *cardo* met. There were, however, exceptions to this rule because of local topography. Thus in Tripolitania (q.v.), the cities of *Sabratha* and *Lepcis Magna* have fora displaced towards the north. But these were maritime cities, and the attraction of the port explains that anomaly.

The fora of cities founded or modernized after the beginning of the Empire were inspired less by the old republican Forum

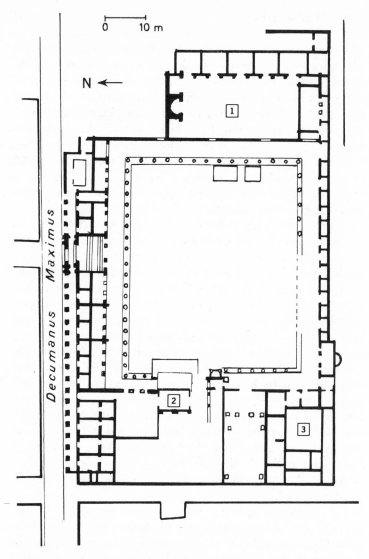

Figure 9. Plan of the Forum at Timgad
Following A. Ballu, *Les ruines de Timgad*[2] (Paris 1911)

1. Basilica   3. Curia
2. Temple

of Rome than by the Imperial Fora, in which colonnades were fully developed, and provincial architects racked their brains to think of original plans. In this respect, the most important forum is without a doubt that of ARLES, in *Gallia Narbonensis.* The paved rectangular area which forms the square is surrounded on the sides by underground corridors which make up the basement (fig. 10A). We no longer have a portico but a *cryptoporticus,* such as were often present in private buildings, especially vacation villas.

The cryptoporticus of ARLES is vaulted and supported by an axial row of pillars, which are linked by surbased arches (see arch, surbased). Daylight is admitted from the side towards the forum by a series of vents at the cornice (q.v.). Above this cryptoporticus was undoubtedly an open portico on three sides of the square. On the north side, in any case, the colonnade stopped in order to frame a temple, of which two columns and part of the rear pediment still remain. It seems to have been the Capitol of the city.

This type of forum, usually completely enclosed, spread and gave birth to clearly characteristic monumental units in the cities of Gaul (Cisalpine and Transalpine [qq.v.], under *Gallia)* and Britain. Recent excavations have revealed an example of this at SAINT-BERTRAND-DE-COMMINGES *(Lugdunum Convenarum* in Aquitania) (fig. 10B): there, as in the Forum of Augustus or that of Nerva, at Rome, the square and the temple form one block, a single *insula* enclosed by a quadruple portico (see city blocks). In front of the temple, an altar. Here and there in the forum, bases, on which statues were once placed. Between the temple and the square itself, a transverse street forms the fourth side of the portico. Like the three other wings, it was covered, and at each of its ends, a large block of stone kept vehicles out: the forum was well protected against intrusion. Only pedestrians could enter the square and go about their business. Behind the portico and parallel to the two long sides of the square, two rows of shops bear witness to the commercial activity of the city. The *insula* is large: 165 meters by 80.

The arrangement of the forum of SAINT-BERTRAND is found again at AUGST *(Augusta Raurica* in Switzerland) and also at

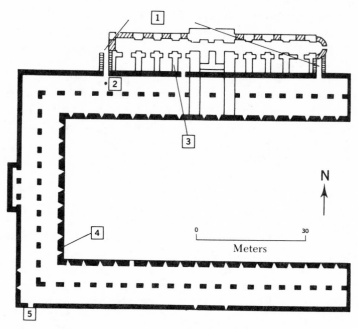

Figure 10A. The Forum at Arles
Following J. Latour, *Revue archéologique* 42 (1953): 49

1. Actual entrances to the corridors
2. Head of Tiberius
3. Temple and buildings of the fourth century
4. Original parts of the corridor
5. Present-day entrance

Lutetia (PARIS), where the forum has been identified at the location of the present-day Rue Soufflot.

Certain indications allow us to suppose that this type of forum was designed around the end of the first century B.C. and spread especially in the Age of the Antonines (the second century after Christ). Most of the cities in Britain adopted it, for example WROXETER *(Viroconium)*, but with a variation, for the British fora do not seem, as a general rule, to have contained a temple.*

---

*R. G. Goodchild, "The Origins of the Romano-British Forum," *Antiquity* 20 (1946): 70-77.

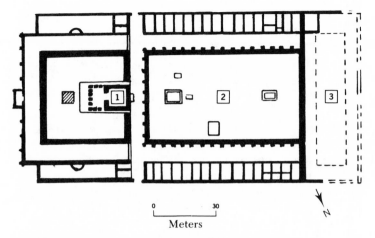

Figure 10B. The Forum of Saint-Bertrand-de-Comminges
Following B. Sapène, *Au forum de Lugdunum Convenarum, Inscriptions du début du règne de Trajan* (Toulouse 1939) pl. 1

1. Temple   3. Basilica
2. Forum

Basilicas and Curiae

Two almost obligatory additional buildings completed the provincial fora: a *basilica* (q.v.) and a *curia* (q.v.). By doing this, the architects reproduced the make-up of the Roman Forum.

We have explained how basilicas had been introduced in Rome at the beginning of the second century B.C.,[7] in order to duplicate the Forum in a way and to provide the citizens with a sheltered place to transact their business during bad weather. In essence, a basilica (so called from a Greek term which means Royal Portico)[8] is a kind of covered market, with sometimes one and sometimes two or more rows of columns, depending on the size. The basilica of TIMGAD is relatively small and corresponds to the first type (fig. 9). The Basilica Aemilia at Rome had three aisles (fig. 7), and the middle one had two stories. The Basilica Iulia was even larger (101 meters by 49), with six secondary aisles, and its central nave was three times larger than the six aisles.

At times, the entrance of the basilica was placed on the longitudinal axis, at the middle of one of the short sides, or there were several of them on one of the long sides. In provincial cities, the basilica usually makes up one of the sides of the forum, and its proportions are analogous to those of the square itself, that is to say that its width varies between a third and a half of its length.

Since the basilica sheltered not only private business but also official functions, it was customary to build there a tribunal, a dais where magistrates sat while serving, and since, under the Empire, this activity became more and more of a judicial nature, the basilica became *par excellence* the place where law-courts were held. At Rome, certain basilicas were even dedicated to one particular court or other: so, in the time of Trajan, the Basilica Iulia was usually used for the tribunal of the *Centumviri,* which heard civil cases.

It is probable that Roman civic basilicas were behind those which the Christians built later as places of worship. The question of the relationship between the two remains very obscure. Certain analogies are obvious: the use of colonnades and the division into aisles and nave, which, for example, is also found in the Basilica of Pompeii (fig. 11) and in the great Christian basilicas of RAVENNA (Sant'Apollinare Nuovo and Sant'Apollinare in Classe), which date from the first years of the sixth century A.D.[9] But Christian basilicas also have noteworthy differences: they only have an axial entrance, they have annexes, especially the apses, and their system of windows is entirely foreign to the legal basilica. All this hinders us from saying that the form was directly borrowed by the Christian architects. It only appears to have provided a general solution to the problem posed by the new religion—the need to assemble large crowds, protected from the weather and near places of pilgrimage, especially at Rome (the tomb of St. Peter, and so forth). But the details of the plan were determined by the special needs of the liturgy.

The second annex of provincial fora was the curia, the hall used for meetings of the local Senate, which, in the West, was called the Order of Decurions. At Rome, the Curia rose beside

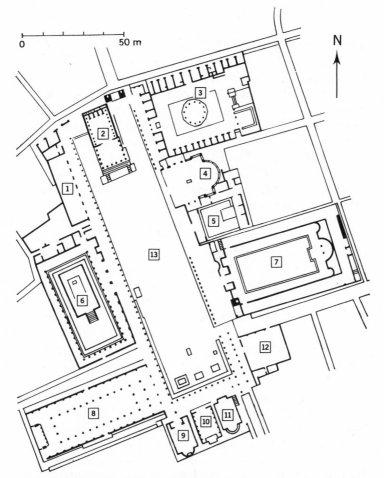

Figure 11. Plan of the Forum at Pompeii
For the Library, following L. Richardson, Jr., *Archaeology* 30 (1977): 400

1. Warehouse
2. Capitol
3. Market
4. Public Library
5. Temple of Vespasian (?)
6. Temple of Apollo
7. Building of Eumachia

8. Basilica
9. Office of the Aediles
10. Curia
11. Office of the Duumviri
12. Comitium (assembly place)
13. Forum

the Roman Forum, where we still see it today, as it was restored
by Diocletian, on the same spot as the Curia of Caesar. The
Roman Curia essentially consisted of a large rectangular hall,
but smaller and shorter than a basilica. In proportion to their
size, curiae are higher than basilicas. Vitruvius tells us that
this must be the case in order to provide an impression of
majesty worthy of the assemblies called to sit there. For this
reason, it is fitting, he says, that they be at least as high as the
width of the front, if the building is square, and even higher,
if it is rectangular. The same impression of size is also the
result of the place usually assigned to the curia: it ought to
dominate the forum. At *Pompeii,* for example, it is symmetrical
with the Capitol and faces the north side of the square (fig.
11). At DJEMILA (ancient *Cuicul,* between SETIF and
CONSTANTINE), it occupies the northeast corner of the older
forum and is entered through an ornate vestibule. At Lepcis
Magna (fig. 12), it looks like a temple, close to the basilica.

It is the curia which symbolizes the oligarchic spirit of the
Roman city. The best supporters of Rome always were the
local aristocrats, who very often owed their political power to
the conquerors. In return, the municipal magistrates strove to
embellish the city as well as they could and to make it a
reflection of Rome. Thus, as the inscriptions tell us, the
members of the chief families of the colonies and *municipia*
(qq.v.) built most of the local monuments at their own expense,
expanded and restored existing buildings and added, here and
there, porticoes and arches of triumph. They paved a street
or a square with beautiful stones; here, they decorated baths,
there they added a marble veneer, and somewhere else they
finished a temple. It was, for the decurions, a way of thanking
the people for the honors which had been granted them. This
building activity, almost obligatory if one wanted to "keep up
his position," was responsible for the magnificence of the
provincial cities during the second century of our era and up
to the dark years which marked the end of the third. It took
place nowhere with more brilliance—and sometimes excess—
than in the surroundings of the forum. Statues were put up
everywhere, on bases where many honorary inscriptions were

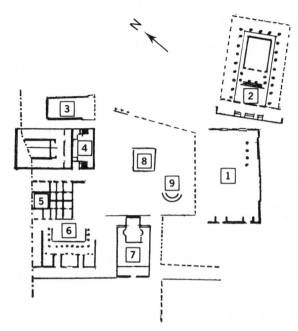

Figure 12. Plan of the Old Forum at Lepcis Magna
Following *Guida della Libia* (Milan 1937): 32a

1. Basilica
2. Curia
3. Unidentified temple
4. Temple of Rome and Augustus
5. Temple of Liber Pater
6. Portico
7. Temple of Magna Mater (later a church)
8. Baptistery
9. Exedra of the Severi

engraved. There was, of course, a statue of the reigning emperor, of members of his family, of his heir apparent, but also there were statues of the patrons of the city, usually a former governor of the province or a native son, who had won honors in the capital and the favor of the Princeps. One could see there the names of the *duumviri* (q.v., equivalent, in a *municipium* or colony, to the consuls at Rome), of their children and indeed of all the notables who, somehow or other, had deserved the gratitude of their fellow citizens. A crowd of images cluttered the square and the porticoes, the surroundings of the basilica and of the curia. However, quick changes in dynasties, revolutions imposed by the armies or the Roman populace and docilely accepted by the provincials, brought about, from time to time, the needed exclusions.

Temples

It was around the forum that the center of the religious life was located. Just as at Rome the Temple of Jupiter Optimus Maximus, in association with Minerva and Juno, dominated the Roman Forum, there was scarcely any provincial forum which did not also contain its Capitol (q.v.), consecrated to the same triad. The law according to which the *Colonia Genetiva Iulia* (Urso, in Spain) was founded expressly mentions the establishment of games in honor of "Jupiter, Juno, and Minerva."[10] We have already explained why this temple was built on a high terrace (see pp. 14-15 above—ed.). Thus it was at *Pompeii* (figs. 4 and 11), at *Ostia* (fig. 5), at DJEMILA and Sabratha and in almost all the provincial cities known to this day, even in the most distant colonies, such as *Banasa* and *Volubilis* (q.v.) in Mauretania Tingitana (present-day Morocco). We have also seen how the Gallic type of forum, such as that at SAINT-BERTRAND-DE-COMMINGES (fig. 10B), had closely integrated the Capitol, with the result that a unit was formed. There are, however, local exceptions: thus at TIMGAD, it is difficult to regard as a Capitol the little temple set just north of the curia (fig. 9). The Capitol of the colony must be sought outside of the original city limits on a hill at the southwest corner (fig. 1). The reason for this unusual location still escapes us. Perhaps there was a previous Numidian cult, set on a "height."

A Capitol may as a rule be recognized because it has a triple *cella*, that is to say three chapels placed side by side inside a single colonnade. It often happens, for that reason, that the plan of a Capitol is squarer and shorter than that of other temples. One proceeds to the terrace and the sanctuary by a monumental stairway, at the foot of which was built an altar— a simple cube of stonework decorated with reliefs—for religious sacrifices. The terrace thus rises above the forum and was used as a rostrum by the magistrates and all who, in the course of their duties, addressed the people. This is the case, among other examples, at Lepcis Magna, where the porch in front of the main temple in the older forum (fig. 12) was used as a speakers' platform.[11]

The Capitol embodied the majesty and the power of the Roman People. But emperor-worship was gradually brought in to the provinces, and we know that this cult eventually took over the sanctuaries of the forum. With respect to this, in Gaul, the history of the Maison Carrée at NIMES does not fail to be instructive. This little temple, miraculously preserved up to our day, dates from the first years of the reign of Augustus. Agrippa (the son-in-law of the Princeps) had given it to the inhabitants of the colony whose protector he was and had (at least this is probable) it dedicated as the Capitol. But when Agrippa died, the Nîmois, in gratitude, dedicated it to his two sons, the young Gaius and Lucius Caesar, whom Augustus had adopted and obviously had chosen as his successors. The new dedication took place in 2 B.C. But, shortly afterwards, the two princes died, and the temple naturally became the shrine of their divinity.

At VIENNE, the inhabitants had first built a temple to the linked divinities of Rome and Augustus. Then, some time after the death of Augustus, Livia, who had been his wife for so many years, also died and was deified, and the temple changed course and was dedicated to Augustus and Livia,[12] divine guardians of the imperial ruling *gens* (q.v.). The provincials could not do better than to install the emperor and his family at the very place where, in the time of the Republic, the supreme god of the Roman people was worshiped. So at Lepcis Magna, in the Augustan forum, the main temple, which dominates the square (fig. 12) and obviously was the Capitol, was transformed into a shrine of Rome and Augustus, around which were placed statues representing all the members of the Julio-Claudian family.

Gradually, the imperial cult occupied a more and more important place in each city. At DJEMILA *(Cuicul)* we find on

the southwest of the first forum a temple of this kind, that of
Venus Genetrix (Mother Venus), divine guardian of the Julian
gens, and a replica of the one which Caesar had built, at Rome,
in his own Forum. At DJEMILA, the location chosen makes it
balance the Capitol, as if the ancient Jupiter of the Roman
People ought to have been duplicated by the goddess
embodying the Destiny of the imperial family.[13]

With the death of Nero and the fall of the Julio-Claudians
in A.D. 68, the process did not stop at all. As dynasties
succeeded each other and the emperors were deified, temples
were added to temples around the provincial fora. The old
temples were neither secularized nor destroyed on this account,
with the result that it was necessary to build new centers in
order to make use of new shrines. This evolution is especially
clear in the North African provinces, where excavations have
now unearthed entire cities and where it is possible to follow
this development step by step. Thus we know that at DJEMILA,
the first forum, with its Capitol, Temple of Venus Genetrix (?),
and Curia, remained the monumental center of the city during
the first and second centuries of our era. But with the arrival
of the Severan emperors at the beginning of the third century,
the city was found to be too small. It was enlarged, and a
second forum was placed outside of the original boundary (fig.
26). This forum is one of the most beautiful examples of imperial
architecture at its apogee. Of much larger proportions than
the old forum, it served as a passage from the old city to the
new neighborhoods on the south. On the north side, it was
supported by the wall, which dominated it. There, in order to
hide the curtain wall, an old defense which the Roman peace
had made needless, was built a terrace, edged by a portico.
In the northwest corner (ed.), a fountain flowed. On the east
was another portico, faced by shops. The south side is almost
completely filled by a temple, the largest and most magnificent
of the entire city; its front is adorned with six Corinthian
columns, ten meters high, still in place today. This temple was
dedicated to the *Gens Septimia*, the whole imperial family. A
monument of loyalty to the reigning dynasty, it originally
adjoined a sanctuary of Saturn, the outstanding North African

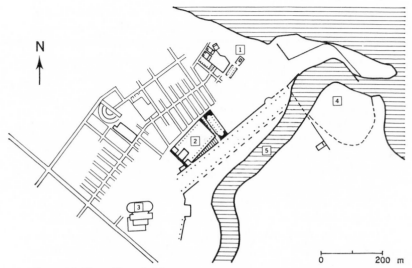

Figure 13. Plan of Lepcis Magna
Following J. B. Ward-Perkins, *Journal of Roman Studies* 38 (1948): 60, fig. 5

1. Old Forum
2. Severan Forum
3. Baths of Hadrian

4. Port
5. Wadi Lebda

god. But soon after the expansion of the city and the increase in its population, the god had to relinquish his place to a second civic basilica. In this way, a forum was created without a Capitol, placed completely under the divine protection of the emperor. On the west, the square was bounded by an arch of triumph dedicated by Caracalla, the son of Septimius Severus, and close to that arch has been found a building shaped like a basilica, in which has been recognized a market for cloth, like those which are still found in our day in the medinas of Morocco.

It was likewise to Septimius Severus that Lepcis Magna owed the building of a new district, comprising a street wholly lined by a double portico and a forum linked with a basilica (fig. 13). It is interesting to see that this Severan forum is very similar to those which we described at SAINT-BERTRAND-DE-COMMINGES and in the cities of Britain. There was a temple on the other short side of the square. Although the dedicatory inscription has not yet been found, it is probable that the family of the Severi was worshiped there.

The examples of DJEMILA and of Lepcis Magna show us according to what process provincial cities grew. Instead of adapting existing buildings to the needs of an increased population, one was content to juxtapose with the old civic center a new one, on land kept open. The emperors did not do otherwise at Rome even when they built the imperial fora.

Shrines to Native Gods

The state religion and the imperial cult did not extinguish all the religious life of the provincial cities. Each city had its *dii patrii*, traditional divinities, often resulting from the assimilation of a native god to a Roman one, which the inhabitants worshiped even inside the city. When it occupied the site of an old native village, people were content with "modernizing" (that is, Romanizing) the previous shrine. But such a temple often kept, in its shape or its location, peculiarities which distinguished it from those dedicated to divinities brought in by the conquerors. Thus one finds, in North Africa, Punico-Roman shrines, where Baal-Saturn and Juno *Caelestis* (the Roman substitute for the Punic Tanit) were worshiped, as well as the *Cereres*, the Greek Goddesses Demeter and Kore, brought from Sicily to CARTHAGE by the Carthaginians themselves after 396 B.C. These shrines are most numerous in the eastern part (present-day Tunisia), the regions which had most deeply felt the influence of CARTHAGE (q.v.). Those of Saturn usually included a large courtyard, surrounded by porticoes, where the sacred processions took place sheltered from profane onlookers, as well as chapels where the chief god dwelt with his assistant divinities. These *cellae* were placed over crypts, where liturgical objects were kept.* An important shrine of this type has been found at El Kenissia (Tunisia). Built well within the Roman period, it has the general

*G. (Charles-)Picard, *Les religions de l'Afrique antique* (Paris 1954).

characteristics of Punic holy places: raised altars, sacred pools, a chapel built on a terrace or "high place" to which one proceeded through a veritable labyrinth. Temples of this type were generally built on the outskirts of the city, while the Roman cults were placed in the center. At DOUGGA (near the present-day Téboursouk, in Tunisia), the Temple of Saturn is built in this way, on the side of the hill to the north and rather far from the forum. Similarly, a small North African temple has been found at TIMGAD on the heights dominated by the Capitol (fig. 1). And one could multiply the examples and show that Roman city planning, in spite of its apparent rigidity, could be adapted to the spiritual needs of the native populations.

The Gallo-Roman cities, unfortunately less well known than the cities of Roman Africa, also had religious buildings in the local style. We shall only mention here one group: temples with a polygonal or circular *cella* dedicated to Celtic divinities. The best known is the partly preserved temple of imposing size which is called the "Tour de Vésone." It most probably was built for the guardian goddess of the city of *Vesunna* (PERIGUEUX in Dordogne). It was twenty-seven meters high and its diameter was nearly eighteen meters. One guesses, from certain indications, that the circular *cella* was surrounded by porticoes. Inside was a rectangular park or large peribolus (fig. 14). The Temple of Janus at AUTUN, the shrine whose foundations were found at MAINZ in 1933,[14] the one at CHASSENON (in the *département* of Charente), the "Moulin du Fâ" at Talmont-sur-Gironde (in the neighboring *département* of Charente-Maritime and not far from BORDEAUX),[15] the temple of SANXAY (in Vienne, the same *département* as Poitiers) are almost copies of the sanctuary of PERIGUEUX. This plan, unknown outside the Celtic area, is obviously the result of adapting Roman architectural forms to the needs of native cults.* Similar buildings have been found outside of Gaul: for example, the octagonal temple of Weycock (Berkshire),[16] a temple which formed a sixteen-sided polygon at SILCHESTER

*J. Formigé, "Le sanctuaire de Sanxay (Vienne)," *Gallia* 2 (1944): 43-120.

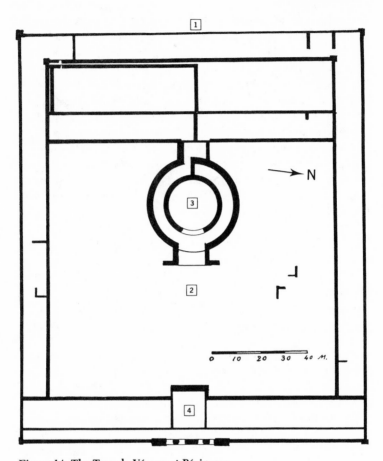

Figure 14. The Tour de Vésone at Périgueux

1. Porticoes   3. Tower
2. Peribolus   4. Entrance

(the ancient *Calleva Atrebatum*, in the Thames Valley), and
that of West Mersea (Essex),[17] whose ground-plan, with its
buttresses, looks like a cogwheel with six teeth.*

The provincial cities certainly had many other places of

---

*J. Ward, *Romano-British Buildings and Earthworks* (London 1911) 236-
238.

worship: temples were built to the Egyptian divinities, Isis and Serapis, to Cybele, to Mithra, to Jupiter Heliopolitanus. The soldiers of the legions and the auxiliary troops had spread their religion everywhere, in the garrisons on the banks of the Rhine and Danube as well as the frontier posts of the Saharan *limes* (q.v.). But it was usually ordinary people who worshiped these exotic gods, and they were not wealthy enough to build monumental temples. The chapels which they were able to build have disappeared, or else we can no longer recognize the remnants, in a ruin which is today anonymous, without an inscription which would make an identification possible. But if, in a provincial city, we often have the impression that only the official gods and especially those relating to the Imperial House were actively worshiped, let us not forget that an entire part—perhaps the most important—of the religious life remains hidden, because the temples which have been preserved for us were not the most-frequented ones but those which, somehow or other, served a political ideal.

Theaters and Amphitheaters

Theaters and amphitheaters figure among the most imposing and often the best-preserved buildings of Roman cities. Under the Empire, each city had at least a theater, and the more important ones had an amphitheater as well.[18] Games, no matter of what kind, were a necessity for the urban masses: the religious aspect never entirely disappeared, and, without them, the worship of the gods would have been incomplete. The law providing for the foundation of the *Colonia Genetiva Iulia,* which we have already cited, provided from the beginning for "theatrical games for Jupiter, Juno, and Minerva and the other gods and goddesses, for a period of four days."[19] When the rites of Roman religion were brought into the provinces, it was also necessary to provide there games and the buildings for holding them. And, moreover, the influence of these entertainments on uneducated people served as an efficient means of Romanization.

Theaters and amphitheaters were not used for the same performances. The former were reserved for comedies, tragedies, and mimes. Shows of a violent nature took place in the latter: gladiatorial combats, hunts in the arena *(venationes)* and all kinds, more or less disguised, of bloody sacrifices. Furthermore, while the amphitheater, like its games, was a typically Italic invention, the theater was a Hellenic sort of building. One, however, would be wrong to believe that the Romans, with their theaters, simply imitated the models offered by the cities of the East. The Roman theater differed from the Greek in several ways. Roman tragedies and comedies were not identical with those of the Greeks, and the theaters, for that reason, had to be adapted to the national literature. It was not at all out of clumsiness or caprice that Roman architects modified the plan and arrangement of Greek theaters.

Rome, as we have said, had no stone theaters before the last years of the Republic, but long before that date, theaters built of permanent material had multiplied in southern Italy in cities under the influence of the Greek colonies, their neighbors. The large theater at *Pompeii*, for example, dated, in the earliest form of its development, from the First Samnite Period (the end of the second century B.C.), and it then had all the essential characteristics of a Greek theater. After the Roman conquest, this theater was modified and adapted to the needs of Latin plays. This was the time when the first Roman theaters were built in southern Italy and in Sicily, even before the capital had one.

A Greek theater (q.v.) essentially consists of a circular space (the *orchestra*), where the chorus performed, surrounded on more than half of its circumference by concentric tiers. At the center of the *orchestra* was an altar, a reminder that tragedies and comedies were religious ceremonies more than literary entertainments. On the side opposite the tiers but touching the *orchestra*, the backdrop was formed by a building called the *skene*, whose length was equal to the diameter of the *orchestra*. In front of the *skene* ran a terrace, the *proskenion*, raised three or four meters above the *orchestra*. It was on the *proskenion* that the actors performed. At least, this was so in the Hellenistic period, the time when the Romans began to be influenced by the models which they saw in the Greek cities.[20]

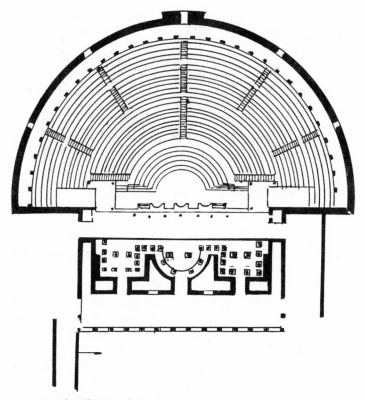

Figure 15. The Theater of Dougga

Roman architects made important changes in this plan: the *orchestra* was no longer a complete circle but a semicircle, and since Roman plays no longer had a chorus, the reduced *orchestra* was invaded by the spectators. In this area were put seats for the most important people of the city. The rest of the audience took their places on the tiers of the *cavea*. This was likewise limited to a semicircle and did not exceed the diameter of the *orchestra* (fig. 15).

Thus the whole performance took place on the *proskenion* (called *pulpitum* by the Romans), lower and closer to the *orchestra*. The supporting wall of the *pulpitum* was not higher than two or three feet. It was usually decorated with small

Figure 16. The *Scena* of the Theater at Sabratha

columns and niches, alternatively rectangular and semicircular. Often fountains flowed there, in order to freshen the air, and the water was drained away by a channel parallel to the *pulpitum*; thus the spectators and actors were separated. Moreover, the use of a curtain was introduced: through a slot on the front part of the *pulpitum*, a sliding partition was raised from the floor and retracted. Thus, just the reverse of our custom, the curtain was lowered at the beginning of the play and was raised at the end. Behind the *pulpitum*, the old *skene* had not disappeared at all, and its façade continued to provide scenery for the play, but its height was much greater than in the Greek theater; the architecture of this back wall—called the *scenae frons* or façade of the *skene*—became complicated and loaded with stereotyped decorative elements.

The *frons scenae* was one of the most characteristic elements of the Roman theater. It represented the front of a palace, which could be as high as three stories (fig. 16). An uneven number of doors—three or five, depending on the magnificence of the theater—was placed there, in order to make possible communication between the *pulpitum* and the inside of the imaginary palace. The central door was called the royal door, and through it appeared the tyrant of a tragedy. The side doors were used for the entrances and exits of the people "from inside" and of less importance. Travelers, messengers, and slaves came and went through the passages at each end of the *pulpitum*, on the audience's right or left, depending on whether they arrived from (or returned to) the city or the port. Each door of the *frons scenae* (except for "temporary" ones) was framed by columns and often topped by a projecting pediment or entablature. It even happened that the royal door was a veritable pavilion surrounded by a concave niche. For each one of these ground-level doors there was, on the upper stories, a window, where, for example, gods appeared.

The fashion of using *frontes scenae* detracted greatly from the realism of the setting. Its monumental nature prevented any changes between one play and another, but there was an invaluable advantage, still appreciated in our day by actors who use Roman theaters: one's voice, reflected by the wall, easily fills the whole *cavea*. It is probable that the prototypes of the *frons scenae* were in Asia Minor, but Rome adopted and perfected them, and, in the most developed forms, *frontes scenae* are found throughout the West. One can be seen as well at ORANGE, in Gallia Narbonensis (the theater goes back to the first century A.D.), as at Sabratha (q.v.) in Tripolitania (fig. 16). Other good examples are at DOUGGA, at DJEMILA, and in Sicily (notably at *Segesta* and TAORMINA).

The *frons scenae* was extraordinarily ornate. Statues were placed in the niches and sculptured friezes on the entablatures. The stone was faced with precious and brightly colored marble. With their splendid and dazzling architecture, Roman theaters surpassed all other buildings in prestige.

Another characteristic distinguished Roman theaters. While Greek theaters were usually placed on the slopes of an acropolis (for example the Theater of Dionysus at Athens) so that tiers could be cut out of the rock, Roman cities, as a rule laid out on a plain, could not use such an expedient. It was necessary to support the *cavea* on a substructure, built upon a system of vaulted passages. Thus a new type of architecture was created: on the outside, the building looks like an immense half-rotunda, whose façade is formed by several levels of arcades, one on top of the other (fig. 17). Looking through the arches, one

Figure 17. The Theater of Marcellus at Rome

could surmise the existence of crossing corridors, of stairways, and of ambulatories set beneath the tiers: one has the impression of an immense framework made of cement and stone. It was all planned so as to allow large crowds to move. In a few moments, thousands of spectators could reach their assigned seats and, in case of a sudden rainstorm, take shelter in the covered passages until the sun returned.

In addition, there was often a large quadrangular portico behind the stage for strolling. Its central area was often made into a garden and decorated with groves and fountains.

In the provincial cities as well as at Rome, the theater formed a particularly impressive unit and, unlike the Greek theaters, was completely independent of the landscape. The *frons scenae* reached the same height as the top of the *cavea*. Thus it became possible to place a frame over the entire building. Covered theaters were imaginable. But the Romans covered only small theaters (sometimes given the name of *odeum* or *auditorium*).

Large theaters were simply sheltered by awnings supported on poles.

It is generally said that the oldest amphitheater is the one at *Pompeii*. At least, until now, it is the oldest one known. It is contemporary with the small theater of the city (about 80 B.C., see fig. 4). Built far from the center, it is at the eastern corner of the city. From a technical point of view, its construction reminds us of that of the small theater, and at first, we have the impression that an amphitheater is nothing more than a double theater: two *caveae* are set together, while each of the two *orchestrae* forms half of the arena. But amphitheaters were not really derived from theaters.[21] They were an original invention which only used some of the technical inventions needed for the latter, and this is clearly seen at *Pompeii*. There, the amphitheater does not yet have the complicated system of vaulted passages and interior staircases characteristic of later theaters and of the great imperial amphitheaters. The architects tried as much as possible to use the natural support of the landscape for the tiers. For that reason, they set the arena lower down than the ground outside, so well that, of the three levels of tiers, only the highest needs supporting walls. The lowest level is entered on gently sloping ramps. The middle level was even with the ground of the city; the top level was made accessible by stairs built on the outside—an unsophisticated expedient which architects soon stopped using.[22]

The Amphitheater of *Pompeii* allows one to suppose that early amphitheaters were formed by a simple earthen embankment, shaped like a funnel and supported, inside and outside, by palisades or walls. Thus the amphitheater was architecturally only a shortened circus, a type of structure which was always set in the bottom of a valley. So in Rome, the *Circus Maximus* was in the *Murcia* Valley, where the track stretches out between the slopes of the Palatine and the Aventine (see fig. 6). But while the circus, because of the dimensions needed for horse races, never stopped depending on the landscape, the amphitheater attained its architectural independence from

the beginning of the first century B.C. The elliptical shape of
the arena—in contrast with the circular orchestra of the Greek
theater—is explained by the need to contain the maximum
number of spectators without overstretching the dimensions
of the structure.

Amphitheaters were, almost certainly, a Campanian
invention, in keeping with the well-known taste of the Samnites
for bloody entertainments, battles between gladiators or wild
beasts. At Rome, these kinds of games took place in the Forum.
This was, we saw, the dictum of Vitruvius. But at about the
time that his *Treatise on Architecture* appeared, a Roman noble,
Statilius Taurus, built on the Campus Martius the first stone
amphitheater at Rome. The City had to wait until the Flavian
dynasty (after A.D. 69) to obtain an amphitheater worthy of its
importance.

The construction of the Colosseum (such was the medieval
name of the Flavian Amphitheater) was begun by Vespasian
and finished by his younger son, Domitian. It would hold at
least 45,000 people. After having been ravaged for centuries
and used as a quarry by the builders of Papal Rome, it still
stands majestically between the Palatine and the Caelian. In
spite of its gaping wounds, it remains the most finished example
of the classical amphitheater and also the largest in the whole
Roman world. Its outer dimensions are 188 meters by 156,
and those of the arena 80 meters by 54. The outer wall reached
a height of 48.5 meters, and the structure was even higher
when a wooden story was added, in cases of need, to the top
of the *cavea*.[23]

The Colosseum, viewed from outside, is very reminiscent
of the Theater of Marcellus, which obviously was used as a
model, but while the outer wall of the theater comprises three
levels of arcades in the three Greek orders (Doric, Ionic and
Corinthian; see figs. 17 and 36), on the Colosseum is
superimposed a fourth level, without openings[24] and decorated
with Corinthian pilasters. Inside, the three tiers rest on a series
of concentric vaulted passages, whose number decreases level
by level. The ground level has five, the second level three,
and the third two. At the fourth level, there is only one passage,

Figure 18. Cross Section (restored) of the Colosseum
Following the restoration by J. Durm, *Handbuch der Architektur* II. 2²
(Leipzig 1905)

mainly filled with staircases. (See fig. 18 for the relationship
between the tiers and the arcade-levels.)

The floor of the arena rested on a basement in which were
put machines used for the spectacle. In it were passages and
access-ramps for the beasts, dressing-rooms, and also a network
of pipes and channels for drainage.

The provincial cities had not waited for the building of the
Colosseum to provide amphitheaters for themselves. The one
in SAINTES (in Charente, the same *département* as Talmont-
sur-Gironde; see p. 55) is thirty or forty years older. Those of
ARLES and NIMES are contemporary with the foundation of

these colonies and go back to the reign of Augustus. And the dimensions of these provincial buildings are not much smaller than those of the Flavian Amphitheater. Thus, for the main Gallic amphitheaters, one finds the following dimensions: AUTUN: 154 meters by 130. Poitiers: 138 by 115. Limoges: 137 by 113. ARLES: 136 by 108. Tours: 135 by 120. BORDEAUX: 132 by 105. NIMES: 131 by 100.[25] The amphitheater of *Italica*, near Seville, was even larger than that of AUTUN (156 meters by 134).

The number of provincial amphitheaters known today is very large. Even relatively unimportant cities had one, where games continued to be given until the beginning of the sixth century after Christ, even at Rome.

In Gaul, these places for shows had a special importance, and one may find a theater or an amphitheater built far from any ancient settlement. These were not therefore planned for the urban populace but for the villagers and peasants. The frontiers of the tribe of the Santoni (the region of SAINTES) thus contained such buildings, of which the best known is the Théâtre des Bouchauds in Charente *département* (about twenty kilometers west of Angoulême).[26] It is very probable that the Romans had found that method to control the large periodic assemblies which were customary for the Gauls and which could have been dangerous if used for hidden political or religious propaganda. The development of games, Romanization by means of the theater or amphitheater and large "pilgrimages" were ways of disciplining the assemblies and gradually substituting Roman influence for that of the druids, while the rites were made more humane.[27]

This policy resulted in the creation of an entirely new type of amphitheater, which seems to have been at first characteristic of Gallic country. The most finished example has been found at the shrine at SANXAY (see p. 55 above) and was studied not long ago.* From the classical amphitheater, this one keeps the arena, which is elliptical or at least in the shape of an elongated oval (fig. 19), but the *cavea*, instead of completely surrounding

*J. Formigé, "Le sanctuaire de Sanxay (Vienne)," *Gallia* 2 (1944): 84 ff.

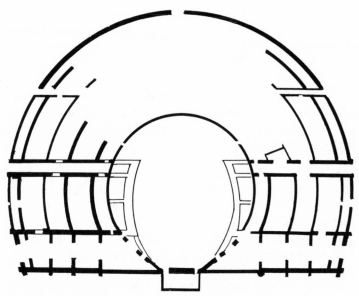

Figure 19. Plan of the Demi-Amphitheater of Sanxay
Following J. Formigé in *Gallia* 2 (1944) 89, fig. 28

the arena, is limited to a semicircle, like the theaters. At the
place where one expects a stage there is only a small platform,
raised very high.

It is obvious that this unusual arrangement, which forms
both a theater and an amphitheater, is the result of an attempt
to save money. It is less expensive to build a *cavea* by placing
the tiers on the side of a hill rather than by supporting it with
an enormous and complicated substructure. But the landscape
can never hold more than a half-circle of tiers, at the most. In
this way, the demi-amphitheater or half-amphitheater was born,
of which a certain number of examples are known. The most
famous—although it is not easily recognizable in its present-
day location—is the one at PARIS. The Arènes de Lutèce are,
in spite of the name, nothing more than a demi-amphitheater
built on the slopes of Montagne Sainte-Geneviève. One can
likewise mention, with the name of the French *département*
in which they are found, the demi-amphitheaters of

Berthouville (Eure), CHASSENON (Charente; see p. 55),
Chènevières (Loiret), Drevant (Cher), Evreux (Eure), Gennes
(Indre-et-Loire), Lillebonne (Seine-Maritime), Néris (Allier),
Valognes (Manche), and Vieux, as well as that of Lisieux (both
in Calvados).[28] From Gaul, this type spread rather far, and we
know that in the Late Empire, the theater of *Iol-Caesarea*
(CHERCHELL, in Algeria) was modified and received an arena.

Baths

Next to the buildings used for shows, the most characteristic
structures of Roman cities were undoubtedly the *thermae* or
public baths.[29] Here again, we are discussing an Italian
architectural invention, which is derived from the Hellenic
gymnasium. Like the Roman theaters and amphitheaters, they
first appeared in southern Italy: the oldest known example is
that of the Stabian Baths (at Pompeii; see fig. 4; the name is
modern). In their earliest form, they antedate the Roman
conquest (about 89 B.C.), but modified several times, they kept
being modernized and enlarged until the end of the city (A.D.
79). One may clearly see there the development of comfort
and luxury, a typical evolution of baths under the Empire. To
the earliest period belong several narrow dark cabins used for
private baths. In addition, the large courtyard surrounded by
columns and used for exercises form part of an old Greek-
style, *palaestra*. Originally, the water was drawn from a
neighboring well. But this rudimentary equipment was
gradually improved. Pipes brought in the water from aqueducts,
and large halls were built, each of which was used for the
various *steps* of the complicated process which a bath then
was. By 89 B.C., the Stabian Baths had already been provided
with the essential parts. But it is particularly in the Forum
Baths, built around 80 B.C., and remarkably preserved, that
we can clearly see the interior plan for buildings of this type
(fig. 20).

The Forum Baths, like the Stabian Baths, are divided into
two parts: the larger one was for men and the smaller for
women. There is still a *palaestra:* it fills up the rear section of
the men's baths, but its dimensions are relatively modest: a

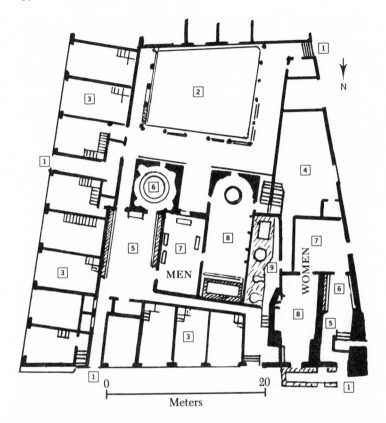

Figure 20. The Forum Baths at Pompeii

1. Entrance
2. Palaestra
3. Shops
4. Garden
5. Apodyterium

6. Frigidarium
7. Tepidarium
8. Caldarium
9. Furnace

square of about twenty meters on each side. It was not used for old-fashioned exercises, but rather for strolling, for playing ball and, especially, the constantly repeated pleasure of conversation. The women's baths had only an uncovered area, perhaps arranged as a garden.

The men's bath is more complete. It has the four parts

necessary for any Roman bath-building: an *apodyterium*, a large cloakroom where the bathers took off and left their clothes, then a cold room, the *frigidarium*, then a warm room, the *tepidarium*, and finally a steam room, the *caldarium*. Everyone went from one to the other according to the customary ritual. The plan of the Pompeian baths shows that the *apodyterium* opened into both the *frigidarium* and the *tepidarium:* thus it was possible for one to go directly into the cold room for the first ablution, accomplished by plunging into a pool which took up almost the whole room, or else one could first enter the warm room, where the body gradually became used to a high temperature. After a few moments, the bather went into the *caldarium*, where the heat caused abundant sweating. A basin was placed there, holding lukewarm water and a tub into which one could plunge. It was then possible, by following the route in the opposite direction, to return to the *frigidarium* for a last cold bath. In the more complicated and sumptuous baths built during the imperial era, other rooms were used for massages, for applying oil, and the rooms for conversation and strolling were multiplied. This is quite apparent, for example, in one of the largest baths of TIMGAD (called the Large North Baths or the Northern Baths; see fig. 1), whose arrangements and symmetry obviously relate to the most magnificent bath-buildings in Rome, those of Caracalla or those of Diocletian (fig. 21). There one finds, next to the *caldarium*, where basins kept the hot room humid, rooms for dry heat, called *laconica* or Spartan baths, where the temperature could climb even higher.

The need to locate in the baths sources of heat, powerful yet still capable of maintaining varied temperatures in the different kinds of rooms, led the architects to invent ingenious methods, of which the most common was the use of pavement supported on pillars of brick, which were called *suspensurae*. Thus, the hot air from the furnace circulated freely and warmed the floor, then it escaped through a large number of vertical pipes built into the walls, while the dust and smoke were carried along. In order to control the temperature of a room, it was sufficient to vary its location along the path of hot air, and the

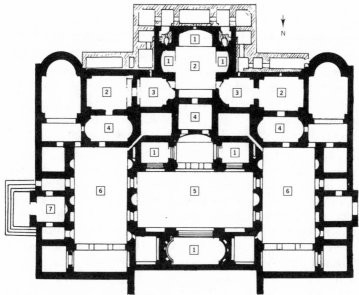

Figure 21. The Large North Baths at Timgad

1. Pool
2. Caldarium
3. Laconicum
4. Tepidarium

5. Frigidarium
6. Promenade
7. Vestibule

rooms closest to the furnace were obviously the hottest. One may note, therefore, that at the Forum Baths at *Pompeii*, the furnace was placed between the two *caldaria*, that of the men's baths and that of the women's (fig. 20).

Each Roman city had a large number of baths,[30] besides the baths in the most costly private homes. Thus at TIMGAD, there were at least a dozen bath-buildings, in a city which certainly had no more than 15,000 inhabitants. And TIMGAD is no exception. The exploration, still incomplete, of the colony of Banasa (q.v.) in Mauretania Tingitana, shows that that modest city, in present-day Morocco, had nothing to envy in the baths of TIMGAD, except perhaps their cost and their sumptuous decoration. In the baths was spent a considerable part of the

Romans' daily life, in the provinces as well as in the capital. At about four o'clock in the afternoon, at the end of the business day, one went to the baths to pass in a leisurely manner the time until dinner. One exercised a little, one relaxed while having a massage, one chatted, one munched on a sweet bought from a strolling candy-seller. It was there that meetings for business or conversation were held, as they previously were in the Forum. During the Empire, the baths were, as has been said, the cafés and the clubs of the Roman cities.

Aqueducts

To provide water for the large number of baths in each city, secure and capacious conduits had to be built.[31] There is no Roman town which did not have, however small it may have been, its aqueduct. For a long time, Rome's inhabitants were satisfied with wells, which were easy to drill in the wet ground of the valleys and, on the hills, with cisterns, many remnants of which have been found. But, towards the end of the fourth century B.C. (in 312), Appius Claudius, the same censor who built the Appian Way between Rome and *Capua*, equipped the city with its first aqueduct, which was called the *Aqua Appia* (Appian Water). It is very likely that the engineers at that time copied the procedures used in the Greek or Hellenized cities of southern Italy. These remained very simple: the aqueduct was still only a channel of stonework, and it rested on the ground or was sunk beneath the level of the earth. It followed the natural slope of the landscape at the cost of interminable curves. It was thus that the *Appia*, although its source was some seven miles from Rome, was, in fact, eleven miles long (11,190 Roman *passus* or 16.55 kilometers from the east), and close to the City, it ran above ground, on supporting walls or arches, for only 60 *passus* (88 meters). Furthermore, it is likely that the elevated sections were built much later. This primitive technique had a serious disadvantage. On leaving its source, the aqueduct very quickly lost altitude, and the water, when it reached the City, was like an underground brook, without any "height," it just flowed into the basin of a fountain. It was impossible to imagine distributing the water under pressure to private houses.[32] Water was common property, and people went to draw it from the nearest fountain. The overflow was lost in sewers or else was sold to dyers, launderers, and the owners of private baths. Such was the water supply at the time of the Punic Wars. At that period, no *thermae* existed, and the need for water was modest. Until the middle of the second century B.C., two aqueducts only were sufficient, the *Appia* and a conduit fed by the *Anio,* the river of *Tibur* (Tivoli), which joins the Tiber some distance upstream from Rome.[33] After the fall of Carthage (in 146 B.C.), when Rome became a Mediterranean capital, its population increased considerably, and a third aqueduct had to be added: this was the *Marcia,* the first modern aqueduct of Rome, and it brought to the City water from springs in the upper valley of the Anio, between TIVOLI and SUBIACO. A kind of veneration was felt for this water from the Sabine country. At the same time, a new custom began: persons of rank, in recognition of their services to the state, were allowed to use the water free of charge. In this way, a significant part of the water carried in by the aqueducts was gradually diverted for the use of private houses. It was then that reservoirs built of masonry or water-castles probably originated; to them were connected private supply-pipes.[34] From that time on, Rome had its underground network, with extensions in all the districts. At the same time, progress was made in the art of civil engineering. A discovery was made, or, at least, it was employed systematically: the (inverted) siphon, that is to say the putting under pressure of a part of the system in order to carry water across a valley without the inconvenience of interminable windings. In spite of much opposition, some of which was colored by religious pretexts, water reached the Capitol and the other hills. The cisterns on the Palatine were abandoned, filled in, or covered. Rome would be, for centuries, dependent on its aqueducts.

At the beginning of the Empire, when private baths multiplied as well as grants to individuals, it was necessary to increase the amount of water brought in. The formation of the little army which maintained the waterways was a result of the administrative talents of Agrippa, who originally recruited them from his own slaves and freedmen. First the friend and later the son-in-law of Augustus, Agrippa put in order the whole network of aqueducts, which, up to that time, had been indifferently administered by censors or aediles. He also built, in the Campus Martius, the first public baths in Rome. He increased the capacity of the existing aqueducts, which he modernized by adding siphons (q.v.) to eliminate the long windings and by multiplying the distance covered above ground on supporting walls and arches. Agrippa furthermore built two completely new aqueducts, the *Aqua Virgo* (Virgin, because, it was said, a young girl had pointed out its excellent source, not much more to the east than that of the *Aqua Appia*). Entering Rome by the Hill of Gardens on the north, it supplied his baths with their large open-air pool. The second, the *Aqua Julia,* from southeast of Rome, is carried on the greater part of its course on the same arches as the *Marcia*. Agrippa multiplied the fountains and the water-castles *(castella aquae),* especially in the new neighborhoods on the Esquiline and even in Trastevere, on the right bank of the river. He standardized the diameters of pipes for private use, and he tried to make a sufficiently precise estimate of the quantities distributed by regulating the water pressure (enough to raise a column of water a few centimeters above the point of connection). It was thus that the water-workers made up for the absence of volumetric measurements. But the water was not distributed under more pressure than before. The Romans had nothing comparable to our lawn-sprinklers or our indoor plumbing with faucets on each story. Fires, numerous at Rome and in all the urban centers, had to be fought by knocking down the threatened buildings (to create a gap) and watering the debris with bucket brigades, done up to a century and a half ago.[35]

Two of the largest and most famous Roman aqueducts, whose stately arches still cross the Campagna today from the Alban Hills, are the *Aqua Claudia* and the *Anio Novus*. Built by the

Emperor Claudius between A.D. 47 and 52,[36] their sources are also in the valley of the Upper Anio, to the north of the Alban Hills. To serve the highest regions of Rome, it was necessary to keep the conduits as high as possible, and for that reason the two channels are now thirty-two meters above the ground at the Porta Maggiore, the southeast corner of Rome.[37]

The amount of water piped into Rome in twenty-four hours (towards the end of the first century after Christ) has been calculated to be about 992,200 cubic meters, a large figure, even if one allows for a total urban population of almost one million, a high estimate.[38] A good portion of this enormous volume was distributed to private individuals, to small businesses (laundries and fulleries), but plenty was left for the public fountains which ran day and night in all the neighborhoods, and especially for the *thermae*. This abundance of sparkling fountains has always been a Roman luxury: the modern city has in no way lost the tradition. But there was another purpose for constantly running water. Gathered in the sewers, it cleaned them by taking along the refuse into the main sewer, the *Cloaca Maxima*, which had been used previously to drain the swamp in the Forum (see p. 35 above). We explained how the *Cloaca*, originally open, had been covered with a vault towards the beginning of the second century before Christ. What we see now, at its outlet into the Tiber, is a reconstruction, the work of Agrippa.[39]

The aqueducts built for the provincial cities followed the same principles as those of the capital. Sometimes their magnificence equalled that of the latter, as is shown by the Pont du Gard, an aqueduct leading to the colony of NIMES, at a height of more than fifty meters above the valley of the Gard. The date is uncertain, but it certainly should be set back to the first century of our era. It comprises three levels of superimposed arcades, and a single arch of the bottom level suffices to cross the river, at least as a rule (fig. 22).

The colony of LYONS had four aqueducts, of which the latest (probably built at the time of the Emperor Hadrian, about A.D. 130) spans seventy-five kilometers. Near NARBONNE, an

Figure 22. The Pont du Gard

ancient aqueduct still runs, and one may spot, every now and then, in the midst of the vineyards, "manholes," which let out the imprisoned air.

City Walls and Triumphal Arches

The origins of Rome were marked by many wars, and for centuries, the City lay in the midst of a hostile Italy. The same was true for most of the provincial cities, especially colonies founded for strategic reasons. Because of these insecure conditions, cities had to be surrounded by walls, and from the sixth century before Christ, Rome had a wall of gray volcanic stone—small blocks of porous tufa called *cappellaccio*, from local quarries—of which some vestiges still remain. This is the wall which has usually been called, since ancient times, the Servian Wall (see p. 30 above).[40] It surrounded, as has recently been shown, all of the urban settlement, mainly extended beyond the *pomerium*, and enclosed, in particular, the Aventine (see fig. 6). It is generally said to have ended at the river, to the west of the Capitol, and to have stopped for some distance along the river bank, only to begin again west of the Aventine. Actually, it seems much more probable that this first wall did not include the plain of the Forum Boarium, bordered the Palatine (on the west), and crossed the valley of the *Circus Maximus*. It used as much as possible the natural escarpments, the slopes of the Capitol, which it crowned, and those of the Quirinal. But if the site of Rome was enclosed on the north, the west, and the south by an almost uninterrupted line of heights, on the east the wide plateau of the Esquiline did not place any natural obstacle in the way of an invader. There, it was necessary to complete the wall with an embankment (the *agger*) and a ditch, about thirty meters across and ten meters deep.

The defensive system of the *agger* was soon faced with a tufa revetment, and at the beginning of the fourth century, after the Gallic invasion, the wall of *cappellaccio* was doubled with another wall, built of much more solid stone (of Grotta Oscura tufa), cut into larger blocks which were used as headers and stretchers. The masons' marks suggest that Greek engineers worked on this, and the Roman wall of the fourth century much resembles those of the Hellenized cities in southern Italy. A similar arrangement is found at *Pompeii*. There, we know that the wall, the oldest parts of which go back to the middle of the fifth century B.C. and latest to the end of the second, was, as at Rome, built with two facings of cut stone, between which was inserted rough masonry made of irregular pieces of stone and cement. The outside facing was equipped with battlements. The inside facing was higher and reinforced with buttresses to resist the blows of battering rams. The battlements were reached by means of stairs built on earthen terraces.

The use of towers was not widespread until the beginning of the second century B.C. At *Pompeii*, they are not much earlier than the siege of the city by Sulla (89 B.C.). These were three-story square towers, projecting from the curtain-wall and topped with battlements. This system was subsequently used in all the provincial cities. We find it, for example, in the time of Augustus, in the fortifications of AOSTA (*Augusta Praetoria*, at the northwestern corner of Italy), at NIMES, and also at

AVENCHES (*Aventicum,* in Switzerland), which was surrounded at the end of the first century after Christ by a very large enclosure. One may also cite for comparison the ramparts of two great North African cities, Tipasa (q.v.) and CHERCHELL (*Iol-Caesarea*), which, at their origins, were roughly contemporary with those of AVENCHES.

As long as the Roman Peace ensured safety in the Empire, fortifications were neglected. Except for some cities in frontier regions or near zones of unrest, the walls were not maintained, and sometimes even, as at Rome, certain sections were destroyed in order to build civil structures in their place. We have explained how Maecenas, at the time of Augustus, had extended his gardens from one end of the Esquiline *agger* to the other (pp. 37-38 above). Two centuries later, the Servian Wall was no more than a memory: the broken lengths which remained (mostly on the Aventine, the Capitol, and Quirinal) were no more than isolated vestiges of the ancient fortification, with no practical use. Moreover, Rome had grown, and the City extended beyond all parts of the royal wall. So when, towards the third quarter of the third century, the threat of barbarian invasions forced the Romans to make provisions for the security of their capital, they had to build a new wall, separate from the ancient one and much longer. This was the Wall of Aurelian, begun around A.D. 272 and finished some years later under the Emperor Probus.[41]

A large number of existing buildings were used for this work: for example, the barracks of the Praetorian Guard, built in the reign of Tiberius, a small amphitheater, called the Military Amphitheater, perhaps simply because it was located near a barracks, also tombs, for example, the pyramid built by a certain Cestius (next to the present-day Protestant Cemetery of Rome), the substructures of the large gardens whose terraces covered the slopes of the Pincian Hill or Hill of Gardens, as well as the main aqueducts on the Esquiline Plateau. This new wall enclosed, besides the districts of the left bank, the triangular plain of Trastevere on the right bank, and it made a kind of forward bastion (see fig. 6).

Although this wall was built hastily, it still was planned and executed with the greatest care: most of it still stands today, and its gates are the same, with some minor modifications, which present-day traffic uses. Along it, projecting quadrangular towers were placed twenty *passus* (about thirty meters) apart. The wall itself was not made, as before, of a solid mass of masonry. Rising about eight meters above ground level, the substructure was solid and supported a series of vaulted rooms, separated by strong buttresses and supported on the exterior (this is to say, facing the enemy) by a solid wall, reaching a thickness of one meter. Above the rooms, there was a circular patrol-route. This system had several advantages. Not only did it allow for numerous armories and protected storehouses, but, most importantly, it decreased the total volume of masonry without weakening the wall's strength. It was not, moreover, invented by Aurelian's engineers, but it followed a long tradition which went back, it would seem, to the Hellenistic period. The same technique may be seen at CHERCHELL (from the first century A.D.), in Britain at *Cilurnum* (Chesters, on Hadrian's Wall),[42] and in still other places.

One ought, of course, to compare the Wall of Aurelian with those built at the middle and the end of the third century A.D. by the great cities of the Empire: BORDEAUX, SAINTES, PERIGUEUX, as well as LONDON and PARIS.[43] We see the same characteristics everywhere: reuse of materials taken from older structures, especially tombs, slabs with inscriptions (which, as a result, have been preserved for us), sculptured capitals, fragments of friezes or columns—all these were good for engineers in a hurry.

Nevertheless, however hasty they may have been, these fortifications were not without their grandeur. The gates, especially, were often built in a monumental style. We have just mentioned, with regard to the Aurelian Wall, the long, partly Hellenistic traditions behind Roman engineers. As a result, Italic architects were also predisposed to vaults and arches. Thus an easily recognizable style existed, which influenced the gates of Roman walls. Most often, they included a court, which gave access to a vaulted passage.[44] Such is the case, for example, at CHERCHELL (fig. 23), for a gate, apparently of the first century after Christ. Sometimes there is a single vault, and sometimes it is double or even triple: then, of the three arches, the one in the center is the largest. Rather often, the gate fits between two towers which complete its protection. This is true of all the large gates of the Aurelian Wall at Rome. But perhaps the most noteworthy example is the famous *Porta Nigra* (or Black Gate) at TRIER, which goes back to the end of the third century or the beginning of the fourth of our era (fig. 24). It has only two arches and a court, flanked by two semicircular towers projecting outwards. The outer side comprises three superimposed levels. Two levels of arcades are supported on the two arches of the gate. The rhythm of the façade resembles that of amphitheaters. The towers have four levels and a flat roof.[45]

The art of the monumental gates, which had such a beautiful renaissance at the end of the Empire, should be compared to that of triumphal arches, which are also gates but separated from any wall. They were designed as independent structures. The Hellenic East did not have arches of triumph, which were an Italian invention. Very probably, they resulted from the triumphal rite: in order to enter the City, the victorious general and his army had to pass through a gate specially built for this purpose on the *pomerium,* after the required sacrifices had been offered to the divinities of the threshold. Thus was born, at the beginning of the second century B.C., the custom of putting up, almost everywhere in the City, symbolic arches, commemorating the victorious return of an army. From the end of the Republic, the Roman Forum was bordered by several arches, the earliest of which was that of Fabius, built in memory of the victory in 121 B.C. over the Allobroges (a tribe from the northeast corner of *Gallia Narbonensis* [q.v.] and VIENNE). But in the time of Augustus, arches were multiplied almost everywhere in Italy, as well as in the provincial cities, especially in Gaul.[46] Next, there was one for each reign, and since they were made for the fora, one may find in the North African

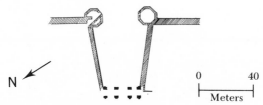

Figure 23. Cherchell, Plan of the South Gate
Entrance to gate at top of plan. Following P.-M. Duval, *Cherchel et Tipasa,
Recherches sur deux villes fortes de l'Afrique romaine* (Paris 1946) p. 101,
fig. 13

Figure 24. The Porta Nigra at Trier

cities, for example, several series of arches, some going back
to the Antonines (emperors A.D. 96-192) and others to the
Severi (A.D. 193-235).

Worthy of mention among the arches in Gaul are those of
Aix-les-Bains, Carpentras, Saint-Chamas (near Aix-en-Provence)
and ORANGE (fig. 25), all of which date from the Augustan

Figure 25. The Arch at Orange

period.[47] The one at SAINTES, at the entrance to the bridge over the Charente River, was built during the reign of Tiberius in A.D. 19. Others, like that at Cavaillon (also in Vaucluse), cannot be dated with certainty.[48]*

---

*On elements of urban architecture omitted by Grimal in this chapter, see note 49 below—Editor.

Chapter Four
Some Important Cities

The study of the principal urban structures has, until now, shown us the similarities among Roman cities: this resemblance was obligatory insofar as it was a tangible expression of the Roman "federation."[1] But it is very certain that this Roman unity, however real and powerful it may have been, could not prevent any diversity from occurring: we have already seen the proof with regard to religious buildings and amphitheaters. But the very life of each city, its evolution, the vicissitudes of its inhabitants were controlled by the geographical conditions in which it was located. And this was equally true of everything which resulted from private initiative (excluding government buildings). It will be sufficient here for us to trace in general outlines the physiognomy and history of some particularly important centers, in North Africa, in Gaul, and in Britain.

Cuicul (DJEMILA)

The founding of *Cuicul* (today DJEMILA, in the central part of northern Algeria) goes back to A.D. 97. It was the work of the Emperor Nerva, who wanted thus to occupy a strategic position, the point in the mountains where two highways crossed.[2] One was the major government road from east to west between the recent towns of *Cirta* (CONSTANTINE) and *Sitifis* (SETIF). The north-south road ran from the port of *Igilgili* (modern JIJEL) to the camp of the Third Augustan Legion at *Lambaesis*. Earlier at *Cuicul*, there had been a native village, inhabited by Numidians (Berbers [q.v.], ancestors of the

83

Kabyles). It occupied a triangular spur, flanked by paths along the wadis, steep-sided or seasonal water-courses. The choice of this site forced the first departure from the rules of laying out a city: *Cuicul* never was a square city and possessed only the beginning of a *decumanus*, oriented in a very approximate way (fig. 26). On account of the landscape, the walls formed a triangle, whose shortest side protected the spur at its base. Very soon, the enclosed area was too small; the choice of site was a happy one. The fertility of the neighboring land, the abundance of the springs, the ease of communications with the interior of a more and more prosperous province caused the city to develop rapidly. Three-quarters of a century after its founding, *Cuicul* built a theater for itself, about 150 meters south of the wall, and twenty years later were built the South Baths, whose splendor and also whose plan remind one of the Large North Baths at TIMGAD. In choosing the locations for these new buildings, the architects followed only the contour lines of the site, without bothering about any geometric rules *a priori*. They foresaw that the city would develop on the plateau in the shape of a fan—and their prediction came true. But, at the same time, as we have seen, they kept free, at the place which, they thought, would become the center of the new city, room for a new forum, which would be the work of the Severi (see pp. 52-53 above). When they built it, they were content to follow the line of the old South Wall, which became the baseline of their plan. There were two arches: one was on the road leading to the theater (it was built in A.D. 161), and the other at the exit from the new forum (it dates from 216). They showed that at these points a monumental zone began. So the growth of the city was limited—by the very landscape—on the east and on the west.[3]

Later, the city continued to grow, even in the midst of the disorder and insecurity which marked the third century of our era, and, when Christianity triumphed, it was in the southern suburb, on the location foreseen by the first architects, that the Christian District was built, two hundred years later, with its basilicas, its baptisteries, and its bishop's palace. Thus, the urban evolution of *Cuicul* shows a remarkable unity. It overcame

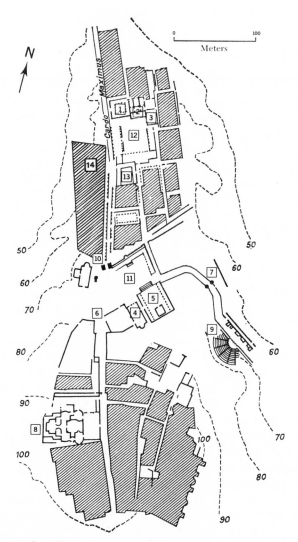

Figure 26. Plan of Djemila: Forum of the Severi

1. Market
2. Capitol
3. Curia
4. Basilica (4th century)
5. Temple to the Severan Family
6. Arch of Caracalla (A.D. 216)
7. Arch of A.D. 161

8. Great baths
9. Theater
10. Original south gate
11. Forum of the Severi
12. Old Forum
13. Temple of Venus Genetrix (?)
14. Newly excavated area

all hindrances and yet remained obedient to the imperatives of the site: the *cardo* was not a true axis, as directed by the rule, but north of the Severan Forum, it was a boulevard in the original sense of the term (the flat top of a rampart), for it was lined with shops which extended to the edge of the western wall. Later, a terrace overlooking the Forum of the Severi was substituted for the old *decumanus*. And fountains were placed throughout; there was one behind the Arch of Caracalla and yet another at some distance from the Large Baths, on the southern extension of the *cardo*. The northwest corner of the New Forum (ed.) was ornamented with a fountain,[4] as was the market, near the Capitol. The courtyards of private houses were likewise made agreeable and civilized by the presence of water; thanks to Roman engineers, the North Africans understood the necessity of placing cool fountains everywhere.

At first sight, one would find the private houses of DJEMILA, and the other North African cities, similar to the classical house, with *atrium* (q.v.) and peristyle (q.v.),* as at Pompeii. Of this Italic house, those at DJEMILA retain the essential element: the central courtyard surrounded by columns (the peristyle). But in reality, there is a great difference. Characteristic of the *atrium* house was an axial series of rooms, but here, one first enters a vestibule of small dimensions and then, directly, the peristyle, which is the heart of the home. Along its four sides are placed rooms, some of which are no more than narrow cells and others, more ornate, serve as rooms for formal occasions. The Italian *atrium* is not seen here, and there is no reason to suppose that it was ever imported into Africa. During the period when the great North African cities were built, the *atrium*, at Rome itself, was no more than a memory, a vestige of the past, which kept diminishing in new structures. Thus, by a natural evolution, the North African houses are much closer than those of Pompeii to the Hellenistic houses which we see on the island of Delos, for example, and which go back to the second century B.C.[5] This same type was continued in

*See P. Grimal, *La vie à Rome dans l'antiquité*³, "Que sais-je?" no. 596 (Paris 1960), pp. 49-59.

the eastern and southern Mediterranean and gave rise to the Arab house. From the first centuries of our era, the Roman city made an indelible mark on North Africa.

LYONS *and* VAISON-LA-ROMAINE

We have already explained why our knowledge of the Roman cities of Gaul is less complete than that of certain North African cities (see pp. 8-9 above). It is, however, not impossible to see in outline the development of one city or another. This is true of the city which was the administrative capital of the Gaul then called *Comata* (long-haired), the colony of *Lugdunum*, LYONS (see *Gallia Comata* in the glossary).

Founded in 43 B.C., one year after the death of Caesar, Lyons probably owed its existence to a plan of the dictator, which was realized, as the Senate decreed, by Lucius Munatius Plancus.[6] The motive of its founders is obvious: here met the two main Gallic routes, one from the Rhine to the Mediterranean and other from the Lake of Geneva to the Atlantic; here the old *Provincia*, Hellenized for more than a century, made contact with the recently conquered peoples. At this place, it was natural to found a colony which would be both an outpost of Roman civilization and soon a crossroads of the Celtic world, unified under the rule of Rome, with its attendant peace. Until a few years before the conquest, VIENNE was the most northern of the great cities in the valley of the Rhône. But the Roman traders who had settled there were driven out by a revolt, and having asked the Segusiavi (a Gallic tribe just to the north) for refuge, they were received favorably and settled at the confluence of the Saône and the Rhône Rivers.[7] It was on this Roman nucleus that Caesar depended at the beginning of his intervention in Gallic affairs, when he campaigned against the Helvetii in 58 B.C. The strategic and economic value of the site was as a result made evident, even before Gaul was annexed.[8] At that time, on the hill which would become that of Fourvière, there was only a Celtic village. The first objective of the founders was to surround the new

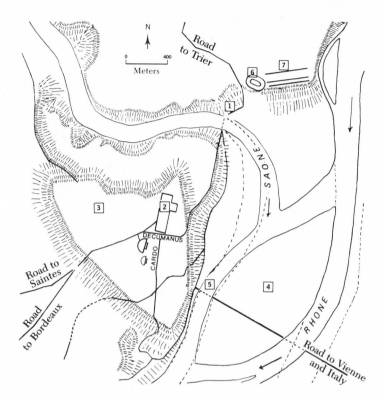

Figure 27. Plan of Lugdunum
Following P. Wuilleumier, *Lyon, métropole des Gaules* (Paris 1953)

1. Condate
2. Forum
3. Fourvière Hill
4. Canabae

5. Ancient harbor
6. Amphitheater
7. Shrine of the Three Gauls

colony with a solid wall which followed the triangular contour of this hill (fig. 27). The wall itself has not been found, but its gates have been recognized. Through them passed the great roads leading to the different regions of Gaul and towards Italy.[9] The forum, which gave the hill its name in French (from Forum Vetus or Old Forum), was set on a terrace; placed above the *decumanus* and the *cardo*, the forum joined them only by means of two ramps. The location of the Capitol and that of the other public buildings escape us.[10] The medieval and modern cities have covered up the traces, perhaps forever. From the colony of LYONS, properly speaking,[11] we know in detail only the magnificent theater of the Fourvière, which recent excavations and restorations have revealed to us. There, on the side of the hill, up to ten thousand spectators could sit. An odeum (q.v.), nearby, could hold three thousand.[12]

Below, outside the walls of the Fourvière were soon placed the residential and business districts, whose memory has at least been preserved by inscriptions.[13] The first was on the island which the Saône *(Arar)* and the Rhône then formed, the suburb of the cabins (or shops, the *Canabae,* q.v.), where the wine-merchants had their warehouses.[14] On the right bank of the Saône the owners of barges had their offices, near the port and the docks. Higher up, just at the confluence, the suburb of *Condate* (in Gallic, the Confluence) welcomed, in 12 B.C., the great shrine consecrated to the divinity of Rome and Augustus by Drusus, the brother of the future emperor Tiberius. This altar, where each year representatives from all the Gallic tribes came to sacrifice, gave birth to an entire district whose center was the federal altar itself, with a temple and, soon, a large amphitheater.

One may see in the history of *Lugdunum* a typical outline of a Roman city's successive functions: a Roman outpost, it became a commercial crossroads by road and by river, and soon the religious center of the new Gallic provinces. And each time, a new district was born in answer to the need which had been created. There also, not *a priori*, no preconceived theory hindered the free play of geographical laws.

If the lasting prosperity of LYONS and the great future which awaited the foundation of Munatius Plancus prevent us from seeing the details of the appearance of a Roman city, we can find in a small town of Provence, VAISON-LA-ROMAINE, some idea of what a Gallo-Roman city was; VAISON was the tribal capital of the Vocontii. There, careful excavations have unearthed the ancient neighborhoods and especially the private houses, and we are allowed a glimpse of urban homes in *Gallia*

Narbonensis. At VAISON are examples of the traditional house
with *atrium* and peristyle, notably the houses called of the
Silver Bust and of the Messii, the latter on the hill of Puymin.
The former is well dated: it was without a doubt built towards
the end of the first century of our era, and it is interesting to
underline here the survival of the *atrium*—perhaps as a result
of the traditionalist spirit which lasted long in the western
provinces. But a new kind of private home was coming in, the
insula (see city blocks in the glossary). Not far from the House
of the Messii has been unearthed a group of apartment buildings
in every respect comparable to those of Ostia and Rome: instead
of receiving light from inner courtyards, the rooms open onto
the street, and the stairs from the upper stories also lead to
the street. Certain neighborhoods—the most crowded—of the
Roman cities in Gaul looked like the old streets of GENOA or
NICE today.

Houses in Roman Britain

As one went farther away from the Mediterranean private
houses gradually became different; more and more, they
resembled the Gallic huts, and it is very probable that, in the
northernmost cities, only a few private mansions were built in
the Roman way. While the evidence is scarce for Gaul itself,
numerous excavations in Britain prove, in that province at least,
that private houses looked very different from those in the
Mediterranean provinces. A first difference is the fact that the
British houses did not cover a city block, but they were
surrounded by a large garden; this was never the case in the
Mediterranean cities. It follows that their plan was not
determined by the landscape on which they were built. The
simplest houses formed a sort of corridor or hallway, whose
front was one of the long sides, bordered by a veranda. The
interior was divided by transverse partitions into separate rooms
which opened onto the veranda in front. Sometimes, at one
end of the house, a room projected out and led to the veranda.
In the larger homes, two hallways were often placed so as to
form a right angle—the start of a house with a patio—with the
rooms simply placed around the open space (fig. 28). At times,

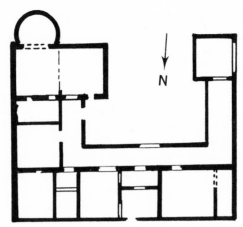

Figure 28. Private House at Silchester
Following J. Ward, *Romano-British Buildings and Earthworks* (London 1911) p. 149, fig. 43

it happened that this space was completely enclosed and became a real courtyard. This arrangement looks like that of the North African house, but its origin and its spirit were entirely different: the courtyard here was nothing but the end, almost accidental, of an evolution and not a central and essential element around which the entire plan was arranged. In fact, it certainly seems that we have in a city like SILCHESTER *(Calleva Atrebatum)* not so much really urban houses as rural homes transported to the city and adapted, somehow or other, to the needs of Roman city planning.[15]

The kinds of public buildings brought into the provinces were direct imitations of those in the capital, but the urban planners could welcome forms of architecture foreign to the Italian tradition and preserve, as much as was necessary, what was original in the local traditions. It was perhaps for this reason, thanks to this flexibility and pragmatism, that Rome could take into account the climates, the social and economic needs, and also the particular talents of each of the peoples welcomed into the Empire and in this way could give birth to so many viable cities, shelters for more than a thousand years and strongholds of Roman civilization.

Part II

Editor's Notes on
Les villes romaines

Introduction (pp. 3-9)

[1] For the shift from the hill to the plain, see Boëthius, "RGTA" 7-8 and Février, "CSG" 18. On new cities built in the West under Roman rule, see Grimal, *Civ. Rome* 353. But some of them were still built on hills, for example, LYONS and DJEMILA.

[2] See Tacitus, *Life of Agricola* 29-30 (= Ogilvie and Richmond, *Agricola* 110-112); translation in N. Lewis and M. Reinhold, *Roman Civilization, Sourcebook II: The Empire* (New York 1966) 415-416. Chapter 21 of the *Life* should be compared with this passage. As governor, Agricola Romanized the southern part of Britain by encouraging the construction of "temples, fora and private houses" (see Chapter III [above] on these). Furthermore, he had the chiefs' sons educated, with the result, says Tacitus, that they preferred the Latin tongue.

For a similar kind of education in Gaul, see AUTUN. On Agricola, see MARSEILLES and + *Verulamium* (under LONDON) below.

[3] An interesting question is why some Roman cities survived to the present, while others did not. The Roman cities of northern Italy (listed in Ward-Perkins, *Cities* 28-29), France, and Western Germany have been continuously occupied. Those of North Africa (on the water supply, Broughton, *RAP* 5-6), Switzerland, and England, for the most part, have not.

[4] A number of Roman colonies were, however, founded in the East. See A. H. M. Jones, *The Cities of the Eastern Roman Provinces*[2] (Oxford 1971), B. Levick, *Roman Colonies in Southern Asia Minor* (Oxford 1967), N. Lewis and M. Reinhold, *Roman Civilization, Sourcebook II: The Empire* (New York 1966) 18 (= Augustus, *Ac-*

95

complishments 28; the document is also translated in A. H. M. Jones, *HR* II pp. 11-23 and in P. MacKendrick and H. M. Howe, editors, *Classics in Translation* II [Madison, Wis., 1952; rpt. 1966] 302-308; called *The Achievements of the Divine Augustus*, the edition by P. A. Brunt and J. M. Moore [Oxford 1967] provides commentary, Latin text and translation). In his *Accomplishments*, the first Roman emperor (died A.D. 14) lists colonies which he founded in the West as well as in the Roman East.

For more on eastern colonies, compare the list in Salmon, *RC* 159-164 under Achaea (southern Greece), Asia Minor, Dacia (Romania), Dalmatia (Adriatic Yugoslavia), Macedonia and Thrace (northern Greece and European Turkey), Moesia (Yugoslavia and Bulgaria), Pannonia (Hungary and Yugoslavia) and Syria (also including Israel and Lebanon); also see Salmon's fig. 12.

Chapter 1 (pp. 10-27)

¹ See Rykwert, *Idea* 65-68. For an example, see A. Audin, *Lyon, miroir de Rome* ... (Paris 1965) 48-51, on the founding of LYONS. For a contrary view, stating that the position of the sun was of no importance, see J. Le Gall, "Les romains et l'orientation solaire," *Mélanges d'archéologie et d'histoire de l'Ecole française de Rome* 87 (1975): 287-320.

² On surveying a Roman city, see Castagnoli, *Orthogonal Town Planning* 75-80, Ward-Perkins, *Cities* 38-40 and, the most helpful, Salmon, *RC* 20-24. Compare centuriation in glossary.

Basic on Roman city planning are: Haverfield, *Town Planning;* K. Lehmann-Hartleben in *RE* III.2 (1929) 2016-2124; P. MacKendrick, "Roman Town Planning," *Archaeology* 9 (1956): 126-133; Crema, *Arch.* 28-33; Wheeler, *RAA* 25-88; Lavedan, *HU;* Harmand, *Occ. rom.* 291-353; Castagnoli, op. cit.; Ward-Perkins, *Cities* and "ERTI." A well-illustrated book for teen-agers will be of value as an introduction: D. Macauley, *City* (Boston 1974).

On planning a Roman army camp and the similarity between that and planning a Roman city, see H. Stuart Jones, *Companion* 226-243; Salmon, *RC* 26-27; Gutkind, *IHCD* V (1970) 184; Boëthius and Ward-Perkins, *ERA* 552, n. 5 (bibl.); Ward-Perkins, *Cities* 28 and Boëthius, *Golden House* 49-54. On the analogy between Roman camps and cities, E. Saglio said, "Thus [orthogonally] planned, the camp became a veritable city, with all its resources joined together, well organized and conveniently located" (Daremberg, *Dar Sag* I.2 [1887] 943, transl. Woloch).

Also see Castagnoli, *Orthogonal Town Planning* 110-113, on TURIN and AOSTA, examples, Castagnoli says, of the "axial plan . . . influenced by the 'encampment plan.'" See ibid. 115-121 on the "encampment plan." On camps, see OSTIA ANTICA, +Caerleon and +Chester (under WROXETER), *Lambaesis* and MAINZ below. Following the *Oxford English Dictionary,* I use the word "camp" throughout rather than "fortress," which Ogilvie and Richmond recommend (*Agricola* 198-199).

[3] More recent examples of orthogonal or checkerboard city planning are Aigues-Mortes (Gard, France, 13th century), New Haven, Connecticut (1638), and Mannheim (Baden-Wuerttemberg, Federal Republic of Germany, 1689). These, like the British outposts in Ireland and France (late 16th and early 17th centuries), were designed to be easily defended, and their plans were influenced by Roman models.

On Aigues-Mortes, see Gutkind, *IHCD* V (1970) 52-56, 475 and Morris, *Urban Form* 85 (air view of Aigues-Mortes). On New Haven, see R. G. Osterweis, *The New Haven Green and the American Bicentennial* (Hamden, Conn., 1976) 12-15; 12, n. 4 cites A. N. B. Garvan, *Architecture and Town Planning in Colonial Connecticut* (New Haven 1951) 1-49.

Also see Boëthius, "RGTA" 18 (Stockholm, Trondheim [Norway] and cities in the Americas). For the orthogonal cities of Spanish America, see Zucker, *Town and Square* 132-140, 274 (bibl.) and C. Gibson, *Spain in America* (New York 1966) 126, especially n. 29 on bibliography and the influence of Vitruvius (listed below under "Ancient Sources").

[4] See Livy 1.6, Fustel de Coulanges, *Ancient City* 134-138 and Rykwert, *Idea* 27-29.

[5] See H. Stuart Jones, *Companion* 14; Salmon, *RC* 24 and 168, n. 27; as well as Ward-Perkins, "Rykwert."

[6] The date is corrected here by the editor, see Grimal, *Search* 181 and MARZABOTTO.

[7] On this area, see Nissen, *IL* II, 437-457.

[8] *Near* Frascati (editor's correction); see *Tusculum* below.

[9] This date is subject to correction. See NAPLES and *Paestum* as well as Etruscans in glossary.

[10] Although Strabo (q.v., 5.4.8) says that the Etruscans once held *Pompeii,* no Etruscan remains have been found there (L. Richardson, Jr. in *PECS* 724). Richardson dates the city wall to the 3rd/2nd centuries B.C.

[11] E. Strong took an opposing view: "That Italic axial planning de-

veloped independently and earlier than the Greek is now accepted"
(*Cambridge Ancient History* IX [1932] 836, n. 1); she said that she
was in agreement with D. S. Robertson. But in both editions of his
Greek and Roman Architecture (Cambridge 1929 and 1945), Robertson was cautious: "The connexion of the Roman scheme with that
popularized by Hippodamus has been much disputed, but they may
have been independent inventions" (p. 193, in both editions).

After summarizing the controversy since 1869 (*Orthogonal Town
Planning* 2-7), Castagnoli takes the view that, in general, orthogonal
systems have no specific predecessors, but the plans of *some* Roman
cities were derived from the works of Hippodamus (pp. 80-81, 124-
125), for example, *Norba, Alba Fucens, Cosa* (pp. 96-99) and *Volsinii
Novi* (p. 137), as they had long and narrow blocks.

The pendulum, however, has swung back to Grimal's position with
Ward-Perkins: "The great achievements of Roman town planning were
built on a solid foundation of Greek theoretical and practical experi-
ence" (*Cities* 20). The same view is held by Wheeler (*RAA* 88), and
that of Boëthius ("RGTA" 7-9) is close to it.

Chapter 2 (pp. 28-39)

[1] Grimal says 754 B.C. here, but see Grimal, *Civ. Rome* 33 and
Ogilvie, *Early Rome* 11, 172. On the origin of the 754 B.C. date
(calculated in the 1st century B.C.), see H. Stuart Jones in *Cambridge Ancient History* VII (Cambridge 1928) 322.

[2] See Livy 1.26. The Sister's Beam was not a real gate.

[3] This is the theory of A. Piganiol, "Les Origines du Forum," *Mélanges . . . Ecole française de Rome* 28 (1908): 233-282 = *Scripta
Varia*, Collection Latomus 133, vol. II (Brussels 1973) 67-104. Even
if we admit that a city could be laid out in an area the size of the
Roman Forum, it would not work out because those streets were not
in fact orthogonal (see fig. 7 above and Nash, *PD* I, 446-449, II, 284).
The theory that Rome's *groma* (q.v.) lay on the Palatine Hill and this
theory, that it was put in the Forum, are summarized and compe-
tently put aside by Castagnoli, *Orthogonal Town Planning* 74-75.
Castagnoli suggests that Rome may not actually have been founded
in the first place (ibid. 124); it was an amalgamation of clusters. Also
see Ward-Perkins, "ERTI" 136-139; Ward-Perkins, "Rykwert"; Boëthius and Ward-Perkins, *ERA* 551, n. 1; F. E. Brown, "Of Huts and
Houses" in L. Bonfante et al. (editors), *In Memoriam Otto J. Brendel* (Mainz 1976) 5-12 and T. J. Cornell, "The Foundation of Rome..."

in H. Blake et al. (editors), *Papers in Italian Archaeology* I.i = British Archaeological Reports Supplementary Series 41.i (Oxford 1978) 131-140, on Rome's origins.

Perhaps it is best to say that Rome, like PALESTRINA, TIVOLI, and *Tusculum* (see p. 20 above), was founded before axial planning became prevalent in Latium. Roman colonies were "images" of Rome in all but their streets.

The inhabitants of Rome kept their irregular street plan after the Gallic invasion (early 4th century B.C.) and after later fires, just as was done in post-medieval LONDON (U. E. Paoli, *Vita Romana*[2] [Paris 1960, translated from the Italian into French] 99, n. 142; cf. Tacitus, *Annals* 15.38 and Boëthius, "RGTA" 19, n. 7). (The traditional date of the Gallic occupation of Rome is 390 B.C., but other ancient chronologies use 387 and 386—see Gauls below, H. Stuart Jones in *Cambridge Ancient History* VII [Cambridge 1928] 321-322 and the table opp. p. 321 and L. Homo in *CAH* VII pp. 561, n.1 and 564, as well as A. Piganiol, *La conquête romaine* [Paris 1967] 142-143, 620-621. Ogilvie says ?386 B.C. in *Early Rome* 9, 172.)

[4] The outline is much clearer on fig. 2 of Grimal's *Civ. Rome*. On the Servian Wall, see pp. 76-77 above; Grimal, *Search* 64-68, *Civ. Rome* 46-49 and *Mélanges ... Ecole française de Rome* 71 (1959): 43-64; G. Saeflund, *Le mura di Roma repubblicana*, Acta Instituti Romani Regni Sueciae 1 (Rome 1932); R. M. Ogilvie, *A Commentary on Livy, Books 1-5* (Oxford 1965) 179 (on Livy 1.44.3); Dudley, *Urbs Roma* 34; Nash *PD* II, 104-116; Piganiol, *HR* 38, 537-538 (further bibliography); and cities (Roman), comparison in area, in glossary.

The existing Servian Wall (e.g., near Rome's main railway station) dates from the early 4th century B.C. (Saeflund), but traces of an embankment behind the "republican" wall have been found on the Quirinal Hill. The earliest phase of this mound was thought to date from c. 550 B.C., the legendary date of Servius Tullius (Ogilvie, op. cit.), but in a later book, *Early Rome*, Ogilvie redates this mound to c. 475 B.C. (pp. 87, 97; cf. Alfoeldi, *Early Rome* 320 ff.).

[5] *Emporion* meant market in Greek; see AMPURIAS, below.

[6] On the new shops, burned in 210 B.C. and rebuilt before 192 B.C., see R. M. Ogilvie, *Commentary* (op. cit. note 4 above) 487-488. They were removed to make way for the restored Basilica Aemilia (early 1st century B.C.; see p. 36 above).

[7] The *Comitia Centuriata* was the political institution, the *Comitium* the place.

[8] See PALESTRINA and TIVOLI.

[9] On the *Tabularium*, see R. Delbreuck, *Hellenistiche Bauten in Latium* I (Strasbourg 1907) 23 ff.; Robertson, *GRA* 240-243; MacDonald, *Arch.* plate 11; Crema, "Arch. rep." in *ANRW* I.4 (1973) plates 40-42; and Nash, *PD* II, 402-408. A good photograph of its interior is used as the frontispiece of Grimal, *Search*. On Michelangelo's palaces, see C. Pietrangeli, *Piazza del Campidiglio* (Milan 1955). For plans of the area, see F. Coarelli, *Guida archeologica di Roma* (Milan 1974) 40-41 and 50-51.

[10] See Chapter III, n. 23 below, ARLES and ORANGE, Nash, *PD* II pp. 418-422, Dudley, *Urbs Roma* 178-180 and Earl, *AA* plate 3 on the Theater of Marcellus.

[11] On the Imperial Fora, see Ward-Perkins, *Cities* 40-42 and K. Schefold in *ANRW* I.4 (1973) pl. 15. On the Forum of Trajan, Ammianus Marcellinus (q.v.) 16.10.15.

[12] On Trajan's Market, see C. Ricci, *Il Mercato di Traiano* (Rome 1929); Carcopino, *Daily Life* 315, n. 6 (bibl. note by H. T. Rowell); Nash, *PD* II pp. 49-58; Grimal, *Civ. Rome* 274-275; (Charles-) Picard, *Roman Architecture* 46, 53-55, plates 37-44; MacDonald, *Arch.* 75-93; Boëthius and Ward-Perkins, *ERA* 239-243, 253-254, figs. 84, 96-97, plates 127-129; and Ward-Perkins, *RA* 124-131, plates 142-149.

Chapter 3 (pp. 40-82)

[1] For all of Chapter III, compare Boëthius and Ward-Perkins, *ERA* 121-180 (Italy) and 341-363 (Gaul, Britain and Roman Germany); also see Ward-Perkins, *RA* 195-261 (northern Italy and the western provinces).

Refer to *forum* and *fora*, comparison in size, in the glossary with regard to this section.

[2] These Fora were on highways in Italy. (Grimal spells them *Appi, Clodi* and *Popili.*) Forum Appii was on the Appian Way in *Latium*. There were two towns called Forum Clodii on the *Via Clodia*, which ran north from Rome through *Etruria* to PARMA in *Aemilia*. One was in the northern part of ancient *Etruria* and the other in the southern. The latter is now called San Liberato in modern Latium (L. Richardson, Jr. in *PECS* 334).

Forum Popilii in *Aemilia* (today Forlimpopoli, Emilia Romagna) became a *municipium* (G. A. Mansuelli, *PECS* 337). It was 70 kilometers southeast of BOLOGNA on the *Via Aemilia*. On it, see G. A. Mansuelli, *Caesena, Forum Popili, Forum Livi,* Italia Romana:

Municipi e Colonie 2.3 (Rome 1948) and H. E. Herzig, "Probleme des roemischen Strassenwesens" in *ANRW* II.1 pp. 602-604. Ward-Perkins discusses two other fora, also *municipia*, on the *Via Aemilia:* Forum Cornelii, Imola today, and Forum Livii, now Forlì. The former provides a notable example of Roman centuriation *(Cities* 121). Also see Brunt, *Italian Manpower* 570-577, "Appendix 11: Fora," especially in Cisalpina" and E. Ruoff-Väänänen, *Studies on the Italian Fora, Historia* Einzelschriften 32 (Wiesbaden 1978).

[3] Forum Iulii for the colony in Gaul; Forum Iulium for the Forum of Caesar in Rome (editor). "Octavian the ... adopted son" added by the editor.

A good example of a provincial forum-town, with the appropriate buildings, is *Octodurus* = Forum Claudii Vallensium = Martigny (Valais, Switzerland). At the opposite end of the Great St. Bernard Pass from AOSTA, the Celtic town was given Latin rights (q.v.) by the Emperor Claudius (A.D. 41-54) and incorporated into the minor province of *Alpes Graiae et Poeninae. Octodurus* was suggested by E. W. Gray; see V. von Gonzenbach in *PECS* 638-639, E. Meyer in *KP* I (1964) 278, *KP* IV (1972) 234-235, J. J. Hatt, *Histoire de la Gaule romaine* (Paris 1959) 88 and F. Wiblé, *Octodurus* (Berne 1976) 61. After the excavation of the forum at Martigny was completed, it was, unfortunately, covered again with earth, and nothing of it can be seen presently—J. H. Farnum, *Guide romain de la Suisse* (Lausanne 1975) 35; we have to depend on the published reports cited by Meyer, von Gonzenbach and Wiblé.

[4] On the Roman merchants, who often preceded colonists, see J. Hatzfeld, *Les trafficants italiens* (Paris 1919); Charlesworth, *Trade-Routes;* O. Schlippschuh, *Die Haendler im roemischen Kaiserreich* . . . (Amsterdam 1974); Frank, *ESAR* (index, see "Traders") and Rostovtzeff, *SEHRE* 796 (index, see "Merchants").

For a contrary view, E. Badian, *Imperialism in the Late Republic* (Oxford 1968) 67-75. On Gaul, see Chapter IV, n. 7 below.

[5] The Roman writer Vitruvius (q.v.) compares Greek *agorai* and Roman fora as follows: "The Greeks lay out their fora in the form of a square surrounded by very spacious double colonnades, adorn them with columns set rather closely together, and with entablatures (the section of wall supported by the columns—ed.) of stone or marble, and construct walks above the upper story. But in the cities of Italy the same method cannot be followed, for the reason that it is a custom handed down from our ancestors that gladiatorial shows should be given in the forum" *(Architecture* 5.1.1; translated by M. H.

Morgan). He goes on to describe the forum, which had to have an open area used for shows only in early Roman times (5.1.2-5.1.10).

[6] Vitruvius 5.1.2.; see finances, city, in glossary.

[7] See p. 36 above and Chapter II, n.6.

[8] The Royal Stoa at Athens was used by the king-archon, a magistrate in charge of legal matters associated with religion. The recent excavation of this stoa has shown that its form was not at all similar to that of the Roman civil basilica (personal communication from Professor Homer Thompson of the Institute for Advanced Study, Princeton, November 5, 1978).

[9] See G. Snider and G. M. Woloch, *The Byzantine Period: Slide Lecture on the Art and Architecture of the Byzantine Period* (Montreal 1977), slides 17-18. Also see J. B. Ward-Perkins, "Constantine and the Origins of the Christian Basilica," *Papers of the British School at Rome* 22 (1954).

[10] For selections from this law, see OSUNA below.

[11] See R. Bianchi Bandinelli, G. Caputo and E. Vergara Caffarelli, *The Buried City: Excavations at Leptis Magna*, transl. D. Ridgway (London 1966) 84-86.

[12] Probably during the reign of Claudius (A.D. 41-54).

[13] We do not know to what divinity this temple in DJEMILA was dedicated. In *PECS*, P.-A. Février calls it "a temple" (p. 249).

[14] An octagonal shrine at MAINZ is described by H. Koethe, *Die keltischen Rund- und Vielecktempel der Kaiserzeit*, Bericht der roemisch-germanischen Kommission 23 (Frankfurt am Main 1934) 80-84. But this reconstruction was unconvincing. In fact, *no* remains of temples have been found at MAINZ (K.-V. Decker and W. Selzer, "Mogontiacum" in *ANRW* II.5.1 [1976] 518 ff.).

In a letter of March 13, 1978, Dr. Decker, Kustos of the Mittelrheinisches Landesmuseum in Mainz, told the editor that ninety more architectural parts of the structure described by Koethe were found in 1973. Decker is of the opinion that these stones came from the main gate of the legionary camp, A.D. 70/96. The results of this research have been published by H. Buesing in his book, *Roemische Militaerarchitektur in Mainz*, Roem.-Germ. Forsch. 40 (Mainz 1982).

[15] This Gallo-Roman *fanum* (Latin for "shrine") was in fact turned into a windmill (Grenier, *Manuel* III 452-457).

[16] See Collingwood and Richmond, *ARB* 156-157, 160.

[17] See Liversidge, *BRE* 499 and Bailey, *Legacy* 452, n. 1. This structure was a tomb; compare A. W. Clapham, "Roman Mausolea of the Cartwheel Type," *Archaeological Journal* 79 (1922): 93-100.

[18] See Caprino, *MAR, Bibl.* 219-235 and H. Bengtson and V. Milojčić, *Atlas* 46 (map).

[19] See n. 10 above.

[20] See Crema, *Arch.* 75-84; Robertson, *GRA* 271-276; Grimal, *Civ. Rome* 504; P. Grimal, *Les villes romaines*[4], "Que sais-je?" no. 657 (Paris 1971) 121 (bibl.); P. Grimal, *Le théâtre antique*, "Que sais-je?" no. 1732 (Paris 1978); and theater, Greek, in glossary.

[21] The Greek-derived word amphitheater does not mean "two theaters together" but rather "space for spectators *(theatron)*," entirely around *(amphi)* the arena (Crema, *Arch.* 95). It is odd that a Greek word was used for a Roman invention. Also see R. Etienne, "La naissance de l'amphithéâtre: le mot et la chose," *Revue des études latines* 43 (1965): 213-220.

[22] For a clear description of this amphitheater, see Robertson, *GRA* 283-285; for an air view, Boëthius and Ward-Perkins, *ERA* plate 99. On a riot there (A.D. 59) against the inhabitants of a neighboring town, who were among the spectators, see Tacitus, *Annals* 14.17.

[23] On the Flavian Amphitheater, see H. Stuart Jones, *Companion* 130-133; Robertson, *GRA* 285-289; Dudley, *Urbs Roma* 142-145; Crema, *Arch.* 293-298; Nash, *PD* I, 17-25 (bibliography); Boëthius and Ward-Perkins, *ERA* 221-224. It is made of concrete faced with travertine stone (see TIVOLI) like the Theater of Marcellus.

[24] The Corinthian order on the top level of the theater is no longer extant except for widely separated rectangular windows (editor).

[25] Poitiers (= *Limonum,* now in the département of Vienne) and Limoges (= *Augustoritum,* now in Haute-Vienne; see Grenier, *Manuel* III 250-252) were in the Roman province of *Aquitania* while Tours (= *Caesarodunum,* now in Indre-et-Loire; see Chevallier in *ANRW* II.3 [1975] 981-982) was in *Gallia Lugdunensis.* On these amphitheaters, see Grenier, *Manuel* III 675-679, 682-684. The writers in *PECS* call into question Grimal's Augustan dates for the amphitheaters of ARLES and NIMES *(PECS* 87, 616). For amphitheaters in general, see H. Kaehler and G. Forni, *Enciclopedia dell'arte antica, classica e orientale* I (1958) 374-390.

One might also look at mainly Celtic Britain: "It may well be the case that all the important towns in Roman Britain had an amphitheatre" (Collingwood and Richmond, *ARB* 119; compare Rivet, *TCRB* 86 and Wacher, *TRB* 51,53-54). These British amphitheaters were all made of earth, and a few had stone revetments.

[26] See Grenier, *Manuel* III 856-859.

[27] Although amphitheaters are important architecturally and his-

torically, the events which took place in them were not humane or
civilized; they were comparable to many programs on American
television today and as important to their audience (editor). See R.
Auguet, *Cruelty and Civilization: The Roman Games* (translated from
the French by L. Edwards; London 1972), and for a bibliography,
Scullard, *Gracchi to Nero* 445, n. 11. Also see L. Friedlaender, *Roman Life and Manners under the Early Empire* II (transl. from the
German 1908; rpt. London 1965) 40-117 and Carcopino, *Daily Life*
223-270 (both on theaters as well).

    ²⁸ On the demi-amphitheaters, see Grenier, *Manuel* III 891-975.
The so-called theater at +*Verulamium* (see LONDON below) was in
fact a demi-amphitheater made of earth with a stone revetment; it is
still visible.

    ²⁹ Roman baths, like aqueducts, were built of concrete faced with
stone. See H. Stuart Jones, *Companion* 115-124; Grimal, *Civ. Rome*
212-213; Wheeler, *RAA* 106-110 and *OCD* 163 (J.B. Ward-Perkins).
Also see Carcopino, *Daily Life* 227-286.

    ³⁰ On how many provincial cities had baths, see Ward-Perkins (note
29) and the map cited in note 18 above. For bibliography, see Caprino, *MAR, Bibl.* 265-269. Some baths were not open to all local
citizens (MacMullen, *Social Relations* 67; 173, n. 39).

    ³¹ Pliny (q.v.) considered the aqueducts of Rome "the most re-
markable achievement anywhere in the world" (*Natural History* 36.
121-122, cited by Dudley, *Urbs Roma* 41). On them, see Frontinus
(q.v.), *The Aqueducts of Rome;* H. Stuart Jones, *Companion* 141-
150; T. Hodgkin, *Italy and Her Invaders* IV (Oxford 1896; rpt. New
York 1967) 150-181; E. B. Van Deman, *The Building of the Roman
Aqueducts* (Washington, D.C., 1934); T. Ashby, *The Aqueducts of
Ancient Rome* (Oxford 1935); E. M. Winslow, *A Libation to the Gods*
(London 1963); H. B. Evans, "Agrippa's Water Plan," *American
Journal of Archaeology* 86 (1982): 401-411; Grimal, *Civ. Rome* 422;
Dudley, op. cit. 38-42; *OCD* 89 (I. A. Richmond and D. E. Strong);
D. R. Blackman, "The Volume of Water Delivered by the Four Great
Aqueducts of Rome," *Papers of the British School at Rome* 46 (1978):
52-72 (the *Aquae Anio Vetus, Marcia, Claudia* and *Anio Novus),* as
well as SUBIACO below.

    Also see LYONS and NIMES (the Pont du Gard) below. On aque-
ducts in Gaul, see Grenier, *Manuel* IV 23-40 and in Spain, R. Menéndez Pidal (ed.), *Historia de España* II³ (Madrid 1962) 597-605, J.
M. Blázquez, *La administración del agua en la Hispania Romana*

(Barcelona 1977). Aqueducts nourished the cities of North Africa (e.g. CHERCHELL) but Broughton remarks, "The Roman development was . . . due to . . . a very careful conservation of water in all parts of the country in cisterns and reservoirs" *(RAP* p. 6).

For aqueducts in general, see Vitruvius (q.v.) 8.6, Grimal, "Vitruve et la technique des aqueducs," *Revue de Philologie* 19 (1945): 162-174 and Crema, *Arch.* 144-147; there are excellent photographs in Cunliffe, *Rome* 130-135. Other general works are *RE* VIIIA.1 (1955) 453-485 (A. W. Van Buren on "Wasserleitungen"), N. Smith, *Man and Water* (New York 1975), N. Smith, "Roman Hydraulic Technology," *Scientific American* 238.5 (1978): 154-161, 172 (bibl.); also N. Schnitter, "Roemische Talsperren," *Antike Welt* 9.2 (1978): 25-32 (on dams).

³² "Modern plumbing began in the early 1880's when the new steam engine was used to supply water under pressure and cheap cast iron pipes were employed to carry it" *(The New Columbia Encyclopedia* [New York 1975] 2170). Also see F. E. Turneaure and H. L. Russell, *Public Water Supplies*² (New York 1911) and H. E. Babbitt and J. J. Doland, *Water Supply Engineering* (New York 1939); (refs. supplied by B. Ward).

Now, electric motors and steel, copper, brass or plastic pipes are used. Roman pipes were made of baked clay and, within cities and for siphons, lead, a practice which Vitruvius condemned as unhealthy (8.6.11); c.f. A. T. Hodge, "Vitruvius, Lead Pipes and Lead Poisoning," *American Journal of Archaeology* 85 (1981): 486-491, a closely reasoned article with extensive references to Roman water supply and technology.

Another contrast with the past is provided by elevators (from 1853/1870; *New Columbia Encyclopedia* 855); buildings can now be taller than five stories.

³³ This aqueduct was called the *Anio Vetus*.

³⁴ On water-castles, see Ward-Perkins, *Cities* 34. He goes on to describe secondary water-tanks for smaller areas.

³⁵ Roman hand-pumps for fighting fires have been found in Italy, France, and England (Homo, *Rome impériale* 185-186).

³⁶ See Hodgkin (note 31) 160-162.

³⁷ The Porta Maggiore (the Italian name) was built by Claudius in A.D. 52 as part of the *Aqua Claudia* (for a picture, see MacDonald, *Arch.* plate 17). "Conduits of both the Aqua Claudia and the Anio Novus were concealed in it; an inscription also recorded Vespasian's

and Titus' restorations; later it was incorporated into the Aurelian walls. The double arches of the gate lead to the ancient Via Praenestina (the road to PALESTRINA) and the Labicana or Casilina (the road to Casino)" (G. Masson, *The Companion Guide to Rome* [London 1970] 304). On the Wall of Aurelian, see p. 78 above and n. 41 below.

[38] For estimates of the population of ancient Rome, see U. E. Paoli, *Vita Romana*[2] (translated from the Italian into French [Paris 1960] 72) = *Rome* (translated from the Italian into English [London 1963] 41-42). They range from 218,000 (F. Lot) to 1,700,000 (J. Carcopino); also see Hodgkin (note 31), vol. I pp. 394-396, "Population of Rome," E. Stein, *Histoire du Bas-Empire* I (Paris/Bruges 1959; rpt. Amsterdam 1968) 408-409, R. Duncan-Jones, *Historia* 13 (1964): 199-208, A. von Gerkan, "Die Einwohnerzahl Roms in der Kaiserzeit," *Mitteilungen des Deutschen Archaeologischen Instituts, Roemische Abteilung* 55 (1940): 149-195, Brunt, *Italian Manpower* 383 (750,000 c. A.D. 1) and J. E. Packer, *Journal of Roman Studies* 57 (1967): 80-95 (number of inhabitants is uncertain). A. G. McKay estimates Rome's population at 700,000 (*Houses* 98-99).

[39] See H. Stuart Jones, *Companion* 151-154, Caprino, *MAR, Bibl.* 217 and Grimal, *Civ. Rome* 296-297. On sewers in general and public toilets (flushed by running water) see Ward-Perkins, *Cities* 34, as well as Carcopino, *Daily Life* 318, nn. 77 and 81 (bibl. notes by H. T. Rowell). In general the streets were lined by covered underground sewers; cf. AOSTA below.

[40] See Chapter II, n. 4 above.

[41] See Hodgkin (note 31) vol. IV pp. 99-106; I. A. Richmond, *The City Wall of Imperial Rome* (Oxford 1930); Crema, *Arch.* 558, 560, fig. 738; Nash, *PD* II, 86-103; and Dudley, *Urbs Roma* 35-37. For plans of the Wall of Aurelian, see Hodgkin's vol. IV, between pp. 96 and 97 and Grimal, *Civ. Rome*, fig. 11.

[42] For Chesters (Northumberland, England) see Finley, *Atlas* 35-39 and *PECS* 370-372. The fort of A.D. 120/132 was manned by an auxiliary unit (q.v.). The site has been excavated and provides the best idea of a fort on this wall. On the name Chesters, see +Chester, listed under WROXETER, below.

[43] Cf. A. Blanchet, *Les enceintes romaines de la Gaule, étude sur l'origine d'un grand nombre de villes françaises* (Paris 1907), R. M. Butler, "Late Roman Town Walls in Gaul," *Archaeological Journal* 116 (1959): 25-50, S. Johnson, "A Group of Late Roman City Walls in Gallia Belgica," *Britannia* 4 (1973): 210-223 and Bruehl, *PC* 245-247.

[44] Local customs duties (see finances, city) could have been collected in the court area. For illustrations of various gates, see R. Schultze, "Die roemischen Stadttore," *Bonner Jahrbuecher* 118 (1909): 280 ff. and Crema, *Arch*. 221-223, figs. 231-239.

[45] The Porta Nigra was used as a church in the Middle Ages (E. Wightman, *Roman Trier and the Treveri* [New York 1971] 94; W. Reusch in *PECS* 120-121).

[46] See I. A. Richmond, "Commemorative Arches and City Gates in the Augustan Age," *Journal of Roman Studies* 23 (1933): 149-174 and Caprino, *MAR, Bibl*. 280-281. On triumphal arches, see R. P. Spiers in *EB* XXVII p. 297, H. Kaehler in *RE* VIIA (1939) 373-493, M. Pallottino, *Enciclopedia dell'arte antica, classica e orientale* I (1958) 588-599 and J. B. Ward-Perkins in *OCD* 1095-1096. In Italy, according to Ward-Perkins, there are over 100 known arches, in France 36 and in North Africa 118, but "examples are recorded for every province of the Empire." Traces of three arches have been found in Britain, all at *Verulamium* (Collingwood and Richmond, *ARB* 120; + *Verulamium* is listed under LONDON below).

The reliefs on triumphal arches, as well as the sculptures on other Roman imperial monuments, were carved according to a well-defined "program," which expressed a certain governmental message.

[47] The dates of these arches are disputed.

[48] On the arches in *Gallia Narbonensis* see Crema, *Arch*. 214-216, 305; M. Pallottino, *Enciclopedia dell'arte antica, classica e orientale* I (1958) 596-597; Kaehler, *Art of Rome* 57-58, 219 and P. Gros, "Pour une chronologie des arcs de triomphe de Gaule Narbonnaise . . .," *Gallia* 37 (1979): 55-83.

Arches in Gallia Narbonensis:

Aix-les-Bains (Savoie) = *Aquae*, a district of Roman VIENNE (q.v.)

Carpentras (Vaucluse) = *Colonia Iulia Meminorum Carpentorate*, tribal capital of the Memini (see MacKendrick, *RF* 98-99; Chevallier in *ANRW* II.3 p. 804 [bibliography]; Cunliffe, *Rome* 242-243 [color photograph of a relief on the arch-Celtic captives]; Latin colony of Julius Caesar, see colonies in *Gallia Narbonensis* in glossary).

Cavaillon (Vaucluse) = *Cabellio*, tribal capital of the Cavari and an honorary Roman colony (41 B.C.-A.D. 14); the full name of the colony is not known. See ORANGE below.

St.-Chamas (Bouches-du-Rhône), Roman name unknown (see Bro-

gan, *Roman Gaul* 33, 71 and Grenier, *Manuel* I 568; compare the
arch at SAINTES).

Arches in Aquitania:
See SAINTES below.

Of some importance is the Augustan arch at + Susa (8 B.C.), listed
under TURIN below.

[49] i) On apartment blocks, see p. 90 above (at VAISON-LA-RO-
MAINE), city blocks in the glossary and OSTIA ANTICA below.
ii) For housing see pp. 86-87 (at DJEMILA) and 90-91 (in Roman
Britain); also see Boëthius and Ward-Perkins, *ERA* 152-162, 312-
336, 356-362 and McKay, *Houses*.
iii) On markets and warehouses, see Crema, *Arch.* 171-173, Ward-
Perkins, *Cities* 35 and G. E. Rickman, *Roman Granaries and Store
Buildings* (Cambridge 1971). For Trajan's Market in Rome, see
Chapter II n. 12 above. For other markets: figs. 4 and 5 and pp. 30-
32 above (at *Pompeii*, OSTIA ANTICA and Rome); also see AUGST (Ward-
Perkins, *Cities)*, DJEMILA and *Lepcis Magna* (Wheeler and Wood,
Roman Africa; Boëthius and Ward-Perkins, *ERA)*. On the Grain
Depot of Epagathus, see (Charles-)Picard in the bibl. for OSTIA
ANTICA.
iv) On highways and bridges, H. Stuart Jones, *Companion* 40-49;
W. W. Hyde, *Roman Alpine Routes*, Memoirs of the American Phil-
osophical Society 2 (Philadelphia 1935); Caprino, *MAR, Bibl.* 245-
250, 252-256; K. Miller, *Itineraria Romana; Tabula Peutingeriana,*
E. Weber (ed.) (qq.v., under "Ancient Sources"); Grenier, *Manuel*
II; V. W. von Hagen, *The Roads That Led to Rome* (London 1967,
bibl. on pp. 282-284); G. Walser (ed.), *Itinera Romana* (a series,
Berne 1967-); Radke, *Viae;* Ziegler, *KP* V (1975) 1243-1246 (G. Radke,
see "Viae Publicae"); Margary, *RRB;* H. E. Herzig, "Probleme des
roemischen Strassenwesns" in *ANRW* II.1 pp. 593-648; Chevallier,
Roman Roads.
v) On public libraries, see R. Cagnat, "Les bibliothèques municipales dans l'Empire romain," *Mémoires...l'Académie des inscriptions et belles-lettres* 38 (1909): 1-26; C. E. Boyd, *Public Libraries
in Ancient Rome* (Chicago 1915); H. Pfeiffer, "The Roman Library at
Timgad," *Memoirs of the American Academy in Rome* 9 (1931): 157-
165; Frank, *ESAR* V p. 102 (in Como and *Volsinii Novi*, Italy); L.
Richardson, Jr., *Archaeology* 30 (1977): 394-402 (probable public li-

brary at *Pompeii);* Nash, *PD* II p. 524 (index, six in Rome); Caprino, *MAR, Bibl.* 378; *OCD* 607-608 (F. G. Kenyon and C. H. Roberts); the map cited in n. 18 above and its *Erlaeuterungen* (Commentary).

Chapter 4 (pp. 83-91)

[1] The Roman Empire was, legally and in practice, a federation of city-states, hence the importance of founding colonies and *municipia* (qq.v.) as well as making treaties with "allied cities" (q.v.).

[2] Grimal says the Emperor Trajan (A.D. 98-117).

[3] *Cuicul* had to expand upwards to the south along the back of the spur (Wheeler and Wood, *Roman Africa* 128).

[4] "The northwest corner ..." is the editor's correction.

[5] See J. Revault, *L'habitation tunisoise...* Et. d'Ant. Afr. (Paris 1978) and R. Rebuffat, "Maisons à péristyle de l'Afrique du Nord," *Mélanges . . . Ecole française de Rome* 81 (1969). Also similar to the Hellenistic houses on Delos (one of the Cyclades, which belong to present-day Greece) are those at *Glanum,* near ST.-REMY-DE-PRO-VENCE (MacKendrick, *RF* 22-24 and McKay, *Houses* 159-161). For Hellenistic houses, see Robertson, *GRA* 300-302 and *OCD* 531-532 (R. E. Wycherley).

On the lack of Roman apartment blocks in North Africa, see Boëthius, "RGTA" 17.

[6] See Frank, *ESAR* III pp. 479-480 (A. Grenier, citing ancient and modern sources).

[7] Enterprising Italian traders often arrived before a Roman colony was actually founded (Chapter III, n. 4 above). See Cicero, *Marcus Fonteius* 5.11 (on Roman traders in Gaul) and Charlesworth, *Trade-Routes* 179-206 (on Gaul).

[8] But why was *Lugdunum* founded at the site on the Celtic *oppi-dum,* on top of a hill and not next to the water? See Introduction, n. 1 above and compare J. Drinkwater, *Britannia* 6 (1975): 133-140.

[9] But also see VIENNE on the Roman highways.

[10] A. Audin, director of the excavations at LYONS, locates the Forum at the present-day Place de Fourvière (only larger) and the Capitol at the site of the Catholic Basilica of Notre Dame de Fourvière *(Lug-dunum dans Lyon* [Lyons n.d.] 11-12). The Capitol is the eastward extension of the rectangle marking the Forum on our figure 27. This temple, which was at least a Temple of Jupiter, if not a Capitol, is known from the finds of sections of columns and a large marble head

and hand of Jupiter (A. Audin, *Essai sur la topographie de Lugdunum*[3] [Lyons 1964] 40-41). It is a pity that archaeological excavations were not undertaken *before* the basilica was begun in 1870. The curia and the Gallo-Roman basilica are more problematic (ibid. 42).

[11] Meaning the hill of Fourvière only.

[12] A temple of Cybele, a little to the north of the odeum, is now under excavation (ibid. 97; A. Audin and M. Leglay, *Bulletin de la Société nationale des antiquaires de France* [May 11, 1966]: 96-99).

[13] The inhabited area of *Lugdunum* grew to 127 hectares (314 acres; Collingwood and Richmond, *ARB* 96; see cities, comparison in area, below).

[14] Early in the 19th century, this island was joined to the mainland to the north and it now forms a peninsula—the central part of LYONS.

[15] On Romano-British town houses, see Collingwood and Richmond, *ARB* 125-129, 132 (bibliography); C. A. F. Berry, "The Dating of Romano-British Houses," *Journal of Roman Studies* 41 (1951): 25-31; Frere, *Britannia* 241, 246-248; Liversidge, *BRE* 68-101; McKay, *Houses* 187-189.

A Descriptive Catalogue of Roman Cities

(With an Index to *Les villes romaines*)

Aix-en-Provence (Bouches-du-Rhône, France): see colonies in *Gallia Narbonensis*

Aix-les-Bains (Savoie, France): see Chapter III, n. 48 above

Alba Fucens (in the ancient region of *Samnium* and the modern region of Abruzzi, Italy; the present-day name is Albe)
p. 20, n. (hilltop orthogonal cities); (see Chapter I, n. 11 above on the city blocks)
    Alba Fucens was a Latin colony of 303 B.C. (see *colonia*, Livy 10.1, Velleius Paterculus 1.14.5), situated just northwest of the Fucine Lake, about eighty kilometers east of Rome on the Via Valeria. (The Fucine Lake was drained in 1876; the Emperor Claudius had attempted this feat in A.D. 41/52—cf. *CAH* X² [1952] 695-696 and *EB* XI.)
    Although on a hilltop, the colony had an orthogonal street plan, with long and narrow blocks. The city was remodeled shortly after 89 B.C., a period of prosperity. Its decline began in the third century A.D. Much of the colony's wall (third to first centuries B.C.) remains.
Alba Fucens I, II = Etudes de philologie, d'archéologie et d'histoire
    anciennes publiées par l'Institut historique belge de Rome 12 and
    13 (Brussels/Rome 1969); bibl. in vol. I, pp. 33-36
Besnier. *Lexique*. 29
Boëthius. *Golden House*. 47, n. 42 (bibl.)
—— and Ward-Perkins. *ERA*. 151-152; 558, n. 42 (bibl.), 605 (index);
    figs. 70, 81 (maps)
Brown, F.E. *Cosa*. Ann Arbor 1980. fig. 12
Castagnoli. *Orthogonal Town Planning*. 96-97; fig. 38; 121
Chevallier. *ANRW*. II.1 pp. 693-694, 700 (bibliography); plate xxxv
    (plan)

Crema. *Arch*. 14 (walls), 173 (market); fig. 66 (basilica)

De Visscher, F. "Alba Fucens: A Roman Colony," *Archaeology* 12 (1959): 123-132

—— et al. *Les fouilles d'Alba Fucens*. . . . = *L'Antiquité classique* 23 (Brussels 1954) and 24 (Brussels 1955)

Dilke. *ANRW*. II.1 pp. 588-589 (bibliography)

Dudley. *RS*. 32; ill. 2 (air view)

EB. I p. 480 (T. Ashby); XI pp. 273-274 (T. Ashby on the Fucine Lake)

Enciclopedia dell'arte antica, classica e orientale. I (1958). 192-194 (V. Cianfarani)

KP. I (1964). 231 (G. Radke)

Lavedan. *HU*. 372 (map)

Lugli. *Tecnica edilizia*. 105-111

MacKendrick. *Mute Stones*. 95-98, 109-110 (centuriation, q.v.), 116; 355 (bibliography)

*Mertens, J. "Etude topographique d'Alba Fucens," in *Alba Fucens* I. Brussels/Rome 1969. 37-118

—— "La stratigraphie et l'évolution planimétrique du centre monumental d'*Alba Fucens* et de *Herdoniae*," in Duval, *Thèmes*. 253-266 (good plans and photographs)

Nissen. *IL*. II pp. 457-461, figs. 25-26 *(Via Valeria)*

OCD. 34 (E. T. Salmon)

Paget. *Central Italy*. 197-199 (with 1 plan)

PECS. 31 (J. Mertens)

Radke. *Viae*

Salmon. *RC*. 27, 33, 34, 38 (compared to *Cosa*, q.v.); 46-47 (map of *Latium);* 60 (foundation); 61 (plan); 110 (list of Latin colonies 334-181 B.C.); plate 15 (air view), 25 (wall), 29 (milestone)

Ward-Perkins. *Cities*. 27

—— "ERTI." 154 (bibl.); fig. 9 (plan)

—— "Republic to Empire." fig. 17

Alba Longa (Latium, Italy)

p. 28 (foundation legend of Rome)

 This site in the Alban Hills, about twenty-five kilometers southeast of Rome and about five kilometers south of *Tusculum* (q.v.), is near the papal summer palace of Castel Gandolfo. The name of the city is thought to refer to its shape, a long line extending up the slope. According to legend, *Alba Longa* was founded in 1152 B.C. (to be the mother-city of Rome four hundred years later; cf. Vergil, *Aeneid* 3.390) and was destroyed by the Romans in 665 (cf. Livy 1.3.3,

1.28.10). Archaeological finds of tombs conform with these dates, but Alfoeldi considers the Roman takeover to have been a gradual process, ending in 338 B.C., when *Alba Longa* was included in the Roman city voting districts. In its prime (until the seventh century), Alba was undoubtedly the chief city of the Latins (q.v.) and the founder of other Latin cities.

After 338 B.C. and far into imperial times, Alba's importance was mostly religious. There were three shrines in the area, the most important of which was the sanctuary of Jupiter Latiaris (no longer extant), where the Roman consuls celebrated the Latin Festival *(Feriae Latinae)* once a year on a movable date (cf. Livy 5.17.2).

Villas were built here, including one belonging to the Emperor Domitian (see Tacitus, *Agricola* 45.1). A legionary camp of the third century A.D. became the nearby town of Albano Laziale (Richardson).

Alfoeldi. *Early Rome*. 236-246
Ashby. *Rom Cam*. 190-193
Ashby, T. "Alba Longa," *Journal of Philology* 27 (1901): 37 ff.
Blue Guide, Rome. 338-340
Dionisi, F. *La scoperta topografica di Alba Longa*. Rome 1961
Gierow, P. *The Iron Age Culture of Latium*. I, Lund 1966; II.1, 1964
Guida d'Italia del Touring Club Italiano, Roma e Dintorni[6]. Milan 1962. 664
KP. I (1964). 231-232 (G. Radke)
McKay, A. G. *Vergil's Italy*. Greenwich, Conn., 1970. 163-164
Nissen. *IL*. II p. 582
OCD. 34 (E. T. Salmon); 569 (H. J. Rose)
Ogilvie, R. M. *A Commentary on Livy, Books 1-5*. Oxford 1965. 43, 120-122, 665
—— and Richmond. *Agricola*. 307 (Domitian's villa)
Pallottino, M. *Archeologia classica*. 1960. 27 ff.
PECS. 32-33 (L. Richardson, Jr.); 33 (G. M. A. Richter)
RE. I (1894). 1301-1302 (C. Huelsen)
RE. Supplement 1 (1903). 50-51 (C. Huelsen; addition to *RE*. I)

ALISE-STE.-REINE (Côte-d'Or, France) = *Alesia, Gallia Lugdunensis*
p. 3 (the *oppidum*, q.v.)
Alesia was an *oppidum* of the Mandubii. This hill-town was the site of Caesar's defeat of Vercingetorix in 52 B.C. (Caesar, *Gallic Wars* 7.69-89). It was surveyed and excavated from 1861 to 1866 by a team under the direction of Napoleon III, and more recent excavations

have taken place (Toutain, *Gallia*). A Roman town succeeded the
Gallic *oppidum* on the same site; the hill is not steep. See *fora*.

Barbet, A. et al. "Peintures murales romaines d'Alésia . . .," *Gallia*
35 (1977): 173-199

Besnier. *Lexique*. 31-32

Brogan. *Roman Gaul*. 17-18, 104-105

Carcopino, J. *Alésia et les ruses de César*. Paris 1958

Chevallier. *ANRW*. II.3 pp. 949-957 (bibliography and plans)

Duval, P.-M. "Alésia et les Gaulois," *Archéologia* 24 (1968): 6-13

Gauthier, A. and G. *Alésia, métropole disparue*. Paris 1963

Greece and Rome. 2nd Ser. 4 (1957)

Grenier. *Manuel*. I 65, 187-225; III 342-346 (the Roman forum), 479-480 (the basilica)

Harmand, J. *Une campagne césarienne, Alésia*. Paris 1967

Holmes, T. Rice. *Caesar's Conquest of Gaul²*. Oxford 1911; rpt. 1931.
170-176 (Caesar's siege); 354-363

KP. I (1964). 241 (J. Le Gall)

Lavedan. *HU*. 391 (maps)

Le Gall, J. *Alésia, archéologie et histoire²*. Paris 1980

—— "Les fouilles d'Alésia de 1944 à 1947," *Gallia* 6 (1948): 96-139

MacKendrick. *RF*. 45-56; 256-257 (bibliography)

OCD. 39 (C. E. Stevens)

PECS. 35-36 (J. Le Gall)

Stier. *Atlas*. 29

Toutain, J. *Alésia gallo-romaine et chrétienne*. La Charité-sur-Loire
1933

—— "Les fouilles exécutées en 1943 à Alise-Ste.-Reine," *Gallia* 2
(1944): 121-140

—— "Les fouilles d'Alésia de 1944 à 1947," *Gallia* 6 (1948): 96-139

Wheeler, R. E. M., and Richardson, K. M. *Hill-Forts of Northern
France*. Oxford 1957

AMPURIAS (Gerona, Spain; region of Catalonia) = in Latin,
Emporiae, Hispania Tarraconensis

p. 3 (the Greek colony)

Emporion (meaning "market") was a Greek colony from *Massalia*
(MARSEILLES) of about 550 B.C. The natives inhabited an adjacent
town, separated from the Greeks by a wall (Livy 34.9). The site was
a port on the Gulf of Rosas, an arm of the Mediterranean. Caesar
settled legionary veterans there, and Augustus made it a Roman
municipium (q.v.). AMPURIAS was on the Roman *Via Domitia* from

NIMES to Tarragona (see *Hispania* below). The Roman city included the Greek and extended inland. Excavations have shown that the street plan of the Roman addition inland was orthogonal.

In Roman times, the harbor silted up, and the city died. Ancient vases, glassware, and sculpture from AMPURIAS may be seen at the Museo Arqueológico at Barcelona; there is also a museum on the site.

Albertini, E. *L'Empire romain*[4]. Paris 1970. 441 (bibl.)

Almagro, M. *Ampurias*. Barcelona 1967; English edition 1956

—— "Estratigrafía de la ciudad helenístico-romana de Ampurias," *Archivo Español de Arqueología* 20 (1947): 179 ff.

Ampurias. Periodical published by Departamento de Barcelona of the Instituto de Arqueología, Consejo Superior de Investigaciones Científicas (Barcelona) from 1940

Blue Guide, Spain. 128,147

Bosch-Gimpera, P. "Katalonien in der Kaiserzeit," *ANRW*. II.3 (1975). 600 (list of plates and figures)

Buisman, H. *Spanien*. Darmstadt 1972. 38-40

CAH. XI[2] (1954). 905 (bibl.)

Finley. *Atlas*. 63-64 (P. MacKendrick)

KP. II (1967). 252-263 (R. Grosse)

MacKendrick. *Iberian Stones*. 42-58

Menéndez Pidal, R., ed. *Historia de España*. II[3]. Madrid 1962. 49, fig. 36 (aerial photograph), 585, 587, 595, 620

OCD. 383 (M. I. Henderson)

PECS. 303 (J. Maluquer de Motes)

RE. V (1905). 2527-2530 (E. Huebner)

RE. Supplement 9 (1962). 34-36 (R. Grosse); (addition to *RE*. V)

Ripoll Perello, E. *Ampurias*. Barcelona 1976 (Engl. transl.)

Rostovtzeff. *SEHRE*. 211 (on the prosperity of Roman *Emporiae*)

Schulten, A. *Ampurias, eine Griechenstadt am iberischen Strande*. Leipzig 1908

Stier. *Atlas*. 21 (plan)

Sutherland, C. H. V. *The Romans in Spain, 217 B.C.-A.D. 117*. London 1939. 11, 13, 15, 66 (historical references)

Wiseman, F. J. *Roman Spain*. London 1956. 7, 72 (history); 53 (linen industry); 109-110 (the city)

Ansedonia, Italy: see *Cosa*

AOSTA (Valle d'Aosta, Italy; capital of the autonomous region) = *Colonia Augusta Praetoria*, region of *Transpadana, Italia;* Piedmont (see TURIN) and the Valle d'Aosta share the same history, but much of the latter's population is French-speaking.

p. 77 (the walls)

The site is in a valley formed by the Dora Baltea River (in Latin, *Duria Maior*), which flows east at this point; it later turns south to join the Po. The surrounding Alps assure a pleasant climate. Near the river's left bank at the junction of roads from the Great (see Chapter III, n.3 above) and Little St. Bernard Passes, the city's strategic location is obvious. (It should be remembered that these passes were closed in winter, except to the most hardy.) The former highway came from Lausanne (see AUGST) and the latter from VIENNE (Mommsen, Staehelin); from AOSTA 's east gate, a road led to the *Via Aemilia* (see Dudley. *RS*. 152 and PARMA).

Augustus founded the colony in 25 B.C. for veterans of his Praetorian Guard (the Roman army corps stationed in Rome) after the conquest of the local Celtic tribe, the Salassi (Strabo 4.206, Cassius Dio 53.25). Those Salassi who had not been killed or enslaved were not granted full civic rights; these were gained gradually (see Salmon, *RC* 169, n. 29 and attributed persons in the glossary below). Both AOSTA and TURIN, its not too distant contemporary, were "bulwarks of empire," says Salmon, for they were "built with strong walls on defensible sites" *(RC* p. 144). They were also bulwarks of Romanization (see *Gallia Cisalpina)*. Besides agriculture in the colony's extensive *territorium* (Rostovtzeff), iron was refined at Roman AOSTA, as it is today (Richmond).

Roman TURIN and AOSTA were (and still, in good part, are) notable for the regularity of their street plans. AOSTA's walls enclosed forty-one hectares (see cities, comparison in area), and there was room for seven *cardines* and seven *decumani* (Castagnoli; see city blocks), but Ward-Perkins's map *(Cities,* fig. 52, comparing ancient and modern AOSTA) shows many double blocks. Ward-Perkins remarks, "The Roman basis of the street plan (today) is confirmed by numerous finds of the corresponding network of street drains" (as at TURIN), and he notes that the main *cardo* was displaced one double block to the west. Also done at TURIN (but to the east), this was a feature of contemporary military camps *(Cities* 120).

On the similarity between the Roman plan of AOSTA and an army camp, see Wheeler, pp. 43-44 ("A Roman colony such as Aosta or Turin or Verona was primarily a copybook War Office fortress ameliorated by an urban content") and Chapter I, n. 2 above.

Unlike ORANGE and other cities in France, a good part of the Roman wall remains at AOSTA, as well as the east gate and part of the south gate. There are many Roman remains besides the fortifications. An arch in honor of Augustus still stands outside the east gate; in Roman times it spanned the approach road (Wheeler, p. 156). The theater has much of the *scaenae frons* (pp. 60-61 above) left, and this is rare in Europe. One may see the cryptoporticus (q.v. and p. 43 above), if not the forum itself. The archaeological museum was closed as of 1978. The words of Frothingham are still correct, after nearly seventy years: "A few of the initiated know that Aosta is one of the best preserved Roman fortified cities in the world."

Barocelli, P. *Aosta*. Ivrea 1936. fig. 1

—— *Augusta Praetoria (Forma Italiae)*. Rome 1948

Beretta, I. *La romanizzazione della Valle d'Aosta*. Milan 1954

Besnier. *Lexique*. 107

Boëthius and Ward-Perkins. *ERA*. 302-304

Caprino. *MAR, Bibl*. 263

Carducci, C. "Il criptoportico di Aosta," *Les cryptoportiques dans l'architecture romaine*. Collection de l'Ecole française de Rome 14 (Rome 1973): 117-129

Castagnoli. *Orthogonal Town Planning*. 112, fig. 49

Chevallier. *ANRW*. II.1 p. 694 (bibliography)

Crema. *Arch*. 657-658 (index)

Dudley. *RS*. ill. 9 (good air view)

EB. II pp. 158; 906 (T. Ashby)

Enciclopedia dell'arte antica, classica e orientale. I (1958). 453-454 (G. Bendinelli)

Eyssenhardt, F. *Aosta und seine Alterthuemer*. Hamburg 1896

Frothingham. *RCID*. 225-243

Grenier. *Manuel*. III p. 313, n. 1 (bibliography); pp. 313-315 (cryptoporticus); 780-783 (theater)

Guida d'Italia del Touring Club Italiano, Torino e Valle d'Aosta[7]. Milan 1959

Gutkind. *IHCD*. IV (1969). 184-185

Haverfield. *Town Planning*. 89-91

Jones, H. Stuart. *Companion*. 450 (index)

KP. I (1964). 737

Lavedan. *HU*. 384 (map), 468 (plan of forum)

Mommsen. *Provinces*. Chapter I

Morris. *Urban Form*. 51; fig. 3.15

Nissen. *IL*. II pp. 167-169 (the Salassi); 170-173

OCD. 147 (E. T. Salmon)

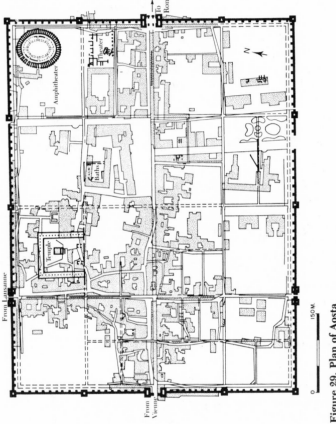

Figure 29. Plan of Aosta
From Salmon, *Roman Colonization*, fig. 11

118

Pais, E. *Dalle guerre puniche a Cesare Augusto*. II. Rome 1918. 375 (Romanization of the Salassi)

Pauli, L. "Denkmaeler roemischer Alpenpolitik," *Antike Welt* 11.2 (1980): 3-14

PECS. 116 (E. T. Salmon)

Promis, C. *Le Antichità di Aosta*. Turin 1862

Radke. *Viae*. fig. 20

Richmond. RAA. 249-259

Robertson. *GRA*. 361, 396 (indexes)

Rostovtzeff. *SEHRE*. 232; 571, n. 5 (bibliography)

Rykwert. *Idea*. 42

Salmon. *RC*. 142-144 (with plan); 169, n. 29

Sommella, P. "Appunti tecnici sull'urbanistica di piano romana in Italia," *Archeologia classica* 28 (1976): 10-29 (AOSTA and Lucca; notes for a course on Roman cities, Rome 1975/1976)

Staccioli, R. A. "I criptoportici forensi di Aosta e di Arles," *Rendiconti dell'Accademia dei Lincei*. *Cl*. *Sc*. *Mor*. ser. VIII. 9 (1954; publ. 1955): 645-657

Staehelin, F. *Die Schweiz in roemischer Zeit*[3]. Basle 1948. 115

Toesca, P. *Aosta*. Rome 1911

Viale V., and Viale Ferrero, M. *Aosta romana e medievale*. Turin 1967

Ward-Perkins. *Cities*. 28, 120, 123; figs. 52-53 (plan and air view)
—— "ERTI." 154 (bibl.); fig. 19 (air view), fig. 20 (plan, nearly the same as my fig. 29)
—— *RA*. 210, pl. 238 ("Porta Praetoria")

Wheeler. *RAA*. 43-44 (the city); 156 (the arch)

Aquae: Aix-les-Bains, q.v.

Aquae Mattiacae: see + Wiesbaden, listed under MAINZ

Aquae Sextiae Salluviorum: Aix-en-Provence, q.v.

Many of the Roman spas had names beginning with *Aquae* (see *PECS* 73-79).

Arausio: see ORANGE

ARLES (Bouches-du-Rhône, France) = *Colonia Iulia Paterna Arelate Sextanorum, Gallia Narbonensis* (see colonies in *Gallia Narbonensis* and mint of the Later Roman Empire) pp. 43-44 (the cryptoporticus), 65-66 (the amphitheater)

Arelate was originally a Celtic *oppidum* (q.v.) on the left bank of the lower Rhône River; the name means "near the marshes." Roman development began here in 103 B.C., when Marius had his troops build a canal (the *Fossae Marianae*) southeast from the Rhône, just below *Arelate*, to the Golfe de Fos, an arm of the Mediterranean; the marshes at the mouth of the Rhône were thus bypassed (compare RAVENNA). A similar canal exists at ARLES today.

Julius Caesar founded the Roman colony on the site in 46 B.C. for veterans of the Sixth Legion; its *territorium* (q.v.) was taken mainly from that of *Massilia* (see MARSEILLES). The *colonia* (c. twenty hectares) was enlarged by Augustus, and it served as a major junction on trade-routes by land and by water.

Arelate could be reached on the canal by seagoing vessels; goods were transferred to or from river-boats there. The principal exports were wine and olive oil. According to Rostovtzeff, ARLES and NARBONNE (q.v.) were great commercial cities of Gaul, whence Gallic products were exported. OSTIA ANTICA was the main destination from ARLES (Grenier, *ESAR* 585). Many inscriptions have been left by trade-guilds and merchants (Charlesworth). In 1964, in the suburb of Trinquetaille on the right bank, was found a portico whose use was comparable to that of the shipping offices in the ancient Piazzale delle Corporazioni at *Ostia* (MacKendrick, *RF*). In contrast, LYONS and TRIER were mainly concerned with supplying the army (Rostovtzeff).

On the left bank of the Rhône, just to the north of *Arelate*, was the end of the *Via Aurelia* from Italy (see FREJUS). As today, the first bridge on the Rhône was here, but it was supported by boats. (A mosaic depicting this bridge was found at the Ostian offices just mentioned.) The highway from the right bank, to NIMES and Tarragona (Spain), was the *Via Domitia*. Another road went north (on the east side of the Rhône) to LYONS. Just south of its junction with the *Via Aurelia*, this road was spanned by a Roman triumphal arch, no longer extant.

The orthogonal Roman city had its aqueducts and sewers as well as two baths, one of which, the so-called Palace of La Trouille, was probably built by Constantine the Great early in the fourth century. Other noteworthy remains are the cryptoporticus (q.v.), the theater and the amphitheater. Sculptures from the theater and elsewhere may be seen in the Musée d'art païen, a seventeenth-century church, near the cryptoporticus. Having become a fortified living-space in the Middle Ages, the amphitheater was well preserved (compare the Theater of Marcellus at Rome on pp. 36-37 above). Bullfights, the successor to gladiatorial combats, are held in ARLES's amphitheater today.

Constantine I and his sons often stayed at ARLES, and the city was given a second name, *Constantina*, in A.D. 330 and again in 353 (compare CONSTANTINE, Algeria). During these years, the letters CON or CONST appear on the coins struck at ARLES, instead of ARL (see P. V. Hill, J. P. C. Kent and R. A. G. Carson, *Late Roman Bronze Coinage* [London 1965] 9 and 54).

About A.D. 400, ARLES became the seat of the Praetorian Prefecture of the Gauls (which extended from Morocco to Britain), an honor which it inherited from TRIER. The Praetorian Prefect was the chief legal officer of a large part of the Later Roman (q.v.) Empire. In the first half of the sixth century, under the Ostrogothic king Theodoric (see RAVENNA and Ostrogoths), the Prefect of the Gauls remained at ARLES, but his jurisdiction covered only the southeastern part of the old province of *Gallia Narbonensis* and was roughly as large as the medieval region of Provence. ARLES was conquered by the Franks (q.v.) in the mid-sixth century.

Present-day ARLES is far overshadowed by MARSEILLES. Having lost its position as a center of trade (a result of the railway), ARLES is an agricultural market, especially for rice. R. Amy sees the Roman orthogonal plan in its somewhat irregular now-existing streets *(PECS* 87). The town is noted for its antiquities, also including the Church (once a Cathedral) of St. Trophime (eleventh-fifteenth centuries).

Amy, R. "Les cryptoportiques d'Arles," *Les cryptoportiques dans l'architecture romaine*. Collection de l'Ecole française de Rome 14 (Rome 1973): 275-291

*Benoît, F. *Arles*. Paris 1954

—— *CAGR*. V *Bouches-du-Rhône* (1936)

—— "Le développement de la colonie d'Arles et la centuriation de la Crau," *Comptes rendus de l'Académie des inscriptions et belles-lettres* (1964): 156-169

—— "Le sanctuaire d'Auguste et les cryptoportiques d'Arles," *Revue archéologique* 39 (1952): 31-67

—— "La voie d'Italie en Espagne à l'époque d'Auguste sur le territoire d'Arles," *Revue des études anciennes* 40 (1938): 133-148

Boëthius and Ward-Perkins. *ERA*. 348; pl. 186 (air view of amphitheater); 606 (index)

Bruehl. *PC*. 234-244

Caprino. *MAR, Bibl.* 241

Charles-Roux, J. *Arles, son histoire, ses monuments, ses musées.* Paris 1914

Charlesworth. *Trade-Routes.* 192

Chevallier. *ANRW.* II.1 plate xl (aerial photograph), xli (plan); II.3 p. 745, fig. 33 (cryptoporticus); 803 (bibliography); plates i, vii, ix, xxvi

—— *Roman Roads.* 94; fig. 15 (the Ostian mosaic of the boat-bridge at ARLES)

Clébert. *Provence antique.* 155-171; cover photo

*Constans, L.-A. *Arles antique.* Bibliothèque des écoles françaises d'Athènes et de Rome 119. Paris 1921 ("a model monograph," Rostovtzeff, *SEHRE* 594)

Crema. *Arch.* 658 (index)

Desjardins. *Géogr.* III pp. 427-429

Dudley. *RS.* ill. 29 (air view)

EB. II pp. 557-558

Février. "CSG." 13-14

—— *Dév. urbain en Provence.* 218 (index); figs. 2, 11, 31, 42

Finley. *Atlas.* 52-53 (P. MacKendrick)

Formigé, J. "L'amphithéâtre d'Arles," *Revue archéologique* (1964): 25-41, 113-163; (1965): 1-46

Frank. *ESAR.* III pp. 473-479, 585 (A. Grenier)

Greece and Rome. 2nd ser. 2 (1955). plates 155a, 157, 159b, 160a

Grenier. *Manuel.* I p. 289, n. 4 (bibliography); pp. 289-295; II 493-509 (on the port); III 157-171; 291-322 (on the forum and cryptoporticus); 515-517 (the basilica); 613-639 (the amphitheater, compared with that at NIMES), 743-753 (the theater), 983-987 (the *circus* for chariot races); IV 254-263 (the baths)

Gutkind. *IHCD.* V(1970). 475 (bibl.)

Jullian, C. "Arles grecque et romaine," *Journal des Savants* (1922): 97-113

KP. I (1964). 525 (P. Wuilleumier)

Latour, J. "Le sanctuaire d'Auguste et les cryptoportiques d'Arles," *Revue archéologique* 42 (1953): 42-51 (see fig. 10A above)

Lavedan. *HU.* 71 (plan of forum)

MacKendrick. *RF.* 61-64; 257-258 (bibliography)

Mommsen. *Provinces.* Chapter III

Notitia Dignitatum, Oc. (West) 42.14: the Rhône fleet's commander at ARLES, c. A.D. 400 (compare VIENNE)

OCD. 102 (C. E. Stevens)

PECS. 87-88 (R. Amy)
Peyre, R. *Nîmes, Arles, Orange*[4]. Paris 1923
(Charles-)Picard. *Roman Architecture*. 50-51; plates 26 and 27 (the cryptoporticus)
Rostovtzeff. *SEHRE*. 167; 613, n. 28 (bibliography)
Staccioli, see AOSTA (comparison of the cryptoporticoes)
Stuebinger, O. *Die roemische Wasserleitungen von Nîmes und Arles*. Heidelberg 1909/1910; rpt. Nendeln, Liechtenstein, 1978
Veran, A. "Arles antique," *Congrès archéologique de France* 43 (1876; publ. 1877): 267-297
Vittinghoff. *Roemische Kolonisation*. 66 (on the epithet "Paterna," shared with NARBONNE)
Ward-Perkins. "Republic to Empire." fig. 9
Wheeler, R. E. M. "The Roman Town-Walls of Arles and Other Roman Town-Walls," *Journal of Roman Studies* 16 (1926): 174-193

Medieval ARLES (references mostly provided by L. Wheeler):
Bruehl. *PC*. general bibl.
Farnarier, F. "La République d'Arles au XIIIe siècle . . .," *Provincia* (1943): 35-68
Fournier, P. *Le royaume d'Arles et de Vienne, (A.D.) 1138-1378*. Paris 1891
Stier. *Atlas*. 88-89 (archbishopric)

ASSISI (Umbria, Italy) = *Asisium* ancient region of *Umbria, Italia*
p. 20 (hill-city)
   This *municipium*, situated on a hill in the Apennines (q.v.) played little part in Roman history.
   Destroyed by the Ostrogoth (q.v.) Totila in A.D. 545, the town was rebuilt, and it prospered during the Middle Ages. St. Francis (1182-1226) is its most famous son. *Asisium* was a "centre . . . of agricultural life with almost no commerce or industry" (Rostovtzeff).
Besnier. *Lexique*. 93
Crema. *Arch*. 277, figs. 317-318 (forum)
Enciclopedia dell'arte antica, classica e orientale. I (1958). 741 (C. Pietrangeli)
Frothingham. *RCID*. 173-187
Harris. *REU*. 100 (allied city); 184-186 (change in language from Umbrian [q.v.] to Latin); 249, 336 (Roman citizenship)
Highet, G. *Poets in a Landscape*. London 1957. 83-86 (Propertius, who was from Umbria)

KP. I (1964). 640 (G. Radke)
Nissen. *IL*. II pp. 394-396
OCD. 131 (E. T. Salmon)
Paget. *Central Italy*. 166-167
PECS. 101 (R. V. Schoder)
Rostovtzeff. *SEHRE*. 58
Zocca, E. *Assisi and its Environs*. Rome 1950

AUGST (Basel-Land, Switzerland) = *Colonia . . . Apollinaris Augusta Emerita Raurica, Germania Superior* (Upper Germany); at first, the colony was in *Gallia Belgica* (Bengtson, *Atlas* 44; cf. ibid. 45); this Augustan colony in the lands of the Raurici was settled by veterans *(emeriti)*.

p. 43 (the forum; also see *fora*, comparison in size)

This Roman colony on the left bank of the upper Rhine was founded in 44 or 43 B.C. by Lucius Munatius Plancus, the same man who founded LYONS *(CIL* X 6087; location, Pliny, *Natural History* 4.106). Both colonies were probably founded at the request of Julius Caesar, who was assassinated on March 15, 44 B.C. *Augusta Raurica* (or *Augusta Rauricorum)* got its name about 15 B.C., during the reign of Augustus. The colony's prosperity reached its height in the second and third centuries. It guarded a bridge over the Rhine and a number of mainly military highways: two of these ran north to MAINZ (q.v.) on both sides of the Rhine (on the right bank c. A.D. 85-260), one east to Augsburg (capital of the Roman province of *Raetia)* by way of Windisch, one west to AUTUN and one southwest to Lausanne (see AOSTA, VIENNE).

For the book *Everyday Life*, J. Liversidge chose AUGST, a well-excavated site, as her typical Roman city. Orthogonally planned, it had two baths, one for men and one for women. The Neben-Forum (or Quasi-Forum) was a market (Ward-Perkins, *Cities* 35). In the first century A.D., a detachment from the legionary camp at Windisch was stationed at AUGST (von Gonzenbach, *PECS* 117). Late in the third century, *Augusta Raurica* was sacked by the Alamans (q.v.), and it never recovered (compare AVENCHES).

A new military fort was built 400 meters to the north, *Castrum Rauricense* or Kaiseraugst today *(castrum* means fort in Latin). This fort was also on the left bank of the Rhine; *Augusta Raurica* was separated from the river by that distance. A new city was also founded at about this time, twenty-two kilometers to the northwest at the place where the Rhine becomes navigable. This was *Basilia* or the present-day Basle, the city which succeeded the Roman colony. There is a museum at AUGST today with a reconstructed Roman house; the Roman theater there has been restored to be used for open-air performances.

Audin, A. *Lyon, miroir de Rome* . . . Paris 1965. 39 (the founding of AUGST)

Besnier. *Lexique*. 107

Boëthius. *Golden House*. fig. 25 (forum)

—— and Ward-Perkins. *ERA*. 343-346; fig. 131

Brogan. *Roman Gaul*. 22, 72; 68 (on the walls); 128 on centuriation (q.v.); 217 *(Castrum Rauricense)*

Brown. *RA*. 34-35, plate 63 (the forum)

Chevallier. *ANRW*. II.1 pl. lviii (plan)

Crema. *Arch*. 658 (index)

Doppelfeld, O. *Die Roemer am Rhein*. Cologne 1967

Duval, P.-M. "Archéologie et histoire de la Gaule," *Annuaire du Collège de France* 75 (1975): 539-545

Farnum, J. H. *Guide romain de la Suisse*. Lausanne 1975. 97-112

Forschungen in Augst

Frei-Stolba, R. "Die roemische Schweiz," *ANRW*. II.5.1 (1976). 345-350

Grenier. *Manuel*. I p. 333, n. 3 (bibliography); pp. 333-336; III 368-374 (the forum); 585-593 (theater and amphitheater)

Howald, E., and Meyer, E. *Die roemische Schweiz*. Zurich 1940. 305-316 (selected Latin inscriptions with German translation), 393 (index to this book of ancient sources)

Jahresberichte aus Augst und Kaiseraugst. (1971-)

KP. I (1964). 737-738 (E. Meyer)

*Laur-Belart, R. *Fuehrer durch Augusta Raurica*⁴. Basle 1966 (bibl. on 178-179)

—— *Ueber die Colonia Raurica und den Ursprung von Basel*. Basle 1959

Lavedan. *HU*. 393 (map); 489 (index)

Lieb, H. "Zur zweiten Colonia Raurica," *Chiron* 4 (1974): 15-23 (As no remains prior to 15 B.C. have been discovered, perhaps the Romans actually built on the site only then.)

Liversidge. *Everyday Life*. 40-50, figs. 5, 8

MacKendrick. *RoR*. 31-46; 252 (bibliography)

OCD. 148 (H. H. Scullard)

PECS. 116-118 (V. von Gonzenbach); 516 (V. von Gonzenbach on the frontier)

Staehelin, F. *Die Schweiz in roemischer Zeit*[3]. Basle 1948. 115-116; 597-604 (topography, with bibliography); 641 (index); map ii

Stier. *Atlas*. 40, fig. III (map of the Upper Rhine frontier from A.D. 369)

Ternes, C.-M. "Die Provincia Germania Superior im Bilde der juengeren Forschung," *ANRW*. II.5.2 (1976). 882-902

Tomasevic, T. "Augusta Raurica, une colonie romaine en Suisse," *Archéologia* 70 (1974): 20-27

Vittinghoff. *Roemische Kolonisation*. 69

Ward-Perkins. *Cities*. 31, 35, 120; figs. 75-77 (plans and a reconstruction)

—— "Republic to Empire." 6-13, fig. 2 (forum of AUGST compared to others, including that of PARIS); 15-16 (the Neben-Forum or market)

—— *RA*. 204, pl. 222 (forum)

Windisch, legionary camp: see list under MAINZ

Augusta Emerita = + Mérida, listed under ITALICA

Augusta Taurinorum: see TURIN

Augusta Treverorum: see TRIER

AUTUN (Saône-et-Loire, France) = *Augustodunum, Gallia Lugdunensis* (see Celtic names of cities below)

pp. 55 (the Temple of Janus); 66 (the amphitheater)

Augustodunum was founded about 12 B.C. to replace the *oppidum* (q.v.) of Bibracte as the tribal capital of the Aedui (compare ENSERUNE). It may have been given colonial status (Salmon, *RC* 160). The new city's walls enclosed a large area, comparable to ARLES or NIMES (see cities, comparison in area). The street plan was orthogonal with large blocks. On the north and east, two of AUTUN's Roman gates survive. Roman roads led west to Poitiers (see SAINTES), east to AUGST and north to PARIS (Chevallier, *Roman Roads* 161).

The city was a center of learning under the Roman Empire; here the élite of "Long-Haired Gaul" (see *Gallia Comata*) studied and became Romanized (Mommsen). AUTUN and LYONS were sacked in A.D. 269 in a civil war, joined by Gallic peasants (Rostovtzeff), but the former was rebuilt by Constantine I (306-337) and took his family name as "Flavia" (Besnier).

Wine was produced in the vicinity; the famous present-day vine-

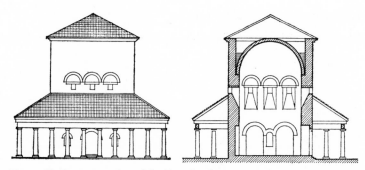

Figure 30. Reconstruction of the Temple of Janus at Autun
From H. J. Eggers et al., *Kelten und Germanen in heidnischer Zeit*, p. 95

yards of Beaune and Nuits-St.-Georges are not far away. These are Burgundy wines (see Burgundians).

Besnier. *Lexique*. 108

Boëthius and Ward-Perkins. *ERA*. plates 183 (model of St.-André Gate); 191 (Temple of Janus)

Brogan. *Roman Gaul*. 104

Bruehl. *PC*. 111-121

Castagnoli. *Orthogonal Town Planning*. 110

Chapot, V. *Le monde romain*. Paris 1951. 380 (twilight after the fourth century)

Chevallier. *ANRW*. II. 3 pp. 1047-1051 (list of figures and plates); 1052 (index)

—— *Roman Roads*. fig. 11 (map)

Clavel and Lévêque. *Villes*. 94-100 (on the schools of AUTUN in the fourth century)

Crema. *Arch*. 658 (index)

de Fontenay, H., and de Charmasse, A. *Autun et ses monuments*. Autun 1889

Desjardins. *Géogr*. III p. 441

Duval, P.-M. *Bulletin de la Société nationale des antiquaires de France* (1950/1951): 26 ff.; 81 ff. (on the gates)

Eggers, H. J., ed. *Kelten und Germanen in heidnischer Zeit*. Baden-Baden 1964. 6 (Bibracte); 95, fig. 2 (the Temple of Janus); (E. Will)

Grenier. *Manuel*. I pp. 337-345 (fig. 86, plan); III 234, nn. 1 and 2 (bibliography); 234-244; 458-463 (the Temple of Janus); 689-691 (the amphitheater, larger than that of ARLES or NIMES); 799-803 (the theater)

Grivot, D. *Autun*. Lyons 1967

Haverfield. *Town Planning*. 121-123
KP. I (1964). 744 (P. Wuilleumier)
Lavedan. *HU*. 489-490 (index)
MacKendrick. *RF*. 118-119
MacMullen, R. *Soldier and Civilian* . . . . Cambridge, Mass., 1963.
  fig. C (the gates)
Mommsen. *Provinces*. Chapter III
Morris. *Urban Form*. 56; fig. 3.24
OCD. 148-149 (C. E. Stevens)
PECS. 122-123 (R. Martin)
Rostovtzeff. *SEHRE*. 498
Thévenot, E. *Autun, cité romaine et chrétienne*. Autun 1932
—— "La voie d'Autun vers la Séquanie," *Latomus* 30 (1971): 1124
  (It led south to LYONS from the AUGST road.)
—— *Les voies romaines de la cité des Eduens*. Brussels 1969
Ward-Perkins. *Cities*. 30
—— "Republic to Empire." fig. 12
Wuilleumier, P. "Le théâtre romain d'Autun," *Revue des études an-
ciennes* 42 (1940): 699-706

AVENCHES (Vaud, Switzerland) = *Aventicum;* after A.D. 74, *Colonia Pia Flavia Constans Emerita Helvetiorum Foederata, Germania Superior* (Upper Germany); it was first in *Gallia Belgica*
(Bengtson, *Atlas* 44; cf. ibid. 45).
p. 78 (the walls, c. A.D. 100)
Aventicum, named after a Celtic goddess, was the chief *oppidum*
of the Helvetii. It lies about ten kilometers south of Lake Neuchâtel,
on the Central Plateau of Switzerland, between the Alps to the south
and the Jura Mountains to the north. Lake Neuchâtel was connected
by waterways to Lakes Bienne and Morat, three kilometers northeast of *Aventicum.* AVENCHES was about 100 kilometers from AUGST
on the Roman road southwest from AUGST to Lausanne.
    A.D. 68 and 69 were tumultuous years in *Gallia Comata* and Ro-
man Germany, with the revolt of several Celtic tribes and the civil
war between the successors of the Emperor Nero. The Helvetii took
the right sides (see Tacitus, *Histories* 1.67-70); Pia and Constans in
the name of the colony (founded A.D. 73 or 74) mean Faithful and
Loyal. Flavia is the *nomen* or family name of the Emperor Vespasian
(69-79) and his sons. Emerita indicates that Roman veterans were
settled there (compare AUGST and + Mérida, listed under ITALICA).
It is unclear what the status of the Helvetii in the colony was; Foe-

derata means allied—-see allied city below. The Celts at *Aventicum* may well have had Latin rights (q.v.) or even been made Roman citizens.

The Roman city's fortifications are comparatively well preserved. They enclosed an area more than twice the inhabited 233 hectares (von Gonzenbach in *PECS*). Over forty insulae have been identified (von Gonzenbach). The colony was sacked by the Alamans (q.v.) in A.D. 259 or 260 and never recovered (cf. Ammianus Marcellinus 15.11.12). In this respect, it is comparable to AUGST, a Roman colony which did not flourish into modern times. The fora at AUGST and AVENCHES have been open to excavation, for no existing buildings are in the way.

But *Aventicum* did last into the sixth century, when it had a bishop, Marius of Avenches (died c. 594). He wrote a chronicle of his century (= *Monumenta Germaniae Historica, Chronica Minora* II. T. Mommsen, ed. Berlin 1894; rpt. 1961, 232-239). This see was under Burgundian (q.v.) and, after about 534, Frankish rule. The bishopric was later moved to Lausanne.

The present-day town of AVENCHES (on the eastern border of French-speaking Switzerland) began in the twelfth century; it is perched on the hill which previously contained the city's Capitol (q.v.). The Musée romain is housed in a medieval tower at the entrance to the Roman amphitheater.

Besnier. *Lexique*. 113

Boegli, H. "Aventicum," *Bonner Jahrbuecher* 172 (1972): 175-184

—— "Aventicum, cité romaine," *Archéologia* 70 (1974): 28-34

—— "Il Capitolium di Aventicum," in *Atti del Convegno internazionale per il XIX centenario della dedicazione del Capitolium e per il 1500 anniversario della sua scoperta, Brescia settembre 1973*. Brescia 1975. II pp. 145-149

—— "Problemi urbanistici di Aventicum," Centro Studi e Documentazione sull'Italia Romana, *Atti* 5 (1974): 271-279

—— and Weidmann, D. "Nouvelles recherches à Aventicum," *Archaeologie der Schweiz* 1 (1978): 71-74

Brogan. *Roman Gaul*. 244 (index)

Dilke. *ANRW*. II.1 pp. 590-591 (bibliography on centuriation, q.v.)

Farnum, J. H. *Guide romain de la Suisse*. Lausanne 1975. 51-62

Frank. *ESAR*. III pp. 589, n. 105; 639 (a goldsmith); (A. Grenier)

Frei, P. *Pro Aventico*. 20 (1969). 5-22

Frei-Stolba, R. "Die roemische Schweiz." *ANRW*. II.5.1 (1976). 384-400

Garzetti. *TA*. 752 (bibl.)

Grenier. *Manuel*. I pp. 350-354; III 375-377 (the forum); 593-599
(theater, amphitheater and temple)
Gutkind. *IHCD*. II (1965). 223; 490 (bibl., see "Vaud")
Howald, E., and Meyer, E. *Die roemische Schweiz*. Zurich 1940.
252-268; 393 (index to this book of ancient sources)
KP. I (1964). 785 (E. Meyer)
Lavedan. *HU*. 392 (map); 490 (index)
Liebundgut, A. *Die roemischen Bronzen der Schweiz*. II, *Avenches*.
Mainz 1976 (Most of these fine pieces are at the Musée romain,
Avenches.)
MacKendrick. *RoR*. 98-99
Morris. *Urban Form*. 56; fig. 3.23
OCD. 155 (H. H. Scullard); 496 (C. E. Stevens, see "Helvetii")
PECS. 130-131 (V. von Gonzenbach)
Pro Aventico. 1- (1949-)
*Schwartz, G. T. *Die Kaiserstadt Aventicum*. Berne and Munich 1964;
bibliography on p. 127
Secrétan, E. *Avenches, son passé et ses ruines*. Lausanne 1919
Staehelin, F. *Die Schweiz in roemischer Zeit*[3]. Basle 1948. 145, 205-
210, 221-232, 457, 604-610 (topography); 641 (index); map iii
Stier. *Atlas*. 43 (plan)
*Tabula Imperii Romani, foglio L32: Mediolanum, Aventicum-Bri-
gantium*. Rome 1966 (map, including Milan, Italy, AVENCHES and
Bregenz, Austria)
Ternes, C.-M. "Die Provincia Germania Superior. . . .," *ANRW* II.5.2
(1976): 902-920
Verzàr, M. *Aventicum II: un temple du culte impérial*. Avenches
1978
Virieux, E. *Avenches, cité romaine*. Neuchâtel 1959

+ Avignon: listed under ORANGE

Banasa = *Colonia A* (......) *Valentia Banasa, Mauretania Tingitana*
(in present-day Morocco)
pp. 50 (the Capitol); 71 (the baths)
On the historical background, see *Volubilis* below. *Banasa* is on
the left or south bank of the Oued (meaning stream) Sebou, not far
from the Atlantic overland, in the fertile Rharb plain. The site had
been occupied for at least three centuries before Octavian-Augustus
(31 B.C.-A.D. 14) founded a colony there for Roman veterans. (Com-

pare the Latin name, *Valentia* [strong, healthy], with Valence [Drôme], France and Valencia, Spain—also colonies.) He founded at least twelve Roman colonies in *Mauretania*, although it was a client-kingdom and not yet a province of the Empire.

Among the ruins of *Banasa*, we may discern the standard elements of a Roman city: forum with basilica, Capitol and baths, as well as streets in a regular pattern. Much of the building dates from the early third century A.D. Later in the same century, the city, it seems, was destroyed by the natives of the Rharb. In 284/5, the Roman frontier was withdrawn to *Lixus* in the north.

A Roman highway led north to +Tangier (q.v., under *Volubilis*) and south to the frontier at *Sala* (near present-day Rabat). To go to *Banasa* from *Volubilis* today by road, one proceeds eighty-five kilometers northwest to Souk-el-Arba-du-Rharb (a farming town whose name means "Wednesday Market of the Rharb" in Arabic), then one travels southwest for twenty kilometers more.

Also see *Volubilis* for bibliography.

Besnier. *Lexique*. 121

Chatelain, L. *Le Maroc des romains*. Bibl. des Ecoles françaises d'Athènes et de Rome 160. Paris 1944. 69-76

Euzennat, M. "Chroniques," *Bulletin d'archéologie marocaine* 2 (1957): 202-205

Jodin, A. "Banasa et le limes méridional de Maurétanie Tingitane," *Actes du 95e Congrès national des Sociétés Savantes* 1970 (Paris 1974): 33-42 (a camp for auxiliary troops in an aerial photograph)

KP. I (1964). 819 (M. Leglay)

Lavedan. *HU*. 429 (map)

Marion, J. (listed under *Volubilis*)

PECS. 140-141 (M. Euzennat)

Salmon. *RC*. 163 (dates of the colonies in *Mauretania*)

Thouvenot, R. *Une colonie romaine de Maurétanie Tingitane, Valentia Banasa*. Paris 1941

Tissot, C. J. *Mémoires présentés à l'Académie des inscriptions et belles-lettres* 9: 277 ff.

—— *Recherches sur la géographie comparée de la Maurétanie Tingitane*. Paris 1878. 141-143

Vittinghoff. *Roemische Kolonisation*. 116-118

On the *Tabula* of *Banasa* (Roman citizenship, A.D. 168 and 177):

Millar, F. *The Emperor in the Roman World*. Ithaca, N.Y., 1977. 261-262, 473

Oliver, J. H. "Text of the Tabula Banasitana, A.D. 177," *American Journal of Philology* 93 (1972): 336-340

Seston, W., and Euzennat, M. "La citoyenneté romaine au temps de Marc Aurèle et de Commode d'après la *Tabula Banasitana*," *Comptes rendus de l'Académie des inscriptions et belles-lettres* (1961): 317-324

—— "Un dossier de la chancellerie romaine, la *Tabula Banasitana*," *CRAI* (1971): 468-490

Sherwin-White. *RC*. 336; 478 (index)

Sherwin-White, A. N. "The *Tabula* of Banasa and the *Constitutio Antoniniana*," *Journal of Roman Studies* 63 (1973): 86-98

+ Béziers: listed under NARBONNE

BOLOGNA (Emilia-Romagna, Italy; capital of the region) = *Bononia*, ancient region of *Aemilia, Italia*

p. 16 (MARZABOTTO)

About 500 B.C., the Etruscans founded Felsina on this site, just at the foot of the eastern slopes of the Apennines and on the right bank of the Reno River (see MARZABOTTO). In the third century B.C., the town was the capital of the Gallic tribe of the Boii, who were expelled by the Romans after their victory in 196. The Latin *colonia* of *Bononia* was founded there on December 30, 189 B.C. (Livy 37.57, Velleius Paterculus 1.15). The city's status was later upgraded to *municipium* and finally, under Augustus, Roman *colonia*. This orthogonal city's location on the *Via Aemilia* (the Aemilian Highway, 187 B.C.) was a strategic one, helping the Romans to control Cisalpine Gaul (see *Gallia Cisalpina*).

In decline since the fifth century A.D., BOLOGNA 's fortunes revived in the thirteenth century, when an independent city-state was formed. This cultural and economic "renaissance" lasted for three centuries. During the past hundred years, the city has become a commercial and industrial center, the result of its location on Italy's roads and railways. Most of the pre-Roman and Roman levels have been destroyed by medieval and later building (Mansuelli in *PECS*), but the orthogonal Roman street plan can still be discerned in the city's center.

Alfoeldi. *Early Rome*. 182 (A flourishing settlement existed on the site before the Etruscans came.)

Andreoli, E. "Bologna nell'antichità," *Atti della Pontificia Accademia Romana di Archeologia, Memorie* 3,6 (1946): 143-182

Bergonzoni, F., and Bonora, G. *Bologna romana*. I. *Fonti letterarie; Carta archeologica del centro urbano*. Istituto per la Storia di Bologna, Testi 9. Bologna 1976

Besnier. *Lexique*. 139

Castagnoli. *Orthogonal Town Planning*. 104, 135-136

Chevallier, R. *ANRW*. II.1 pp. 694, 698-699 (bibliography); plates xxiii-xxiv (aerial photograph and maps)

—— "Notes sur trois centuriations romaines; Bononia, Ammaedara, Vienna," in *Hommages à A. Grenier*, edit. M. Renard. Collection Latomus 58. Brussels 1962. 403-418

—— *Roman Roads*. 135-136

Chilver. *Cisalpine Gaul*. 6 (Latin colony), 17 (*colonia* under Augustus); 31 (use of the Reno River three kilometers west of *Bononia* as a waterway)

Coarelli. *Le città etrusche*. 325 (bibl.)

Ducati, A. *Storia di Bologna*. I. Bologna 1928

EB. IV pp. 178-179 (T. Ashby)

Ewins, U. *Papers of the British School at Rome* (1952). 54 ff.

Frank. *ESAR*. I pp. 114, 118 (primary sources for the Latin colony); V p. 117

Grenier, A. *Bologne villanovienne et étrusque*. Paris 1912

Lavedan. *HU*. 490 (index)

KP. I (1964). 927 (G. Radke)

Mansuelli, G. A. *Mostra dell'Etruria Padana*. 2 vols. Bologna 1960. I pp. 1-39; II pp. 22-25 (bibliography)

—— "Permanence et discontinuité urbaines dans la région de Bologne," in *Thèmes* by Duval. 73-80

*—— et al. "Lo sviluppo urbano di Bologna," *Bologna, centro storico*. Bologna 1970. 21-36

Nissen. *IL*. II pp. 262-264

OCD. 172 (E. T. Salmon)

Ogilvie. *Early Rome*. 11 (pre-Etruscans); 160 (Etruscan towns in north Italy)

PECS. 158 (G. A. Mansuelli)

Rykwert. *Idea*. 79, 80, 83

Salmon. *RC*. 23 (centuriation; q.v.); 86, 102-106 (After 189 B.C., the Roman policy was to found citizen colonies in *Gallia Cisalpina*); 110 (list of Latin colonies 334-181 B.C.); 138 (the Augustan colony)

Scullard. *Etruscan Cities*. 198-205

Ward-Perkins. *Cities*. 29 (on the continuity of settlement—to the present day—in cities on the *Via Aemilia*)

+ Bolsena *(= Volsinii Novi):* listed under *Volsinii*

BORDEAUX (Gironde, France) = *Burdigala, Aquitania*
pp. 8 (continuity of settlement); 66 (amphitheater); 79 (Late Roman wall)

   Burdigala was made the capital of *Aquitania* by Augustus (see *Gallia Comata*). Almost certainly, the city became a *municipium* A.D. 69/ 79 (Etienne in *PECS*). Here was and is the first bridge over the Garonne River (compare ARLES on the Rhône), before the river enters the Gironde estuary, an arm of the Atlantic. Both a river and an ocean port, *Burdigala* was a major commercial center in Roman times (Charlesworth). Highways led north to SAINTES, northeast to LYONS, southeast to TOULOUSE and NARBONNE and south to Pamplona (Charlesworth 156; Chevallier; Menéndez Pidal).

   Speaking of his native city, the Late Roman poet Ausonius (q.v.) said, "Burdigala is my native soil, where skies are temperate and mild, and the well-watered land generously lavish.... Her goodly walls four-square raise lofty towers so high that their tops pierce the soaring clouds. Within her, you may marvel at streets clearly laid out, at houses regularly plotted out ... as, where the channel of her spring-fed stream divides the city, as soon as old Ocean has filled it with his flowing tide, you shall behold a whole sea gliding onward with its fleets" *(Ordo* 20, transl. Evelyn-White).

   In the Later Empire, the university at BORDEAUX rivaled that of AUTUN (Mommsen, *Provinces*). The vineyards nearby were almost as famous in Roman times as they are today (Besnier).

   BORDEAUX was taken by the Visigoths (q.v.) in the fifth century A.D. and the Franks (q.v.) in the sixth. Under English control from 1154 to 1453, it then became part of the French kingdom. Owing to continuous settlement and building, little is known of the Roman plan of what is now the sixth largest city in France and still a major port (Etienne in *PECS*).

Besnier. *Lexique*. 149

Brogan. *Roman Gaul*. 108-109

Charlesworth. *Trade-Routes*. 288 (index)

Chevallier. *Roman Roads*. 161

Crema. *Arch*. 507; fig. 662 (amphitheater); 520, fig. 681 ("Piliers de la Tutelle" = ?a forum portico, c. A.D. 200, see Etienne in *PECS;* it was destroyed 1643/1715)
Desgraves, L. *Evocation du Vieux Bordeaux*. Paris 1960
Enciclopedia dell'arte antica, classica e orientale. II (1959). 137-139 (R. Etienne)
Etienne, R. *Bordeaux antique*. Bordeaux 1962. = vol. I of an eight-volume series, *Histoire de Bordeaux*, edit. C. Higounet (There is a good general bibliography for Gaul in vol. I pp. 373-376.)
—— "Burdigala et Garumna," in *Thèmes* by Duval. 329-340 (Bordeaux and the Garonne; excellent plans)
Grenier. *Manuel*. I pp. 410-411; III 434-439 ("Piliers de la Tutelle," ?a Gallo-Roman temple); 658-662 (the amphitheater, now called the Palais Gallien)
Gutkind. *IHCD*. V (1970). 136-137, 208-215; 475-476 (bibl.)
Hammond. *The City*. 321 (the poet Ausonius, q.v.)
Higounet, C., ed. *Histoire de l'Aquitaine*. Toulouse 1971 (see especially pp. 65-127 by R. Etienne)
Jullian, C. *Histoire de Bordeaux*. . . . Bordeaux 1895
KP. I (1964). 972 (M. Leglay)
Lavedan. *HU*. 490 (bibliography)
MacKendrick. *RF*. 60
Menéndez Pidal, R., ed. *Historia de España*. II³. Madrid 1962. plate following p. 568 (road)
Mommsen. *Provinces*. Chapter III
OCD. 185 (C. E. Stevens)
PECS. 172 (R. Etienne)
Stier. *Atlas*. 88-89 (archbishopric)

+ Caerleon: listed under WROXETER

Calleva Atrebatum: see SILCHESTER

CAPUA (Campania, Italy) = *Casilinum*, ancient *Campania, Italia* p. 16 (the location of modern CAPUA)
The city was founded around 600 B.C., probably by the Etruscans. In the fifth century B.C., it became the chief city of the Samnites (q.v.). The Romans in turn conquered *Casilinum* by 341 B.C. *Casilinum* guarded the bridge over the Volturnus River of the *Via Appia* (the Appian Highway of c. 312 B.C.) and the junction with the *Via*

Latina. The latter was a very old road, an alternate route to the east of the *Via Appia;* both highways joined again at Rome. *Casilinum* was destroyed in the ninth century A.D. by the Arabs. It was soon rebuilt by refugees from CAPUA VETERE (q.v.), and its name was changed to CAPUA. Today CAPUA is an agricultural center.
Besnier. *Lexique*. 183 (? a colony of Caesar in 58 B.C.)
Enciclopedia Italiana. VIII. Rome 1949. 918-919 (M. Schipa on the Principality of Capua, A.D. 900/910-1134)
KP. I (1964). 1065-1066 (G. Radke)
McKay, A. G. *Vergil's Italy*. Greenwich, Conn., 1970. 230 (an illegal colony founded on the site by Mark Anthony)
OCD. 210 (E. T. Salmon)
Paget. *Central Italy*. 225
Radke. *Viae*. 74 (the *Via Latina*)
Stier. *Atlas*. 88-89 (archbishopric, A.D. 966)

CAPUA VETERE (meaning Ancient Capua) or SANTA MARIA CAPUA VETERE (Campania, Italy) = *Capua;* from 27 B.C./A.D. 14, *Colonia Iulia Felix Augusta*, ancient region of *Campania, Italia*
pp. 16-18 (the orthogonal city)
    The site is about five kilometers southeast of present-day CAPUA (q.v.). Ancient *Capua* was founded before 600 B.C. by the Etruscans; it was conquered by the Samnites (q.v.) c. 423 and by the Romans c. 338. The Etruscan name for their Campanian stronghold was "*Volturnum*"; "Capua" may have been a second Etruscan name and not have begun with the Samnites (Ogilvie; compare Livy 4.37). The date of the orthogonal or chessboard city is still not certain. Ward-Perkins places it somewhere in the sixth century B.C.
    After 312 B.C., *Capua* was linked to Rome (about 180 kilometers to the northwest) by the *Via Appia*. In 211, as punishment for supporting Hannibal (see CARTHAGE), Rome confiscated its *territorium*, in which the Romans settled for the next 150 years (Livy 26.11, 16; Cicero, *On the Agrarian Law* 1.19, 2.88). The inhabitants of *Capua* received Roman citizenship after 90 B.C. Roman colonies on the site date from 59 B.C., 36, 27 B.C./A.D. 14, 54/68 and an honorary one in 284/305 (Salmon p. 161).
    The slave-revolt led by Spartacus (73-71 B.C.) began at the school for gladiators of *Capua*. Rostovtzeff draws attention to the local bronze and silverplate industry, whose unrivaled wares were exported as far as the Caucasus. The city was still prosperous in the fourth century A.D. (de Franciscis in *PECS*, citing Ausonius, q.v.). Arab invaders

destroyed it in 841, when its inhabitants settled in the present-day CAPUA. The ruins at CAPUA VETERE include a very large amphitheater of the first century A.D.; the orthogonal plan of ancient Capua has been studied by aerial photography (Castagnoli, figs. 18-20; Ward-Perkins, *Cities* 25; compare MARZABOTTO). Today Santa Maria Capua Vetere is an agricultural market-town.

Alfoeldi. *Early Rome*. 183-186 (the Etruscan invasion of Campania); 279-280 (the Etruscan god Volturnus)
Besnier. *Lexique*. 171-172
Boëthius and Ward-Perkins. *ERA*. plates 164-165 (mausoleums)
Castagnoli. *Orthogonal Town Planning*. 46-51
Christ. *Bibl*. 117, 119-120
Coarelli. *Le città etrusche*. 325-326 (bibl.)
Dilke. *ANRW*. II.1 p. 584 (bibl.)
EB. V pp. 294-295 (T. Ashby)
Enciclopedia dell'arte antica, classica e orientale. II. 1959. 335-336 (A. de Franciscis)
Frederiksen, M. W. "Republican Capua," *Papers of the British School at Rome* N.S. 14 (1959): 80-130
*Guida d'Italia del Touring Club Italiano, Campania*³. Milan 1963. 165-173
Guido. *Southern Italy*. 79-84
*Heurgon, J. *Recherches sur l'histoire, la religion et la civilisation de Capoue préromaine*. Bibliothèque des Ecoles françaises d'Athènes et de Rome 154. Paris 1942
Hodgkin, T. *Italy and her Invaders, 376-814*. V. Oxford 1895; rpt. New York 1967. 36-45
KP. I (1964). 1048-1049 (G. Radke)
McKay, A. G. *Vergil's Italy*. Greenwich, Conn., 1970. 228-230
Nissen. *IL*. II pp. 696-717
OCD. 203-204 (E. T. Salmon)
Ogilvie, R. M. *Commentary on Livy, Books 1-5*. Oxford 1965. 591-592
PECS. 195-196 (A. de Franciscis)
Radke. *Viae*. 95 (map), 99, 107; figs. 5, 9
RE. III (1899). 1555-1561 (C. Huelsen)
Rostovtzeff. *SEHRE*. 36, 70-71
Rykwert. *Idea*. 42
Salmon. *RC*. 201 (index)
Scullard. *Etruscan Cities*. 188-197
Vermaseren, M. J. *The Mithraeum at Santa Maria Capua Vetere*.

Etudes préliminaires aux religions orientales dans l'empire romain 16. Leiden 1971
Ward-Perkins. *Cities*. 24-25, 117

Carpentras (Vaucluse, France): see Chapter III, n. 48 above and colonies in *Gallia Narbonensis* below

CARTHAGE (near Tunis, the capital of Tunisia) = Kart Hadshat (meaning New City) to 146 B.C.; from 44 B.C. *Colonia Iulia Carthago, Africa Proconsularis;* mint of the Later Roman Empire (q.v.) p. 54 (cult of Demeter and Kore brought to CARTHAGE from Sicily)
    The site is on a peninsula in the Bay of Tunis, an arm of the Mediterranean. The legendary date for settlement by colonists from Tyre in Lebanon is 814 B.C. The Carthaginians (q.v.) established trading posts and colonies on the Mediterranean coasts of Spain and North Africa (west from *Lepcis Magna*, q.v.) and the islands of the western Mediterranean. This activity led to military conflicts with the Greeks (off Corsica c. 535 B.C.; in Sicily in 480, 409 and 250 B.C. — see *Selinus)* and with Rome from 264 to 146 B.C., when the Romans razed CARTHAGE.
    A Roman colony there was authorized in 123 B.C. (Salmon 119-120), but its charter was soon revoked although some colonists had already settled. (NARBONNE, therefore, must be called the first permanent Roman colony outside of Italy.) Another colony was founded at CARTHAGE in 44 B.C. for the Roman proletariat, in the same year and for the same purpose as those at CONSTANTINE and OSUNA. Part of this colony was displaced during the civil war of 44-31, but it was reinforced by Octavian (soon to become Augustus) in 29 B.C. with a settlement of veterans (Cassius Dio 43.50, 52.43).
    On the orthogonal street plan of the colony, see Castagnoli and Grimal in the bibliography below. Under the Empire, CARTHAGE developed into one of the five major provincial capitals; the others were Alexandria (Egypt), Antioch of *Syria* and Ephesus of *Asia* (both are in present-day Turkey) in the East and LYONS in the West (Rostovtzeff 139). With Alexandria and *Ostia* (see OSTIA ANTICA), it was one of the Empire's three main ports (Rougé 123-124). By c. A.D. 220, indeed, CARTHAGE was the second or third city of the Empire in population—over 300,000 (Duncan-Jones, citing Herodian 7.6.1). Olive oil and wheat were exported to *Ostia* to meet the needs of the imperial capital. On the main highways in Roman Africa, see DOUGGA below, and Chevallier, *Roman Roads* 152.

The Roman governor of *Africa Proconsularis* was a *proconsul* sent every year by the Senate. One cohort (one-tenth) of the Third Augustan Legion was transferred from its camp to guard the governor (Cagnat; see *Lambaesis*). The *procurator,* the emperor's chief financial officer, similarly had an Urban Cohort, a squad from the city police of Rome (Cagnat; compare LYONS; these military arrangements were unique). The Emperor Septimius Severus (193-211) honored CARTHAGE by granting it the exemption from taxes called *ius Italicum* (q.v.; Ulpian, *Digest* 15.8.11; Frank V pp. 64).

Conquered by the Vandals (q.v.), CARTHAGE was their capital from A.D. 429 to 533, when it was reconquered by the Byzantines (q.v.). Under Constantinople, it became a western enclave similar to RAVENNA. The Arabs took CARTHAGE in 698. There are now hardly any ancient remains left above ground level. The British Museum and the Bardo Museum of Tunis have mosaics from Roman CARTHAGE.

Tunis is presently expanding from the southwest, and the site will be subject to urban development again. For that reason, the UNESCO International Campaign to Save Carthage was recently organized, and excavations are being undertaken by teams from Bulgaria, Canada, Denmark, France, Germany, Italy, Tunisia, the U.S.A. (2), and the United Kingdom. Publication of their reports is under way.

I. Bibliography for the period 814-146 B.C. :

Christ. *Bibl.* 121-139

Dorey, T. A., and Dudley, D. R. *Rome Against Carthage.* London 1971

Hammond. *The City.* 501 (basic bibliography)

Scullard, H. H. "Carthage," *Greece and Rome.* 2nd ser. 2 (1955). 98-107

Warmington, B. H. *Carthage*[2]. London 1969

II. Bibliography for the period 146 B.C.-A.D. 698:

Audollent, A. *Carthage romaine.* Bibliothèque des Ecoles françaises d'Athènes et de Rome 84. Paris 1901

Belkhodja, M. et al. *Histoire de la Tunisie: L'antiquité.* Tunis 1900

Bengtson, H., and Milojčić, V. *Grosser historischer Weltatlas.* I[5]. Munich 1972. 37b (plan); also see *Erlaeuterungen* (commentary; contains bibl.)

Besnier. *Lexique.* 180-181

Bouchier. *LLRA.* 13-21 (outline of the Roman city); 105-117 (the Vandal and Byzantine cities); 127 (index)

Broughton. *RAP*. 229 (index)

Broughton, T. R. S. "The Territory of Carthage," *Revue des études latines* 97bis (1970): 265-275

Cagnat. *Armée romaine*. 211-215 (the garrison); 340 (the mint; but a mint earlier than A.D. 270 is questionable—Woloch)

Cagnat, R. *Carthage, Timgad, Tébessa et les villes antiques de l'Afrique du nord*. Paris 1909. 3rd ed. Paris 1927

CAH. IX² (1951). 957 (bibl.)

Carcopino, J. *Revue historique* 158 (1928): 2, n. 2 (dates the *Colonia Iulia* later than 44)

——— "L'Afrique au dernier siècle de la république romaine," *Revue historique* 162 (1929): 86-95

Castagnoli. *Orthogonal Town Planning*. 112, 115 (plan of long rectangular city blocks, 35.28 by 141.12 meters or 120 by 480 Roman feet—worked out by C. Saumagne and P. Davin from ruins of the sewer system); fig. 50

Courtois, C. *Les Vandales et l'Afrique*. Paris 1955

Cunliffe. *Rome*. 131-133 (map and color photographs of the aqueduct)

Davin, P. "Etude sur la cadastration de la Colonia Iulia Carthago," *Revue tunisienne* N.S. 1 (1930)

Debbasch, Y. "Colonia Iulia Karthago," *Revue historique de droit* 31 (1953): 30-53; 335-337

Duncan Jones. *ERE*. 67, n.3 and 260, n.4

EB. V pp. 426-431 (E. Babelon)

Ennabli, A., and Slim, H. *Carthage, A Visit to the Ruins*. 1974

Finley. *Atlas*. 67-69 (C. R. Whittaker)

Frank. *ESAR*. IV pp. 31, 102-103 (R. M. Haywood, foundation of the Roman colony); V 64 (T. Frank, *ius Italicum*); 243, 292 (trade with Ostia); index p. 13

Grimal. *Civ. Rome*. 434-435 (urban plan studied by 1963: streets, baths, theater, odeum, *circus*, aqueduct, harbor; summary)

Gsell, S. "Les premiers temps de la Carthage romaine," *Revue historique* 156 (1927): 225-240

Haverfield. *Town Planning*. 113-115

Hours-Miédan, M. *Carthage²*. "Que sais-je?" no. 340. Paris 1959. bibl. on p. 118

Humphrey, J. H. "North-African Newsletter I," *American Journal of Archaeology* 82 (1978): 511-520, bibl. on 520

——— et al. *Excavations at Carthage Conducted by the University of Michigan*. I-IV. Tunis/Ann Arbor 1975-1978

—— "Roman Carthage," *Scientific American* 238.1 (1978): 111-120; 140 (bibl.)

Hurst, H. "Excavations at Carthage 1974," *Antiquaries Journal* 55 (1975): 11-40 (harbor and fifth century A.D. wall)

—— *AJ* 56 (1976): 177-197

—— *AJ* 57 (1977): 232-261

—— "Excavations at Carthage 1977-78. Fourth Interim Report," *AJ* 59 (1979): 19-49

Institut géographique national. *Atlas des centuriations romaines de Tunisie*. Paris 1954

Karthago. 1- (1950-)

KP. III (1969). 135-138 (G. Schwabl)

Lancel, S., ed. *Byrsa I*. *Rapports préliminaires des fouilles (1974-1976)*. Collection de l'Ecole française de Rome 41. Rome 1979 (Byrsa was the Punic citadel on its hill, where Late Roman fortifications were also built.)

—— et al. "Fouilles françaises à Carthage (1974-1975)," *Antiquités africaines* 11 (1977): 11-130 (The French excavation is divided into three zones, one of which is Roman.)

Lapeyre, G. G., and Pellegrin, A. *Carthage latine et chrétienne*. Paris 1950

Lavedan. *HU*. 442-443 (maps); 490 (index)

Lengyal, A., and Poulton, R. "Geographical Survey in Carthage, 1976," *Journal of Field Archaeology* 3 (1976): 368-469 (aims of the UNESCO project)

Lézine, A. *Carthage-Utique: Etudes d'architecture et d'urbanisme*. Paris 1968

—— "Sur la population des villes africaines," *Antiquités africaines* 3 (1969): 69-82

Liversidge. *Everyday Life*. 233 (index)

Mahjoubi. *CRT*

OCD. 208-209 (W.N.W., B. H. Warmington and H. H. Scullard)

PECS. 201-202 (A. Ennabli)

Picard, C. *Carthage*. Paris 1951

(Charles-)Picard, G. *La Carthage de Saint Augustin*. Paris 1965; "an excellent survey of the ruins, history, and life of Roman Carthage" (Hammond, *The City* 523)

Piganiol. *HR*. 207, 356 (bibl.)

Poinssot, L. *Atlas historique, géographique, économique et touristique de Tunisie*. Paris 1936

Raven. *Rome in Africa*. 183 (bibl.); 186 (index)

RE. X (1919). 2150-2242 (R. Oehler and Lenschau)

Romanelli, P. "Della popolazione di Cartagine...," *Accademia dei Lincei, Rendiconti* (Jan.-Feb. 1971)

—— *Storia*

Rostovtzeff. *SEHRE*. 593-595 (bibl.); 767-768 (index)

Rougé. *Recherches*. 123-124

Salmon. *RC*. 119-121 (attempted colony of 123 B.C.); 135-136 (colony of Julius Caesar and Octavian); 159 (date); 201 (index)

Saumagne, C. "Colonia Iulia Karthago," *Bulletin archéologique du Comité des travaux historiques et archéologiques* (1924); (1930-1931)

Senay, P. et al. *Carthage I = Cahier des études anciennes* 6 (1976). (a circular Roman monument, of uncertain date, perhaps a market)

—— *Carthage II = CEA* 9 (1978)

—— *Carthage III = CEA* 10 (1979)

—— *Carthage IV = CEA* 12 (1980). 2 fascicles

—— "Carthage 1978: Fouilles du monument circulaire," *Classical News and Views* 23 (1979): 9-14

Stager, L. E. "Carthage 1977: The Punic and Roman Harbors," *Archaeology* 30 (1977): 198-200

Stier. *Atlas*. 21 (plan)

Toutain, J. *Les cités romaines de la Tunisie*. Paris 1896

—— *La colonisation romaine en Tunisie*. Paris 1904

Vittinghoff. *Roemische Kolonisation*. 81-82 (calls it the *Colonia Iulia Concordia* and questions the date of 44 B.C.); 111 (Octavian's settlement); 140 (index)

Wells, C. et al. "Carthage, Site 2: The Theodosian Wall," *Classical News and Views* 22 (1978): 9-12 (fortification of A.D. 379/395)

—— "Carthage 1978: La muraille théodosienne," *CNV* 23 (1979): 15-18

—— *CNV* 25 (1981): 1-10

III. Bibliography A.D. 698 to the present:

Abun-Nasr, J. M. *A History of the Maghrib*. Cambridge 1971

Cavaillon (Vaucluse, France): see Chapter III, n. 48 above and colonies in *Gallia Narbonensis* below

CHASSENON (Charente, France) = *Cassinomagus, Aquitania*
pp. 55 (the Gallo-Roman temple); 68 (the demi-amphitheater)
This was a Gallo-Roman village, known for its sacred spring, on

the Roman road between SAINTES and Limoges (see Chapter III, n. 25). There are now museums on the site and at Rochechouart, six kilometers away.

Barrière, P. "Une bourgade gallo-romaine: Chassenon, ses monuments et ses puits," *Revue des études anciennes* 39 (1937): 241-255
Besnier. *Lexique*. 183
Crema. *Arch*. 403; fig. 492 (the temple)
Eydoux, H.-P. *Résurrection de la Gaule*. Paris 1961. 251-278
Grenier. *Manuel*. III pp. 572-577
MacKendrick. *RF*. 180-183; 261 (bibl.)
PECS. 203-204 (J.-H. Moreau)

CHERCHELL (wilaya of El Asnam, Algeria) = *Iol* (Carthaginian name) = *Caesarea* (name given by Juba II) = from A.D. 42/54, *Colonia Claudia Caesariensium Iol, Mauretania Caesariensis*
pp. 68 (the theater, which was transformed into an amphitheater after A.D. 300), 78-79 (the city walls), 80 (the south gate)
This city, now with a population of 15,000, is on the Mediterranean coast, 100 kilometers west of Algiers. For the Roman coastal road, see TIPASA. CHERCHELL began as a Carthaginian trading station with a harbor, and it grew into a town. Here Juba II, the client-king (q.v.) of Mauretania and Numidia (25 B.C.-A.D. 23), built the new city of *Caesarea*, as he did *Volubilis* (q.v.). The former was his capital. Juba built *Caesarea's* temples, baths, theater, and amphitheater, a separate, rectangular building. There are a few indications that his street plan was orthogonal. The wall, 7 kilometers long and enclosing 400 hectares, was probably begun by him. One hundred and fifty of these hectares became inhabited in ancient times.

This *Caesarea* should be distinguished from *Caesarea* in present-day Israel, built by Herod the Great (41-4 B.C.). Both cities were built by client-kings and named after Augustus Caesar. But, even if their street plans were orthogonal and they contained the standard features, were they really Roman cities?

When the Emperor Claudius transformed Mauretania into two Roman provinces in A.D. 42/44, he made *Caesarea-Iol* the capital of one of them. He founded a Roman colony here (Pliny, *Natural History* 5.20), but it is unclear whether it was a veteran or honorary colony (Vittinghoff). Auxiliary Roman troops were stationed here, and the harbor was used for a Roman naval base (Cagnat). The colony had the usual magistrates *(duoviri*, q.v.) and priests (Bouchier), in contrast with RAVENNA, a naval base but not a Roman colony; also

compare FREJUS. *Caesarea's* population grew to about 40,000 (Leveau 22), and some of its aqueducts may be seen today.
The city was plundered by the Berber (q.v.) Prince Firmus in 364 and conquered by the Vandals (q.v.) in 429. The Byzantines (q.v.) built new fortifications in the mid-sixth century, but their control was short-lived.
Not much of the ancient city still remains. A new Museum of Antiquities is planned to contain some of the fine statues with which Juba II adorned his city. Of the present-day town, Valerie and Jon Stevens say, "If there is a strange element it is that in spite of the beauty and opportunity (for tourism) there is no sign of a holiday atmosphere about CHERCHELL, which remains a town to live in and to work in."

Besnier. *Lexique*. 156-157
Bouchier. *LLRA*. 28-31
Cagnat. *Armée romaine*. 275-284 (the fleet); 520-521 (the auxiliary army); 281 (map of the Roman harbor)
*Duval, P.-M. *Cherchel et Tipasa, Recherches sur deux villes fortes de l'Afrique romaine*. Institut français de Beyrouth, Bibliothèque archéologique et historique 43. Paris 1946
EB. VI pp. 82-83
Frank. *ESAR*. IV p. 70 (R. M. Haywood, trade); 111 (commercial and a naval harbor)
Gsell. *AAA*. fasc. 4 ("Cherchel")
—— *Cherchel, antique Iol*. Rev. by M. Leglay, Algiers 1952
KP. I (1964). 1003-1004 (M. Leglay)
Lassus, J. *Bulletin d'archéologie algérienne*. 1 (1962-1965); (on the mosaics)
Leveau, P., and Paillet, J.-L. *L'alimentation en eau de Caesarea en Maurétanie et l'aqueduc de Cherchel*. Paris 1976
Libyca. 1953-1960
Liversidge. *Everyday Life*. 233 (index); ill. 52 (a mosaic showing plowing)
Mann. *ANRW*. II.1 p. 528 (the frontier)
Nagel's Guide, Algeria. 171-175
OCD. 191 (W.N.W.)
PECS. 413-414 (J. Lassus; see "Iol")
(Charles-)Picard, G. "La date du théâtre de Cherchel . . .," *Comptes rendus de l'Académie des inscriptions et belles-lettres* (1975): 386-397 (The theater dates from 25-15 B.C.; others are compared.)
Raven. *Rome in Africa*. 186 (index)

Rebuffat, R. "Notes sur les confins de la Maurétanie Tingitane et de la Maurétanie Césarienne," *Studi Magrebini* 4 (1971): 33-64
Salama, *Voies*. 105
Stevens. *Algeria*. 104-107
Vittinghoff. *Roemische Kolonisation*. 28, n.1

+Chester: listed under WROXETER

+Cimiez: listed under FREJUS

Cirta: see CONSTANTINE

Colchester (Essex, England): mentioned under LONDON below and colonies in *Britannia* in the glossary

+Cologne: listed under MAINZ

CONSTANTINE (wilaya of Constantine, Algeria) = *Cirta* (from the Carthaginian word for City); from 44 B.C., *Colonia Iulia Iuvenalis Honoris et Virtutis Cirta, Africa Proconsularis* (ancient region of *Numidia,* q.v.)
pp. 48, 83 (location of DJEMILA on the Roman highway)
The city began in the late third century B.C. as the capital of the Numidian kingdom. CONSTANTINE has been continuously occupied since that time, and, for that reason, virtually the only aspect of the ancient city which can be seen today is its position atop a natural fortress. It is protected on the north and east sides by the deep gorge of the Oued (meaning "stream") Rhumel. The Stevenses call this "the most stupendous gorge in the whole of North Africa" (p. 145). The plateau on which the city was built extends for eighty hectares.

An unauthorized Roman colony was founded here in the mid-first century by Publius Sittius, who handed it over to Julius Caesar. The date of the official Roman colony is probably 44 B.C. (cf. Appian, *Civil War* 4.230-242), the year of the foundations at CARTHAGE and Corinth. The area governed by the colony at *Cirta* was extremely large, extending well inland from the Mediterranean. It contained some of the best land for grain in North Africa as well as three other colonies, whose precise status has, naturally enough, caused debate among modern scholars. The city had an unusual government, headed by triumvirs rather than duovirs, to administer this confederation.

Cirta was an important crossroads in Roman times. The highway west to *Sitifis* (SETIF) has been mentioned by Grimal above. Another road ran south from Skikda, the city's port on the Mediterranean eighty kilometers away, through CONSTANTINE to TIMGAD. *Cirta* was rebuilt and renamed by the Emperor Constantine I. Fortified CONSTANTINE was taken by the French Foreign Legion in the epic raid of 1837. It is now the third largest city in independent Algeria.

Roman-period artifacts and inscriptions from the district are kept in the Constantine Museum.

Besnier. *Lexique*. 215-216
Bouchier. *LLRA*. 22-28
Broughton. *RAP*. 230 (index)
Chevallier. *Roman Roads*. 152
Duncan-Jones. *ERE*. 69 (prices)
EB. VII pp. 2-3
Finley. Atlas. 72 (C. R. Whittaker)
Frank. *ESAR*. IV pp. 31, 77-78 (R. M. Haywood—political); 32 (agriculture); 68, n.20 (highways); 103 (veterans settled at *Cirta* by Augustus)
Gsell. *AAA*. fasc. 17 ("Constantine")
KP. I (1964). 1196 (M. Leglay)
Nagel's Guide, Algeria. 309-317 (with one plan)
OCD. 242 (W.N.W. and B. H. Warmington)
PECS. 224-225 (P.-A. Février)
Piganiol. *HR*. 356 (political bibliography)
Raven. *Rome in Africa*. 186 (index)
Rostovtzeff. *SEHRE*. 34, 315, 317-319, 323; 682 nn. 69-70
Salmon. *RC*. 159; 166, n.4; 195, n. 294 (political history)
Stevens. *Algeria*. 142-146
Vittinghoff. *Roemische Kolonisation*. 112-114 (political history)

Cosa (Etruria, Italia)
p. 20, n. (hilltop orthogonal cities); (see Chapter I, n. 11 above on the city blocks)

The present-day name is Ansedonia. The site is about 125 kilometers northwest of Rome on a rocky promontory overlooking the Tyrrhenian Sea (cf. Strabo 5.2.8). The coastal Latin colonies of *Cosa* and *Paestum* (q.v., in *Lucania*, well southeast of Rome) were both founded in 273 B.C. (Salmon 173, n. 63; on *Cosa*, Velleius Paterculus 1.14.6, Pliny, *Natural History* 3.5.1). By the end of the third century, the Romans had conquered all of *Etruria*.

The buildings in and beside *Cosa's* forum date from 273-125 B.C., and the Capitol (q.v.) 175-150 (Brown in *PECS*). *Cosa's* street plan had long and narrow blocks. Cisterns had to be used to hold rain water; there were no wells in the limestone or aqueducts. Sand could be flushed out of the harbor by clean water from a natural reservoir (Paget). The *Via Aurelia* (second century B.C.) passed nearby (Besnier). Of *Cosa*, Scullard says, "Its fine walls, temples, and other buildings make it for us the very paradigm of a Latin colony. For the Etruscans, it was a symbol of Roman power which cut their coastline in half."

The city's decline began when it was destroyed in the 60s B.C.; we do not know by whom (Brown in *PECS*). Rebuilding took place 27 B.C.-A.D. 14, but *Cosa* from then on was only a religious center. In the fourth century A.D., the forum served as the center of a large estate (ibid.), and a small building at one end of the forum was used as a Bacchic shrine. As *Cosa* was out of the way on its hilltop, pagan worship took place there even after the edicts of 391 and 392 (Collins-Clinton).

An American team excavated *Cosa* 1948-1954 and 1965-1972. Because it was abandoned in antiquity (to be followed only by Ansedonia, a short-lived town of the ninth century [Ashby in *EB*]), archaeologists have been able to form a clear idea of a Roman city of this early date—and its orthogonal plan. On September 17, 1981, the American Academy in Rome presented the Antiquarium at Cosa, which houses exhibition and work areas, to the Italian government.

Bengtson. *Atlas*. 33d (plan)
Besnier. *Lexique*. 238 ("Cossa")
Boëthius. *Golden House*. 38
—— and Ward-Perkins. *ERA*. 151-152; 522, n. 1 (bibl.); 603 (index); figs. 24, 64, 65; plates 60 (gate); 96 (villa)
Brown, F. E. *Archaeology* 2 (1949): 2-10
—— "Cosa I, History and Topography," *MAAR* 20 (1951): 7-113
*—— *Cosa: The Making of a Roman Town*. Ann Arbor 1980
—— *RA*. 120-121 (index)
—— Richardson, E. H., and Richardson, Jr., L. "Cosa II, The Temples on the Arx," *MAAR* 26 (1960); (includes the Capitol)
Castagnoli, F. "La Centuriazione di Cosa," *MAAR* 24 (1956): 147-165
—— *Orthogonal Town Planning*. 98; fig. 39 (the city's blocks vary in size, but some are 32/37 meters [roughly 120 Roman feet] by 82 meters; see city blocks below); 121
Chevallier. *ANRW*. II.1 p. 695 (bibliography)
Coarelli. *Le città etrusche*. 120-128; 321 (bibliography)

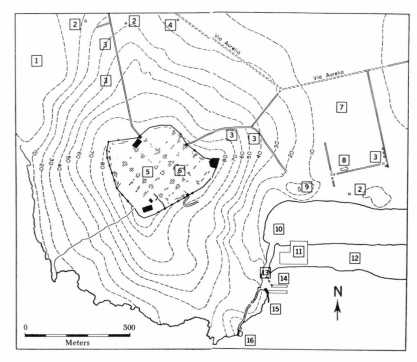

Figure 31. Plan of the District of Cosa
From Salmon, *Roman Colonization*, fig. 3

1. Tombolo di Feniglia (hill)
2. Spring
3. Tombs
4. Well
5. Cosa
6. Forum
7. Succosa
8. San Biagio
9. Port temple
10. Port of Cosa
11. Villa
12. Petrified sand dunes
13. Channel
14. Jetties
15. Tagliata Etrusca (fissure)
16. Spacco della Regina (fissure)

Collins-Clinton, J. *A Late Antique Shrine of Liber Pater at Cosa.*
Etudes préliminaires aux religions orientales dans l'empire ro-
main 64. Leiden 1977
Crema. *ANRW.* I.4 "Arch. rep."
—— *Arch.* 660 (index)
Dennis. *CCE.* II pp. 237-255

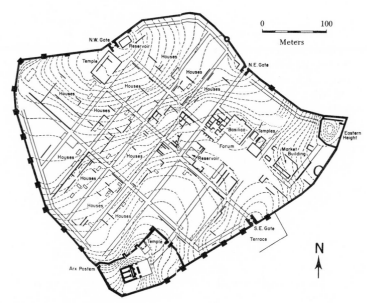

Figure 32. Plan of Cosa
From Salmon, *Roman Colonization*, fig. 4

Dyson, S. L. "Survey Archaeology: Reconstructing the Roman
Countryside," *Archaeology* 34 (1981): 31-37 (on the area of *Cosa*)
EB. VII p. 212 (T. Ashby)
Forma Italiae, Cosa. Rome 1968
Frederiksen, M. W. *Journal of Roman Studies* 52 (1962): 266-267
(review of Brown et al., "Cosa II")
KP. I (1964). 1326 (G. Radke)
Lavedan. *HU*. 373 (map); 491 (index)
Lugli. *Tecnica edilizia*. 111-115
MacKendrick. *Mute Stones*. 98-115; 354-355 (bibl.)
McCann, A. M., and Lewis, J. D. "The Ancient Port of Cosa," *Ar-
chaeology* 23 (1970): 200-211
McKay. *Houses*. 60-63; plate 23
McKay, A. G. *Vergil's Italy*. Greenwich, Conn., 1970. 88-89
Nissen. *IL*. II pp. 310-311
OCD. 293-294 (J. B. Ward-Perkins)
Paget. *Central Italy*. 127-128
PECS. 245-246 (F. E. Brown)

Richardson, L., Jr. "Cosa and Rome: Comitium and Curia," *Archae-
ology* 10 (1957): 49-54
—— "Excavations at Cosa in Etruria," *Antiquity* 27 (1953): 102-103
Rykwert. *Idea*. 117-121
Salmon. *RC*. 23; 29-39; 62-63; 110-111; figs. 3 and 4 (good maps);
plates 28, 30-33
Scullard. *Etruscan Cities*. 276
Stier. *Atlas*. 21 (plan)
Ward-Perkins. *Cities*. 27; 39; 120; fig. 45
—— "ERTI." 154 (bibl.); figs. 7-8 (maps—fig. 8 is the same as my fig.
32)
—— *RA*. 348 (index)
—— "Rykwert" (The *mundus* [q.v.] has been found.)

Cuicul: see DJEMILA

Deva (+Chester): listed under WROXETER

+Die: listed under VAISON

DJEMILA (wilaya of Constantine, Algeria) = (*?Colonia Nerviana)
Cuicul, Africa Proconsularis* (ancient region of *Numidia*, q.v.)
pp. 48 (the curia), 50 (the Capitol), 51-52 (so-called Temple of Venus
Genetrix), 52-53 (the New Forum), 54 (comparison with *Lepcis Magna*,
which also had a second forum), 61 (the theater), 83-86 (the Roman
city), 86 (houses)

Grimal has described medium-sized *Cuicul* more extensively than
any other Roman city save Rome itself. Nerva's colony for Roman
veterans (*CIL* VIII 20,713) was built on a defensive site by the Third
Augustan Legion (see *Lambaesis*, TIMGAD and SETIF). Previously,
DJEMILA was the location of a *castellum* or fort belonging to *Cirta*
(see CONSTANTINE), eighty kilometers to the east (Rostovtzeff 323).
The built-up area of ancient *Cuicul* was only twelve hectares (see
cities [Roman], comparison in area, below). It is not known when
the city was abandoned; a bishop from *Cuicul* is recorded for A.D.
553 (Whittaker). Excavations from 1909 to 1957 brought the Roman
colony to light. There is a new museum on the site containing its
mosaics.

The ground on which the city was built precluded a strictly orthogonal plan (Ward-Perkins, *Cities* 121). In that author's words,
"Anyone who thinks that Roman provincial planning was efficient
but dull need only travel seventy miles from the staid, copybook

proprieties of (TIMGAD) to view the breathless, cliff-top improvisations of its sister foundation, *Cuicul* (DJEMILA), founded only three years earlier" (ibid. 33).

Allais, Y. *Djemila*. Paris 1938

—— "Le quartier occidental de Djemila," *Antiquités africaines* 5 (1971): 95-119 (a study of new excavations)

Ballu, A. *Revue africaine* (1921)

—— *Les ruines de Djemila (antique Cuicul)*. Algiers 1921

Blanchard-Lemée, M. *Maisons à mosaïques du quartier central de Djemila (Cuicul)*, *Etudes d'antiquités africaines* of the Institut d'archéologie méditerranéenne with the Centre national de la recherche scientifique. Aix-en-Provence 1975

Boëthius and Ward-Perkins. *ERA*. plates 241 (market), 254 (air view), 255 (Temple of the Severi); 486-490

Broughton. *RAP*. 129-130 (political)

Cagnat, R. "La colonie romaine de Djemila," *Musée belge* 27 (1923): 113-129

—— *Comptes rendus de l'Académie des inscriptions et belles-lettres* (1916): 548

Cunliffe. *Rome*. 230 (air view in color)

Duncan-Jones. *ERE*. 71 (prices)

Février, P.-A. *Djemila²*. Algiers 1971 (also see bibl. for SETIF below)

Finley. *Atlas*. 72-73 (C. R. Whittaker)

Frank. *ESAR*. IV pp. 38, 76 (R. M. Haywood)

Grimal. *Civ. Rome*. 447 (one-paragraph summary)

Gsell. *AAA*. fasc. 16 ("Sétif")

KP. I (1964). 1338-1339 (M. Leglay)

Leschi, L. *Djemila²*. Algiers 1953

Libyca. 1953-

Liversidge. *Everyday Life*. 235 (index)

Monceaux, P. *Cuicul chrétien*. 1923

Nagel's Guide, Algeria. 283-293 (with 1 plan)

OCD. 300 (W.N.W.)

PECS. 249-250 (P.-A. Février)

(Charles)-Picard. *Roman Architecture*. 177 and plan 178 (Arch of Caracalla)

Raven. *Rome in Africa*. 186 (index)

Rostovtzeff. *SEHRE*. 323; 594 (bibl.); 685, n. 81 (bibl.); 686, n. 84 (local benefactor); 701, n. 21 (granary)

Ward-Perkins. *Cities*. 3, 121; figs. 67-68

—— *RA*. 348 (index)

Wheeler and Wood. *Roman Africa*. 126-138; plates 43 (the *cardo maximus*, q.v.), 44 (the Arch of Caracalla and the new town), 45-46 (the Temple of the Severi), 47 (the "Rue du théâtre" or Street of the Theater), 48 (weights-office in the "Market of Cosinius"), 49 (a mosaic)

DOUGGA (seven kilometers south of Téboursouk, Tunisia) = *Thugga, Africa Proconsularis:* from A.D. 261, *Colonia Licinia Septimia Aurelia Alexandriana Thugga* (Licinius was the family name of the Emperor Gallienus 253-268.)

pp. 55 (Temple of Baal-Saturn), 61 (the theater of A.D. 169, also shown on fig. 15)

DOUGGA overlooks the Oued (or stream) Khalled, which soon joins the Oued Medjerda in its course of 100 kilometers to the Gulf of Tunis. The Medjerda valley was one of the best agricultural areas (grain and olives) in Roman Africa. Like CONSTANTINE and DJEMILA, DOUGGA is set on a fortresslike position, a height above the Khalled valley. The Téboursouk Mountains run further north. The ancient site has been preserved because it was away from communications routes, after Roman times. A Roman highway ran via Musti to CARTHAGE, 100 kilometers to the northwest (H. Bengtson and V. Milojčić, *Grosser historischer Weltatlas* I⁵, Munich 1972, 40-41).

Settlement on DOUGGA's sloping site began in prehistoric times. In the early second century B.C., a Berber prince (to whom an impressive monument still stands) ruled the district as a part of the kingdom of *Numidia* (q.v.). The bilingual inscription from this monument, in ancient Berber and Carthaginian (now it is in the British Museum), shows that the two cultures were alive in this area then. Following the Roman conquest of CARTHAGE in 146 B.C., Italian settlers occupied the better farmlands here.

After 146 B.C., the native inhabitants of *Thugga* were recognized by the Roman governments as a *civitas* (q.v.), just inside the province of *Africa* (Haywood 3, 14 on the boundary). The Roman farmers were organized as a *pagus* (see *paganus* below for *pagus;* Rostovtzeff 319; 683, n. 73 and *Année epigraphique* [1963] 94). Ownership of the area's farms was gradually taken over by the emperor (Rostovtzeff 686, n. 87; 743, n.42). The Romans and the natives were united in a *municipium* (q.v.) in A.D. 205, fifty-six years before the honorary colony (Ennabli).

The buildings which appear so impressive and well preserved today date from 166/167 (the *Capitolium*) up to 222/235 (the Temple of Juno Caelestis, who succeeded the Carthaginian goddess Tanit

[Wheeler and Wood]). The irregular street plan (with a forum at the center) was partly the result of the land-contours, but the streets of *Thuburbo Maius*, sixty-five kilometers to the east and on level ground, are also not orthogonal. Ancient *Thugga* was about twenty hectares in area (see cities [Roman], comparison in area, below). Mosaics from *Thugga* may be seen at the Bardo Museum in Tunis.
The city was abandoned by A.D. 600. Of it in its prime, Haywood says, "Thugga may perhaps be singled out as the richest city of the proconsular province after Carthage" *(ESAR* 112). That the wealthier residents of the Roman period were eager to adorn it is indicated by the inscriptions as well as the buildings themselves.
See CARTHAGE for additional bibliography.

Broughton. *RAP.* 85, 113 *(civitas* under Claudius); 214-216 ("Aurelia" added to name of *civitas* A.D. 180/192, from the family name of the Emperor Commodus; *municipium* formed by Septimius Severus, 193/211— "Septimia")
CAH. X² (1952). 968 (bibl.)
Carton, M. *Dougga.* Tunis 1929
—— *Le théâtre romain de Dougga.* Paris 1902
Finley. *Atlas.* 69-70 (C. R. Whittaker)
Frank. *ESAR.* IV (R. M. Haywood; see index, p. 71)
Golfetto, A. *Dougga.* Basle 1961
Grimal. *Civ. Rome.* 449 (monuments)
KP. V (1975). 791-792 (M. Leglay)
Lavedan. *HU*
Lézine, A. "Sur la population des villes africaines," *Antiquités africaines* 3 (1969): 69-82
Mahjoubi. *CRT*
OCD. 1070 (B. H. Warmington)
PECS. 917-919 (A. Ennabli)
Poinssot, C. *Comptes rendus de l'Académie des inscriptions et belles-lettres* (1962): 55-76
—— *Les ruines de Dougga.* Tunis 1958
Raven. *Rome in Africa.* 190 (index)
RE. Supplement 7 (1940): 1567-1571 (F. Windberg)
Robertson. *GRA.* 280-281 (theater); 356 (bibliography on temples)
Rostovtzeff. *SEHRE.* 817 (index)
Seston, W. "Des 'portes' de Thugga à la 'constitution' de Carthage," *Revue historique* 237 (1967): 277-294 (on the gates of DOUGGA)
Tlatli, S. *Antique Cities in Tunisia.* 1971
Ward-Perkins. *RA.* 83, pl. 275 (Capitol); p. 353 (index)

Wheeler. *RAA*. 46-47

—— and Wood. *Roman Africa*. 100-108; plates 30 (Temple of Juno
Caelestis), 31 (the *Capitolium*), 32 (the Piazza of the Winds), 33
(the theater), 34 (the monument of a Numidian prince)

Emerita (Augusta) = +Mérida, listed under ITALICA

Emporiae = AMPURIAS

ENSERUNE (Hérault, France)
p. 3
    Ensérune (the modern name) was a typical native *oppidum* (q.v.)
on a plateau 120 meters above the coastal plain. After the Roman
conquest and the foundation of the colony at *Narbo* nearby, it be-
gan to fade away; the *oppidum* came to an end early in the first
century A.D.
Chevallier. *ANRW*. II.3 pp. 786, 787, 805 (bibliography)
Février. "CSG." 7, fig. 2.1 (map); 11, n. 85 (bibl.)
Finley. *Atlas*. 61 (P. MacKendrick)
Formigé, J. "L'oppidum d'Ensérune," *Gallia* 1 (1943; rpt. Paris 1964):
    5-14
Gallet de Santerre, H. *Ensérune*. ECNMHS. Paris n.d.
—— "Ensérune, An Oppidum in Southern France," *Archaeology* 15
    (1962): 163-171
*Jannoray, J. *Ensérune*. 2 vols. Bibliothèque des Ecoles françaises
    d'Athènes et de Rome 181. Paris 1955
KP. II (1967). 277 (M. Leglay)
MacKendrick. *RF*. 16-18
PECS. 305 (H. Gallet de Santerre)

FLORENCE (Tuscany, Italy; capital of the region; in Italian, Fi-
renze) = *Colonia Florentia, Etruria, Italia*
p. 8 (continuity of settlement)

+Fiesole

    The site on the Arno River's right or north bank and the *Via Cassia*
was a small agricultural settlement before the Roman colony of *Florentia* was founded there (in 41 B.C., according to Hardie). To the
northeast of FLORENCE, *Faesulae* (or Fiesole in Italian) looks down
on it from a hilltop. A much older Etruscan town and a Roman col-

ony from the 80s B.C., *Faesulae* continued to exist after 41 although
obviously weakened. + Fiesole did not die away as did ENSERUNE.
As the result of continuous occupation, little of Roman Florence
remains, except for the street plan (Paget, Higson; compare BOR-
DEAUX, where not even the Roman street plan is certain). *Florentia*
was a walled city of 480 by 420 meters (Richardson), and the blocks
were usually about 60 meters (200 Roman feet) on a side (Castagnoli). The surrounding farmland underwent centuriation (q.v.). Finds
from the Roman city are kept in the National Archaeological Museum; it also contains Etruscan material from FLORENCE, TARQUI-
NIA, Orvieto (see *Volsinii)* and *Vetulonia.*

FLORENCE:
Besnier. *Lexique.* 314-315
Caprino. *MAR, Bibl.* 264
Castagnoli. *Orthogonal Town Planning.* 108
Coarelli. *Le città etrusche.* 148-156 (the National Archaeological
    Museum); 322 (bibl.)
Dilke. *ANRW.* II.1 p. 584 (bibliography on centuriation)
Ducati, P. *Etruria antica.* I. Turin 1925. 131
Engel, J., ed. *Grosser historischer Weltatlas.* II. Munich 1970. 128
    (plan of the medieval city)
Gutkind. *IHCD.* IV (1969). 327-337; 625 (bibl.)
*Hardie, C. "The Origin and Plan of Roman Florence," *Journal of
    Roman Studies* 55 (1965): 122-140
Harris. *REU.* 302-303, 307
Haverfield. *Town Planning.* 91-95
Higson, Jr., J. W. *A Historical Guide to Florence.* New York 1973
KP. II (1967). 580 (G. Radke)
Lake, A. K. *Memoirs of the American Academy in Rome* 12 (1935):
    93-98
Lavedan. *HU.* 382 (map), 491 (index)
MacKendrick. *Mute Stones.* 111-112 (centuriation)
Maetzke, G. *Florentia.* Italia Romana: Municipi e Colonie 1.5. Rome
    1941
Nissen. *IL.* II pp. 270-271
OCD. 442 (E. T. Salmon)
Paget. *Central Italy.* 148-150 (with plan)
PECS. 331 (L. Richardson, Jr.)
Pucci, E. *A Short History of Florence.* Florence 1939

Rykwert. *Idea*. 235 (index); fig. 165 (painting by G. Vasari, "The Foundation of Florence")

Salmon. *RC*. 138-139 (with plan)

Schevill, F. *History of Florence from the Founding of the City through the Renaissance*. New York 1961

Stier. *Atlas*. 88-89 (archbishopric)

Ward-Perkins. *Cities*. 29 (continuity of settlement)

—— "ERTI." figs. 15 (air view), 25 (map)

+ Fiesole:

Crema. *ANRW*. I.4 "Arch. rep." pl. 3

Coarelli. *Le città etrusche*. 30-34; 318 (bibl.)

Dennis. *CCE*. II pp. 106-120

Ducati, P. *Etruria antica*. II. Turin 1925. 130

KP. II (1967). 507-508 (G. Radke)

Nissen. *IL*. II pp. 293-296

OCD. 429 (D. W. R. Ridgway)

Paget. *Central Italy*. 150

PECS. 322-323 (P. Bocci Pacini)

Robertson. *GRA*. 365 (bibliography)

Frascati: see *Tusculum*

FREJUS (Var, France) = *Forum Iulii Octavanorum Colonia Pacensis Classica, Gallia Narbonensis* (see colonies in *Gallia Narbonensis*)
p. 40 (Caesar's Forum and the colony)

+ Cimiez (Alpes-Maritimes département, France)

Forum Iulii began as a market-town founded by Julius Caesar on land that had previously been ceded to the Romans by MARSEILLES (Mommsen, *Provinces*). The colony of ARLES was also established on former Massaliot land, but while *Arelate* developed into a major commercial port, *Forum Iulii* soon became a naval base.

We learn from Tacitus (*Annals* 4.5) that Octavian (before he was hailed as "Augustus") sent there galleys captured from Cleopatra in 31 B.C. It must have become a base for military ships by then.

Grenier (*Manuel* I) and Salmon date the colony, with the settlement of veterans from the Eighth Legion, to 30 B.C. "Classis" in Latin means "fleet," and the word "Classica" in the name is indicative of the colony's naval function. During the early Empire, at least, the fleet which guarded what is now the French Riviera was stationed there (compare RAVENNA). Fishing was a local industry, and *garum*, a popular paste made of fish and used for seasoning, was manufactured near *Forum Iulii* (Besnier; Grenier, *ESAR*).

FREJUS was destroyed several times, most notably by the Arabs at the beginning of the tenth century. In Roman times, the *Via Aurelia*, running from Rome to ARLES, served as the *decumanus*, dividing the northern and southern parts of *Forum Iulii*, which had an area of about forty hectares. Today's city occupies mainly its southern half and the street plan is no longer the same (Clébert 108).

Several Roman ruins survive, including the theater, the amphitheater, the east and west gates, and sections of the walls and aqueducts (Grenier, *Manuel* and Goudineau in *PECS*). Two columns, made of Carrara marble from Italy and found in 1954 in a shipwreck in the nearby Gulf of St. Tropez, were set up southwest of the amphitheater in 1968.

The Argens River has silted up the Roman harbor, whose former entrance is now traversed by trains between MARSEILLES and Nice. Present-day FREJUS is now over one kilometer from the Mediterranean. The site lies between Esterel Massif (Peaks) to the northeast and the Maures Massif, where cork oaks are carefully grown, to the southwest.

FREJUS:
Besnier. *Lexique*. 317
Brogan. *Roman Gaul*. 69, 83, 94-97
Chevallier. *ANRW*. II.1 plate xliv; II.3 p. 734 (plan), 805 (bibl.)
Clébert. *Provence antique*. 105-113
Coussin, P. et al. *CAGR*. II, *Var* (1932; publ. 1933)
Crema. *Arch*. 217; fig. 225 (gates)
Donnadieu, A. "Les fouilles récentes du 'Forum Julii' à Fréjus," *Congrès archéologique de France* 95 (1932; publ. 1933): 264-276
—— *Fréjus, le port militaire de Forum Iulii*. Paris 1935
—— *La Pompéi de la Provence, Fréjus*[2]. Paris 1928
Février. "CSG." 20-24; 21, fig. 3 (map)
—— *Dév. urbain en Provence*. 221 (index); figs. 3, 18, 33, 35, 54, 67, 69
Février, P.-A. *Forum Iulii (Fréjus)*. Bordighera/Cuneo 1963
Formigé, J. "Le comblement du port romain de Fréjus," *Mémoires de la Société nationale des antiquaires de France* (1937): 67
—— "Fréjus, Forum Julii Octavanorum Colonia," *Congrès archéologique de France* 95 (1932; publ. 1933): 244-263

Frank. *ESAR*. 586 (A. Grenier)
Fustier, P. *La route: Voies antiques, chemins anciens, chaussées modernes*. Paris 1968. 124 (Pont des Esclopes)
Greece and Rome. 2nd ser. 2 (1955). plate 158b
Grenier. *Manuel*. I pp. 298-314; III 99-114; 606-612 (amphitheater); 734-741 (theater); IV 41-55 (aqueducts)
Lavedan. *HU*. 491 (index)
Lenthéric, C. *The Riviera: Ancient and Modern*. Transl. from the French by C. West. London 1895; rpt. Chicago 1976. 225-306
MacKendrick. *RF*. 72-74; 258 (bibl.)
Mommsen. *Provinces*. Chapter III
OCD. 446 (C. E. Stevens)
PECS. 335-336 (C. Goudineau)
Radke. *Viae*. figs. 5, 27
Salmon. *RC*. 161 (date of the colony); 194, n. 283
Starr, C. G. *The Roman Imperial Navy, 31 B.C.-A.D. 324*. 2nd ed. Cambridge 1960. 11-13; 26, n. 4 (bibliography)
Vittinghoff. *Roemische Kolonisation*. 100

+ Cimiez:
Sixty-five air-kilometers northeast of *Forum Iulii* was *Cemenelum*, capital of the minor province of the Maritime Alps. It guarded the highway from Italy to FREJUS, ARLES, and Spain. The site of *Cemenelum* or Cimiez is three kilometers northwest of Nice.
The Emperor Nero granted Latin rights (q.v.) to the tribes of the Maritime Alps in A.D. 63 (Tacitus, *Annals* 15.32.1).

*Benoît, F. *Fouilles de Cemenelum I: Cimiez, la ville antique*. Paris 1977
—— *Nice et Cimiez antiques*. Paris 1968
Besnier. *Lexique*. 192
Chevallier. *ANRW*. II.3 p. 808 (bibl.)
Clébert. *Provence antique*. 86-94
Duval, P.-M. "Rapport préliminaire sur les fouilles de *Cemenelum* (Cimiez, 1943)," *Gallia* 4 (1946): 77-136
Février. "CSG." 27, nn. 182-185 (bibl.)
Grenier. *Manuel*. III pp. 599-606 (amphitheater); IV 55-60 (aqueduct); 251-254 (baths)
KP. I (1964). 1103-1104 (M. Leglay)
MacKendrick. *RF*. 83-86; 258 (bibl.)

PECS. 211 (C. Goudineau)

On the minor province of the Maritime Alps:
Février, P.-A. "Géographie historique des alpes méridionales," *La communità alpina nell'antichità*. Centro studi e documentazione sull'Italia Romana, Atti 7. Milan 1975/1976. 269-301
Laguerre, G. *Fouilles de Cemenelum II: Inscriptions de Nice-Cimiez*. Paris 1975. 87-88 (An auxiliary unit [q.v.] is mentioned in inscription 58, *Cohors prima Ligurum et Hispanorum civium Romanorum*.)
—— "L'occupation militaire de Cemenelum," *Revue archéologique de Narbonnaise* 2 (1969): 165-184
Lamboglia, N. *Liguria romana*. Alassio (Liguria, Italy) 1939
Prieur, J. "L'histoire des régions alpestres (Alpes Maritimes, Cottiennes, Graies et Pennines) sous le haut-empire romain," *ANRW*. II.5.2 (1976): 630-656

+ Geneva: listed under VIENNE

Glanum: see ST.-REMY-DE-PROVENCE

Glevum (+ Gloucester): listed under WROXETER

Hispalis (+ Seville): listed under ITALICA

Igilgili: see JIJEL

Isca Silurum (+ Caerleon): listed under WROXETER

ITALICA (or Santiponce; province of Sevilla, Spain) = *Italica, Baetica;* from A.D. 117/138, its full name was *Colonia Aelia Augusta Italica* (Aelius was the *nomen* or family name of the Emperor Hadrian, who was born there, probably in 76).
p. 66 (the amphitheater)

+ León, + Mérida (Badajoz), + Seville

Roman settlement began at *Italica* in 206 B.C., when Scipio Africanus left soldiers and camp followers behind to build an outpost against the Celtic Lusitanians. This was not, however, a formal *colonia* (q.v.); the first Roman colony outside of Italy and *Gallia Cis-*

alpina (q.v.) was NARBONNE. *Italica* became a Roman *municipium* 27 B.C. /A.D. 14, and it was made an honorary colony by its native son, the Emperor Hadrian (117-138). His predecessor Trajan (98-117) was also born there.

Italica was only about nine kilometers northwest of + Seville and about eight from the right bank of the *Baetis* (from which the province of *Baetica* took its name; from Arab times, the river has been called the Guadalquivir). During the Empire, + Seville *(Colonia Iulia Romula Hispalis,* on the left bank of the *Baetis)* eclipsed ITALICA. Twice founded as a Roman colony (in 45 B.C. and A.D. 68/69), + Seville overtook even Cádiz (on the Atlantic Ocean and the terminus of the *Via Augusta* from Tarragona) as the main port of the region (compare ARLES, also on a river).

The *Via Augusta* went north from Cádiz to Seville, mostly along the *Baetis.* There it turned east to a point opposite Cordova *(Corduba),* the provincial capital (on the right bank of the same river); then it continued to the Mediterranean (Stier; cf. Chevallier, *Roman Roads* 156). A road from Seville to Itálica continued to + Mérida, while Itálica had its own road to Cordova.

Italica had the standard elements of a Roman city: a forum, orthogonal streets with porticoes and sewers, walls enclosing about thirty hectares (Roldán in *PECS),* two baths, temples, and the largest amphitheater in *Hispania* (q.v.). A theater, like the amphitheater outside the city wall, has been excavated recently (Roldán). Detachments from the Seventh Legion were stationed at Itálica and Tarragona *(Tarraco),* the capital of *Hispania Tarraconensis* (Mommsen). The only legion (q.v.) left in *Hispania* after A.D. 71/74, its camp was at + León (which takes its name in Spanish from *Legio,* from the legion; compare + Caerleon, listed under WROXETER). Auxiliary units (q.v.) posted at + Tangier (listed under *Volubilis)* also protected *Baetica* (Mommsen).

The products of *Baetica* were wine, wheat, honey, sheep, fish, copper, lead, silver, and mercury. The landowners during the Empire seem to have been descendants of immigrants from Italy (Rostovtzeff). Attesting to the export of olive oil to Rome are pieces of amphorae or jars found at the Monte Testaccio (composed of such shards) on the left bank of the Tiber, near the *Emporium* (Van Nostrand, *ESAR* 184).

The decline of *Italica* began during the fifth century. In 584, the Visigothic (q.v.) king Leovigild built an outpost there to harass the

Byzantines (see Byzantine) at + Seville (Thompson 71). *Italica* died under Arab rule, and now it is an insignificant village (Santiponce), where sculptures and columns have been found (to be taken to the Museo Arqueológico de Sevilla). Some of its small finds are at the Hispanic Society in New York (Broadway and W. 156th Street). A new site-museum has been built at ITALICA for future finds. Household mosaics may be seen *in situ*, as well as the architectural ruins. Seville continued to exist under Vandals (q.v.), Visigoths, Byzantines, Berber-Arabs (A.D. 712), and Spaniards. It was conquered by St. Ferdinand III, king of Castile in 1248. Castile developed into the Spanish kingdom about 250 years later. First Seville and later Cádiz (1718) were the main ports for trade with Spanish America. Seville today is the fourth largest city in Spain. Jerez de la Frontera, famous for the production of sherry wine, lies between Seville and Cádiz.

ITALICA:

Archivo Español de Arqueología. 50/51 (1977/1978)

Besnier. *Lexique*. 402-403

Blanco Freijeiro, A. *Mosaicos romanos de Itálica*. Corpus de Mosaicos de España 2. Madrid 1978.

Blue Guide, Spain. 524

Bouchier, E. S. *Spain Under Roman Rule*. Oxford 1914. 144-147

CAH. XI² (1954). 905 (bibl.)

Castillo García, C. "Staedte und Personen der Baetica," *ANRW*. II.3 (1975). 651-654 (bibl.)

Crema. *Arch*. 440 (amphitheater)

de Collantes Terán, F. *Catálogo arqueológico y artístico de la Provincia de Sevilla*. IV (1965)

Finley. *Atlas*. 63 (P. MacKendrick on "The Iberian Peninsula")

Frank. *ESAR*. III pp. 184, 200, 566 (J. J. Van Nostrand)

*García y Bellido, A. *Colonia Aelia Augusta Itálica*. Bibliotheca Archeológica 2. Madrid 1960.

—— "Las colonias romanas de España," *Anuario de Historia del Derecho Español* 29 (1959)

—— "La Itálica de Adriano," *Les empereurs romains d'Espagne*. Madrid/Itálica 1965. 7 ff.

KP. II (1967). 1485 (R. Grosse)

Lavedan. *HU*. 350 (population); 426 (map); 492 (index)

MacKendrick. *Iberian Stones*. 168-176

Maxwell, G. "Roman Towns of the Valley of the Baetis," *Archaeological Journal* 56 (1899): 245-305

Menéndez Pidal, R., ed. *Historia de España*. II³. Madrid 1962. 632 (amphitheater); 639 (baths); 670; 691-693, 695, 800 (sculptures); 780, fig. 6 (plan of a city villa); 839 (index)

Millar. *REN*. pl. 11 (the amphitheater)

Mommsen. *Provinces*. Chapter II

OCD. 556 (J. J. Van Nostrand); 159 (J. J. Van Nostrand and M. I. Henderson on "Baetica")

PECS. 419-420 (J. M. Roldán Hervás)

Rostovtzeff. *SEHRE*. 213

Salmon. *RC*. 164 (date of the colony)

Stier. *Atlas*. 38 (roads)

Sutherland, C. H. V. *The Romans in Spain*.... London 1939. 192, 202

Syme, R. "Hadrian and Italica," *Journal of Roman Studies* 54 (1964): 142-149

Thouvenot. *Essai*. 426 (theater); 442 (amphitheater); 461 (baths); 720-721 (index)

Vittinghoff. *Roemische Kolonisation*. 72

+ León:

Besnier. *Lexique*. 422

Chevallier. *ANRW*. II.1 p. 723 (bibl.) and plate xc

Garzetti. *TA*. 749 (bibl.)

Legio VII Gemina. León 1970 (a collection of articles)

Menéndez Pidal. 840 (index)

PECS. 495 (R. Teja)

Richmond, I. A. *Journal of Roman Studies* 21 (1931): 91-94 (the wall); fig. 15 (plan)

+ Mérida:

Mérida (*Colonia Augusta Emerita*, a veteran-colony of 25 B.C.) is the best-preserved Roman city of *Hispania*. As is common, however, in Spanish cities still inhabited after the Arab period, the present street plan diverges somewhat from the orthogonal Roman one.

Almagro, M., ed. *Guide of Mérida*². Madrid 1965

Augusta Emerita. *Actas del Simposio internacional conmemorativo del bimilenario de Mérida, 16-20 de noviembre de 1975*

Bailey. *Legacy*. fig. 65 (extant Roman bridge at Mérida)
Blanco Freijeiro, A. *Mosaicos romanos de Mérida*. Corpus de Mo-
  saicos de España 1. Madrid 1978
CAH. XI² (1954). 905 (bibl.)
Caprino. *MAR, Bibl*. 333
Finley. *Atlas*. 64-65 (P. MacKendrick)
KP. I (1964). 737 (R. Grosse)
MacKendrick. *Iberian Stones*. 129-143
Menéndez Pidal. 829, 842 (index)
PECS. 114-116 (L. G. Iglesias)
Ward-Perkins. *RA*. 347 (index)

+ Seville:
Besnier. *Lexique*. 369-370
Blue Guide, Spain. 501-523
Buisman, H. *Spanien*. Darmstadt 1972. 213-240
Charlesworth. *Trade-Routes*. 152-164
Gutkind. *IHCD*. III (1967). 498-502; 526 (bibl.)
Henderson, M. I. "Julius Caesar and Latium in Spain," *Journal of
  Roman Studies* 32 (1942): 13
KP. II (1967). 1184-1185 (R. Grosse)
Menéndez Pidal. 838, 848 (index)
OCD. 520 (M. I. Henderson)
Salmon. *RC*. 136 (Caesar's colony); 164 (dates)
Stier. *Atlas*. 88-89 (archbishopric)
Thompson, E. A. *The Goths in Spain*. Oxford 1969. 353 (index)
Vittinghoff. 74

JIJEL (until recently, "Djidjelli"; wilaya of Constantine, Algeria) =
Igilgili, Mauretania Caesariensis
p. 83 (Roman highway from JIJEL to *Lambaesis* via DJEMILA)
  A Roman colony was founded here in 27 B.C./A.D. 14. The site had
previously been a Carthaginian trading post, and it has been a fairly
important port on the Mediterranean from Roman times on. The city
was at the junction of the Roman road along the coast and a road
inland through a pass in the Petite Kabylie Mountains.
  The harbor today is used for fishing, and there are beautiful beaches
nearby. Roman mosaics, sculptures and artifacts from the site are in
the museum at Skikda.
Gsell. *AAA*. fasc. 7 ("Bougie")

KP. II (1967). 1356 (M. Leglay)
Nagel's Guide, Algeria. 305-307
PECS. 405-406 (M. Leglay)

Lambaesis (in the present-day wilaya of Batna, Algeria); in Roman *Africa Proconsularis* (ancient region of *Numidia*, q.v.)
p. 83 (Roman road south from JIJEL to *Lambaesis* via DJEMILA)

Lambaesis, the walled camp of the Third Augustan Legion, should be compared and contrasted with MAINZ, which began as another Roman legionary camp in a strategic location. The Roman highway from *Lambaesis* east to TIMGAD (q.v.) ran just to the north of the Aurès Mountains. This highway continued east to Tébessa and then northeast to CARTHAGE, where one cohort (one-tenth) of the Third Augustan Legion was posted. Roman roads to the desert also went southwest through two passes in these mountains, one from *Lambaesis* and the other from TIMGAD.

The Third Augustan Legion moved from Tébessa (in Algeria, near the Tunisian border) to *Lambaesis* probably in A.D. 81, when it built the original camp. The second camp, measuring 500 by 420 meters (21 hectares), was begun early in the second century, 2 kilometers to the east. Its plan was orthogonal (cf. chapter I, n.2 above). It is the finest and best-preserved example extant today, although the southwest quadrant was built over by the French army in 1851.

In Roman times, the inevitable camp followers arrived at *Lambaesis* and they settled on the rising ground to the south of the camp (see *canabae* below). Their status was regularized when the Emperor Septimius Severus (193/211) allowed Roman soldiers to marry before discharge. This settlement became a *municipium* (q.v.) c. A.D. 200. Its baths, arches, and temples were built along an irregular street plan.

Various auxiliary units (q.v.) were also stationed at *Lambaesis*. The camp housed the Third Augustan Legion until late in the third century, except for A.D. 238-253 when it was temporarily disbanded. The site was abandoned after the Vandal (q.v.) invasion. Some of the artworks, transferred to the Louvre by the French, are now in Algiers. There is a museum on the site.

The Third Augustan Legion built nearby SETIF, TIMGAD, and DJEMILA, where its veterans could settle. This was the only legion in North Africa, outside of Egypt. Of it Parker says, "The development of the province of Africa from one of the most backward to one of the most Romanized districts of the Empire in the third century was due to the uninterrupted settlement of the legion III *Aug.* in the country" (p. 225).

Ballu, A. *Tébessa, Lambèse, Timgad.* Paris 1894

Besnier. *Lexique.* 412

Bouchier. *LLRA.* 5 (the *municipium*)

Broughton. *RAP.* 135-138 (plan); 203-208 (political history)

Cagnat. *Armée romaine.* 434-519 (definitive)

Cagnat, R. *Musée de Lambèse.* Paris 1895

Castagnoli. *Orthogonal Town Planning.* 116 (the camp plan)

Crema. *Arch.* 662 (index)

Duncan-Jones. *ERE.* 67, n. 2 (bibl.); 70 (prices of buildings and statues)

Euzennat, M. "Equites Secundae Flaviae," *Antiquités africaines* 11 (1977): 131-135 (About an auxiliary unit and Hadrian's speech at *Lambaesis:* see Hadrian's speech below.)

Finley. *Atlas.* 75 (C. R. Whittaker)

Germain, S. "Mosaïques florales de Lambèse (Algérie)," *Antiquités africaines* 11 (1977): 137-148

Gsell. *AAA.* fasc. 27 ("Batna")

Gsell, S. *Les monuments antiques de l'Algérie.* I. Paris 1901. 115; 115, n. 2 (bibl.)

Janon, M. "Lambaesis—Ein Ueberblick," *Antike Welt* 8.2 (1977): 3-20; bibl. on p. 20

—— "Recherches à Lambèse," *Antiquités africaines* 7 (1973): 193-254

Jones, H. Stuart. *Companion.* 240-242; 456 (index)

KP. III (1969). 463 (M. Leglay)

Leschi, L. *Algérie antique.* Paris 1952. 88-101

Nagel's Guide, Algeria. 349-352

OCD. 576-577 (W.N.W.), 591-593 (G. R. Watson on the various Roman legions)

Parker, H. M. D. *The Roman Legions.* Oxford 1928; rpt. Cambridge 1961. 224-225

PECS. 478-479 (J. Marcillet-Jaubert)

Rakob, F., and Storz, S. "Die Principia des roemischen Legionslagers in Lambaesis," *Mitteilungen des Deutschen Archaeologischen Instituts, Roemische Abteilung* 81 (1974): 253-280

Raven. *Rome in Africa.* 188 (index)

Robertson. *GRA.* 193; 355 (bibl.)

Romanelli. *Storia.* 300-301

Wheeler and Wood. *Roman Africa.* 118; plate 39 (the four-sided arch)

On Hadrian's speech at the camp in A.D. 128 (*CIL* VIII 2532 and
18,042):
Garzetti. *TA*. 693 (bibl. on Hadrian's speech)
Jones. *HR*. II pp. 153-155 (translation)
Leglay, M. "Les discours d'Hadrien à Lambèse (128 apr. J.-C.)," *Ak-
ten des XI. Internationalen Limeskongresses*, (1976; publ. Buda-
pest 1977): 545-558 (commentary; bibliography on 557-558)
Lewis, N., and Reinhold, M. *Roman Civilization, Sourcebook II:
The Empire*. New York 1966. 507-509 (translation)
Piganiol. *HR*. 304-305 (bibl.)
Smallwood, E. M. *Documents Illustrating the Principates of Nerva,
Trajan and Hadrian*. no. 328. Cambridge 1966 (Latin text)

Africa Proconsularis and *Numidia*, the Frontier (cf. *Volubilis*):
Baradez, J. *Fossatum Africae. Recherches aériennes sur l'organisa-
tion des confins sahariens à l'époque romaine*. Paris 1949
—— *Vue-aérienne de l'organisation romaine dans le Sud algérien.
Fossatum Africae*. Paris 1949
Christ. *Bibl*. 399 (the frontier)
Fentress, E. W. B. *Numidia and the Roman Army* = British Ar-
chaeological Reports International Series 53. Oxford 1979
Jones, G. D. B., and Mattingly, D. J. "Fourth-Century Manning of
the 'Fossatum Africae,'" *Britannia* 11 (1980): 323-326
KP. III (1969). 660-662 (H. Volkmann, see "Limes")
Mann. *ANRW*. II.1 pp. 526-527
Webster. *Army*. 286; 316-317 (index)

+ León: listed under ITALICA

Lepcis (or *Leptis*) *Magna* (A.D. 98/117 *Colonia Ulpia Traiana Fidelis
L.M.*), *Africa Proconsularis* (today in the region of Tripolitania [q.v.],
a part of Libya); the village of Al Khums is on the western outskirts
of the ancient city.
pp. 41, 51 (the Old Forum), 48 (the curia, q.v.), 53-54 (the Severan
Forum), 54 (comparison with DJEMILA)
   The Carthaginian (q.v.) port-town was founded in the sixth century B.C., due south of Sicily on the Mediterranean coast. This harbor is 190 kilometers east of the one at *Sabratha* (q.v.). Tripolitania
was peaceful under Roman rule only in the second half of the first
century A.D., and then it became truly prosperous. A Roman highway ran along the North African coast from *Lepcis* west to CAR-

THAGE, the provincial capital. Local olive oil and grain were exported to Rome (via *Ostia*), as well as ivory, brought by camel across the Sahara Desert and originating in Central Africa. Agriculture in Tripolitania depended on irrigation systems, which were destroyed by the Arab invaders in the seventh century (Rostovtzeff 335, 339; Hammond 295).

To visualize the growth of *Lepcis* from Carthaginian times to the early third century A.D., see Ward-Perkins, *Cities* fig. 73. (The scale, however, is wrong.) Successive orthogonal districts were added to the original Punic settlement, which has not yet been excavated. The city expanded southward from the sea and reached the highway to CARTHAGE in the early first century A.D. *Lepcis* probably became a *municipium* (q.v.) in A.D. 69/79 and an honorary colony (see *colonia*) in 98/117. The bilingual inscriptions (Latin and Carthaginian) of the Roman period and use of "suffes" for *duovir* (q.v.) are worthy of note (Liversidge 64-65).

Lepcis has been brought to light by Italian archaeologists in the 1920s and 30s, as well as British ones in the 1950s, but the task has not been completed. The extensive ruins were preserved by the sand which covered the city after the seventh century A.D. They would be magnificent in any case, but are even more so because the Emperor Septimius Severus (193-211), a native of the city, granted it a privileged tax status, *ius Italicum* (q.v.), and presented it with a new district (see p. 54 above) and an improved harbor, which still silted up. Summarizing, Hammond says, "Leptis came into being for economic reasons but achieved through private and imperial munificence a grandeur far beyond its economic significance" (p. 295).

Africa italiana. 8 vols. (1926-1941); especially P. Romanelli in vol. I (1926) on Lepcis

Apolloni, B. M. *Il Foro e la Basilica Severiana di Leptis Magna*. Rome 1936

Aurigemma, S. *L'Italia in Africa. Le scoperte archeogiche (1911-1943): Tripolitania*. I.1-2. Rome 1960-1962 (on mosaics and paintings)

Bartoccini, R. *Guida di Lepcis*. Rome/Milan 1927

Besnier. *Lexique*. 425-426

*Bianchi Bandinelli, R., Caputo, G., and Vergara Caffarelli, E. *The Buried City: Excavations at Leptis Magna*. Transl. from the Italian by D. Ridgway. London 1966. bibl. on pp. 121-122

Boëthius and Ward-Perkins. *ERA*. 465-471; 475-479; 599 (bibl.); plates 196; 240 (market); 242-248

Broughton. *RAP*. 131-132 (political history)

Brown. *RA*. 33-35, plate 64 (Severan Forum); 37-38, plates 70-71 (baths)

Cagnat, R. "Les ruines de Leptis Magna à la fin du XVIIe siècle," *Mémoires de la Société nationale des antiquaires de France* 60 (1901)

Caprino. *MAR, Bibl*. 332

Caputo, G., and Traversari, G. *Le sculture del teatro di Leptis Magna*. Rome 1976

Christ. *Bibl*. 399 (the frontier)

Crema. *Arch*. 662 (index)

Cunliffe. *Rome*. 150-151 (color photograph of the market)

Degrassi, N. "L'ordinamento di Leptis Magna nel primo secolo dell'impero...," *Epigraphica* 7 (1945): 3-21

Di Vita, A. *Tripolitania ellenistica e romana alla luce delle più recenti scoperte*. Monografie di Archeologia Libica 12 (1977)

Duncan-Jones. *ERE*. 68 (prices of buildings and statues); 266, n. 1 (bibl.)

Earl. *AA*. plates 44, 45, 47

EB. XVI p. 482 (E. Babelon)

Finley. *Atlas*. 76-77 (C. R. Whittaker)

Frank. *ESAR*. IV pp. 46, 48 (olives); 61, 62; 67 (roads); 69, 75, 110 (R. M. Haywood)

Goodchild, R. G. "The *Limes Tripolitanus* II," *Journal of Roman Studies* 40 (1950): 30-38; rpt. in *Libyan Studies: Select Papers of the Late R. G. Goodchild*. Edit. J. Reynolds. London 1976

Goodchild, R. G., and Ward-Perkins, J. B. "The *Limes Tripolitanus* in the Light of Recent Discoveries," *Journal of Roman Studies* 39 (1949): 81-95

────── "The Roman and Byzantine Defences of Leptis Magna," *Papers of the British School at Rome* 21 (1953): 42-73

────── *Tabula Imperii Romani: Lepcis Magna*. London 1954 (map of the region)

Grimal. *Civ. Rome*. 355, 470; illustration 127 (air view of the harbor)

Gsell, S. *Tripolitanie et Sahara au IIIe siècle de notre ère*. Mémoires de l'Académie des inscriptions et belles-lettres 43 (1926)

Guida della Libia. Milan 1937 (see fig. 12 above)

Hammond. *The City*. 295

*Haynes, D. E. L. *An Archaeological and Historical Guide to the Antiquities of Tripolitania*². London 1959. 71-100

Kaehler. *Art of Rome*. 171-172 (Arch of Septimius Severus at *Lepcis*); 222 (bibl.)
KP. III (1969). 581-582 (M. Leglay)
Kraeling, C. H. *Leptis Magna* (1963)
Lavedan. *HU*. 446, 448 (maps); 492 (index)
Liversidge. *Everyday Life*. 64-66; fig. 21 (reconstruction of the market)
Mann. *ANRW*. II.1 p. 526 (the frontier)
Mathews, K. D. *Cities in the Sand: Leptis Magna and Sabratha in Roman Africa*. Ann Arbor 1957
McKay. *Houses*. 267-268 (bibl.)
Menen, A. *Cities in the Sand: Leptis Magna, Timgad, Palmyra, Petra*. New York 1972. 67 ff.
Millar. *REN*. pl. 14
OCD. 596 (O. Brogan)
PECS. 499-500 (J. B. Ward-Perkins)
(Charles-)Picard. *Roman Architecture*. 14-15; 147-148; 151-152 (plans)
Piganiol. *HR*. 419, 593 (bibl.)
Raven. *Rome in Africa*. 189 (index)
Rivista della Tripolitania
Romanelli, P. *Leptis Magna*. Rome 1925
—— *Storia*
—— Also see *Africa italiana* above
Rostovtzeff. *SEHRE*. 332-339; 594-595, n. 4 and 688, n. 99 for bibl.
(Floriani)-Squarciapino, M. *Leptis Magna*. Ruinenstaedte Nordafrikas 2. Basle 1966 (in German)
Wacher. *TRB*. 60 (market at *Lepcis* compared with those in Britain)
Ward-Perkins, J. B. "The Art of the Severan Age in the Light of the Tripolitanian Discoveries," *Proceedings of the British Academy* 37 (1951)
—— *Cities*. 30-31; 35 (the warehouses); 121-122; figs. 73-74b
—— *RA*. 350 (index)
—— "Severan Art and Architecture at Lepcis Magna," *Journal of Roman Studies* 38 (1948): 59-80
—— and Toynbee, J. M. C. "The Hunting Baths at Lepcis Magna," *Archaeologia* 93 (1949): 165-195
Wheeler. *RAA*. 52-59
—— and Wood. *Roman Africa*. 58-79; plates 9-19 (10 is of the harbor, 12 the theater, 13-14 the market, 15 the Hunting Baths and Al Khums, 16 the Hadrianic Baths, 17 the amphitheater)

Wright, J. *Libya*. New York 1969 (mentions second Arab migration
of the eleventh century)

LONDON (England, U.K.) = *Londinium, Britannia* (after A.D. 326/
365, *Londinium Augusta*, province of *?Maxima Caesariensis*), mint
of the Later Roman Empire (q.v.)
p. 79 (the city walls)

+ *Verulamium*

In spite of its Celtic name (cf. Rivet, *PNRB* 397-398), there is no
evidence of a pre-Roman *oppidum* (q.v.) at LONDON. The Roman
city was on the left bank of the Thames, at the site of the first bridge,
made of wood, across the river (compare ARLES; much of LONDON's
trade was by river).

Londinium must have been founded soon after the Romans invaded Britain in A.D. 43. Bits of the orthogonal street plan have
come to light; just north of wharves by the bridge were probably
four *insulae* (see city blocks) of 72 meters (240 Roman feet) by 144
meters (480 Roman feet; Wheeler 84 and Finley 22; compare Margary 58). North of them was the forum (A.D. 69/96) in a block 150
meters square on the summit of Cornhill (see *fora*, comparison in
size, below). The forum's east-west basilica was half again as long as
the Basilica Iulia in Rome (see p. 36 and fig. 7 above).

Excavating in 1949, W. F. Grimes found a fort of the early second
century in the Cripplegate district (part of northwest *Londinium*); it
was manned by an auxiliary unit (q.v.) or by a legionary detachment
(compare ITALICA). The fort's north and west walls formed part of
the city's wall, which was built about A.D. 200. The wall enclosed
the then inhabited area of the city, which had grown to about 134
hectares (330 acres; see cities, comparison in area, below). McKay
estimates the population at 45,000 (p. 188).

Londinium was the node of the Roman highway system. One road,
now called Ermine Street, its Saxon name, led north to Lincoln and
York (see colonies in *Britannia*). Other roads ran northeast to Colchester (another colony), west to SILCHESTER and northwest to
WROXETER by way of + *Verulamium* (Watling Street is its Saxon name);
after crossing the Thames bridge, one could go southwest to Chichester (Stane Street) and southeast to Canterbury (this road is also
called Watling Street). From Canterbury, one could travel east to
the main Channel port at Richborough (both are in Kent; on the
roads see Margary 34-68).

The pattern of streets connecting the Roman highways to the forum in *Londinium* is unclear to us, and what happened there after the Saxon invasion is very uncertain (see Grimes). The scarcely orthogonal street plan with which central LONDON is now provided would seem to be indicative of destruction, abandonment and gradual resettling. Besides the topographical puzzles about *Londinium*, there are the political ones. We neither know for certain what its civic status was (cf. Tacitus, *Annals* 14.33.1) nor when it became the capital of Roman Britain. Basing his words soundly on the literary and archaeological evidence, Rostovtzeff says, "The richest commercial city was Londinium, which played in the life of Britain the same part as Trèves (TRIER) and Lyons (qq.v.) in the life of Gaul and Germany" (p. 229). As such, LONDON probably was, in the first century, a Roman *municipium* (compare *Verulamium* below) and perhaps later an honorary colony.

The original capital of *Britannia* was Colchester. In view of LONDON's importance as a financial center, perhaps the *procurator* or imperial financial officer moved his office there during the first century (Liversidge 105; compare TRIER). In 211/212, *Britannia* was divided into two provinces, with York the capital of Lower Britain and London that of Upper Britain (Wacher 84). It is quite likely that *Londinium* was the capital of the undivided province before that date, with the imperial shrine (somewhat like that at LYONS) left behind at Colchester. Under Diocletian, A.D. 284-305, the British provinces were divided further. In today's London, besides the incomparable British Museum, the new Museum of London (London Wall, London E.C. 2) should be visited to see the Romano-British finds.

LONDON:

Alcock, J. P. *Londinium* ². London 1977 ("a practical guide to the visible remains of Roman London"; bibl. on 37-39)

Besnier. *Lexique*. 439

Biddle, M., ed. *The Future of London's Past*. London 1973 (our present knowledge of Roman, Anglo-Saxon and medieval London)

Brooke, C. *London 800-1215: The Shaping of a City*. Berkeley 1975

CAH. X² (1952). 989 (bibl.)

Caprino. *MAR, Bibl.* 241

Charlesworth. *Trade-Routes*. 211-215, 219

Collingwood, R. G. *Roman Britain*. Oxford 1932

—— and Myres. *RBES*

—— and Richmond. *ARB*. 129-132 (bibl.), 343 (index)

Finley. *Atlas*. 22-23 (J. J. Wilkes)

Frank. *ESAR*. III (see index); (R. G. Collingwood)

Frere. *Britannia*. 386 (general bibliography for Britain); 424 (index)

Grimes, W. F. *The Excavation of Roman and Medieval London*. London and New York 1968

Gutkind. *IHCD*. VI (1971). 451-473; 501-502 (bibl.)

Hammond. *The City*. 333 (on continuity of settlement in England)

Haverfield, F. "Roman London," *Journal of Roman Studies* 1 (1911): 141-172

Hibbert, C. *London*². London 1977

Hobley, B. "Recent Rescue Archaeology in London," *Archaeology* 31 (1978): 56-58

KP. III (1969). 730-731 (F. M. Heichelheim and ?J. Ward)

Lavedan. *HU*. 420 (map)

Liversidge. *BRE*. 517-518 (index); plate 20 (drawing of London in the third century)

Lobel, M. D. *Historic Towns, Maps and Plans of Towns and Cities in the British Isles, with Historical Commentaries from the Earliest Times to 1800*. Oxford 1969

Mann, J. C. "The Administration of Roman Britain," *Antiquity* 35 (1961): 316-320

Margary. *RRB*. 34-68; map 11

Marsden, P. R. V. *Roman London*. London 1980

McKay. *Houses*. 188

Merrifield, R. *A Handbook to Roman London*. London 1978 (bibl. on 48-49)

——— The Roman City of London. London and New York 1965

——— *Roman London*. London 1969 (a condensation of the above)

——— review of *Southwark Excavations 1972-4*. *Britannia* 11 (1980): 445-447

Mommsen. *Provinces*. Chapter V

Morris. *Urban Form*. 57-58; fig. 3.27

OCD. 618-619 (?C. E. Stevens)

OSMRB

PECS. 524-525 (S. S. Frere)

Philp, B. J. "The Forum of Roman London: Excavations 1968-9," *Britannia* 8 (1977): 1-64

RE. XIII (1927). 1396-1399 (Macdonald)

Richmond. *RB*. 236 (index)

Rivet. *TCRB*. 137-138; 163 (bibl.); 189 (index)

Rostovtzeff. *SEHRE*. 229; 231 (on the army as the main market for the businessmen of LONDON); 594 (bibliography)

Royal Commission on Historical Monuments. *An Inventory of the Historical Monuments in London*. III: *Roman London*. 1928

Shepherd, J. W. "London: Metropolitan Evolution and Planning Response," in *World Capitals*, edit. H. W. Eldredge. Garden City, N.Y., 1975. 90-136 (present-day geography)

Stier. *Atlas*. 109 (plan)

Wacher. *TRB*. 79-87 (administration of Britain); 87-103 (the city); 454 (index)

Ward-Perkins. *Cities*. 30 (comparison of LONDON's location with Rome's)

Wheeler, R. E. M. *London in Roman Times*. London 1930 (Roman collection of the London Museum)

—— *RAA*. 82-88; 233, n. 27 (bibl.)

Wilson, D. M. *The Archaeology of Anglo-Saxon England*. London 1976

+*Verulamium*, near St. Albans (Hertfordshire):

Verulamium lay thirty-five kilometers (twenty-two miles) northwest of LONDON on Watling Street and on the southwest bank of the little River Ver, which, in Roman times, was crossed by a ford to go northeast by road. Located in a valley below the pre-Roman *oppidum*, orthogonal *Verulamium* in its first stage was laid out in A.D. 43-54 by the Romans. It filled 48 hectares (119 acres). The city continued to expand, and the third-century wall enclosed a larger area (more than eighty hectares), mainly filled by the grid of streets. From the southwest gate, one could go west to Gloucester (on Akeman Street) or southwest to SILCHESTER.

The orientation of the orthogonal city is unusual in that it did not correspond to the cardinal points of the compass but was more in accord with Watling Street and the river. Watling Street, nevertheless, changed direction within the city, and there was a section of it oblique to the southern part of the grid; Ward-Perkins compares it to Broadway in nineteenth-century Manhattan (pp. 29-30).

Verulamium was both the tribal capital of the Catuvellauni and also, most probably, a Roman *municipium* by A.D. 60 (see Tacitus, *Annals* 14.33). Liversidge compares this arrangement with the Roman colony at AVENCHES (p. 30). The Catuvellauni may well have had Latin rights (q.v.) or even Roman citizenship by A.D. 60 (also compare TRIER).

A fragmentary inscription serves to date the forum (with a basilica) in the center of the city, as it mentions Julius Agricola, governor of Britain A.D. 77/78-83/85 (cf. Ogilvie and Richmond, *Agricola* 316 [on

the inscription] and 317-320 [on these dates]; Agricola was the fa-
ther-in-law of the historian Tacitus and a native of FREJUS). On the
second-century theater, actually a demi-amphitheater, see Chapter
III, n. 28 above). The continuing excavations at *Verulamium* have
unearthed a number of houses with mosaic floors (compare + St.-
Romain-en-Gal, under VIENNE). One may be seen at its location,
and other mosaics have been moved to the site-museum, which also
contains wall-paintings.

Verulamium was abandoned in the fifth century and remains so
except for St. Michael's Church, which adjoins the forum; in its basilica, St. Alban (a Roman soldier of ? A.D. 200; from yet another
Roman fort) was condemned to martyrdom. The Benedictine Abbey
(see SUBIACO) founded on a hilltop across the River Ver in 793 by
King Offa (see Angles) to house the saint's remains became the nucleus of the medieval and modern town of St. Albans.

+ *Verulamium:*
Anthony, I. *The Roman City of Verulamium*. St. Albans 1978 (bibl.
on p. 24)
Birley, A. R. *The* Fasti *of Roman Britain*. Oxford 1981. 73-81 (the
career of Agricola)
Blue Guide, England. 305-308
Branigan, K. *Town and Country: The Archaeology of Verulamium
and the Roman Chilterns*. Bourne End, Buckinghamshire, 1973
Burn, A. R. *Agricola and Roman Britain*. London 1953. 58 (plan of
the demi-amphitheater)
Collingwood and Richmond. *ARB*. 109-110 (the forum); 115-116 (the
demi-amphitheater); 120 (the three arches on Watling Street are
the only ones to have come to light in Britain); 129-132 (bibl.); 346
(index; see St. Albans)
Enciclopedia dell'arte antica, classica e orientale. VII (1966). 1145-
1146 (J. M. C. Toynbee)
Finley. *Atlas*. 25-27 (J. J. Wilkes)
Frere. *Britannia*. 201 (the forum inscription); 393, 401 (bibliography); 431 (index); plate 21 (mosaics)
Frere, S. S. *Britannia Romana*. Accademia dei Lincei. Rome 1971
—— "*Verulamium* and Canterbury: Continuity and Discontinuity,"
in *Thèmes* by Duval. 185-195
—— "Verulamium and the Towns of Roman Britain," *ANRW*. II.3
(1975). 290-327; general bibliography for Britain on pp. 324-326

—— "Verulamium, Three Roman Cities," *Antiquity* 38 (1964): 103-112

—— et al. *Verulamium Excavations*. I. Reports of the Research Committee of the Society of Antiquaries of London 28. 1972

Kenyon, K. M. "The Roman Theater at Verulamium," *Archaeologia* 84 (1934): 213-261

KP. VI (1975). 1221 (E. Olshausen)

Liversidge. *BRE*. 70-73 (mosaics); 94-99 (wall-paintings); 368-380 (on the "theater"); 524 (index); plates 7 (forum inscription); 8-9 (reconstructed gate); 10 (a cellar); 15 (a floor-mosaic); 17b, 18 (wall-painting); 19 (floor-mosaic)

Margary. *RRB*. 156, 172-180, 198; map 7b

McKay. *Houses*. 181 (ancient city visible from the air); 187 (town plans); 197-199 (wall-paintings); 200

Morris. *Urban Form*. 60; fig. 3.33

OCD. 1114-1115 (S. S. Frere); 217 (S. S. Frere on the Catuvellauni)

Ogilvie and Richmond. *Agricola*. 221, 223, 226 (plans)

PECS. 971-972 (S. S. Frere)

RE. VIIIA.2 (1958). 2425-2428 (I. A. Richmond)

Richmond. *RB*. 106 (aqueduct); 240 (index)

Rivet. *TCRB*. 145-148 (on the Catuvellauni); 167 (bibliography); 192 (index)

Stier. *Atlas*. 40 (map)

Wacher. *TRB*. 202-225; 458 (index)

Ward-Perkins. *Cities*. 29-30, 123; figs. 69-70

Wheeler. *RAA*. 69, 116 (the "theater"); 155-156 (on the commemorative arches over Watling Street)

Wheeler, R. E. M., and Wheeler, T. V. *Verulamium: A Belgic and Two Roman Cities*. Society of Antiquaries Research Report 11. London 1936

Lugdunum: see LYONS

Lugdunum Convenarum: see SAINT-BERTRAND-DE-COMMINGES

Lutetia Parisiorum: see PARIS

LYONS (in English, often; in French, Lyon; Rhône, France) = *Lugdunum, Gallia Lugdunensis;* from A.D. 48, its full name was *Colonia Copia Claudia Augusta Lugdunum (Claudius* was the family name of the Emperor Claudius, A.D. 41-54, who was born there in 10 B.C.,

when his father Drusus was in charge of *Gallia Comata);* mint of the
Empire; mint of the Later Roman Empire (q.v.).

pp. 8 (resemblance of the present city plan to the Roman); 75 (the
four aqueducts); 87-89 (general description)
Like many of the towns in Europe which were later colonized by
the Romans, *Lugdunum* was named after a Celtic god (Lug, of light
or sun; see Celtic names of cities below and Rivet, *PNRB* 401-402).
The city is located at the confluence of the Rhône River, which flows
westward from the Lake of Geneva and turns south at this point
towards the Mediterranean, and the Saône, which runs from the
north. The colony was founded in 43 B.C. by Lucius Munatius Plancus, who was then governor of *Gallia Comata* (q.v.; Cassius Dio
46.50; compare AUGST, VIENNE; see Audin, *Lyon, miroir* below). In
about 27 B.C., Augustus divided *Gallia Comata* into three provinces,
and *Lugdunum* was made the capital of *Gallia Lugdunensis.* It was
the center of *Aquitania* and *Lugdunensis* for taxation (compare TRIER)
and of all three for the state cult (Brogan 23-25).

Except for two columns of Egyptian granite (sawn in half and placed
in the eleventh-century church of St.-Martin-d'Ainay), virtually
nothing of the shrine of the "three Gauls" (see p. 89 above) survives
today; the associated amphitheater has been excavated recently (A.
Audin and M. Leglay, "L'amphithéâtre..."). A similar shrine was built
at +Cologne (listed under MAINZ) 9 B.C./A.D. 4 for the projected
provinces of Upper and Lower Germany (Mommsen, Chapter II;
Scullard 243). The theater and odeum of Fourvière Hill (p. 89 above)
have been well excavated and partly restored. The excellent Gallo-
Roman Museum, inaugurated in 1975, was built next to them.

An interesting question is the location of the imperial mint, which
began under Augustus, and that of the barracks of the Urban Cohort,
a squad of the city police from Rome, which was stationed in LYONS
to protect the mint (for the only other such squad outside of Rome,
see CARTHAGE). Our only archaeological evidence for the barracks is
an altar dedicated by a soldier in A.D. 207 and found on the southern
spur of Fourvière Hill, called St.-Just (Audin, *Essai sur la topographie* 111, citing Fabia, *La garnison romaine* 73-76).

A major find at LYONS is the bronze inscription of a speech given
to the Roman Senate in A.D. 48 by the Emperor Claudius, who favored the admission of senators from *Gallia Comata* (*CIL* XIII 1668;
Fabia, *La Table claudienne).* Discovered in 1528, it is now in the
Musée de la civilisation gallo-romaine, just mentioned.

Citing C. Jullian, *Histoire de la Gaule romaine,* A. Grenier estimated the population of Roman LYONS at 200,000 *(ESAR* 530, n. 65). Although this figure is perhaps four times too large (Audin, *Lugdunum dans Lyon* 31), we still can say that LYONS was in the first rank (see cities [Roman] population of, below and compare Rostovtzeff 139). On the area of colonial *Lugdunum,* see Chapter IV, n. 13 above. The walls and gates have been discussed by Grimal on pp. 87-88.

Of the city's economic importance in Roman times, Rostovtzeff says, "Lyons was not only the great clearing-house for the commerce in corn (wheat), wine, (olive-) oil and lumber; she was also one of the largest centres in the Empire for the manufacture and distribution of most of the articles consumed by Gaul, Germany and Britain" (166). Much of this trade was with TRIER and originated from the legions on the Rhine frontier (ibid. 223; compare LONDON).

River traffic was supplemented by the Roman highways from LYONS. They went south, east of the Rhône, to ARLES and north, by way of the Saône and Moselle valleys, to TRIER. Two roads led westward: one to Limoges and SAINTES and the other, more southerly, to BORDEAUX, by way of Agen on the Garonne River (see Grenier, *Manuel* I p. 330, fig. 84 and Grenier in *ESAR* III pp. 482-484, citing Strabo [q.v.] 4.6.11). For the routes to the east, see VIENNE. This system of highways, with LYONS (and VIENNE) at its center, was planned by Agrippa, Augustus' right-hand man, in 27 B.C. The intercity rivalry with nearby VIENNE was fierce (see Tacitus, *Histories* 1.65 and Salmon, *RC* 197, n. 318; compare *Pompeii* in Tacitus, *Annals* 14.17).

That which was destroyed by fire at LYONS in A.D. 65 (cf. Tacitus, *Annals* 16.13) was quickly rebuilt, and the colony continued to prosper until 197, when it was sacked in a civil war. The economic place of LYONS was taken over by ARLES, VIENNE, and TRIER, and it was plundered again in A.D. 269 (see AUTUN). In yet another civil war of the early fourth century, the city's aqueducts were destroyed. As a result, the Lyonnais moved from Fourvière Hill to the city's lower districts. But the Basilica of St.-Just (destroyed in the sixteenth century) was built on the hill in the sixth (Sidonius Apollinaris, *Letters* 2.10, cited by Hodgkin 322-324).

LYONS was the capital of the kingdom of the Burgundians (q.v.) from c. 460 to the Frankish conquest in c. 534 (Boehm; see Franks). Two major fifth-century churches have been found, one probably a cathedral (Leglay in *PECS).*

The scene of two Catholic Church councils in the thirteenth century, LYONS became a center for manufacturing silk in the fifteenth. Devastated in 1793 during the French Revolution, LYONS again recovered, thanks to an improved method of weaving silk. The commercial enterprise of its citizens (textiles, metals, and chemicals) and its geographic location have made LYONS the third largest city of France today. If the entire metropolitan areas are counted, LYONS overtakes MARSEILLES for second place. Much of the orthogonal Roman street plan can be traced in the medieval (and modern) streets of western LYONS.

Audin, A. "L'amphithéâtre des Trois Gaules à Lyon," *Gallia* 37 (1979): 85-100

—— *César et Plancus à Lyon*. Lyons 1951

*—— *Essai sur la topographie de Lugdunum*[3]. Lyons 1964

—— *Lugdunum dans Lyon*. Lyons n.d.

*—— *Lyon, miroir de Rome dans les Gaules*. Paris 1965 (annotated bibliography on pp. 215-219; the day of *Lugdunum*'s foundation, 9 October, calculated by the position of the *decumanus* — see p. 11 above — towards the sun 48-50)

—— "Les voies cardinales de Lugdunum," *Revue des études anciennes* 16 (1965): 159-164

—— and Leglay, M. "L'amphithéâtre des Trois-Gaules à Lyon: Première campagne de fouilles," *Gallia* 27 (1970): 67-89

—— "Découvertes archéologiques récentes à Lugdunum, métropole des Gaules," *Bulletin de la Société nationale des antiquaires de France* (May 11, 1966)

Bazin, H. *Villes antiques, Lyon et Vienne gallo-romaines*. Paris 1891

Besnier. *Lexique*. 442-443

Blanchet, A. *Recherches sur les aqueducs et cloaques de la Gaule romaine*. Paris 1908. 7; 80-86

Boehm, L. *Geschichte Burgonds*. Urban Taschenbuecher 134. Stuttgart 1971. 60-61 (citing the *Burgundian Laws*) LYONS as the Burgundian capital; Godomar II and Chilperich II ruled in VIENNE and had the title of king, but they acknowledged the supremacy of their brother, King Gundobad (480-516) in LYONS; 71-72 (Frankish conquest)

Boëthius and Ward-Perkins. *ERA*. pl. 182 (air view of theater and odeum)

Boucher, S. *Bronzes romains figurés du Musée des Beaux-Arts de Lyon*. Lyons 1973

—— et al. *Bronzes antiques du Musée de la civilisation gallo-romaine à Lyon*. Lyons 1977

Brogan. *Roman Gaul*. 101-104

Bruehl. *PC*. 201-222

Burdy, J. *Promenades gallo-romaines.* I. Lyons 1977

Cary. *Geogr. Backgr.* 250 (river and highway traffic)

Charlesworth. *Trade-Routes.* 292 (index)

Chevallier. *ANRW*. II.3 pp. 912-939 (description with bibliography and plans)

—— *Roman Roads*. 243 (bibl.)

Christ. *Bibl.* 262 (government); 313 (Christianity)

Christopherson, A. J. "The Provincial Assembly of the three Gauls . . .," *Historia* 17 (1968): 351-366 (on the provincial assembly of notables from the three Gauls at the federal shrine)

Coville, A. *Recherches sur l'histoire de Lyon*. . . . Paris 1928 (early medieval; "basic"—Bruehl, *PC* 201)

Desjardins. *Géogr*. III pp. 441-448

Dragendorff, H. "Der Altar der Roma und des Augustus in Lugdunum," *Jahrbuch des Deutschen Archaeologischen Instituts* 52 (1937): 111-119

Drinkwater, J. F. "Lugdunum: 'Natural Capital' of Gaul?" *Britannia* 6 (1975): 133-140 (see Chapter IV, n. 8 above); (*Lugdunum* was not a typical foundation for the period, as its center was on a hill.)

Fabia, P. *La garnison romaine de Lyon*. Lyons 1918

—— *Mosaïques romaines de Lyon*. Lyons 1923

Fishwick, D. "The Temple of the Three Gauls," *Journal of Roman Studies* 62 (1972): 46-52 (the Temple is later than the Altar)

Frank. *ESAR*. III pp. 479-486 (A. Grenier)

Germain de Montauzon, C. *Les aqueducs antiques de Lyon*. Paris 1909

Grenier. *Manuel*. I pp. 329-332; III 220-223; 685-688 (amphitheater), 786-798 (theater and odeum), 993 (*circus* for chariot races); IV 118-143 (aqueducts and sewers), 506-516 (Altar of Rome and Augustus)

Grimal. *Civ. Rome*. 353, 473

Guey, J. "A propos de la fondation de Lyon," *Bulletin de la Société des antiquaires de France* (1959): 128 ff.

—— and Audin, A. "L'amphithéâtre des Trois-Gaules à Lyon," *Gallia* 20 (1962): 117-145; 21 (1963): 125-164; 22 (1964): 37-61

Gutkind. *IHCD*. V (1970). 135-136, 226-228; 477 (bibl.)

Hatt, J. J. *Histoire de la Gaule romaine*. Paris 1959. 81-83, 96-99; 84, 100 (bibliographies)

Hodgkin, T. *Italy and her Invaders*. II. London 1892; rpt. New York 1967. 291-374 (on the Lyonnais nobleman, later Bishop of Clermont, Sidonius Apollinaris)

Jones, C. P. "A Syrian in Lyon," *American Journal of Philology* 99 (1978): 336-353 (Greek epitaph, probably of the third century A.D., an inscription from LYONS, where there were many Eastern traders)

Jones, H. Stuart. *Companion*. 150-151 (the aqueducts)

Kleinclausz, A. J. *Histoire de Lyon*. 4 vols. Lyons 1939 (ref. provided by J. Brooke)

KP. III (1969). 770-771 (M. Leglay)

Latreille, A., ed. *Histoire de Lyon*. . . . Toulouse 1975

Lavedan. *HU*. 389 (map); 492 (index)

Leglay, M. "Le culte impérial à Lyon, au IIe siècle après J.-C.," in *Les Martyrs de Lyon (177)*. Colloques internationaux du Centre National de la Recherche Scientifique 575, Lyons 1977. Paris 1978. 19-31

Leglay, M. et al. "Lyon, capitale archéologique," *Archéologia* 50 (1972)

—— *Notes d'épigraphie et d'archéologie lyonnaises*. Travaux édités sous les auspices de la ville de Lyon 5. Paris 1976

MacKendrick. *RF*. 64-72

McKay. *Houses*. 265 (bibl.)

Mommsen. *Provinces*. Chapter III

OCD. 625 (A. L. F. Rivet)

PECS. 528-531 (M. Leglay); (good for ancient sources)

Pelletier, A. "Lyon et sa région dans l'antiquité à la lumière des études récentes," *Cahiers d'histoire* 19 (1974): 161-187

Rambaud, M. "L'origine militaire de la colonie de Lugdunum," *Comptes rendus de l'Académie des inscriptions et belles-lettres* (1964): 252-277

Raynaud, J.-F. et al. "Lyon du IIIe siècle au haut moyen âge," *Archéologia* 112 (1977): 50-59; bibl. on 58-59

RE. XIII.2 (1927). 1718-1723 (Cramer)

Reid. *Municipalities*. 184-185 (on the federal shrine)

Ritter, J. *Le Rhône*. "Que sais-je?" no. 1507. Paris 1973 (geography; bibl. on 127)

Rostovtzeff. *SEHRE*. 139; 165-166; 223; 407 (sack of A.D. 197); 498 (sack of 269); 593, n. 3, 607, n. 21 (bibl.); 794 (index)

Scullard. *Gracchi to Nero*. 243; 487 (index)

Steyert, A. *Nouvelle histoire de Lyon*. I, II. Lyons 1895, 1899

Stier. *Atlas*. 88-89 (archbishopric)

Vittinghoff. *Roemische Kolonisation*. 67-69

Wuilleumier, P. *Fouilles de Fourvière à Lyon*. *Gallia*. Suppl. 4 (1951)

—— *Lyon, métropole des Gaules*. Paris 1953

—— and Audin, A. "Les voies axiales de Lugdunum," *Gallia* 2 (1943): 125-131

On Claudius' speech of A.D. 48:
(also see bibl. for VIENNE, below)
Abbott and Johnson. *Municipal Administration*. no. 50 (Latin text and commentary)
Arnold. *RSPA*. 144-150
CAH. X² (1952). 976-977 (bibl.)
Carcopino, J. *Les étapes de l'impérialisme romain*. Paris 1961. 174-208
Fabia, P. *La Table claudienne de Lyon*. Lyons 1929
Garzetti. *TA*. 591 (bibl.)
Hardy, E. G. *Roman Laws and Charters*. Oxford 1912. Part II, pp. 133-154 (translation and discussion of Claudius' speech)
Hatt, J. J. *Histoire de la Gaule romaine*. Paris 1959. 132-135; 140 (bibl.)
Jones. *HR*. II pp. 111-114 (translation)
Lewis, N., and Reinhold, M. *Roman Civilization, Sourcebook II: The Empire*. New York 1966. 133-134 (part of the text of Claudius' speech in translation); 622 (bibl.)
Momigliano, A. *Claudius* . . .². Cambridge 1961. 11-13, 64; 122, 123 (index); 84-85, 129 (bibl.)
Piganiol. *HR*. 264, 574 (bibl.)
Riccobono. *FIRA²*. I no. 43
Scramuzza, V. M. *The Emperor Claudius*. Cambridge, Mass., 1940. 99-110
Scullard. *Gracchi*.... 467, n. 14 (bibl.)
Sherwin-White. *RC*. 237-241
Smallwood, E. M. *Documents Illustrating the Principates of Gaius, Claudius and Nero*. no. 369. Cambridge 1967 (Latin text)

MAINZ (capital of Rhineland-Palatinate, Federal Republic of Germany) = *Mogontiacum*, capital of *Germania Superior* (Upper Germany)
p. 55 (shrine like that at PERIGUEUX, but no such temple existed; see Chapter III, n. 14 above)

+ Cologne, + Wiesbaden

Taking their name from the Celtic god Mogon (compare LYONS), the army camp and city were located on the left bank of the Rhine,

opposite the confluence of the River Main. A permanent camp for
two legions (q.v.) was built there in 18/13 B.C., and it was rebuilt in
stone A.D. 50/100. On the resemblance between the Roman plans
for army camps and for cities, see Salmon, *RC* 26-27, Castagnoli,
Orthogonal Town Planning 115-116, and Chapter I, n. 2 above. The
camp at MAINZ was about one kilometer from the Rhine and the
Roman bridge to Kastel, a fort on the opposite bank just upstream
from the confluence.

Called the *Canabae* (q.v.), the civilian settlement of camp followers grew up in a disarranged fashion in the region between the camp
and the river (see Abbott and Johnson, *Municipal Administration*
13-14). The river port was an important section of this settlement
(Grenier, *ESAR*). No traces of Roman MAINZ, camp or town, remain
above ground, other than portions of the theater, the aqueduct and
the city wall of the third and fourth centuries A.D.

The Roman government did not recognize the settlement at MAINZ
as a municipality until very late, perhaps after A.D. 300, when no
legions remained. The city of MAINZ was called a *civitas* by an inscription of 293/305, *CIL* XIII 6727, and a *municipium* by Ammianus
Marcellinus (q.v.), 15.11.8 (see *civitas* in the glossary below). MAINZ
had two legions until A.D. 89/90, and thereafter one. When the Roman army was reorganized c. A.D. 300, it was replaced by other
units. While a legion was still adjacent, the town would have been,
as Mommsen pointed out, subordinate to it.

Roman highways led south from + Cologne through MAINZ to
AUGST, along the left bank of the Rhine. Both MAINZ and + Cologne
had their own roads to TRIER (west of MAINZ), and when the entire
right bank of the Rhine was inside the Roman frontier (A.D. 74/98 to
259/263), there was a parallel road from MAINZ to AUGST on the east
side of the river. Across the Rhine but near MAINZ was the spa of
Aquae Mattiacae (or *Aquae Mattiacorum*), today + Wiesbaden, the
capital of Hesse. As Mommsen mentioned, it was used by the troops
from MAINZ for rest and recreation; these mainly military spas (such
as Bath in England) were not mentioned by Grimal in his *Les villes
romaines*.

MAINZ was raided by the Alamans (q.v.) in 259/260 and destroyed
in 406 by the Vandals (q.v.), who subsequently migrated to Spain
and North Africa. By about 460, this area was ruled by the Franks
(q.v.). Viticulture was introduced to the Rhine valley by the Romans, and MAINZ today is the largest wine-market in Germany.

The history of Roman + Cologne provides a contrast to that of

MAINZ because the former's legions were removed before A.D. 50, when the Emperor Claudius founded a Roman colony for veterans there: *Colonia Claudia Ara Augusta Agrippinensium* or *Colonia Agrippina*. (Agrippina was the emperor's wife.) The altar *(ara)* at Cologne has been mentioned in connection with the federal shrine at LYONS. Unlike MAINZ, the colony had an orthogonal street plan, which can be traced in the streets of modern Cologne. But despite these differences of political status and city plan, Roman MAINZ was the capital of Upper Germany, as + Cologne was that of the province of Lower Germany.

Speaking of the two Germanies, Rostovtzeff said, "The division of the Rhine lands into a lower and an upper Germany appears purely artificial. In fact, the lands on the left bank of the river formed one unit, those on the right another. The former, especially those in the South, did not differ greatly from the rest of Gaul, to which they originally belonged." The military districts gradually became politically more self-sufficient until it was time to make provinces of them. On the change of the two German military districts into provinces, in 89/90, see H. Bengtson, *Grundriss der roemischen Geschichte* I (Munich 1967) 323-324 and Piganiol, *HR* 279.

Rostovtzeff went on to discuss the cities of Roman Germany, quite validly except for + Cologne, whose foundation has been explained above. "It is true that the large cities of the left bank...were all of military origin. Colonia Agrippinensis, Castra Vetera (Birten), Novaesium (Neuss), Mogontiacum, Bonna (Bonn) &c., all developed out of the settlements which arose around the great military fortresses, the so-called *canabae*" *(SEHRE* p. 222).

There are a number of excellent museums relating to provincial Roman civilization in the Rhineland: at + Cologne, the Roemisch-Germanisches Museum; at Bonn, the Rheinisches Landesmuseum; and at MAINZ, the Roemisch-Germanisches Zentralmuseum and the Mittelrheinisches Landesmuseum.

A useful outline of the Roman Rhine-Danube frontier is given in Finley, *Atlas* 40-41 by J. J. Wilkes. He makes a comparison between the legionary camps of c. A.D. 14 and A.D. 117. Going up the Rhine, we find the following camps (Woloch's adaptation) in A.D. 14:
Roman Lower Germany
North Rhine-Westphalia, Federal Republic of Germany
    Birten two legions
    + Cologne two legions (the First; the Twentieth,
    later at WROXETER [q.v.] and + Chester)

Roman Upper Germany
  Rhineland-Palatinate, FRG
    MAINZ two legions (the Fourteenth, later at
    WROXETER; the Sixteenth)
  France, region of Alsace
    Strasbourg (Bas-Rhin département) one legion
  Switzerland
    Windisch (Aargau canton) one legion (see AUGST)
and in A.D. 117:
Roman Lower Germany
    Birten one legion
    Bonn (North Rhine-Westphalia) one legion
Roman Upper Germany
    MAINZ one legion (the Twenty-second)
    Strasbourg one legion
compare WROXETER, below

MAINZ:
Baatz, D. *Mogontiacum*. Limesforschungen. 4. Berlin 1962 (=
    Frontier-Research)
Bengtson, H., and Milojčić, V. *Grosser historischer Weltatlas*. I⁵.
    Munich 1972. 45
Besnier. *Lexique*. 497
Brogan. *Roman Gaul*. 117-118
Caprino. *MAR, Bibl*. 241
Chevallier. *ANRW*. II.1 p. 915 (bibliography)
Christ. *Bibl*. 329, 358-360, 512
*Decker, K.-V., and Selzer, W. "Mogontiacum: Mainz vor der Zeit
    des Augustus bis zum Ende der roemischen Herrschaft," *ANRW*.
    II.5.1 (1976): 457-559
Duval, P.-M. "Archéologie et histoire de la Gaule," *Annuaire du
    Collège de France* 75 (1975): 539-545
Esser, K. H. "Mogontiacum," *Bonner Jahrbuecher* 172 (1972): 212-
    227
Frank. *ESAR*. III pp. 482, 505 (A. Grenier, on the port)
Grenier, A. *Quatre villes romaines de la Rhénanie*. Paris 1925 (on
    MAINZ, TRIER, Bonn, +Cologne)
Gutkind. *IHCD*. I (1964). 272-275; 482 (bibl.)
KP. III (1969). 1389-1390 (H. Cueppers)
Lavedan. *HU*. 344 (map); 493 (index)
MacKendrick. *RoR*. 59-76; 252-253 (bibl.)

Mommsen. *Provinces*. Chapter IV

OCD. 697 (P. Salway)

PECS. 586-587 (D. Baatz)

RE. XV.2 (1932). 2422-2433 (M. Besnier)

Rostovtzeff. *SEHRE*. 222

Stier. *Atlas*. 88-89 (archbishopric)

Stuempel, B. "Zur Datierung der roemischen Stadtmauer in Mainz," *Bonner Jahrbuecher* 178 (1978): 291-303

Ternes, C.-M. "Die Provincia Germania Superior...," *ANRW*. II.5.2 (1976): 831-835

Vittinghoff, F. "Die Entstehung von staedtischen Gemeinwesen in der Nachbarschaft roemischer Legionslager," *Legio VII Gemina*. León 1972 (see + León under ITALICA above)

*von Elbe, J. *Roman Germany*. Mainz 1975. 253-265

Webster. *Army*. 291 (bibl.), 319 (index)

Weidemann, K. "Die Topographie von Mainz...," *Jahrbuch, Roemisch-Germanisches Zentralmuseum, Mainz* 15 (1968): 146-199

Wells, C. M. *The German Policy of Augustus*. Oxford 1972. 138-146

+ Cologne:

Borger, H. *Das Roemisch-Germanische Museum, Koeln*. Munich 1977

Brogan. *Roman Gaul*. 118-119; 150-151 (on the manufacture of glass, a leading industry from the second century A.D.); 242 (bibliography)

Caprino. *MAR, Bibl.* 241

Dilke. ANRW. II.1 pp. 591-592 (bibl.)

Doppelfeld, O. *Roemische und fraenkische Zeit*. Cologne 1958 = vol. I of *Ausgewaehlte Quellen zur Koelner Stadtgeschichte*, edit. R. Frohn et al. (source-books)

—— et al. "Das roemische Koeln," *ANRW*. II.4 (1975): 715-782

Eydoux, H.-P. *The Buried Past*. London 1966. 103-119, 184 (bibl. transl. from the French)

Fremersdorf, F. *Urkunden zur Koelner Stadtgeschichte aus roemischer Zeit²*. Cologne 1963

Grenier. *Manuel*. I pp. 345-351

Gutkind. *IHCD*. I (1964). 260-265; 481 (bibl.)

Hellenkemper, H. "Architektur als Beitrag zur Geschichte der Colonia Ara Agrippinensium," *ANRW*. II.4 (1975): 783-824

Herrnbrodt, A. *Uebersichtskarte der archaeologischen Denkmaeler im Rheinland/Koeln*. Bonn 1969

Koelner Roemerillustrierte. 2 vols. 1974-1975

KP. I (1964). 1248-1249 (H. Cueppers)

La Baume, P. *Colonia Agrippinensis*[3]. Cologne 1964

—— "Oppidum Ubiorum . . .," *Gymnasium* 80 (1973): 333-347

MacKendrick. *RoR*. 46-58; 252 (bibl.)

OCD. 264 (O. Brogan and P. Salway)

PECS. 231-232 (O. Doppelfeld)

Raepset-Charlier, M.-T., and Raepset-Charlier, G. *"Gallia Belgica et Germania Inferior,"* ANRW. II.4 (1975): 93-95; 139

Rykwert. *Idea*. 42

Schmitz, H. *Colonia Claudia Ara Agrippinensium*. Cologne 1956

—— *Stadt und Imperium: Koeln in roemischer Zeit*. Cologne 1948

Signon, H. *Die Roemer in Koeln*[3]. Frankfurt am Main 1972

—— *Die Roemer zwischen Koeln, Bonn und Trier*. Frankfurt 1977

Stier. *Atlas*. 78 (plan); 88-89 (archbishopric)

*von Elbe. *Roman Germany*. 183-228

+ Wiesbaden (= *Aquae Mattiacae):*
Besides being a spa, it was the tribal capital of the Mattiaci.

Christ. *Bibl*. 362-363

EB. XXVIII pp. 623-624

KP. I (1964). 476 (H. Cueppers)

PECS. 76-77 (H. Schoppa)

Schoppa, H. *Aquae Mattiacae: Wiesbadens Roemische und Alaman-nisch-Merowingische Vergangenheit*. Wiesbaden 1974

Wurm, K., and Schoppa, H. *Aus Wiesbadens Vorzeit*. Bonn 1972

The Roman-German Frontier:

Baatz, D. *Der roemische Limes*[2]. Berlin 1975

—— et al. *Die Roemerstaedte in Deutschland. Gymnasium*. Suppl. 1. Heidelberg 1960

Bengtson. *Atlas*. 45 (maps); also see *Erlaeuterungen* (contains bibl.)

Brogan, O. "The Roman Limes of Germany," *Archaeological Journal* 92 (1935): 1-41

CAH. XI[2] (1954). 884 (bibl.)

Chapot. *MR*. 52-55; 340-387

Christ. *Bibl*. 358-363, 397; 511, 512 (Late Roman)

Christ, K. *Die Roemer in Deutschland*[3]. Stuttgart 1967

Gelzer, M. "Roemische Rheinpolitik," *Elsass-Lothringisches Jahr-buch* II (1932): 1-20

Germania Romana, Ein Bilderatlas. 2 vols. Bamberg 1924-1930
Hagen, J. *Roemerstrassen der Rheinprovinz²*. Bonn 1931
Harmand. *Occ. rom.*
Koepp, F. *Die Roemer in Deutschland³*. Bielefeld/Leipzig 1926
Kossack, G. "The Germans," in Millar. *REN*. 294-320
KP. III (1969). 652-654 (H. Cueppers; see Limes)
MacKendrick. *RoR*. 100-138; 254-255 (bibl.)
Mann. *ANRW*. II.1 pp. 518-521
Parker, H. M. D. *The Roman Legions²*. Cambridge 1958
PECS. 511-513 (H. von Petrikovits and H. Schoenberger)
Piganiol. *HR*. 649 (index)
Rostovtzeff. *SEHRE*. 594, n. 4 (bibl.)
Schleiermacher, W. *Der roemische Limes in Deutschland²*. Berlin
    1961
Schoenberger, H. "The Roman Frontier in Germany," *Journal of Roman Studies* 59 (1969): 144-197
Syme, R. "Rhine and Danube Legions under Domitian," *Journal of Roman Studies* 18 (1928): 41-55
Webster. *Army* (bibl. on pp. 282-284, 286-288)
Wells, C. M. *The German Policy of Augustus*. Oxford 1972
—— "The Impact of the Augustan Campaigns in Germany," in Pippidi. *Assimilation*. 421-431
Woloch, G. M., review of P. La Baume. *Romans on the Rhine*. Chicago 1967 (transl. from the German) *Classical World* 62 (1968): 21

Málaga, charter of: see OSUNA

MANTUA (in Italian, Mantova; Lombardy, Italy) = *Mantua, Venetia, Italia*
pp. 20-21 (on terramara, q.v.)
    Perhaps of Etruscan origin (compare BOLOGNA and MARZABOTTO), Mantua became a Roman *municipium* (q.v.). It is bordered on three sides by lakes which the Mincio River forms, and it is north of the Po River. Until 49 B.C., Mantua was part of the province of *Gallia Cisalpina* (q.v.).
    Little of the ancient city remains.
Besnier. *Lexique*. 462
Chilver. *Cisalpine Gaul*. 210; 215-216 (Vergil's birthplace)
Gutkind. *IHCD*. IV (1969). 293-297
Highet, G. *Poets in a Landscape*. London 1957. 56-64 (Vergil)

KP. III (1969). 980 (G. Radke)

McKay, A. G. *Vergil's Italy*. Greenwich, Conn., 1970. 68-69 (comparison with nearby VERONA)

Nissen. *IL*. II pp. 202-204

OCD. 644 (E. T. Salmon)

PECS. 550 (D. C. Scavone)

Scullard. *Etruscan Cities*. 215-216

Tozzi, P. *Storia padana antica*. Milan 1972

MARSEILLES (in English, often; in French, Marseille; Bouches-du-Rhône, France) = *Massilia, Gallia Narbonensis*

p. 3 (the Greek colony)

Massalia was the Greek name, *Massilia* the Latin. The Greek colony was founded c. 600 B.C. by settlers from *Phokaia* in Ionia (q.v.). The site was an excellent port, on a bay of the Mediterranean coast of what is now France, and was well suited for sea-trade, the primary raison d'être of the colony. The Massaliots themselves founded colonies at AMPURIAS to the west, as well as Antibes, Nice, and Monaco to the east. Trade by sea from Greek *Massalia* extended as far as the northeast coast of Spain in addition to Britain. These Greeks also introduced viticulture to what is now southern Provence.

In 124 B.C., the Massaliots called in the Romans to help them against the Gauls. The result was that MARSEILLES became an allied city (q.v.) in the Roman Empire. As a *civitas libera et foederata* (free and allied city), MARSEILLES was, at least in theory, free from interference by the governor of *Gallia Narbonensis* (q.v.), but it never received the status of colony, considered more prestigious.

Having sided with Pompey, who lost to Caesar in that civil war, in 49 B.C., *Massilia* was stripped of most of its territory, to the benefit of ARLES and FRÉJUS. The former replaced it as a civilian port and the latter as a military one. Concerning this decline, Mommsen said, "In a political aspect there is nothing more to be said of Massilia after its capture in the civil war; the town was thenceforth for Gaul only what Neapolis (NAPLES) was for Italy—the centre of Greek culture and Greek learning."

Under Roman rule, MARSEILLES was in fact best known for its Greek schools (Grenier, *ESAR* 416-417). About A.D. 98, speaking of the education of Julius Agricola (cf. + *Verulamium*), the historian Tacitus said, "The *alma mater* of his studies was Massilia, a blend and happy combination of Greek refinement and provincial simplicity" (*Agricola* 4, transl. M. Hutton).

Clébert's view that a topographical description of *Massilia* in Roman times is completely impossible (130-131) is overstated but not far from the truth. The Greek city was more or less orthogonal (Clavel-Lévêque 184-185), and what the Romans destroyed in the siege of 49 B.C. had to be rebuilt. Located to the north of the Greco-Roman port (called the Vieux Port today), the ancient city contained about fifty hectares. Because of the continuous settlement and building, little can be known of the ancient city plans (but see Février, *Dév.*, fig. 4).

Among other structures, one may see traces of the ancient port, which was to some extent still used after 49 B.C. In the Musée des docks romains, near the present city hall, there is material which came to light after World War II.

MARSEILLES today is the first port of France and of the Mediterranean. The much larger present-day port lies northwest of the Vieux Port. The return to preeminence began with the French conquest of Algeria (1834-1837; see CONSTANTINE) and the opening of the Suez Canal in 1869. Supported by its harbor and its factories, MARSEILLES is the second largest city in France (but see LYONS).

Baratier, E., ed. *Histoire de Marseille*. Toulouse 1973

Benoît, F. *CAGR*. V, *Bouches-du-Rhône* (1936).

—— "L'évolution topographique de Marseille, le port et l'enceinte à la lumière des fouilles," *Latomus* 31 (1972): 54-70 (The Greek walls were discovered in 1966-1967.)

—— "Les fouilles de Marseille," *Comptes rendus de l'Académie des inscriptions et belles-lettres* (1947): 528-585

—— *Musée des docks romains et du commerce antique de Marseille²*. Marseilles 1970

—— "The New Excavations at Marseille," *American Journal of Archaeology* 53 (1949): 237-240

Besnier. *Lexique*. 469-470

Brogan. *Roman Gaul*. 86-87

Chevallier. *ANRW*. II.3 pp. 702-706; 709-715 (with 2 plans); 806-807 (bibliography)

Clavel-Lévêque, M. *Marseille grecque*. Marseilles 1977 (ref. provided by D. Snyder)

Clébert. *Provence antique*. 125-136

Clerc, M. "Marseille et Jules César," *Musée belge* 27 (1923): 145-156

—— *Massalia: histoire de Marseille dans l'antiquité*. 2 vols. Marseilles 1927, 1929 ("a model monograph," Rostovtzeff, *SEHRE* 594)

Ebel. *TG*. 111-112 (index)

*Euzennat, M. "Ancient Marseille in the Light of Recent Excavations," *American Journal of Archaeology* 84 (1980): 133-140 (basic; see notes for bibl.)

—— "Les fouilles de la Bourse à Marseille," *Comptes rendus de l'Académie des inscriptions et belles-lettres* (1976): 529-552

—— and Salviat, F. "Les découvertes archéologiques de la Bourse de Marseille," *CRAI* (1968): 145-159

—— *Gallia* 27 (1969): 423-430

—— "Marseille retrouve ses murs et son port grecs," *Archéologia* 21 (1968): 5-17 (bibl. in notes and on p. 16)

Février. "CSG." 6, fig. 1 (map), 8; 8, nn. 38-44 (bibl.); plates i-ii (air views)

—— *Dév. urbain en Provence*. 222-223 (index); figs. 4, 43

Frank. *ESAR*. III pp. 416-425 (A. Grenier)

Grenier. *Manuel*. I pp. 284-287; II 476 ff.

Gutkind. *IHCD*. IV (1969). 610 (the Greek city); V (1970). 236-237; 477 (bibl.)

KP. III (1969). 1066-1068 (H. Volkmann)

MacKendrick. *RF*. 10-14

Mommsen. *Provinces*. Chapter III

OCD. 654 (A. L. F. Rivet)

PECS. 557-558 (F. Salviat)

RE. XIV.2 (1930). 2130-2152 (H. G. Wackernagel)

Woodhead. *Greeks in the West*. 66-68; plate 30 (Greek theater, exc. 1946, no longer extant)

Martigny (Valais, Switzerland): discussed in Chapter III, n. 3 above

MARZABOTTO (Emilia-Romagna, Italy); ancient name unknown

pp. 16 (the orthogonal city); 21 (earlier Greek orthogonal cities)

The site is on the left bank of the Reno River, a tributary of the Po, and is twenty-five kilometers southwest of BOLOGNA, also on the Reno. The city was laid out in 525/500 B.C. by the Etruscans (q.v.) on an orthogonal plan aligned with the cardinal compass points and with elongated blocks, as at CAPUA VETERE. In the words of Ward-Perkins, "It is hard to avoid the conclusion that for the Etruscans, as for the Greeks, orthogonal planning was the product of a colonizing situation, involving the formal establishment of new urban centers" (*Cities* p. 25). For the Greek influence on this plan, see Grimal, above, Castagnoli p. 54 and Ogilvie p. 30.

MARZABOTTO guarded an important trans-Apennine route down the Reno (Ward-Perkins, *Cities* 118). The city traded with the Greek world through the Etruscan port at + *Spina* (Castagnoli 54; see RA-VENNA). Etruscan MARZABOTTO was captured and laid waste by the Gauls (q.v.) early in the fourth century B.C. Little excavation has taken place there (Ogilvie, ibid.), and the plan is known mainly from air photography.

Alfoeldi. *Early Rome*. 180-181
Boëthius. *Golden House*. 47, n. 41 (bibl.)
—— and Ward-Perkins. *ERA*. 60-61; 590 (bibl.); pl. 29
Brizio, E. "Relazione sugli scavi eseguiti a Marzabotto presso Bologna," *Monumenti antichi pubblicati per cura dell'Accademia dei Lincei* 1 (1889): 249-426; rpt. Mainz 1980
Castagnoli. *Orthogonal Town Planning*. 51-54; fig. 21 (map); 133; 51, n. 132 (bibl.)
Chevallier. *ANRW*. II.1 pp. 687-692; plates vi-vii
Coarelli. *Le città etrusche*. 325 (bibl.)
Crema. *Arch*. 29-30 (orthogonal plan)
Enciclopedia dell'arte antica, classica e orientale. IV (1961). 896-899 (P. E. Arias and G. A. Mansuelli)
Grimal. *Search*. 181-185
Gutkind. *IHCD*. IV (1969). 25-27; 625 (bibl.)
Haverfield. *Town Planning*. 61-62
Holloway, R. R. *American Journal of Archaeology* 81 (1977): 255 (comparison with contemporary and "unplanned" Acquarossa)
Lugli. *Tecnica edilizia*. 378-397; 460-461
MacKendrick. *Mute Stones*. 29-33; 353 (bibl.)
Mansuelli, G. A. "La cité étrusque de Marzabotto," *Comptes rendus de l'Académie des inscriptions et belles-lettres* (1960): 66 ff.; (1962): 62-84
—— *Guida alla città etrusca ed al Museo di Marzabotto*[2]. Bologna 1974
—— "Marzabotto: dix années de fouilles et de recherches," *Mélanges...Ecole française de Rome* 84 (1972): 111 ff.
—— "Marzabotto. I problemi della città etrusca e i criteri metodici per una pubblicazione scientifica degli scavi," *Rendiconti della Classe di Scienze morali, storiche e filologiche dell'Accademia dei Lincei* 28. Rome 1973. 745-753
—— *Mostra dell'Etruria Padana e della Città di Spina*. 2 vols. Bologna 1960. I pp. 214-219; II p. 25 (bibl.)
OCD. 653 (D. W. R. Ridgway)

Ogilvie. *Early Rome*. 30; 160 (list of Etruscan cities in north Italy)
PECS. 584-585 (G. A. Mansuelli; see "Misano")
Robertson. *GRA*. 191; 366 (bibl.)
Rykwert. *Idea*. 42, 79-87; figs. 47-52
Scullard. *Etruscan Cities*. 205-208 (map on 207)
Ward-Perkins. *Cities*. 25; 118 (with bibl.); fig. 42
—— "ERTI." figs. 5 and 6 (maps)
Wheeler. *RAA*. 30; 232, n. 12 (bibliography)

Mediolanum meant Clearing in the Middle in Celtic (Chevallier, *Roman Roads* 130).

Mediolanum = Milan (Lombardy, Italy)

Mediolanum Aulercorum = Evreux (Eure, France): see p. 68 above

Mediolanum Santonum: see SAINTES

+ Mérida: listed under ITALICA

MODENA (Emilia-Romagna, Italy) = *Mutina, Aemilia, Italia*
pp. 20-21 (on terramara, q.v.)
    There was a Roman fort on this site as early as 218 B.C. (Livy 21.25). The Roman colony of *Mutina* was founded in 183 B.C., on the *Via Aemilia*, thirty-six kilometers northwest of *Bononia* (see BO-LOGNA). *Parma* (q.v.) was also founded in 183, and the three cities guarded separate passes in the Apennines (q.v.) on the side more distant from Rome.
Besnier. *Lexique*. 503
Castagnoli. *Orthogonal Town Planning*. 98, 100
Chevallier. *ANRW*. II.1 plates xxvi-xxvii (centuriation, aerial photo-graph, and plan of *Mutina*)
Chilver. *Cisalpine Gaul*. 6 (the *colonia*), 163-164 (the wool trade)
Dilke. *ANRW*. II.1 p. 586 (bibl. on centuriation, q.v.)
EB. XVIII pp. 641-642
Enciclopedia dell'arte antica, classica e orientale. V (1963). 137-138 (N. Alfieri)
Frank. *ESAR*. V pp. 116-117 (agriculture); 188 (pottery); 108, 164-165, 184, 202, 276 (sheep and wool)
Gutkind. *IHCD*. IV (1969). 309-313
Haverfield. *Ancient Town Planning*. 69 (cited by Castagnoli 98, n. 9)

Lavedan. *HU*. 376 (map)
Nissen. *IL*. II pp. 264-267
OCD. 713 (E. T. Salmon)
PECS. 600 (D. C. Scavone)
Salmon. *RC*. 24 (on centuriation, q.v.); 104-106; 107 (map of *Gallia Cisalpina*, q.v.)
Scullard. *Etruscan Cities*. 213 (?early Etruscan settlements)
Ward-Perkins. *Cities*. 29 (continuity of settlement, to the present day)

MONTPELLIER (Hérault, France)
p. 3 (on ENSERUNE)
The Roman history of Montpellier is very hard to discern. The city is now the capital of Hérault département.
Arbaret, C. "Montpellier, système urbain médiéval," in Y. Barel, *La ville médiévale*. Grenoble 1975. 619-700
Bonnet, E., and Blanchet, A. *CAGR*. X, *Hérault* (1946)
Chevallier. *ANRW*. II.3 p. 725 (map)
EB. XVIII pp. 788-789
Gutkind. *IHCD*. V (1970). 477 (bibl.)
Richard, J. C. M. "Le problème des origines de Montpellier," *Revue archéologique de Narbonnaise* 2 (1960): 49-63

Mutina: see MODENA

NAPLES (in Italian, Napoli; Campania, Italy: capital of the region)
= *Neapolis, Campania, Italia*
p. 25 (orthogonal plan; no Etruscan influence when the Greek colony was founded, see Chapter I, n. 9 above)
Greeks from nearby *Cumae* founded NAPLES c. 600 B.C. on the Bay of Naples, an arm of the Tyrrhenian Sea. About 150 years later, the orthogonal "New City" (Neapolis) was laid out, northeast of the original settlement and north of the modern port (Ward-Perkins, *Cities* 118). NAPLES was conquered by the Samnites (q.v.) and next, in 327 B.C., by Rome, 240 kilometers to the northwest; it became an allied city (q.v.). In the late Republic, Naples became a *municipium* (q.v.; Roman citizenship was made universal in Italy in 89 B.C.), and under the Empire, it received the title of *colonia* (q.v.).
The city nevertheless maintained its Greek institutions. The extent to which Greek continued to be spoken at NAPLES under the Empire is debated, but the settlement of Roman veterans there c.

A.D. 80 would have contributed to the decline of that language. The city's Greek schools under Roman rule were, however, comparable to those at MARSEILLES.

The Roman and medieval cities occupied the fifth-century site, and the orthogonal street plan is preserved in the modern city. The present-day port is Italy's most important for passengers, and NAPLES is now that country's third largest city, after Rome and Milan.

Acton, H. *The Bourbons of Naples (1734-1825)*. London 1956
—— *The Last Bourbons of Naples (1825-1861)*. London 1961
Bérard. *Bibl. topogr.* 71
Besnier. *Lexique*. 518-519
Buchner, G. *Metropoli e colonie di Magna Grecia*. Naples 1964
Caprino. *MAR, Bibl.* 263
Castagnoli. *Orthogonal Town Planning*. 35-39; 35, n. 90 (bibliography); 53 (comparison with MARZABOTTO, not valid in detail); figs. 13-14
Crema. *Arch.* 29-30 (the orthogonal city)
Croce, B. *History of the Kingdom of Naples*. Bari 1925; transl. Chicago 1970
D'Arms, J. H. *Romans on the Bay of Naples*. Cambridge, Mass., 1970. 247 (index); (The book is on villas.)
De Seta, C. *Storia della Città di Napoli*. Rome/Bari 1973
Enciclopedia dell'arte antica, classica e orientale. V (1963). 332-339 (M. Napoli and A. Maiuri)
Finley. *Atlas*. 132-133 (G. D. B. Jones); (see "The Bay of Naples")
Gleijeses, V. *La Storia di Napoli*. Naples 1974
Guida d'Italia del Touring Club Italiano, Nápoli e Dintorni[4]. Milan 1960
Gutkind. *IHCD*. IV (1969). 384-389, 603; 626 (bibl.)
Haverfield. *Town Planning*. 100-102
Highet, G. *Poets in a Landscape*. London 1957. 74-82 (Vergil)
KP. IV (1972). 30-32 (G. Radke)
McKay, A. G. *Naples*. 40-69; 231 (bibl.)
—— *Vergil's Italy*. Greenwich, Conn., 1970. 195-201
Napoli, M. A. *Napoli greco-romana*. Naples 1959
Nissen. *IL*. II pp. 746-748
OCD. 725 (E. T. Salmon)
PECS. 614-615 (W. D. E. Coulson)
Pirro, A. *Le origini di Napoli*. Salerno (Campania, Italy) 1906
Pugliese Carratelli, G. et al. "Napoli antica," *La Parola del Passato*. 25/27. 1952; rpt. Amsterdam 1971. 241-447
RE. XVI.2 (1935). 2112-2122 (H. Philipp)

Rykwert. *Idea*. 42
Salmon. *RC*. 149 (the decline of Greek)
Ward-Perkins. *Cities*. 23-25, 118-119; fig. 39 (air view)
—— "ERTI." fig. 4 (plan), fig. 16 (air view)

NARBONNE (Aude, France); *Colonia Narbo Martius* was its name
when founded; its full name after the middle of the first century A.D.
was *Colonia Iulia Paterna Claudia Narbo Martius Decumanorum;*
in *Gallia Narbonensis* (see colonies in *Gallia Narbonensis* below).
pp. 3 (ENSERUNE); 3-4 (foundation); 175-176 (the underground aqueduct)

+ Béziers (Hérault)

Founded in 118 B.C. below the native hill-fort of Montlaurès, *Narbo*
was the first permanent Roman colony outside of what, in 42 B.C.,
became Italy (on the controversy about the date of Narbo's foundation, see Scullard, *Gracchi to Nero* 399, n. 40). Like ENSERUNE,
Montlaurès was abandoned in the years after 118. *Gallia Narbonensis* (q.v.) was annexed by Rome in 121 B.C., but MARSEILLES was the
province's most important city until 49 B.C., when it was crushed in
a civil war.

Cicero called *Narbo* "a colony which stands as a watch-tower and
bulwark of the Roman people" *(For M. Fonteius* 5.13, ?69 B.C.; he
also alluded to the allied city of Marseilles; transl. N. H. Watts, London and New York 1931). Cicero thought of the colony as a defense
against those Gallic tribes which had not yet been conquered. In 45
B.C., Caesar's Tenth Legion was settled in NARBONNE, which became the capital of the province and, later, the center of its imperial
cult.

The colony was a crossroads on the *Via Domitia* from ARLES to
Spain and the Roman road from TOULOUSE. Its port traded with
Spain, especially *Baetica*, and with OSTIA ANTICA, where its traders
had an office (Rostovtzeff 607, n. 22 [bibliography] and Grenier, *ESAR*
471-472). In its heyday, *Narbo* was a major commercial center comparable to *Arelate* (Rostovtzeff 167). The former was first in popu-
laion in Narbonensis and second only to LYONS in all of Gaul (see
cities [Roman], population of, below).

The extent of NARBONNE's decline, which began with a fire in
A.D. 145, is debated. In the fourth and fifth centuries, Ausonius (q.v.)
and the Lyonnais, Sidonius Apollinaris, spoke of it as flourishing
(Grenier, ibid. 469). Although its port silted up in the fourteenth

century, the city has been continuously inhabited to the present day. It was conquered by the Visigoths (q.v.) in 462, after they tried for fifty years, later by the Arabs in 719 and the Franks (q.v.) in 759. The Roman forum, the cryptoporticus (q.v.) and the Capitol, all in the same area, have been excavated (Grenier, ibid. 468; Crema). The outline of ancient Narbo is known from the plan of the medieval city; the *Via Domitia* formed the *cardo* (Gayraud and Solier in *PECS*). Bannert. "Volcae."

Benedict, C. H. *A History of Narbo*. Lancaster, Pa., 1941

Besnier. *Lexique*. 512

Brogan. *Roman Gaul*. 88-89

Charlesworth. *Trade-Routes*. 193

Chevallier. *ANRW*. II.1 plate xlv (plan); II.3 pp. 690 and 728 (maps), 807-808 (bibl.)

Christ. *Bibl*. 141

Crema. *Arch*. 165; fig. 160 (the cryptoporticus)

Desjardins. *Géogr*. III p. 420

Ebel. *TG*. 89-98

Février. "CSG." 16

Frank. *ESAR* III pp. 466-473, 585 (A. Grenier)

Gayraud, M. *Narbonne antique des origines à la fin du IIe siècle*. *Revue archéologique de la Narbonnaise*. Suppl. 8 (1981)

——— "Narbonne aux trois premiers siècles après Jésus-Christ," *ANRW*. II.3 (1975): 829-859

Giry, J., and Mare, A. F. *Narbonne, son histoire, ses monuments*. Paris 1969

Grenier, A. "Essai de topographie narbonnaise," *Comptes rendus de l'Académie des inscriptions et belles-lettres* (1955): 352-362

——— "Les capitoles romains: La Gaule et le capitole de Narbonne," *CRAI* (1956): 316-323

——— *Manuel*. I pp. 287-288; II 483, 486 (roads); III 128-142; 272-279 (the Capitol)

——— et al. *CAGR*. XII, *Aude* (1959)

Guy, M. "Vues aériennes montrant la centuriation de la colonie de Narbonne," *Gallia* 13 (1955): 103-108

Héléna, P. *Les origines de Narbonne*. Toulouse/Paris 1937

Hermon, E. "La date de la fondation de la colonie Narbo Martius en Gaule Narbonnaise," *Revue historique de Droit français et étranger* 54 (1976): 229-239

KP. III (1969). 1570-1571 (M. Leglay)

MacKendrick. *RF*. 18, 34-35

Mattingly, H. B. "The Foundation of Narbo Martius," *Hommages à A. Grenier.* Collection Latomus 58. Brussels 1962. 1159-1171
OCD. 722 (C. E. Stevens)
PECS. 607-608 (M. Gayraud and Y. Solier)
Perret, V. "Le Capitole de Narbonne," *Gallia* 14 (1956): 1-22
Radke. *Viae.* 265; figs. 5, 27
RE Supplement 7 (1940). 515-548 (P. Goessler)
Rostovtzeff. *SEHRE.* 167, 218
Salmon. *RC.* 121-123, 136 (Salmon dates the colony to c. 114 B.C., p. 121.)
Solier, Y. "Note sur les galeries souterraines de Narbonne," *Les cryptoportiques dans l'architecture romaine.* Collection de l'Ecole française de Rome 14. Rome 1973. 315-324
Stier. *Atlas.* 88-89 (archbishopric)
Vittinghoff. *Roemische Kolonisation.* 55 (general); 66 (on the epithet *Paterna*, shared with ARLES)
von Hagen, V. W. *The Roads that Led to Rome.* London 1967. 204-205 (photographs of a Roman bridge)

+ Béziers (= *Colonia Iulia Victrix Baeterrae Septimanorum):*
This colony was twenty-five kilometers northeast of NARBONNE on the *Via Domitia;* see colonies in *Gallia Narbonensis* below. Locating Roman Béziers on a hill distorted its ancient orthogonal plan, which was aligned northwest-southeast (Clavel-Lévêque).
The wine-trade supports the present-day city, as it did the Roman one.
Besnier. *Lexique.* 118
Bonnet, E. *CAGR.* X, *Hérault* (1946). 30 ff.
Chevallier. *ANRW.* II.3 p. 804 (bibl.)
*Clavel, M. *Béziers et son territoire dans l'Antiquité.* Paris 1970
Frank. *ESAR.* III pp. 581-582 (A. Grenier on the wine)
Grenier. *Manuel.* I p. 288; III 643, n. 1 (bibl.); 643-645 (amphitheater)
KP. I (1964). 804 (M. Leglay)
PECS. 134-135 (M. Clavel-Lévêque)

NIMES (Gard, France) = *Colonia Augusta Nemausus, Gallia Narbonensis* (see colonies in *Gallia Narbonensis)*
pp. 51 (the Maison Carrée), 66 (the amphitheater), 75 (the Pont du Gard), 77 (the walls)
The colony was founded in 28 B.C. at an *oppidum* (q.v.) near the

shrine of the Celtic water-god Nemausus. The *Via Domitia,* the highway from ARLES (twenty-eight kilometers to the southeast) into Spain (see AMPURIAS), served as the city's *decumanus* (q.v.). *Nemausus* was one of the last Latin colonies (compare VIENNE) (see *colonia).*

The colonists were mainly sailors and marines from the fleet of Octavian (Augustus from 27 B.C.) and perhaps also from that of Mark Anthony; they came from the Greek East but were rapidly Romanized. The local Celts, the Volcae Arecomici, were probably integrated with them immediately and also given Latin rights (q.v.; they had been under Roman rule for a century).

Nemausus had its own mint (for bronze coins) from 28 B.C.; this was a privilege. The city's symbol, a crocodile under a palm tree, appears on these coins; it recalls the colonists' military service in Egypt.

In 16 B.C., the walls were built at *Nemausus;* two gates remain, one of which is later. A large area was enclosed, nearly 225 hectares (or 550 acres); (see cities, comparison in area, below). In the same year, Agrippa, Augustus' son-in-law and right-hand man, donated the temple now known as the Maison Carrée to the city. (It now contains the city's Musée des Antiques; the Musée archéologique is in the former Collège de Jésuites.) The amphitheater here was designed by the architect of the one in ARLES; the two were of similar plan and underwent similar fates; they became fortified dwelling-places in the Middle Ages and thus survived.

The aqueduct of *Nemausus* had its source twenty-four air-kilometers to the north, but it covered twice the distance by land, followed by a secondary Roman road. The famous Pont du Gard, taking the aqueduct over the Gard River, stands about half-way along this route. The bridge was built of large unmortared stone blocks, whose quarry was about 600 meters away (? c. 20 B.C., but see Robertson, p. 341).

Nemausus obtained the title of Roman colony at an unknown date. In the second century, it may have replaced NARBONNE as the capital of *Gallia Narbonensis* (Stevens, *OCD).*

Continuously inhabited, NIMES is now the capital of Gard département.

Amy, R., and Gros, P. *La Maison Carrée de Nîmes. Gallia.* Suppl. 38. 2 vols. (1979)

Balty, J.-C. *Etudes sur la Maison Carrée de Nîmes.* Collection Latomus 47 (1960)

Bannert. "Volcae"

Bazin, H. *Nîmes gallo-romain*. Nîmes 1891

Besnier. *Lexique*. 520

Boëthius and Ward-Perkins. *ERA*. 347-348; plates 179 (the Pont du Gard), 184 (Maison Carrée), 185 (amphitheater)

Bon, A. "La fontaine de Nîmes," *Revue des études anciennes* 42 (1940): 580-592

Brogan. *Roman Gaul*. 92-94; 248 (index)

Brown. *RA*. 27, pl. 34 (Maison Carrée); 30-31, pl. 60 (Pont du Gard)

Charlesworth. *Trade-Routes*. 192-193

Chevallier. *ANRW*. II.1 pl. xlvi (plan); III.3 pp. 808-809 (index to figures and plates; long bibliography)

Clébert. *Provence antique*. 176-189

Crema. *Arch*. 663 (index)

Cunliffe. *Rome*. 134-135 (color photograph of the Pont du Gard)

Desjardins. *Géogr*. III pp. 420-422

Earl. *AA*. plates 41, 46

Espérandieu, E. *L'amphithéâtre de Nîmes*. Paris 1933

—— *La Maison Carrée à Nîmes*. Paris 1929

—— *Le Pont du Gard et l'aqueduc de Nîmes*. Paris 1926

Etienne, R. "La date de l'amphithéâtre de Nîmes," *Mélanges Piganiol*. Paris 1966. 985-1010

Finley. *Atlas*. 54-55 (P. MacKendrick)

Giard, J.-B. "Nîmes sous Auguste," *Schweizer Muenzblaetter* 21 (1971): 68-73, 1 pl. (on the coins)

Goudineau, C. "Le statut de Nîmes et des Volques Arécomiques," *Revue archéologique de Narbonnaise* 9 (1976): 105-114

Greece and Rome. 2nd ser. 2 (1955). plates 153, 154, 155b, 159a

Grenier. *Manuel*. I 314-323; II 680-683; III 143-156; 388-392 (Maison Carrée), 613-639 (amphitheaters at ARLES and NIMES compared), 988-989 *(circus* for chariot races); IV 88-101 (Pont du Gard); 493-506 (Sanctuary of Nemausus)

Kaehler. *Art of Rome*. 54-58

KP. IV (1972). 44-45 (M. Leglay)

Kraay, C. M. "The Chronology of Colonia Nemausus," *Numismatic Chronicle* (1955). 75 ff.

Lassale, V. *Nîmes*. Paris n.d.

Lavedan. *HU*. 493 (index)

Louis, M., and Blanchet, A. *CAGR*. VIII, *Gard* (1941)

MacKendrick. *RF*. 74-79; 257-258 (bibl.); 271 (index)

Naumann, R. *Der Quellbezirk von Nîmes*. Denkmaeler antiker Architektur 4 (Berlin/Leipzig 1937); (Sanctuary of Nemausus, and district)
OCD. 726 (C. E. Stevens)
PECS. 616-617 (P. Gros)
Peyre, R. *Nîmes, Arles, Orange*[4]. Paris 1923
(Charles-)Picard. *Roman Architecture*. 48-50, figs. 17, 21-23 (Pont du Gard); 98-99, figs. 75-78 (Maison Carrée); 103-104, figs. 64, 79-82 ("Temple of Diana" near the Sanctuary of Nemausus)
Piganiol. *HR*. 360 (bibl.)
Portal, F. *Nîmes, la Rome française, et le Gard pittoresque*. Lyons 1931
Radke. *Viae*. 43 (map), 265; figs. 5, 27
Robertson. *GRA*. 369 (bibl.); 401 (index)
Roux, J. C. *Nîmes*. Paris 1908
Stuebinger, O. (listed under ARLES)
Vittinghoff. *Roemische Kolonisation*. 100-101; 141 (index)
Ward-Perkins. *Cities*. 30 (Like LYONS, see p. 87 above, NIMES included a pre-Roman settlement.)
—— *RA*. 350 (index)
—— "Republic to Empire." 1 (the walls)
Woloch, G. M., ed. *The McGill University Collection of Greek and Roman Coins*. I. Amsterdam 1975. coins: Augustus, S6 to S8 (coins of *Nemausus*, 2 B.C.)

Norba (Italy)
p. 20, n. (hilltop orthogonal cities); (see Chapter I, n. 11 above on the city blocks)
   More than one ancient city was called Norba. The city in question was in *Latium*, forty-five kilometers southeast of Rome; it was built on the Lepini Mountains and overlooked the Pomptine Marshes. E. T. Salmon classifies it as one of the *Priscae Latinae Coloniae* (early Latin colonies, before 338 B.C.; see *colonia*, below); he dates its foundation to 492 B.C. (cf. Livy 2.34.6). It is the *earliest* city founded from Rome discussed in this book; *Ostia* (see OSTIA ANTICA) is the earliest Roman colony in our list. Ward-Perkins dates the orthogonal city of *Norba* to soon after 342 B.C. (*Cities* 27).
   Norba in *Latium* was destroyed by Sulla in 82 B.C. (Appian, *Civil Wars* 1. 94). The city's plan (walls, two acropoleis, and yet streets at right angles) has been studied by aerial photography.

Alfoeldi. *Early Rome*. 16, 395
Besnier. *Lexique*. 530
Boëthius. *Golden House*. 47, n. 42 (bibl.)
—— and Ward-Perkins. *ERA*. 613 (index); fig. 65 (plan of temple);
pl. 59 (gate)
Brown, F. E. *Cosa*. Ann Arbor 1980. fig. 11
—— *RA*. 16, pl. 11 (gate)
Castagnoli. *Orthogonal Town Planning*. 96; fig. 37 (air view)
Chevallier. *ANRW*. II.1 plate xxxvi (plan based on an aerial photo-
graph)
EB. XIX p. 738 (T. Ashby); (near the modern Norma)
Frothingham. *RCID*. 80-97
Grimal. *Search*. 131-133 (on the aerial photography); 255 (bibliog-
raphy)
KP. IV (1972). 156 (G. Radke)
Lugli. *Tecnica edilizia*. 137-142
Nissen. *IL*. II pp. 644-645
OCD. 737 (E. T. Salmon)
Ogilvie, R. M. *A Commentary on Livy, Books 1-5*. Oxford 1965. 322
(on 2.34.6)
PECS. 628-629 (L. Richardson, Jr.)
Salmon. *RC*. 29, 33, 34, 42, 51, 84; 46-47 (map of *Latium*); 110 (list
of the *Priscae Latinae Coloniae*); plate 27 (gate)
Schmiedt, G., and Castagnoli, F. "L'antica città di Norba," *L'Univ-
erso* 37 (1957): 125-148

Noviomagus meant New Market; see Celtic names of cities below.

Noviomagus Batavorum = Nijmegen, Gelderland, Netherlands (see
WROXETER, for the legionary camp)

Noviomagus Lexoviorum = Lisieux (see p. 68 above, on the demi-
amphitheater)

Noviomagus Regnensium = Chichester (mentioned under SILCHES-
TER)

Noviomagus ?Tricastinorum = + Nyons, listed under ORANGE

ORANGE (Vaucluse, France) = *Colonia Firma Iulia Secundorum Arausio, Gallia Narbonensis* (see colonies in *Gallia Narbonensis*) pp. 61 (the theater, *scaenae frons* extant); 81-82 (the arch, dated 27 B.C./A.D. 14)

+ Avignon (Vaucluse), + Nyons (Drôme)

Arausio began as a Celtic *oppidum*, named after the water-god of a local spring (Grenier; compare NIMES). The Roman colony was founded in 35/33 B.C. (Salmon's date; *Roman Colonization* 160) by Octavian for veterans of the Second Legion. The walls, of which there are only minor remains, enclosed an area of 70 hectares (173 acres), including the hill of St.-Eutrope in the southern quarter. Otherwise, the land is flat, for ORANGE is on the plain which follows the east bank of the Rhône. The site is five kilometers east of the Rhône and sixty-five kilometers north of ARLES on the Highway of Agrippa from LYONS, which formed the city's *cardo* (the *cardo* may still be seen in the present-day street plan of ORANGE). The road from the *decumanus* went northeast to VAISON-LA-ROMAINE.

A discovery of major importance from ORANGE is the land-register, which was engraved in marble and kept for all to see in the colony's basilica. The marble from the register found so far weighs about 500 kilograms (1,100 pounds; MacKendrick 104). Finds of the marble have been published since 1856 (Piganiol, *Documents*, p. 12). In 1904 a section relating to the "downtown" area was found (see finances, city, below), but most of the register turned up in 1949, when a cellar to contain the strongroom of a local bank was being dug out. The excavation of these fragments took place from 1949 to 1955 under the direction of Abbé Sautel, who was also responsible for the discovery of VAISON. A. Piganiol has interpreted the register and has found on it three units of centuriated land (in addition to the downtown area) or cadasters, which map out an area in the Rhône Valley sixty-three kilometers from north to southwest and thirty-one from east to west (see centuriation below). The date of these three cadasters is disputed, but it seems that the main part dates to A.D. 77, in the reign of Vespasian, who reaffirmed grants by Octavian. The land-register of ORANGE is fundamental for our understanding of centuriation. The stone fragments are in the Musée de la ville at ORANGE.

We learn from this register that land for the colony and its *territorium* was actually bought from the local Celtic tribe, the Tricastini. The least fertile lots on the register were assigned to them, and it seems that they made *Noviomagus* their new *oppidum*. +Nyons is sixteen kilometers north of VAISON and is a beautiful spot in the foothills of the Maritime Alps, where olive trees and truffles grow. The principal Roman structures visible today at ORANGE are the theater and an arch, filled with reliefs, about fifty meters beyond the site of the Roman north gate. MacKendrick dates the arch to A.D. 26 and compares it to that at Carpentras, twenty-three kilometers southeast of ORANGE (see Chapter III, n. 47 above). J. Formigé, in charge of the excavations at ORANGE for many years after 1912, found remains which complete a semicircular structure, directly to the west of the theater. This structure surrounded a temple, also excavated by Formigé. The shape of a stadium, in a "U" (for foot-races), may be outlined by drawing two parallel straight lines for 400 meters north of the semicircle (compare the Piazza Navona at Rome, which was the Stadium of Domitian; see Nash, *PD* II pp. 387-390). Formigé thought of the stadium at ORANGE as the center of the *"ludus"* or school mentioned in the land-register. Behind the stadium on the lower slopes of the hill of St.-Eutrope stood the colony's Capitol (q.v.); remains of the triple *cella* (q.v.) have been found.

The post-Roman history of ORANGE merits a brief summary. Sacked by the Alamans (q.v.) and Visigoths, the city became much later— in the thirteenth century—the center of a small principality, which William the Silent inherited in 1544. In the following year, William became the stathouder of Holland, where he led a successful revolt against the Spanish occupiers. The Dutch royal family is descended from him, and one of the squares of ORANGE today (1978) is named after Queen Juliana. Maurice of Nassau, William's son and successor, built a wall around ORANGE and in so doing destroyed most of the Roman remains left by the barbarians. The theater was immured in his wall, and the arch had previously been fortified. Louis XIV took over ORANGE in 1672, and, under his rule, the wall was razed.

The present city, smaller than *Arausio*, is still a center for agriculture, especially for early vegetables and wine-grapes. Rostovtzeff compared Roman ORANGE to VIENNE, the centers of well-cultivated rural districts, in contrast with the commercial Roman cities of ARLES and NARBONNE *(SEHRE* 218). The area which became the famous vineyard region of Châteauneuf-du-Pape was mapped on the most southerly of the three cadasters of the ancient land-register; it is 9 kilometers south of ORANGE and contains about 3,000 hectares (7,500 acres). The wine-district takes its name from a castle built there in the fourteenth century by the papal state of Avignon.

The medieval history of + Avignon is a direct contrast to that of neighboring ORANGE. The city is on the Rhône, twenty-eight kilometers south of ORANGE, and lay on the Highway of Agrippa to ARLES. Gallo-Roman *Avenio* lies buried beneath the famed medieval buildings of + Avignon. Both Avignon and Carpentras were temporal possessions of the popes from the fourteenth century to the French Revolution (1791). Today, Avignon is the capital of the département of Vaucluse and its chief commercial center.

ORANGE:

Amy, R. et al. *L'arc d'Orange*. *Gallia*. Suppl. 15. Paris 1962
Besnier. *Lexique*. 71
Boëthius and Ward-Perkins. *ERA*. pl. 188 (the arch)
Brogan. *Roman Gaul*. 99-100
Châtelain, L. *Les monuments romains d'Orange*. Bibliothèque de l'Ecole des Hautes Etudes, Sciences historiques et philologiques 170. Paris 1908
Chevallier. *ANRW*. II.1 plate xxxix (map of the cadasters of Rhône Valley, with ORANGE, + Avignon, Cavaillon and ST.-REMY-DE-PROVENCE); II.3 pp. 796 (bibliography on the centuriation); 810 (list of figures and plates, bibl.)
Clavel and Lévêque. *Villes*. 155-160 (the arch)
Clébert. *Provence antique*. 222-229
Crema. *Arch*. 663 (index)
Desjardins. *Géogr*. III p. 426
Dilke, O.A.W. *The Roman Land Surveyors*. Newton Abbot, Devon, 1971. 159-177
—— *ANRW*. II.1 p. 583 (bibl. on centuriation)
Earl. *AA*. plate 22 (the theater)
Finley. *Atlas*. 56-57 (P. MacKendrick)
Formigé, J. "Le prétendu Cirque d'Orange," *Mémoires présentés par divers savants à l'Académie des inscriptions et belles-lettres* 13 (1917): 201-225 (on the stadium; it was not a *circus* for chariot races, like the *Circus Maximus* at Rome; on the latter, see Nash, *PD* I pp. 236-240)
—— "Remarques sur les dates de construction des théâtres d'Arles, d'Orange et de Vienne," *Revue archéologique* 29/30 (publ. 1949): 382-386
—— "Théâtre d'Orange (Vaucluse)," *Mémoires présentés...à l'Académie des inscriptions...* 13 (1933): 697-712
Frank. *ESAR*. III p. 512, n. 9 (A. Grenier on the arch)

Greece and Rome. 2nd ser. 2 (1955). plates 156, 158a, 160b

Grenier. *Manuel*. I 296 (the arch); III 172-193 (the temple inside the semicircle of the stadium); 398-402; 754-765 (the theater); 646 (the amphitheater—nothing remains)

Gutkind. *IHCD*. V (1970). 229-231; 477 (bibl.)

Haverfield. *Town Planning*. 107-108

KP. I (1964). 489 (P. Wuilleumier)

Lavedan. *HU*. 493 (index)

MacKendrick. *RF*. 99-105

OCD. 92 (A. L. F. Rivet)

PECS. 83-84 (C. Goudineau)

Pelletier, A. "La superficie des exploitations agraires sur le cadastre d'Orange," *Latomus* 35 (1976): 582-585

Peyre, R. *Nîmes, Arles, Orange*[4]. Paris 1923

Piganiol, A. *Les documents cadastraux de la colonie romaine d'Orange*. *Gallia*. Suppl. 16 (1962)

—— "L'inscription de l'arc de triomphe d'Orange," *Comptes rendus de l'Académie des inscriptions et belles-lettres* (1954): 20-21 = *Scripta Varia*, Collection Latomus 133, vol. III. Brussels 1973. 40-41 (He dates the arch c. 25 B.C. and the inscription A.D. 26/27.)

Richmond, I. A. "Commemorative Arches and City Gates in the Augustan Age," *Journal of Roman Studies* 23 (1933): 149-174

—— and Stevens, C. E. "The Land-Register of *Arausio*," *Journal of Roman Studies* 32 (1942): 65-77

Robertson. *GRA*. 279-282 (theater); 293-294 (arch)

Salmon. *RC*. plate 12 (part of the land-register)

Sautel, J. *CAGR*. VII, *Vaucluse* (1939)

Ward-Perkins. *Cities*. 35, 39, 119-120; figs. 47-48 (on the land-register, with a short explanation of how to read it)

—— "ERTI." 150-151

Wheeler. *RAA*. 35 (the *cardo*); 116 (theater); 156 (arch)

+ Avignon:

Brun, R. *Avignon au temps des papes*. Paris 1928

Chevallier. *ANRW*. II.3 p. 804 (bibl.)

Desjardins. *Géogr*. III pp. 425-426

EB. III pp. 63-64

Gagnière, S. *Le Palais des Papes*. ECNMHS. Paris n.d.

Gagnière, S., and Granier, J. *Avignon de la Préhistoire à la Papauté*. Avignon 1970

Girard, J. *Avignon*. Paris

Gutkind. *IHCD*. V (1970). 232-235; 475 (bibl.)
Labande, L. H. *Le Palais des Papes et les monuments d'Avignon au 14e siècle*. 2 vols. Marseilles 1925
Mommsen. *Provinces*. Chapter III (Latin colony)

+ Nyons:
Nyons should be distinguished from Nyon (= *Noviodunum*) Vaud, Switzerland.

Piganiol. *Documents*. 30-31 (He believes that the Tricastini received Latin rights [q.v.] from Augustus.)
Sautel, J. *CAGR*. XI, *Drôme* (1957). 25

Orvieto (modern Umbria, Italy): see *Volsinii*

OSTIA ANTICA (Latium, Italy) = *Ostia*, ancient region of *Latium, Italia*
pp. 27 (orthogonally planned colony founded early fourth century B.C.); 33 *(Via Ostiensis*, the highway from Rome); 50 (the Capitol)
Twenty-five kilometers southwest of Rome, the site was at the mouth of the Tiber River, on the left bank. Because of silting, the modern beach, Ostia Lido, is now five kilometers farther west. Like *Antium* (Anzio, 338 B.C.) and *Tarracina* (Terracina, 329 B.C.), *Ostia* (c. 338 B.C.) was one of the very earliest citizen *coloniae* (q.v.; Salmon's dates, pp. 161-162). These three were *coloniae maritimae*, guarding the coast of *Latium*. In its earliest form, *Ostia* was essentially a military camp of a little more than five acres (two hectares; ibid. 71). Besides being responsible for defense, the citizen-soldiers of *Ostia* had to collect harbor taxes and prevent smuggling.
During the wars with CARTHAGE (264-146 B.C.), *Ostia* was a major naval base. After the defeat of Carthage as well as the Mediterranean pirates (67 B.C.), *Ostia* prospered and grew as the seaport of Rome. Goods—most notably grain and wine—were transferred onto barges to be shipped upriver. Protection of the harbor had become the responsibility of the Roman navy. New walls built around the colony early in the first century B.C. enclosed sixty-four hectares (Meiggs in *PECS*). The *cardo* and *decumanus* of the camp both remained important as the city expanded (Robertson 192). Only the north and east sections of the enlarged city were orthogonal (Ward-Perkins, *Cities* 122).
Under the Emperor Claudius (A.D. 41-54), a new harbor, *Portus*,

was built across the Tiber three kilometers to the north; this was extended and improved by Trajan (98-117). The district was considered by the ancient Romans to be part of the city of *Ostia*. It was purchased from the Pope by the aristocratic Torlonia family in 1856 and remains largely unexcavated (Casson). During the Empire, *Ostia* was one of its three main ports, with CARTHAGE and Alexandria. Shipping routes to *Ostia* ran from Gaul, North Africa, Spain, and the East (Rougé, *Recherches* 124-126). People moved there for work, living in *insulae* or apartment blocks inside the town walls (Packer in *MAAR;* see city blocks below). This area was excavated mainly from 1938 to 1942, and its population has been estimated at from 20,000 (McKay, *Houses* 98-99) to 58,000 (Meiggs; see Duncan-Jones, *ERE* 276). *Ostia's* decline began late in the third century A.D., when an emperor no longer resided at Rome, and it was finally abandoned in the ninth, when malaria and pirates' attacks made it uninhabitable. Because the site was deserted, the daily life of its ancient residents may be surmised much better at *Ostia* than at Rome. No amphitheater has as yet been found at *Ostia*, but there are several baths, various temples, and a forum; there is an excellent site-museum. The ruins, in fact, rival those at *Pompeii*. Outstanding at OSTIA ANTICA is the so-called Piazzale delle Corporazioni (first and second centuries A.D.), behind the (relatively small) theater; over sixty shipping companies from around the Mediterranean (see ARLES, NARBONNE, *Sabratha)* had offices there.

Ashby. *Rom. Cam.* 214-219
Bagnani. *Rom. Cam.* 3-9
Becatti, G. *Case ostiensi del tardo impero.* Rome 1949 (Late Roman houses)
Besnier. *Lexique.* 556-557
Blue Guide, Rome. 310-325
Boëthius. *Golden House.* fig. 14 (plan)
—— "RGTA." 6 and fig. 3 (nonorthogonal sections); 10 *(insulae)*
—— and Ward-Perkins. *ERA.* 148-151; 279-289; 334-336; plates 93 (republican temple); 150-151 (houses), 152 (Grain Depot of Epagathus); 153 *(decumanus),* 154 (shops)
Bradford. *Ancient Landscapes.* 237-256; plates 60-61 (on Portus)
Calza, G. *Ostia: Historical Guide to the Monuments* (transl. from the Italian). Milan/Rome n.d.
—— and Becatti, G. *Ostia⁴.* Rome 1957
—— Becatti, G. et al. *Scavi di Ostia.* I-VIII. Rome 1953-1977

Calza, R., and Nash, E. *Ostia*. Florence 1959 (in Italian; it has 163 illustrations)
Carcopino. *Daily Life*. 312 (bibl.), 315, n. 2 (bibl. note by H. T. Rowell on the *duoviri* and the *Fasti*, A.D. 108-113); 356 (index)
Carcopino, J. *Virgile et les origines d'Ostie*. Bibliothèque des Ecoles françaises d'Athènes et de Rome 116. Paris 1919; rpt. 1968
Casson, L. "Ancient Port to Modern Zoo," *Archaeology* 31 (1978): 44-51
—— "Harbour and River Boats of Ancient Rome," *Journal of Roman Studies* 55 (1965): 31-39
Castagnoli. *Orthogonal Town Planning*. 100; fig. 40
Charlesworth. *Trade-Routes*. 293 (index)
Chevallier. *ANRW*. II.1 p. 695 (bibl.)
Christ. *Bibl*. 93, 292 (cults)
Crema. *Arch*. 663 (index)
Dudley. *RS*. ills. 25 (air view), 26-28 (reconstructions)
Earl. *AA*. plates 15-16 (views of the *decumanus maximus*); 31 (theater)
Enciclopedia dell'arte antica, classica e orientale. V (1963). 782-796 (G. Becatti)
Février, P.-A. "Ostia et Porto à la fin de l'Antiquité: topographie religieuse et vie sociale," *Mélanges...Ecole française de Rome* 70 (1958): 295-330
Finley. *Atlas*. 111-113 (G. D. B. Jones)
Frank. *ESAR*. V pp. 236-252
Frank, T. "The People of Ostia," *Classical Journal* 29 (1934): 481-493
Grimal. *Civ. Rome*. 482 (the site and its ruins)
—— *Rome*. 210-217
—— *Search*. 119-127
*Guida d'Italia del Touring Club Italiano, Roma e Dintorni*⁶. Milan 1962. 573-582
Gutkind. *IHCD*. IV (1969). 188-191
Hammond. *The City*. 231, 269, 293-294
Helbig, W. *Fuehrer durch die oeffentlichen Sammlungen klassischer Altertuemer in Rom*⁴. IV. Tuebingen 1972. 3-151 (the Museo Ostiense)
Jones, H. Stuart. *Companion*. 157-158; 458 (index)
KP. IV (1972). 374 (G. Radke); (with bibl.)
Lavedan. *HU*. 368-369 (maps)
Lugli, G., and Filibeck, G. *Il Porto di Roma imperiale e l'Agro portuense*. Rome 1935

MacDonald. *Arch*. (bibl. on 193)
MacKendrick. *Mute Stones*. 251-265; 358 (bibl.)
McKay. *Houses*. 77-79; 95-99; 262 (bibl.); plates 30-36
McKay, A. G. *Vergil's Italy*. Greenwich, Conn., 1970. 152; plate 34
*Meiggs, R. *Roman Ostia²*. Oxford 1974
Morris. *Urban Form*. 54, fig. 3.20
Nissen. *IL*. II pp. 566-571
OCD. 760-762 (R. Meiggs)
Packer, J. E. "Housing and Population in Imperial Ostia and Rome,"
Journal of Roman Studies 57 (1967): 80-95
——— "The Insulae of Imperial Ostia," *Memoirs of the American
Academy in Rome* 31 (1971)
Paget. *Central Italy*. 96-106
Paschetto, L. *Ostia: Colonia romana*. Rome 1912
Pasini, F. *Ostia Antica: Insule e classi sociali*. Rome 1978
PECS. 658-661 (R. Meiggs)
(Charles-)Picard. *Roman Architecture*. 52-53 (the Grain Depot of
Epagathus, plan on 53, plates 32-36); 52 (plans of Trajan's harbor
and an *insula*)
Piganiol. *HR*. 354, 591, 629 (bibl.)
Piganiol, A. "Les Fastes d'Ostie," *Bulletin de la Société nationale des
antiquaires de France* (1938): 148-153 = *Scripta Varia*, Collection
Latomus 133, vol. III. Brussels 1973. 121-124 (the *duoviri* [q.v.]
A.D. 115-151)
Pohl, I. "Piazzale delle Corporazioni ad Ostia . . .," *Mélanges . . .
de l'Ecole française de Rome* 90 (Paris 1978): 331-355
RE. XVIII.2 (1942). 1654-1664 (G. Calza)
Rickman, G. E. *Roman Granaries and Store Buildings*. Cambridge
1971
Robertson. *GRA*. 369 (bibl.); 402 (index)
Rostovtzeff. *SEHRE*. 159 and 607, n. 22 (on the Piazzale delle Cor-
porazioni); 568, n. 36 (bibl.); 800 (index)
Salmon. *RC*. 53, 71, 75; plates 41-43
Schaal, H. *Ostia*. Bremen 1957
(Floriani-)Squarciapino, M. *Bolletino d'Arte del Ministero della pub-
blica instruzione* 46 (1961): 326-337 (synagogue)
Starr, C. G. *The Roman Imperial Navy 31 B.C.-A.D. 324*. 2nd ed.
Cambridge 1960. 17-18; 27, n. 22 (bibliography)
Stier. *Atlas*. 32 (plan)
Testaguzza, O. "The Port of Rome," *Archaeology* 17 (1964): 173-179
——— *Portus*. Rome 1970

Van Buren. *Bibl.* 31

Vitelli, G. "Grain Storage and Urban Growth in Imperial Ostia: A
  Quantitative Study," *World Archaeology* 12.1 (1980): 54-68 (ref.
  supplied by L. Fox)

Ward-Perkins. *Cities.* 28, 32, 34-36, 122; figs. 49-51, 80, 83, 85

—— *RA.* plates 198-218

Wheeler. *RAA.* 31-32, 34-42, 131-134; ills. 11, 12, 14, 15, 17-21,
  110-112, 114-117

Wilson, F. H. "Studies in the Social and Economic History of Ostia,"
  Papers of the British School at Rome 13 (1935): 41-68; 14 (1938):
  152-163

OSUNA (province of Sevilla, Spain) = *Colonia Iulia Genetiva Urbanorum Urso, Baetica*

pp. 50 (the charter and the Capitol); 57 (the charter and the theater)

   In historical times, settlement began on this site, about 100 kilometers east of Seville, with a native *oppidum.* A Roman colony was
founded there in 44 B.C., at the request of Julius Caesar, but after
his assassination in that year (Pliny, *Natural History* 3.12). According to Caesar's plan, the colony was settled by the urban poor of
Rome (the *Urbani*); similar colonies were founded at Corinth in
Greece and CARTHAGE in the same year.

   OSUNA today is a town of over 20,000 people. The Roman predecessor, *Urso,* is best known for its colonial charter, the only one of
which has come down to us *(CIL* II, Suppl., no. 5439 = *CIL* I² no.
594). The existence of the colony's Capitol and the theater are im-
plied by this charter, and the theater has been found. Four bronze
tablets, found at OSUNA in 1870 and 1873, contain only part of the
text, which dates from A.D. 69/96 and is, in general, a faithful copy
of the original law of 44 B.C. (Salmon, Hardy).

   The Emperor Vespasian (69-79) bestowed Latin rights on all three
provinces in *Hispania* (q.v.), and we also have charters of two new
municipia which resulted from Vespasian's action, confirmed by his
sons Titus (79-81) and Domitian (81-96): Salpensa and Málaga. These
charters are also incomplete and on bronze tablets, and all three are
in the Museo Arqueológico Nacional at Madrid.

   In view of the light which the charter of *Urso* casts on the government of a Roman city, selections from the translated text are printed
here, with the permission of the Columbia University Press, which
holds the copyright to the work by Lewis and Reinhold cited in the

bibliography below. G. M. Woloch has expanded some of their notes, has added other notes and some q.v. references, and has changed references to conform with the present book.

THE CHARTER OF THE COLONY GENETIVA JULIA

(URSO)

Adapted from E. G. Hardy, Three Spanish Charters

[The beginning of the charter is lost as far as clause LX.]

LXI. [This clause deals with legal procedures in the execution of judgments against debtors.]

LXII. In respect to all *duoviri* (q.v.), each *duovir* shall have the right and power to employ two lictors, one attendant, two clerks, two apparitors, a secretary, a herald, a soothsayer, and a flute player.[a]

In respect to the aediles (q.v.) in the said colony, each aedile shall have the right and power to employ one clerk, four public slaves in girded aprons,[b] a herald, a soothsayer and a flute player. In this number they shall employ persons who are colonists of the said colony. The said *duoviri* and the said aediles, so long as they shall hold their magistracy, shall have the right and power to use the *toga praetexta*,[c] wax torches, and wax tapers.

In respect to the said clerks, lictors, attendants, apparitors, flute players, soothsayers, and heralds employed by each of the same, all the said persons, during the year in which they shall perform such services, shall have exemption from military service. And no person shall, during the year in which they perform such services for magistrates, make any such person a soldier against his will, or order him to be so made, or use compulsion against him, or administer the oath, or order such oath to be administered, or swear in such person

[a] The lictors carried *fasces*, the magistrate's symbol of power (cf. *Vetulonia* below). Apparitor is the translation of the Latin word *viator*, summoner. The heralds were public criers. The flute player accompanied the magistrate on all public occasions, including sacrifices.

[b] The dress of slaves. Slaves were assigned to the aediles because of duties connected with the care of streets, extinguishing fires, etc.

[c] A toga bordered with a band of purple.

or order such person to be sworn in with the preliminary oath, except on the occasion of sudden military alarms in Italy or Gaul. The following shall be the rate of pay for such persons as perform services for the *duoviri:* for each clerk 1,200 sesterces;[d] for each attendant 700; for each lictor 600; for each apparitor 400; for each secretary 300; for each soothsayer 500; for a herald 300. For persons serving the aediles the pay shall be: for each clerk 800 sesterces; for each soothsayer 500; for each flute player 300; and for each herald 300. And the aforesaid sums it shall be lawful for the said persons to receive without risk of personal penalty.

LXIII. [This clause deals with the prorating of pay for the staff of the *duoviri* who serve until the end of the year 44 B.C.]

LXIV. All *duoviri* holding office after the establishment of the colony shall, within the ten days next following the commencement of their magistracy, bring before the decurions (q.v.) for decision, when not less than two thirds shall be present, the question as to the dates and number of the festal days, the sacrifices to be publicly performed, and the persons to perform such sacrifices. Whatever a majority of the decurions present at such meeting shall have decreed or determined concerning the said matters shall be lawful and valid, and such sacrifices and such festal days shall be observed in the said colony.

LXV. [This clause allocates to sacrificial purposes all fines levied in connection with the collection of municipal taxes.]

LXVI. In respect to pontiffs and augurs[e] appointed from the Colonia Genetiva by Gaius (Julius) Caesar or the person who by his command shall establish the colony, such persons shall be pontiffs and augurs of the Colonia Genetiva Julia, and shall be members of the colleges of pontiffs and augurs within the said colony with all the rights and privileges appertaining to pontiffs and augurs in every colony. And the said pontiffs and augurs who shall be members of the several colleges, and also their children, shall have exemption from military service and compulsory public services solemnly guaranteed, in such wise as a pontiff in Rome has or shall have the same, and all their military service shall be accounted as discharged. Respecting the auspices (q.v.) and matters appertaining to the same, jurisdiction and adjudication shall belong to the augurs. And the said pontiffs and augurs shall have the right and power to use the *toga*

---

[d]Under the Roman Empire, a brass coin, weighing about 25 grams. Accounts were often stated in sesterces.

[e]Colonies copied Rome in establishing these two colleges of priests.

praetexta at all games publicly celebrated by magistrates, and at public sacrifices of the Colonia Genetiva Julia performed by themselves, and the said pontiffs and augurs shall have the right and power to sit among the decurions to witness the games and the gladiatorial combats.

LXVII-LXVIII. [These clauses deal with the election of pontiffs and augurs.]

LXIX. [This clause deals with the payment of moneys due contractors providing the requisites for religious ceremonies.]

LXX. All *duoviri*, except those first appointed after this law, shall during their magistracy at the discretion of the decurions celebrate a gladiatorial show or dramatic spectacles in honor of Jupiter, Juno, Minerva,[f] and the gods and goddesses, as far as possible during four days, for the greater part of each day; and on the said spectacles and the said shows each of the said persons shall expend of his own money not less than 2,000 sesterces, and out of the public money it shall be lawful for each several *duovir* to appropriate and expend a sum not exceeding 2,000 sesterces, and it shall be lawful for the said persons so to do without risk of personal penalty. Always provided that no person shall appropriate or make assignment of any portion of the money which in accordance with this charter shall be properly given or assigned for those religious ceremonies which are publicly performed in the colony or in any other place.

LXXI. [On games to be given by the aediles of the colony.]

LXXII. [On the expenditure of moneys collected for religious purposes.]

LXXIII. No person shall, within the boundaries of the town or colony, within the area marked round by the plow,[g] introduce a dead person, or bury or cremate the same therein, nor build therein a monument to a deceased person. Any person acting in contravention of this shall be condemned to pay to the colonists of the Colonia Genetiva Julia 5,000 sesterces, and may be sued or prosecuted at will by any person for that amount. Any monument so built a *duovir* or aedile shall cause to be demolished, and if, in contravention of this law, a dead person has been introduced and placed therein, they shall make the proper expiation.

LXXIV. [This clause forbids the building of new crematories within one half mile of the town.]

LXXV. No person shall unroof or demolish or dismantle any build-

---

[f] The Capitoline Triad (see Capitol below).

[g] The *pomerium* is meant (q.v.).

ing in the town of the Colonia Julia, unless he shall have furnished sureties, at the discretion of the *duoviri*, that he has the intention of rebuilding the same, or unless the decurions have allowed such act by decree, provided that not less than fifty shall be present when the said matter is discussed. Any person acting in contravention of this shall be condemned to pay to the colonists of the Colonia Genetiva Julia a sum of money equal to the value of the said building, and may, in accordance with this charter, be sued or prosecuted at will by any person for that amount.

LXXVI. [Restrictions on the size of pottery and tile works in the town.]

LXXVII. If any *duovir* or aedile shall desire in the public interest to make, lay down, alter, build, or pave any streets, gutters, or sewers within the boundaries belonging to the Colonia Julia, it shall be lawful for the said persons to do the same, provided that no injury be done to private persons.

LXXVIII. Respecting public roads and footpaths which were within the boundaries assigned to the colony, all such thoroughfares, roads, and footpaths which exist or shall exist or have existed in the said territories, shall be public property.

LXXIX. Respecting all rivers, streams, fountains, lakes, springs, ponds, or marshes within the territory divided among the colonists of this colony, the holders and possessors of such land shall have the same right of access, carriage and drawing of water in respect to the said streams, fountains, lakes, springs, ponds, and marshes, as belonged to former holders and possessors. In like manner, the persons who own or possess or shall own or possess the said land shall have legal right of way to the said waters.

LXXX. Whatever public business in the colony is given to any person by decree of the decurions, the person to whom such business shall be given shall produce and render an account of the said matter to the decurions in good faith as far as possible within the 150 days next following his completion of the said business or his ceasing to carry it on.

LXXXI. In respect to all clerks of the *duoviri* and aediles of the Colonia Julia to be employed in making entry of public money and in writing the accounts of the colonists, every *duovir* and every aedile shall, before the said clerks make up or handle public records, administer to each publicly and openly, in the daytime, on a market day in the Forum, an oath by Jupiter and the *Penates*[h] that they will

---

[h]Gods who protected state property.

conscientiously and in good faith guard the public money of the said colony and keep true accounts, and that they will not knowingly and with malice aforethought defraud the colony by false entries. As each clerk shall so take the oath, the said magistrate shall cause him to be entered in the public records. Clerks failing to take such oath shall not make up the public accounts, nor shall they receive the money or the pay due attendants for such service. Magistrates failing to administer such oath shall be fined 5,000 sesterces, and may be sued or prosecuted for that amount by any person at will in accordance with this charter.

LXXXII. In respect to all lands or woods or buildings granted or assigned to the colonists of the Colonia Genetiva Julia for public use, no person shall sell the said lands or woods, or lease the same for a longer period than five years, or bring a proposal before the decurions or carry a decree of the decurions whereby the said lands and woods shall be sold or leased otherwise than as aforesaid. Nor, in case they are sold, shall they thereby cease to be the property of the Colonia Genetiva Julia. And any person using the produce of the same on the ground of such purchase shall be condemned to pay to the colonists of the said colony 100 sesterces for every *iugerum*[i] for each year of use, and may be sued or prosecuted by any person at will for that amount in accordance with this charter.

[The remainder of this section is lost.]

XCI. Respecting any person in accordance with this charter appointed or elected *decurio*, augur, or pontiff in the Colonia Genetiva Julia, whatsoever *decurio*, augur, or pontiff of the said colony shall fail within the next five years to possess in the colony or town, or within a mile of the town, a domicile whence a sufficient pledge can be taken,[j] the same shall cease to be an augur, pontiff, or *decurio* in the said colony; and the *duoviri* in the said colony shall conscientiously cause the names of such persons to be struck from the public lists of decurions and priests; and it shall be lawful for the said *duoviri* so to do without risk of personal penalty.

XCII. [This clause concerns public embassies dispatched by the colony.]

XCIII. No *duovir* appointed or elected after the establishment of the colony, and no prefect left in charge by a *duovir* in accordance with the charter of the colony, shall, concerning public ground or for

---

[i]A rectangle 240 Roman feet long and 120 Roman feet wide (cf. measurements of distance, Roman, below).

[j]That is, within five years after appointment.

public ground, receive or accept from a contractor or leaseholder or surety any gift or present or remuneration or any other favor; nor shall he cause any such favor to be bestowed upon himself or upon any member of his family. Any person acting in contravention of this shall be condemned to pay to the colonists of the Colonia Genetiva Julia 20,000 sesterces, and may be sued or prosecuted by any person at will for that amount.

XCIV. [This clause limits legal jurisdiction to authorized officials.]

XCV. [Legal procedures in a case involving the collection of fines due to the colony.]

XCVI. [Decurions may vote a public investigation of the administration at any time.]

XCVII. [Limitations on the selection of patrons of the colony by decree of the decurions.]

XCVIII. In the case of any compulsory public service[k] decreed by the decurions of the said colony, a majority of the decurions being present when the said matter is discussed, it shall be lawful for such work to be carried out, provided that in any one year not more than five days' work be decreed for each adult male, nor more than three days' work for each yoke of draught animals. The said public work shall by decree of the decurions be superintended by the incumbent aediles. They shall see that the work is carried out in accordance with the decree of the decurions, provided that no labor be required, without his own consent, from any person less than fourteen or more than sixty years of age. Persons possessing a domicile or land in the said colony, or within the boundaries of the said colony, who are not colonists of the said colony shall be liable to the same amount of labor as a colonist.

XCIX. Respecting any public aqueducts brought into the town of the Colonia Genetiva the incumbent *duoviri* shall make proposal to the decurions, when two thirds of the same are present, as to the lands through which an aqueduct may lawfully be brought. Whatever lands a majority of the decurions then present shall have determined upon, provided that no water be brought through any building not constructed for that purpose, it shall be lawful and right to bring an aqueduct through the said lands, and no person shall do aught to prevent an aqueduct from being so brought.

C. [Concerns the granting by the decurions of permission to private individuals to use public water overflowing from a reservoir.]

---

[k]Such as fortification work and, most commonly, road construction and repair.

CI. [Disqualified persons not to be entered in elections to magistracies.]

CII. [On the amount of time for pleading allotted to accusers and defendants in trials.]

CIII. Whenever a majority of the decurions present at a meeting shall have decreed to call out armed men for the purpose of defending the territories of the colony, it shall be lawful, without risk of personal penalty, for the responsible *duovir* or prefect invested with judicial power in such manner to call out under arms colonists, resident aliens, and attributed (q.v.) persons. And the said *duovir* or any person placed in command of such armed forces by the *duovir* shall have the same authority and the same power of punishment as belongs to a military tribune of the Roman people in an army of the Roman people; and he shall lawfully and properly exercise such authority and power without risk of personal penalty, provided that this is done in accordance with the decree of a majority of the decurions present at the said meeting.

CIV. [Forbids the blocking up of boundary roads, crossroads, and drainage ditches.]

CV. [Expulsion of disqualified decurions from the local senate.]

CVI. [Forbids unlawful assembly.]

CVII-CXXII. [This section is lost.]

CXXIII and CXXIV. [On procedures connected with accusations of conduct unbecoming a *decurio*.]

CXXV and CXXVI. [On persons permitted to sit in the place assigned to decurions for viewing games in the circus; on places assigned to decurions at theatrical performances.]

CXXVII. Respecting any dramatic spectacles in the Colonia Genetiva Julia, no person shall sit in the orchestra to view the performance, save a magistrate or promagistrate of the Roman people, or a Roman official invested with legal jurisdiction, or one who is or has been a senator of the Roman people, or the sons of such senator, or the *praefectus fabrum*[1] of the magistrate or promagistrate governing the province of Farther Spain or Baetica, or those persons who are or shall be allowed by this law to sit in the place assigned to the decurions. Nor shall any person, acting conscientiously and in good faith, introduce into the said place or allow to sit therein any other persons.

---

[1] This high-ranking former army officer was appointed by the governor to supervise skilled workmen and engineers. Before Augustus' division of *Hispania* (q.v.), Farther Spain included *Lusitania* and *Baetica*.

CXXVIII. [On the annual appointment by the magistrates of officers in charge of shrines and of the conduct of religious services.]

CXXIX. All *duoviri*, aediles, and prefects of the Colonia Genetiva Julia, and likewise all decurions of the said colony, shall diligently and in good faith observe and obey the decrees of the decurions,[m] and they shall use their diligence to do and perform, conscientiously and in good faith, all things whatsoever it shall be proper for the said persons respectively to do or perform in accordance with the decree of the decurions. Any person failing so to act, or knowingly and with malice aforethought acting in contravention of this, shall for every such act or omission be condemned to pay to the colonists of the Colonia Genetiva Julia 10,000 sesterces, and may be sued or prosecuted for that amount in accordance with this charter through *recuperatores*[n] before a *duovir* or prefect by any person at will.

CXXX. [Additional severe restrictions on the adoption of Roman senators as patrons of the colony.]

CXXXI. [Severe restrictions on the adoption of Roman senators as honorary public guests *(hospites)* of the colony.]

CXXXII. No person in the Colonia Genetiva Julia who is a candidate for election to any magistracy within the said colony shall, after the promulgation of this charter, with a view to seeking such magistracy, or during the year in which he shall be a candidate or shall stand for or intend to stand for such magistracy, knowingly and with malice aforethought provide entertainments, or invite any person to dinner, or hold or provide a banquet, or knowingly and with malice aforethought cause another person to hold a banquet or invite any person to dinner with a view to his candidature, except that the said candidate himself who shall be seeking a magistracy may, if he so desire, in good faith invite during the said year daily any persons not exceeding nine.[o] No candidate seeking office shall knowingly and with malice aforethought give or make largess of any gift or present or any other thing with a view to his candidature. Nor shall any person, with a view to the candidature of another, provide entertainments, or invite any person to dinner, or hold a banquet, or knowingly and with malice aforethought give or make largess of any gift or present or any other thing. Any person acting in contravention of

---

[m]Note the continuation by Caesar of the Roman policy, traditional both in Italy and in the provinces, of vesting supreme power in the town council, which was made up of the local aristocracy.

[n]A special jury.

[o]The usual number of guests at the formal Roman *cena*, "dinner."

this shall be condemned to pay to the colonists of the Colonia Genetiva Julia 5,000 sesterces, and may be sued or prosecuted in accordance with this charter for that amount through *recuperatores* before a *duovir* or prefect by any person at will.

CXXXIII. Respecting all persons who, in accordance with this charter, are or shall be colonists of the Colonia Genetiva Julia, the wives of all such persons who are within the colony in accordance with this charter shall obey the laws of the Colonia Genetiva Julia and of their husbands, and shall in good faith enjoy, in accordance with this charter, all such rights as are specified in this charter.

CXXXIV. No *duovir* or aedile or prefect of the Colonia Genetiva shall after the promulgation of this charter make proposal to the decurions of the said colony, or consult the same, or carry a decree of the decurions, or enter such a decree, or order such a decree to be entered in the public records, and no *decurio* when such matter is discussed among the decurions shall declare his vote, or frame a decree of the decurions, or enter such a decree, or cause such a decree to be entered in the public records, whereby any public money or anything else is given or granted to any person as a reward for holding office, or for giving or promising a gladiatorial show, or for the sake of giving or setting up a statue. . . . [The rest is lost.]

OSUNA:
Besnier. *Lexique*. 799
Blue Guide, Spain. 482-483
Castillo García, C. "Staedte und Personen der Baetica," *ANRW*. II.3 (1975). 651-654 (bibl.)
KP. V (1975). 1072 (E. Olshausen)
Menéndez Pidal, R., ed. *Historia de España*. II³. Madrid 1962. 844, 850 (index)
OCD. 1103-1104 (J. J. Van Nostrand and M. I. Henderson)
PECS. 948-949 (C. Fernández-Chicarro)
Piganiol. *HR*. 206 (bibl.)
RE. IXA.1 (1961). 1064-1066 (R. Grosse)
Salmon. *RC*. 135; plate 11 (the charter)
Scullard, H. H. *Scipio Africanus: Soldier and Politician*. Ithaca, N.Y., 1970. 104-105; 106-107 (map)
Sutherland, C. H. V. *The Romans in Spain*. . . . London 1939. 127-128 (on the charter)
Thouvenot. *Essai*. 190, 298, 367; 438-440 (theater); 732 (index)
Vittinghoff. *Roemische Kolonisation*. 59, n. 2 (*Urbanorum* in the colony's name is correct; it is not *Ursaonum*); 74

Text of the OSUNA charter:

Abbott and Johnson. *Municipal Administration*. no. 26, pp. 300-317 (Latin text and discussion)

CAH. IX² (1951). 708-710 (commentary by F. E. Adcock); 956-957 (bibl.)

d'Ors, A. *Epigrafía jurídica de la España romana*. Madrid 1953. 167-280

Hardy, E. G. *Three Spanish Charters and Other Documents*, in *Roman Laws and Charters*. Oxford 1912. 7-60 (translation and valuable commentary)

Jones. *HR*. I pp. 314-330 (translation)

Lewis, N., and Reinhold, M. *Roman Civilization, Sourcebook I: The Republic*. New York 1966. 420-428 (translation reprinted here); also see p. 533 (bibl.)

Menéndez Pidal. between pp. 416 and 417 (Latin text, drawing of Latin text and photograph); discussion on 407-408; bibl. on 817-818

Oersted, P. *Vespasian og Spanien*. Copenhagen 1977

Riccobono. *FIRA²*. I no. 21

On new fragments, found in 1941, see de Ruggiero, *Diz. ep*. IV (1957). 727-728

Texts of the Salpensa and Málaga charters:

Abbott and Johnson. no. 64 (Salpensa) and 65 (Málaga), pp. 369-381 (Latin text and discussion)

d'Ors, A. *Epigrafía jurídica*. . . . 281-346

Hardy, E. G. 61-118 (translation and valuable commentary)

Jones. *HR*. II pp. 212-223 (translation)

Lewis, N., and Reinhold, M. *Roman Civilization, Sourcebook II*. 320-326 (translation)

McCrum, M., and Woodhead, A. G. *Select Documents of the Principates of the Flavian Emperors*.... Cambridge 1961. nos. 453-454 (Latin text)

Menéndez Pidal (as for the Osuna charter); discussion on 408

Oersted, P. *Vespasian*. . . .

Riccobono. *FIRA²*. I nos. 23-24

Paestum (the Latin name; the site is in the present-day region of Campania, Italy; the Roman region was *Lucania*); the Greek name was *Pos(e)idonia* pp. 22, 25 (no Etruscan influence when the Greek colony was founded; see Chapter I, n. 9 above)

Paestum is on the Gulf of Salerno, an arm of the Tyrrhenian Sea, and is seventy-five air-kilometers southeast of NAPLES (q.v.). Ward-Perkins dates Poseidonia's founding to c. 700 B.C., while Salmon and Grimal place it c. 600. Castagnoli dates the orthogonal street plan to c. 600. The colonists came from *Sybaris* (see *Thurii*). The city was held by the Oscan-speaking (see Samnites) Lucani from c. 390 B.C. to 273, when the Latin colony (see *colonia*) of *Paestum* was founded on the site (Velleius Paterculus 1.14.7). (A similar Latin colony, *Cosa*, q.v., was founded in the same year.)

At the time of Strabo (q.v.), this area was marshy and unhealthy, and the soil poor (5.4.13; 6.1.1, cited by Frank). *Paestum* was abandoned in the fourth century A.D. because of encroaching malarial swamps. Three important Greek temples, in good condition, may be seen here, as well as the city wall (all sixth century B.C., except for one temple, c. 450).

Besnier. *Lexique*. 561
Boëthius. *Golden House*. 35, n. 22 (bibl.); 42; fig. 20 (plan)
Bradford. *Ancient Landscapes*. 218-227
Caprino. *MAR, Bibl.* 243 (the baths)
Castagnoli. *Orthogonal Town Planning*. 39-46; figs. 15-17; 132
Chevallier. *ANRW*. II.1 p. 674 (bibl.); plate xxxiv (plan)
Crema. *Arch*. 28-29, 42; figs. 39-40
de Rosa, G. *La Chiesa dell'Annunziata a Paestum*. 1971 (church of the fifth century A.D.)
Finley. *Atlas*. 128-130 (G. D. B. Jones)
Frank. *ESAR*. V p. 136
Grimal. *Search*. 206-207 (on eighteenth-century travelers)
Guido. *Southern Italy*. 193-203, figs. 29, 30, 31
Gutkind. *IHCD*. IV (1969). 602-603
KP. IV (1972). 1079 (G. Radke)
Krauss, F. *Paestum, Die griechischen Tempel*[2]. Berlin 1943
—— *Die Tempel von Paestum*. I.1 *Der Athenatempel*. Berlin 1959; rpt. 1978
Lo Piccolo, S. *Paestum*. Narni/Terni 1972 (guidebook, in English transl.)
MacKendrick. *Greek Stones*. 203-204; 426 (index)
—— *Mute Stones*. 112; 113 (aerial photograph)
McKay, A. G. *Vergil's Italy*. Greenwich, Conn., 1970. 243-246; plate 66

Mello, M. *Paestum romana: Ricerche storiche*. Studi pubblicati dall'Istituto italiano per la Storia antica 24. Rome 1974
Napoli, M. *Civiltà della Magna Grecia*. Rome 1969. plates 21-24
—— *Paestum*. Novara (Piedmont, Italy) 1967
Nissen. *IL*. II p. 893
OCD. 767 (E. T. Salmon)
Pareti, L. *La Lucania antica*. 2 vols. Rome 1972
PECS. 663-665 (W. D. E. Coulson)
Randall-MacIver, D. *Greek Cities in Italy and Sicily*. Oxford 1931. 9-20; plates ii-iii
RE. XXII.1 (1953). 1230-1254 (H. Riemann)
Robertson. *GRA*. 73-81; 402 (index)
Rykwert. *Idea*. 42; 238 (index); figs. 140-144
Salmon. *RC*. 29, 34, 74; 111 (list of Latin colonies); 23 (on centuriation, q.v.); 182, n. 137 (on the *duoviri*, q.v.); 62 (paired with *Cosa*); 86 (on the quaestors, q.v.)
Salmon, E. T. *Samnium and the Samnites*. Cambridge 1967. 288-289 (the Latin colony)
Sestieri, P. C. "The Antiquities of Paestum," *Archaeology* 7 (1954): 206-213
—— *Paestum*[8]. Rome 1967 (English translation)
—— *Paestum*[9]. Rome 1966
Ward-Perkins. *Cities*. 22, 24, 119; figs. 29-30
Wheeler. *RAA*. 29-30; fig. 10 (map)
Woodhead. *Greeks in the West*. 61-62; 123, fig. 17 (map); plates 23, 24, 52, 57 (air view), 63, 64; p. 168 (bibliography)

PALESTRINA (Latium, Italy) = *Praeneste, Latium, Italia*
p. 20 (early nonorthogonal hill-town)
A city of the Latins (q.v.), like *Tibur* (see TIVOLI) and *Tusculum*, *Praeneste* lies thirty-seven kilometers southeast of Rome, on a spur of the Apennines (q.v.), facing the Alban Hills. The earliest known Latin inscription (c. 625 B.C. — Warmington; Richardson in *PECS*) has been found on a gold *fibula* or brooch from this site. The extensive cemeteries have yielded a number of treasures (Richardson, ibid.; Foerst).
An allied city (q.v.) of Rome from the fourth century B.C. (Livy 23.19), *Praeneste* received Roman citizenship in 90 B.C. Sulla sacked it in 82 B.C. and founded a colony of veterans below the older site. *Praeneste*, joined to Rome by the *Via Praenestina*, was a country resort and was famous for its temple of Fortuna Primigenia, whose

ruins can still be seen. Finished c. 80 B.C. (cf. Gullini), it was perhaps the largest sanctuary in Italy. There is an archaeological museum in the Palazzo Barberini on the upper terrace of the temple.
Alfoeldi. *Early Rome*. 385-391
Ashby. *Rom. Cam*. 139-142 (the Temple); 255 (index)
Bagnani. *Rom. Cam*. 191-204
Besnier. *Lexique*. 623
Blue Guide, Rome. 343-347
Boëthius. *Golden House*. 27, n. 3 (bibl.); fig. 26
—— and Ward-Perkins. *ERA*. plates 84-87
Brown. *RA*. 20-21, plates 18-20 (Sanctuary of Fortune)
Chevallier. *ANRW*. II.1 p. 696 (bibl.)
Crema. *ANRW*. I.4 "Arch. rep."
—— *Arch*. 663 (index)
EB. XXII pp. 243-244 (J. G. Frazer et al.)
Foerst, G. *Die Gravierungen der Praenestinischen Cisten*. Rome 1978 (engraved small bronze boxes)
Forma Italiae, Praeneste. Rome 1970
Frank. *ESAR*. I pp. 51, 178 (bronze industry, third/second centuries B.C.); 368 (large farms nearby); 372 (buildings); V pp. 127 (Strabo on the Temple of Fortune); 129 (garden products); 412 (bibl.)
Frothingham. *RCID*. 10-37
Grimal. *Rome*. 200-201
Gros. *Architecture*. . . . 1978 (listed under Rome, below)
Guida d'Italia del Touring Club Italiano, Roma e Dintorni[6]. Milan 1962. 631-645
Gullini, G. "La datazione e l'inquadramento stilistico del santuario della Fortuna Primigenia a Palestrina," *ANRW*. I.4 (1973): 746-799 + 36 plates
Hammond. *The City*. 231
Kaehler, H. *Art of Rome*. 49; 218 (bibl.)
—— *Das Fortunaheiligtum von Palestrina Praeneste*. Saarbruecken 1958
KP. IV (1972). 1110-1111 (G. Radke)
Lavedan. *HU*. 485 (drawing of the shrine)
Lugli. *Tecnica edilizia*. 116-121
MacDonald. *Arch*. 7-8; plates 7-10
MacKendrick. *Mute Stones*. 116-132 (on the Temple of Fortuna); 355-356 (bibl.)
McKay, A. G. *Vergil's Italy*. Greenwich, Conn., 1970. 170-171; plate 41

Nissen. *IL*. II pp. 620-624

OCD. 873 (E. T. Salmon)

Ogilvie, R. M. *A Commentary on Livy*. Oxford 1965. 285 (early history)

Paget. *Central Italy*. 210-214

PECS. 735-736 (L. Richardson, Jr.)

Randall-MacIver, D. *The Iron Age in Italy*. Oxford 1927

RE. XXII.2 (1954). 1549-1555 (G. Radke)

RE. Supplement 8 (1956). 1241-1260 (H. Besig)

Robertson. *GRA*. 371 (bibl.)

Romanelli, P. *Palestrina*. Naples 1967

Salmon. *RC*. 46-47 (map of Latium); 50-53 (the Latin city); 131, 196, n. 307 (the colony of Sulla); plate 54 (the Temple)

Ward-Perkins. *RA*. plates 47-51

On the inscribed *fibula:*

Cornell, T. J. in Prag. *AR*. 88

Gordon, A. E. *The Inscribed Fibula Praenestina: Problems of Authenticity*. Berkeley 1975 (There is a "slight shadow of a doubt."— J. Heurgon, *Journal of Roman Studies* 70 [1980]: 219)

Guarducci, M. "La cosiddetta fibula prenestina . . .," *Atti dell' Accademia dei Lincei, Memorie*. Ser. VIII. 24.4 (1980); (says that the inscription is a forgery; favorably reviewed by A. E. Gordon, *Classical Journal* 78 [1982]: 64-70)

Ogilvie. *Early Rome*. 49

Warmington, E. H. *The Remains of Classical Latin*. IV, *Archaic Inscriptions*. London/Cambridge, Mass., 1940. 196, no. 1; plate opp. p. 151

PARIS (France) = *Lutetia Parisiorum, Gallia Lugdunensis*
pp. 8-9 (continuity of settlement); 44 (forum); 67 (demi-amphitheater); 79 (Late Roman wall)

Lutetia was the tribal capital of the Parisii, a Celtic tribe of *Gallia Comata* (q.v.). Their *oppidum* was on the Ile de la Cité. Under Roman rule the town expanded on both banks of the Seine, but especially on the south or left bank, where the forum (see *fora*, comparison in size) and demi-amphitheater were. The city blocks of the Gallo-Roman town were irregular. Three baths have been found, of which the Cluny Baths are the best preserved (Fleury in *PECS*). In contrast with *Londinium* (LONDON), *Lutetia* had an aqueduct. A Roman highway led from AUTUN to the English Channel by way of PARIS (Chevallier, *Roman Roads* 161).

Sacked about A.D. 275, PARIS nevertheless became more important in the Late Empire; it was one of the imperial residences in the fourth century. Julian, who was proclaimed emperor there in 360 by his troops (Ammianus Marcellinus 20.4), said of it three years earlier, "I have spent a winter in dear Lutetia, for so the Gauls term the little town of the Parisii, a small island lying in the river and walled all around....The water there is excellent and pure to look at and drink;...the inhabitants have a pretty mild winter...and good wine is grown among them." *(Misopogon* pp. 340-341, abridged, quoted by Mommsen in *Provinces* Chapter III. The Late Roman wall enclosed only the Ile de la Cité. In this passage, Julian also said that the bridges were of wood.)

The Frankish King Clovis (see Franks) who conquered PARIS in 493, made it his capital (on the capital see Gregory of Tours, *History of the Franks* 2.38). For most of the time thereafter, Paris has been the capital of France.

Bastié, J. "Paris: Baroque Elegance and Agglomeration," in *World Capitals*, edit. H. W. Eldredge. Garden City, N.Y., 1975. 55-89 (present-day geography)

Bazin, H. *Les monuments de Paris.* . . . Paris 1905 ("souvenirs of twenty centuries")

Besnier. *Lexique.* 446

Brogan. *Roman Gaul.* 106-108; 242 (bibl.)

Bruehl. *PC.* 6-33

Caprino. *MAR, Bibl.* 241

Chambart de Lauwe, P.-H. et al. *Paris et l'agglomération parisienne.* Paris 1952 (a sociological critique of the urban plan)

Champigneulle, B. *Paris de Napoléon à nos jours.* Paris 1969

Chevallier. *ANRW.* II.3 pp. 939-949 (description, bibl. and plans)

Chevallier, R. et al., eds. *Tabula Imperii Romani, feuille M31: Lutetia.* Paris 1975 (map of northern Gaul)

Couperie, P. *Paris au fil du temps.* Paris 1968 (historical atlas, on city planning) = *Paris through the Ages.* New York 1968 (English translation)

Crema. *Arch.* 364; fig. 422 (forum); 540 (Cluny Baths)

de Pachtere, F.-G. *Paris à l'époque gallo-romaine.* Paris 1912 ("brilliant and reliable," Duval, below, p. 312; has ten plans)

Dossiers de l'archéologie 7 (1974); *(Dans le sol de Paris)*

Druon, M. *The History of Paris from Caesar to St. Louis*. London 1969 (transl. from the French)

*Duval, P.-M. *Paris antique, des origines au IIIe siècle*. Paris 1961 (excellent bibl. on 303-338)

EB. XX pp. 804-822 (H. de Blowitz)

Engel, J., ed. *Grosser historischer Weltatlas*. II. Munich 1970. 77 (plan of the medieval city)

Fleury, M. *Carte archéologique de Paris*. 1er sér. Paris 1971

—— *Paris monumental*. Paris 1974

George, P. et al. *La région parisienne*[2]. Paris 1964 (urban geography)

Gibbon, E. *The History of the Decline and Fall of the Roman Empire*. II. Edit. J. B. Bury. London 1901. 286-287 (Julian at PARIS)

Grenier. *Manuel*. I pp. 414-419 (walls); III 363-369 (forum); 815-818 (theater on the Rue Racine); 899-903 (amphitheater); IV 180-191 (aqueduct); 310-319 (baths)

Grimal. *Civ. Rome*. 472

Gutkind. *IHCD*. V (1970). 238-285; 477-478 (bibl.)

Hatt, J. J. *Histoire de la Gaule romaine*[2]. Paris 1966

—— "Les monuments gallo-romains de Paris," *Revue archéologique* 39 (1952): 68-83

Hillairet, J. *Dictionnaire historique des rues de Paris*[2]. 2 vols. Paris 1964

Jullian, C. *Le Paris des romains*. Paris 1924

KP. III (1969). 793-794 (M. Leglay)

Lavedan. *HU*. 493 (index)

Lavedan, P. *Histoire de l'urbanisme à Paris*. "Nouvelle Histoire de Paris." Paris 1975

—— *Histoire de Paris*[2]. "Que sais-je?" no. 34. Paris 1967

—— *Nous partons pour Paris*. Paris 1964

Lombard-Jourdan, A. *Paris, genèse de la ville. La rive droite de la Seine des origines à 1223*. Paris 1976

MacKendrick. *RF*. 142-147; 211-245, 264 (Roman influence on the architecture of PARIS, seventeenth to nineteenth centuries)

Malet, H. *Le Baron Haussmann et la rénovation de Paris*. Paris 1973

Millar. *REN*. pl. 9 (the Cluny Baths)

OCD. 626 (C. E. Stevens)

Paris, croissance d'une capitale. Paris 1961

PECS. 534-535 (M. Fleury)

Picard, C. "The Romans in Paris," *Archaeology* 3 (1930): 112-118

Pinkney, D. H. *Napoleon III and the Rebuilding of Paris*. Princeton 1958

RE. Supplement 12 (1970). 986-990 (P.-M. Duval; see Parisii)

Roblin, M. *Le terroir de Paris aux époques gallo-romaine et franque*. Paris 1978 (with nine tables and forty-one maps)

Saalman, H. *Haussmann: Paris Transformed*. New York 1971 (nineteenth-century plan; bibl. on pp. 121-122)

Stier. *Atlas*. 103, 109 (plans)

Ward-Perkins. *Cities*. 31 (forum); 38 (modern circular street plan)

Wheeler. *RAA*. 65-70; ills. 46-49 (excellent general description)

PARMA (Emilia-Romagna, Italy) = *Parma, Aemilia, Italia;* after 31 B.C., it was called *Colonia Iulia Augusta Parmensis (CIL* XI 1059).

pp. 20-21 (on terramara, q.v.)

This Roman colony was founded in 183 B.C. (Livy 39.55.6), forty-five kilometers northwest of *Mutina* (see MODENA) on the *Via Aemilia*. The colony of *Mutina* was also founded in 183. PARMA lies on the right bank of a seasonal tributary which flows north to the Po River. The *Via Clodia* from Rome (see Chapter III, n. 2 above) joined the *Via Aemilia* at PARMA. After 31 B.C., Augustus founded a new colony for his veterans on the same site. The orthogonal Roman street plan may be easily recognized in that of the modern city (Frova in *PECS*).

Bazzi, T., and Benassi, U. *Storia di Parma*. Parma 1908

Besnier. *Lexique*. 574-575

Castagnoli. *Orthogonal Town Planning*. 104, 106

Chevallier. *ANRW*. II.1 plate xxv (centuriation and aerial photograph)

Chilver. *Cisalpine Gaul*. 6, 18 (the *colonia);* 164 (the wool trade)

Dilke. *ANRW*. II.1 p. 588 (bibl. on centuriation, q.v.)

EB. XX pp. 850-851

Enciclopedia dell'arte antica, classica e orientale. V (1963). 960-961 (N. Alfieri)

Frank. *ESAR*. I p. 119 (Livy on the colony's foundation)

Gutkind. *IHCD*. IV (1969). 297-299

KP. IV (1972). 517 (G. Radke)

Nissen. *IL*. II pp. 268-270

OCD. 782 (E. T. Salmon)

PECS. 233 (A. Frova)

Rossignani, M. P. *Decorazione architettonica romana a Parma*. Rome 1975 (the most important Roman remains)

Salmon. *RC*. 24 (centuriation); 104-106; 107 (map of *Gallia Cisalpina*, q.v.); 138 (the colony of Augustus)

Scullard. *Etruscan Cities*. 213 (?Etruscan settlement, relatively early)

Testi, L. *Parma*[3]. Bergamo 1934
Tozzi, P. *Saggi di topografia storica*. Florence 1974
Ward-Perkins. *Cities*. 29 (continuity of settlement, to the present day)

PERIGUEUX (Dordogne, France) = *Vesunna Petrucoriorum, Aquitania*
pp. 55-56 (the Tour de Vésone or Temple of Vesunna); 79 (the Late Roman wall)

At the center of the more-or-less orthogonal Gallo-Roman town stands the Tour de (or Tower of) Vésone. Grenier dates the Tower to the reign of Hadrian (117-138). The local tribe, the Petrucorii, for whom this was the capital (Ptolemy [q.v.] 2.7.9) gave its name to PERIGUEUX (compare PARIS). The Roman road north from ST.-BER-TRAND-DE-COMMINGES ran through on the way to Limoges.

Across the river from the original *oppidum*, *Vesunna* lay on the right bank of the Isle River, which flows west into the Gironde estuary (see BORDEAUX). As was usual for the Celts, baths were associated with the shrine. The amphitheater, north of the Tower, was dismantled in the third century to build a wall around the nearby area against the Germanic invaders. Some of its stones remain on the original site.

The medieval cathedral and town were built on a hill to the northeast of ancient *Vesunna*. It was also on the right bank of the river, which flows from northeast to southwest here. In more recent times, the town has expanded to the north. Situated in the fertile valley of the Isle, PERIGUEUX is famous for its gastronomic specialties, truffles and foie gras. It is the capital of Dordogne département.

Barrière, P. *Vesunna Petrucoriorum, histoire d'une petite ville à l'époque gallo-romaine*. Périgueux 1930
Besnier. *Lexique*. 813
Bournichon. *Vesunna: Périgueux à l'époque gallo-romain*. 1952
Brogan. *Roman Gaul*. 109
Coupry, J. *Gallia* 21 (1963): 514-525
Crema. *Arch*. 664 (index)
Eggers, H. J., ed. *Kelten und Germanen*. Baden-Baden 1964. plate 18 (the Tower)
Grenier. *Manuel*. I 553-555 (the Porte de Mars, a city gate which has now disappeared); II 683-686; III 252-254; 440-447 (the Tour de Vésone); 670-674 (the amphitheater); fig. 232 (plan of the town); IV 154-163 (the aqueduct)

Koethe, H. *Die keltischen Rund- und Vielecktempel der Kaiserzeit.* Bericht der roemisch-germanischen Kommission 23. Frankfurt am Main 1934. 47-53
KP. IV (1972). 676-677 (M. Leglay, see "Petrucorii")
Lavergne, G. *Histoire de Périgueux.* Périgueux 1945
MacKendrick. *RF.* 121-122
PECS. 972-973 (A. Blondy)
RE. Supplement 15 (1978). 298-306 (H. Bannert; see Petrucorii)
Stier. *Atlas.* 43 (plan)
Ward-Perkins. *RA.* plates 270-271 (Tour de Vésone)

Pompeii (in the ancient and modern regions of Campania, Italy); the full name of the Roman colony (c. 80 B.C.) was *Colonia Veneria Cornelia Pompeianorum* (Cornelius was Sulla's *nomen* or family name). pp. 25-27 (general description), 41 (Main Forum, c. 210 B.C.), 46 (basilica), 46 (curia), 50 (Capitol), 58 (theater, c. 100 B.C.), 63 (amphitheater, c. 80 B.C., oldest known), 68-71 (Stabian and Forum Baths), 77 (towers added to the city walls, c. 90 B.C.), 86 (the Italic houses)

The site is on the Bay of Naples, an arm of the Tyrrhenian Sea, and just northeast of the mouth of the Sarno River. It lies about twenty kilometers southeast of NAPLES. As Grimal states, *Pompeii* was founded by the Oscans (q.v.) at the end of the sixth century B.C. (also see Chapter I, n. 10 above). About 425, it was taken by the Samnites (q.v.), who greatly increased the size of the city. The city walls of the third/second centuries B.C. (Richardson in *PECS* 724) enclosed sixty-five hectares (Duncan-Jones, *ERE* 276, n. 7). The southwest section of the city, containing the main forum, is closest to the port, which seems to have been on the Sarno (Richardson, ibid.).

After the defeat of the Samnites, Pompeii came under Roman control, but it remained an Oscan-speaking city until Sulla planted there a Roman colony, into which the local inhabitants were integrated. (On the colony, see Cicero, *For Sulla* 60-62.) At this point, the names of the city's magistrates and measurements were changed from Oscan ones to Roman. The city's orthogonal plan was not altered then, but new structures took on a Roman look. Many Romanized buildings date from after the earthquake of A.D. 62. As is clear from his many references, Grimal considers *Pompeii* to have been a good example of a Roman city, but we should remember that originally it was Italic (q.v.) rather than Roman.

On the city's economic base, Rostovtzeff said, "There is no doubt that Pompeii, which had always been the centre of a flourishing agricultural region and a harbour of some importance for the group of inland cities that lay near, gradually became a centre of local industry which sold goods produced in her workshops to customers not only in the city but also in neighbouring cities and in the homesteads of the country round" (*SEHRE* 72). Under Roman rule, the industries were woolen textiles, clothes, and *garum* fish sauce (ibid. 73, Moeller). In addition, it became a fashionable resort, surrounded by villas. There were good road connections to the nearby cities.

The population of Pompeii grew to under 20,000, and it is most famous for its houses, which range from mansions to one-room shops with lofts (Richardson in *PECS* 724, 726). No slums have been found, and Rostovtzeff remarked that at Pompeii or at TIMGAD there are no houses in which one would not care to live (*Rome* 256).

Pompeii was covered with lava by the eruption of the volcano Vesuvius in A.D. 79, and the ruins were preserved until discovered in 1748. The site has been excavated since that time, with increasing precision (Richardson in *PECS* 724). About three-fourths of the city has been uncovered. Much of the material (including most of the wall-paintings) is in the National Museum at NAPLES, but the local antiquarium or site-museum is well worth a visit.

A modern town, called "Pompei," has grown up one kilometer southeast of the excavated city. It contains hotels and restaurants, as well as the Catholic Basilica of Our Lady of the Rosary (1876/1891).

Andreae, B., and Kyrieleis, H., eds. *Neue Forschungen in Pompeji*. . . . Recklinghausen 1975

Andrews, I. *Pompeii*. Cambridge 1977

Besnier. *Lexique*. 616-617

Boëthius. *Golden House*. 46-47; fig. 15 (plan), figs. 27-28 (forum)

—— and Ward-Perkins. *ERA*. 290-297; 591-592 (bibl.); fig. 62 (map); plates 54, 70 (streets), 66; 69 (Forum Baths), 73 (basilica); 89, 94, 95; 99 (amphitheater); 155 (forum), 157 (Central Baths); 173 (houses)

Brilliant, R. *Pompeii, A.D. 79*. New York 1979

Brion, M. *Pompeii and Herculaneum: The Glory and the Grief*. New York 1960 (transl. from the French)

Cagnat, R., and Chapot, V. *Manuel d'archéologie romaine*. I. Paris 1916. 62 (streets)

Caprino. *MAR, Bibl.* 257-259 (houses); 332

Carcopino. *Daily Life*. 358 (index)

Carrington, R. C. *Pompeii*. Oxford 1936

Castagnoli. *Orthogonal Town Planning*. 24-35; figs. 9-12

Castrén, P. *Ordo Populusque Pompeianus. Polity and Society in Roman Pompeii.* Rome 1975 (bibliography on pp. 15 ff.); "Castrén has included the name of every (recorded) person who was resident in Pompeii." J. Corbett, *Phoenix* 32 (1978): 267

Chevallier. *ANRW.* II.1 p. 696 (bibl.)

Christ. *Bibl.* 345-348

Coarelli, F., ed. *Guida archeologica di Pompei.* Milan 1976 (good bibl. on pp. 349-354)

—— *Le città etrusche.* 326 (bibl.)

Corti, E. C. *The Destruction and Resurrection of Pompeii and Herculaneum.* London 1951 (transl. from the German)

Crema. *Arch.* 664-665 (index)

—— *ANRW.* I.4 "Arch. rep."

D'Arms, J. H. *Romans on the Bay of Naples.* Cambridge, Mass., 1970 (on the villas)

Day, J. "Agriculture in the Life of Pompeii," *Yale Classical Studies* 3 (1932): 165-208

Della Corte, M. *Case ed abitanti di Pompei*[3]. Pompei/Rome 1965

Eschebach, H. "Die bauliche Struktur des antiken Pompeji," *Antike Welt* 6.2 (1975): 2-14

—— *Pompeji.* Leipzig 1978

*—— *Die Staedtebauliche Entwicklung des antiken Pompeji.* Mitteilungen des Deutschen Archaeologischen Instituts, Roemische Abteilung, Ergaenzungsheft 17. Heidelberg 1970

Etienne, R. *La vie quotidienne à Pompéi.* Paris 1966

—— *Archéologia.* 54 (1973). 8-14, 34-41

Finley, M. I. *Atlas.* 126-128 (G. D. B. Jones)

Frank, T. *An Economic History of Rome*[2]. Baltimore 1927. Chapter XIV

—— *ESAR.* I pp. 282 (the harbor probably encouraged by low local customs duties); 288 (buildings); V 252-266

Grant, M. *The Cities of Vesuvius: Pompeii and Herculaneum.* New York 1971

Grimal. *Guide.* 276 (bibl.)

—— *Search.* 137-157

Guida d'Italia . . . (see NAPLES). 419-462; 496-497 (modern Pompei)

Guido. *Southern Italy.* 56-61, 64-77

Gutkind. *IHCD.* IV (1969). 191-201, 603; bibl. on 191 and 627

Hammond. *The City.* 231, 293

Haverfield. *Town Planning.* 63-68

Jashemski, W. F. *The Gardens of Pompeii.* New Rochelle, N.Y., 1979

Jones, H. Stuart. *Companion.* 459 (index)

Kaehler. *Art of Rome*. 85-88, 106, 108-109; 220 (bibliography on wall-painting)

KP. IV (1972). 1020-1022 (G. Radke)

Kraus, T., and von Matt, L. *Pompeii and Herculaneum*. Transl. from the German by R. E. Wolf. New York 1975. 7-117, 150-226; 227-228 (bibl. of 192 entries)

Krischen, F. *Die Stadtmauern von Pompeji und griechische Festungsbaukunst in Unteritalien und Sizilien*. Die hellenistiche Kunst in Pompeji 7. Berlin 1941

Lavedan. *HU*. 467 (map); 494 (index)

Ling, R. "Pompeii and Herculaneum: Recent Research and Future Prospects," in H. Blake et al., eds. *Papers in Italian Archaeology* I.i = British Archaeological Reports Supplementary Series 41.i. Oxford 1978. 153-174 (bibl. on 168-173)

MacKendrick. *Mute Stones*. 196-223; 357 (bibl.)

Maiuri, A. *Pompei*[14]. Rome 1967

—— *Pompei ed Ercolano fra case ed abitanti*[2]. Milan 1959

—— "Pompeii." *Scientific American* 198.4 (1958): 69-78

—— *Pompeii, the New Excavations*[7]. Transl. by V. Priestly. Rome 1965

—— *Roman Painting*. Transl. by S. Gilbert. Geneva 1953

Mau, A. *Pompeii, Its Life and Art*[2]. Transl. from the German by F. W. Kelsey. London 1908

McKay. *Houses*. 30-51, 106, 108-110; 286 (index); plates 15, 16, 18, 20, 22, 46-48

—— *Naples*. 89-135; 238-239 (bibl.); 260-261, 263-264 (bibl.)

Moeller, W. O. *The Wool Trade of Ancient Pompeii*. Studies of the Dutch Archaeological and Historical Society 3. Leiden 1976

Morris. *Urban Form*. 52-53, figs. 3.16-3.19

Nairn, J. A. *A Classical Handlist*[3]. Oxford 1960. 116 (bibl.)

Nissen. *IL*. II pp. 762-766

OCD. 856-857 (R. C. Carrington)

Overbeck, J., and Mau, A. *Pompeji*[4]. Leipzig 1884

Patroni, G. "Vetulonia, Pompei e la sua storia," *Studi etruschi* 15 (1941)

PECS. 724-726 (L. Richardson, Jr.)

Pernice, E. *Pompeji*. Leipzig 1926

Piganiol. *HR*. 591 (bibl.)

Piganiol, A. "Notes d'histoire pompéienne. I. Le plan de Pompéi. II. Sur une peinture de Pompéi," *Revue des Etudes latines* (1929): 3-12 = *Scripta Varia*, Collection Latomus 133, vol. III. Brussels 1973. 84-92

Raper, R. A. "The Analysis of the Urban Structure of Pompeii: A Sociological Examination of Land Use (Semi-Micro)," in *Spatial Archaeology*. Edit. D. L. Clarke. London 1977. 189-221 (ref. provided by J. Ramsey)

RE. XXI.2 (1952). 1999-2038 (A. W. Van Buren)

Richardson, L., Jr. "The Libraries of Pompeii," *Archaeology* 30 (1977): 394-402

Robertson. *GRA*. 191 (plan); 370 (bibl.); 403 (index)

Rostovtzeff. *SEHRE*. 804 (index)

Salmon. *RC*. 131 (the Sullan colony); plate 56 (the Forum)

Scullard. *Etruscan Cities*. 188

Sogliano, A. *Pompei nel suo sviluppo storico: Pompei preromana*. Rome 1937

Spano, G. "L'illuminazione delle vie di Pompei," *Atti della Reale Accademia di Archeologia, Lettere e Belle Arti di Napoli* (1920)

Spinazzola, V. *Pompei alla luce degli scavi nuovi di Via dell'Abbondanza (anni 1910-1923)*. 3 vols. Rome 1953

Staccioli, R. A. "Sulla destinazione e l'uso dei criptoportici," *Les cryptoportiques dans l'architecture romaine*. Collection de l'Ecole française de Rome 14. Rome 1973. 65 (on the House of the Cryptoporticus)

Stier. *Atlas*. 32 (plan)

Tanzer, H. H. *The Common People of Pompeii*. Johns Hopkins Univ. Studies in Archaeology 29. Baltimore 1939

Taylor, D. *Pompeii and Vesuvius*. London 1969

Tran Tam Tinh, V. *Essai sur le culte d'Isis à Pompéi*. Paris 1964

Van Buren, A. W. *A Companion to the Study of Pompeii and Herculaneum*[2]. Rome 1938

von Gerkan, A. *Der Stadtplan von Pompeji*. Berlin 1940

Ward-Perkins. *Cities*. 24 and figs. 40-41 (plan); 34 and fig. 79 (secondary water-tanks); 35 (the market); 41 (Capitol); 118-119 (general)

—— *RA*. 351 (index)

Ward-Perkins, J. B. et al. *Pompeii, A.D. 79*. 2 vols. Boston 1978 (catalogue of the traveling exhibition of treasures from Pompeii; based on the edition of London 1976; bibl. in vol. II pp. 219-221)

Wheeler. *RAA*. 32-33 and fig. 13 (plan); 249 (index)

Pos(e)idonia: see *Paestum*

Praeneste: see PALESTRINA

RAVENNA (Emilia-Romagna, Italy; the historic region of Romagna
originated with the Byzantine [q.v.] occupation of RAVENNA in the
sixth century A.D.) = *Ravenna, Aemilia, Italia;* mint of the Later
Roman Empire (q.v.)
p. 46 (the Christian basilicas)

+ *Spina*

The name of RAVENNA is not Indo-European, and it may be
Etruscan. About 500 B.C., nearby *Spina* (forty-five kilometers to the
north, on the then southern mouth of the Po River) was colonized
by the Etruscans (q.v.; compare MARZABOTTO and BOLOGNA), but
the city only barely survived the Gallic invasions of c. 390 (Chilver
53). The orthogonal plan of *Spina* was identified by aerial photography in 1956 (D. W. R. Ridgway). The finds from *Spina* are kept in
the National Archaeological Museum at Ferrara *(PECS)*. This collection was first exhibited in 1935.

RAVENNA was probably first settled by Umbrians (q.v.; cf. Pliny,
Natural History 3.15 and Strabo 5.1.7) coming from the south. It
became an allied city (q.v.) of Rome and in 49 B.C., less than a century later, a *municipium* (q.v.; L. R. Taylor; also see *Gallia Cisalpina).*

About 39 B.C., Octavian located the permanent headquarters (in
camp format) of the Eastern Fleet three kilometers southwest of the
city, near the harbor (Appian, *Civil Wars* 5.80, cf. Tacitus, *Annals*
4.5.1; for the Western Fleet, see FREJUS and OSTIA ANTICA). Soon a
canal was built north to the Po, and navigation was possible along
the river all the way to TURIN. Vitruvius (q.v.) mentioned the trans-
port of wood down the Po to RAVENNA and the Adriatic *(Architecture* 2.9.16).

Because of silting, RAVENNA is now eight kilometers from the Adriatic coast of Italy, but the Umbrian orthogonal city was quite near
the sea. It was surrounded by water-courses and marshes (as had
been *Spina)* but was not unhealthy (as yet, they were not malarial).
The Romans built a coastal highway, which was constantly liable to
be closed by floods. The supply of fresh water never was very good
and was disparaged by the poet Martial (of the first century A.D.;
3.56-57). Its wine, he said, was cheaper. In A.D. 467, the Lyonnais
nobleman, Sidonius Apollinaris also complained about the water
(Letters 1.5, a description of RAVENNA cited by Hodgkin I pp. 440-
442). An aqueduct was built by the Emperor Trajan (A.D. 98-117)
and restored by Theodoric in 503 (see Ostrogoths), one of his several
projects of restoring or completing Roman structures (cf. *CIL* XI 10).

Although, under the Roman Empire, there was no other city at the mouth of the Po, RAVENNA was not primarily a commercial city but a naval one (Chilver). Its inhabitants then were mainly sailors (from Dalmatia and Thrace). Only the framework of municipal government existed, under the control of the Prefect of the Fleet *(Praefectus Classis)*. Ship-building was the major industry (Frank, *ESAR* V 117-118).

In the Late Roman period (A.D. 404), the Emperor Honorius made RAVENNA the *de facto* center of his government; Rome remained the capital of the Western Empire only in theory. In that age of barbarian invasions, RAVENNA had the advantage of being nearly inaccessible, because of the silting (see Hodgkin I pp. 433-434). But the *Notitia Dignitatum* (q.v.) tells us that a fleet was still kept at RAVENNA c. A.D. 400 *(Oc.* [West] 42.6-7).

The Germanic King Odovacar (476-493) and the Ostrogothic kings of Italy, most notably Theodoric (489-526; see VERONA), ruled from RAVENNA, which was conquered by the Eastern Emperor Justinian in 540. For some two hundred years afterward, RAVENNA remained an important Byzantine enclave in Italy.

After a short period of rule by the Lombards (q.v.), RAVENNA came under the control of Pope Stephen II in 756, with the help of the Frankish King Pippin the Short. Papal rule of RAVENNA was ratified by Charlemagne in 774 (see Franks); this was one of the origins of the temporal power of the popes in Italy.

Some major Byzantine churches may be seen at RAVENNA, as well as the Mausoleum of Galla Placidia (A.D. 388-450, sister of Honorius) and the Tomb of Theodoric. RAVENNA today is an agricultural center for grain, wine-grapes, hemp, and maize, and, although it is off the main trading routes, petroleum is refined there.

RAVENNA:
Bengtson. *Atlas*. 56c (plan)
Besnier. *Lexique*. 637-638
Boëthius and Ward-Perkins. *ERA*. 600 (bibl. on the Palace of Theodoric)
Bovini, G. *Eglises de Ravenne*. Novara 1960 (Trans. from the Italian)
—— *Monumenti antichi di Ravenna*. Milan 1952
—— "Le origini di Ravenna e lo sviluppo della città in età romana," *Felix Ravenna* 19 (1956): 38-60; 21 (1958): 27-68
—— "Il Problema della ricognizione archeologica del 'Portus Augusti' di Ravenna e del 'Castrum Classis,'" *Atti del I. Congresso Internazionale di Archeologia dell'Italia Settentionale*. Turin 1963

—— *Saggio di bibliografia su Ravenna antica*. Bologna 1968
Chevallier. *ANRW*. II.1 pp. 696-701 (bibl.)
Chierichetti. *Ravenna*. Milan 1958
Chilver. *Cisalpine Gaul*. 18-19, 28-29, 32, 58, 126-127, 138-139
Christ. *Bibl*. 259 (the fleet); 460-461 (art); 492, 506 (Late Roman and Byzantine)
Deichmann, F. W. *Ravenna, Geschichte und Monumente*. I. Wiesbaden 1969. II. 1976
Diehl, C. *Ravenna*. Paris 1903
Duranti, E. "Lo stato municipale di Ravenna in età romana," *Felix Ravenna* 39 (1964): 49-83
Felix Ravenna (1911-)
Finley. *Atlas*. 100-103 (G. D. B. Jones on RAVENNA and *Spina)*
Galassi, G. *Roma e Bisanzio*. Rome 1955
Hodgkin, T. *Italy and her Invaders, 376-814*. Oxford 1892-1899; rpt. New York 1967. I (Honorius and Galla Placidia), pp. 432-454 (description of RAVENNA); II (Odovacar); III (Theodoric); IV (Justinian); VII (Pippin the Short and Charlemagne)
Hutton, E. *The Story of Ravenna*. London 1926
Kaehler. *Art of Rome*. 92-94; 220 (bibl. on the "Apotheosis of Augustus" relief)
KP. IV (1972). 1342-1343 (G. Radke)
MacDonald, W. L. *Early Christian and Byzantine Architecture*. New York 1962
Mansuelli, G. A. "Elementi organici e razionali nell'urbanistica ravennate," *Felix Ravenna* N.S. 1 (1970): 27-37
—— *Geografia e storia di Ravenna antica*. Corsi di Cultura sull'Arte ravennate e bizantina 14. Ravenna 1967. 157-190
Moss, H.St.L.B. *The Birth of the Middle Ages, 395-814*. Oxford 1935; rpt. 1961. 54-56 (description of RAVENNA c. A.D. 500); 217 (bestowed on Papacy); 290 (index)
Nissen. *IL*. II pp. 251-256
OCD. 909-910 (R. Browning)
PECS. 751 (D. C. Scavone)
Perogalli, C. *Ravenna paleocristiana e altomedioevale*. Milan 1966
Radke, G. *Latomus* 24 (1965): 815 ff. (on the harbor)
Rostovtzeff. *SEHRE*. 652 (wine exported from Scyros, Greece, to RAVENNA)
Scagliarini, D. *Ravenna e le ville romane in Romagna*. Collana di Quaderni di Antichità Ravennati . . . 10. Ravenna 1968 (Roman villas)
Scullard. *Etruscan Cities*. 215

Snider, G., and Woloch, G. M. *The Byzantine Period*. Montreal 1977
(accompanying text to a slide lecture on the art and architecture
of the Byzantine period)
Starr, C. G. *The Roman Imperial Navy, 31 B.C.-A.D. 324*. 2nd ed.
Cambridge, England, 1960. 21-23; 28, n. 46 (bibl.)
Stier. *Atlas*. 88-89 (archbishopric)
Taylor. *Voting Districts*. 124, n. 19; 271
Uggeri, G. *La romanizzazione dell'antico delta padano*. Ferrara 1975
(The delta changed in 1152.)
Ward-Perkins. *RA*. plates 114, 170, 414, 415

+ *Spina:*
Alfieri, N., and Arias, P. E. *Spina*. Florence 1958
Alfieri, N. et al. *Spina*. Munich 1958
Aurigemma, S. *Il R. Museo di Spina in Ferrara*[2]. Ferrara 1936
—— *Scavi di Spina*. I. 2 fascicles. Rome 1960, 1965
Besnier. *Lexique*. 716
Chilver. *Cisalpine Gaul*. 53
Coarelli. *Le città etrusche*. 325 (bibl.)
Enciclopedia dell'arte antica, classica e orientale. VII (1966). 446-
453 (N. Alfieri and P. E. Arias)
Eydoux, H.-P. *The Buried Past*. London 1966. 24-44, 182 (bibl.);
ills. 5-6 (good air views) (transl. from the French)
Istituto di studi etruschi ed italici, Atti del I convegno di studi etrus-
chi. *Spina e l'Etruria padana*. Florence 1959 = *Studi etruschi*.
Suppl. to vol. 25
KP. V (1975). 313 (W. H. Gross)
Mansuelli, G. A. *Mostra dell'Etruria Padana e della Città di Spina*.
2 vols. Bologna 1960
OCD. 1009-1010 (D. W. R. Ridgway)
Ogilvie. *Early Rome*. 11 (pre-Etruscans); 160
PECS. 857 (N. Alfieri and G. V. Gentili)
Rykwert. *Idea*. 82-85; figs. 53-54
Scullard. *Etruscan Cities*. 209-212, 215

ROME (Latium, Italy) = *Urbs Roma, Italia;* mint of the Republic
and Empire; mint of the Later Roman Empire (q.v.)
topographical references only: pp. 5 (*pomerium* and Capitol), 28-39
(Chapter II, on the urban development of ancient Rome), 41, 46
(basilicas in the Forum); 46 (tomb of St. Peter), 48 (the Curia), 63
(Circus Maximus), 64-65 (Flavian Amphitheater), 70 (baths of Cara-

calla and of Diocletian), 72-76 (aqueducts), 75 (Cloaca Maxima), 76-77 (Servian Wall), 78-79 (Wall of Aurelian), 80 (Arch of Fabius); on the population, see Chapter III, n. 38 above

Latin speakers and writers used to call Rome the "Urbs Aeterna," the "Eternal City" (e.g. Ammianus Marcellinus 14.6.1, 28.1.1, 29.6.17). This terminology is still correct.

On Augustus' buildings, see N. Lewis and M. Reinhold, *Roman Civilization, Sourcebook II: The Empire*, New York 1966, 15-16 (= Augustus, *Accomplishments* 19-21; other translations are listed in Introduction n. 4 above). On the most noteworthy sights of Rome in A.D. 357, see Ammianus 16.10.14-15.

Also see ITALICA (on Monte Testaccio) and SUBIACO (on the aqueducts).

Abbott, F. F. *The Common People of Ancient Rome*. London 1912
Albertini, E. *L'Empire romain*[4]. Paris 1970. 436 (bibl.)
Alfoeldi. *Early Rome*. esp. 193-206 (Alfoeldi places the Etruscan domination of Rome c. 600-455 B.C. [archaeological finds]; during this period, the Forum was drained and its streets laid out); also see pp. 320 ff. (The Servian Wall is a "myth.")
Anderson, W. J. *The Architecture of Ancient Rome*. Rev. by T. Ashby. London 1927
Bengtson. *Atlas*. 33c, 35 (plans)
Besnier. *Lexique*. 648-649
Bianchi Bandinelli. *Rome*. I
Bloch, R. *Les origines de Rome*. "Que sais-je" no. 216. Paris 1959
—— *The Origins of Rome*. London 1960 (transl. from the French) (not the same book as the preceding)
Blue Guide, Rome. 1-309
Boëthius and Ward-Perkins. *ERA*. 84-278; 497-515; 551, notes 1-5 (bibl. on early Rome); 587-589, 591-593, 600 (bibl.); plates 8 (early iron-age hut), 55 (Via Sacra), 63 ("Servian" Wall on the Aventine 87 B.C.), 67-68, 71; 72 (Tabularium), 75 (Forum Holitorium), 76-77, 79 (republican temples), 102; 103 (Via Appia), 104 (Forum), 105 (Theater of Marcellus), 106-114; 115 (Porta Maggiore); 116-118, 120; 121 (Flavian Amphitheater); 122-126; 127-129 (Trajan's Market); 130-133; 138-146; 258-265, 267
Brown. *RA*
Caprino. *MAR, Bibl*. 332 ("a reconstruction of imperial Rome")
Carcopino. *Daily Life*
Carettoni, G. et al. *La pianta marmorea di Roma antica*. Rome 1960
Castagnoli, F. *Foro romano*. Milan 1957
—— *Roma antica, profilo urbanistico*. Rome 1978

—— *Topografia di Roma antica.* Turin 1980
—— et al. *Topografia e urbanistica di Roma.* Istituto di Studi Romani, Storia di Roma 22. Bologna 1958
Chiarini, M., ed. *Vedute romane: disegni dal XVI al XVIII secolo.* Rome 1971 (exhibition catalogue)
Christ. *Bibl.* 46-48; 504-505 (Christian archaeology)
*Coarelli, F. *Guida archeologica di Roma*[3]. Milan 1980. good bibliography 345-351
—— "Public Buildings in Rome between the Second Punic War and Sulla," *Papers of the British School at Rome* 45 (1977): 1-19
Cozzi, L. G. *Le porte di Roma.* Rome 1968
Crema. *ANRW.* I.4 "Arch. rep."
—— *Arch.* 23-27 (early Rome); 665-667 (index)
Curtius, L., Nawrath, A., and Nash, E. *Das antike Rom*[3]. Vienna 1957
Dudley. *Urbs Roma*
Earl. *AA*
Enciclopedia dell'arte antica, classica e orientale. VI (1965) (article on "Roma," also printed separately)
Evans, H. B. "The 'Romulean' Gates of the Palatine," *American Journal of Archaeology* 84 (1980): 93-96
Finley. *Atlas.* 105-111 (G. D. B. Jones)
Florescu, F. B. *Die Trajanssaeule.* Bucharest/Bonn 1969 (the Column of Trajan; bibl. on pp. 293-295)
Fowler, W. Warde. *Social Life at Rome in the Age of Cicero.* London 1908; rpt. London 1965
Frank. *ESAR.* V pp. 218-236
Frank, T. *Roman Buildings of the Republic.* Papers and Monographs of the American Academy in Rome 3. Rome 1924
Fried, R. C. *Planning the Eternal City: Roman Politics and Planning since World War II.* New Haven 1973 (general bibl. on 321-331; bibl. on planning ancient Rome in the notes on 10-15, on papal Rome 15-19, on Rome after 1870 as the capital of Italy 19 ff.; ref. provided by P. Sabetti)
Frier, B. *Landlords and Tenants in Imperial Rome.* Princeton 1980
—— "The Rental Market in Early Imperial Rome," *Journal of Roman Studies* 67 (1977): 27-37
Frutaz, A. P. *Le carte del Lazio.* Rome 1972
—— *Le piante di Roma.* 3 vols. Rome 1962
Garzetti. *TA.* 814 (bibl. on topography and planning)
Gilbert, O. *Geschichte und Topographie der Stadt Rom im Altertum.* Leipzig 1883-1890 (reprint forthcoming)

Gjerstad, E. *Early Rome*. I. Lund 1953 (on the *Forum Romanum* and the *Sacra Via*); II-IV. Lund 1956-1966

——, ed. *Les origines de la République romaine*. Fondation Hardt, Entretiens 13. Vandoeuvres/Geneva 1966; publ. 1967

Grant, M. *The Roman Forum*. London 1970

Gregorovius, F. A. *History of the City of Rome in the Middle Ages*[2]. 8 vols. London 1894-1910 (transl. from the 4th German ed.)

Grimal. *Civ. Rome*. 494 (index)

—— *Guide*. 250-251 (bibl.)

—— *Les jardins romains*. Paris 1969; 1st edition was Bibliothèque des Ecoles françaises d'Athènes et de Rome 155. Paris 1944 (the gardens of Rome; cf. pp. 37-38, 78 above)

—— *Rome*

—— *Search*. 9-109

Gros, P. *Architecture et société à Rome....* Collection Latomus 156. Brussels 1978 (useful review by R. Ling, *Journal of Roman Studies* 70 [1980]: 227-228)

—— *Aurea Templa: Recherches sur l'architecture religieuse de Rome à l'époque d'Auguste*. Bibl. des Ecoles françaises d'Athènes et de Rome 231. Rome 1976

Guida d'Italia del Touring Club Italiano, Roma e Dintorni[6]. Milan 1962

Gutkind. *IHCD*. IV (1969). 414-441; 627-628 (bibl.)

Hammond. *The City*. 493-529 (bibliography); 614 (index)

Helbig, W. *Fuehrer durch die oeffentlichen Sammlungen klassischer Altertuemer in Rom*[4]. I-IV. Tuebingen 1963-1972

Henze, A. *Rom*. Graz 1965 (a book with 224 photographs from Anderson, Alinari, W. Henze et al.)

Homo, L. *Lexique de topographie romaine*. Paris 1900

—— *Rome impériale* (201, map of aqueducts; bibl. on pp. 678-687)

—— *Rome médiévale*. Paris 1954

Huelsen, C. *The Forum and the Palatine*. New York 1928

—— and Jordan, H. *Topographie der Stadt Rom im Altertum*. 4 vols. Berlin 1878-1907; rpt. 1970

Istituto Nazionale di Urbanistica. *Roma: Città e piani*. Turin n.d.

Iversen, E. *The Obelisks of Rome*. Copenhagen 1968

Jones, H. Stuart. *Companion*

Jordan, H. *Topographie der Stadt Rom im Alterthum*. 2 vols. Berlin 1871-1885

Kaehler. *Art of Rome*

KP. IV (1972). 1444-1451 (R. Grosse)

Krautheimer, R. *Rome, Profile of a City, 312-1308*. Princeton 1980 (bibl. 329-333)

Laurand. *Manuel*. 18-19 (bibl.)

Lavedan. *HU*. 315 (map of the two walls); 328 (map of the main streets); 336 (map of the aqueducts); 494 (index)

Lugli, G. *Fontes ad topographiam veteris Urbis Romae pertinentes*. Rome 1952-

—— *I Monumenti antichi di Roma e suburbio*. 3 vols. Rome 1930-1938. Suppl. Rome 1940

—— *Roma antica, il centro monumentale*. Rome 1946 (supersedes *The Classical Monuments of Rome*)

*—— *Topografia di Roma antica* = Enciclopedia classica. III. x.3. Turin 1957

—— and Gismondi, I. *Forma Urbis Romae imperatorum aetate*. Novara 1949 (plan)

MacDonald. *Arch*. (bibl. on p. 194)

MacKendrick. *Mute Stones*

Magdelain, A. "L'inauguration de l'urbs et l'imperium," *Mélanges…Ecole française de Rome* 89 (1977): 11-29

Masson, G. *The Companion Guide to Rome*. London 1965

—— *A Concise History of Republican Rome*. London 1973 (bibl. on 182-183)

Matz, F., and von Duhn, F. *Antike Bildwerke in Rom*. 3 vols. Rome 1968

Maury, J., and Percheron, R. *Itinéraires romains*. Paris 1950 (medieval Rome)

McKay. *Houses*. 64-77, 83-89, 98-99; plates 25, 26, 49, 50; 286 (index)

McKay, A. G. *Vergil's Italy*. Greenwich, Conn., 1970. 122-146; 350-351 (index)

Muratori, S. et al. *Studi per una operante Storia urbana di Roma*. Rome 1963

Nairn, J. A. *A Classical Handlist*[3]. Oxford 1960. 116-117 (bibl.)

*Nash. *PD*. 2 vols.

Nissen. *IL*. II pp. 495-550

OCD. 935-936 (I. A. Richmond, F. Castagnoli)

Ogilvie, R. M. *A Commentary on Livy, Books 1-5*. Oxford 1965

—— *Early Rome* (esp. 30-35)

Pallottino, M., and Vallet, G. "Du Latium primitif aux origines de Rome," *Archéologia* 112 (1977): 14-17

Paoli, U. E. *Vita Romana*[2]. Paris 1960 (French translation); see Première Partie: *Urbs*. 21-138; 473-474 (bibliography) = *Rome*. London 1963 (transl. from Italian into English but shortened)

PECS. 763-770 (E. Nash)

(Charles-)Picard. *Roman Architecture*. 189-190 (bibliography)

Pietrangeli, C. *Piazza del Campidoglio*. Milan 1955 (The Piazza designed by Michelangelo lies atop the Capitol, "Campidoglio" in Italian.)

Piganiol, A. *La conquête romaine*. Paris 1967. 627 (bibl.)

—— *Essai sur les origines de Rome*. Bibliothèque des Ecoles françaises d'Athènes et de Rome 110. Paris 1917

Platner, S. B., and Ashby, T. *A Topographical Dictionary of Ancient Rome*. Oxford 1929

Pressouyre, S. *Rome au fil des temps*. Paris 1973 (historical atlas, on city planning)

Radke. *Viae*. esp. p. 10 (map)

RE. IA (1920). 1008-1061

Richardson, L., Jr. "The Approach to the Temple of Saturn in Rome," *American Journal of Archaeology* 84 (1980): 51-62

Richter, O. *Topographie der Stadt Rom*. Handbuch der klassischen Altertumswissenschaft. III.3.2. Munich 1901

Robathan, D. M. *The Monuments of Ancient Rome*. Rome 1950

Robertson. *GRA*. 371-373 (bibl.); 404 (index)

Rounds. *AAF*. 430-431 (bibl.)

Rowell, H. T. *Rome in the Augustan Age*. Norman, Okla., 1962

Rykwert. *Idea*. 239-240 (index)

Sabetti, P. "The Politics and Bureaucracy of Planning Modern Rome," *Il Politico* [University of Pavia] 43 (1978): 144-149

Saeflund, G. *Le mura di Roma repubblicana*. Acta Instituti Romani Regni Sueciae 1 (1932)

Scott, I. "Early Roman Tradition in the Light of Archaeology," *Memoirs of the American Academy in Rome* 7 (1929): 7-118

Stier. *Atlas*. 32-33 (plan)

Strong, D. S. *Roman Art*. Harmondsworth, Middlesex, 1976

Studi di topografia romana. Quaderni dell'Istituto di Topografia Antica dell'Università di Roma 5. Rome 1966

Todd, M. *The Walls of Rome*. 1977

Touring Club Italiano. *Roma*. 2 vols. Milan 1960 ("a photographic synthesis")

Van Buren, A. W. *Ancient Rome*. London 1936

Van Deman, E. B. "The Sullan Forum," *Journal of Roman Studies* 12 (1922): 1-31

Vinaccia, G. *Il problema dell'orientamento nell'urbanistica dell'antica Roma*. Rome 1939

Ward-Perkins. *Cities*. 29-36, 40-42, 122; 126-127 (index)

—— *RA*. 11-154; 295-320 (Late Roman)

Wheeler. *RAA*

Wiesel, J. M., and Cichy, B. *Rom, Veduten des 14.-19. Jahrhunderts*. Stuttgart 1959 (engravings by Piranesi et al.)

Yavetz, Z. "The Living Conditions of the Urban Plebs in Republican Rome," *Latomus* 17 (1958): 500-517 = *The Crisis in the Roman Republic*. Edit. R. Seager. Cambridge 1969. 162-182

Sabratha, Africa Proconsularis (today in the region of Tripolitania [q.v.], a part of Libya)

41 (the forum), 50 (the Capitol, q.v.), 61 (the theater)

Like *Lepcis Magna* (q.v.) *Sabratha* began as a Carthaginian harbor-town, but it was founded about a century later (fifth century B.C.). Under Roman rule, *Sabratha* also exported local olive oil and grain to Rome, as well as ivory from Central Africa. Consequently, there is a mosaic of an elephant at the office of the traders from *Sabratha* in the Piazzale delle Corporazioni at OSTIA ANTICA (Rostovtzeff 338; 688, n. 99).

In addition to its theater, *Sabratha* was distinguished by a fine amphitheater (Haywood in *ESAR* 111). It was granted the honor of colonial status (see *colonia*), perhaps by the Emperor Trajan (A.D. 98-117; *Antonine Itinerary* [q.v.] 61; Broughton, *RAP* 132, Haywood 75; Salmon, *RC* 159). As at *Lepcis*, the extensive, sand-covered remains have been excavated, but not completely, by Italian archaeologists.

For bibliography, also see *Lepcis Magna*.

Bartoccini, R. *Guida di Sabratha*. Rome/Milan 1927

Besnier. *Lexique*. 656

Bianchi Bandinelli, R., Caputo, G., and Vergara Caffarelli, E. *The Buried City: Excavations at Leptis Magna*. Transl. from the Italian by D. Ridgway. London 1966. 121-122 (bibliography)

Boëthius and Ward-Perkins. *ERA*. 465, 471-474; fig. 175B (the theater); plates 249-250 (theater)

Brown. *RA*. 28-29, pl. 45 (the theater)

Caputo, G. *Il teatro di Sabratha e l'architettura teatrale africana*. Monografie di archeologia libica 6. Rome 1959

Crema. *ANRW*. I.4 "Arch. rep." pl. 45

—— *Arch*. 667 (index)

Di Vita, A. *Sabratha*. Basle 1969

Duncan-Jones. *ERE*. 266, n. 1 (bibl.)

Enciclopedia dell'arte antica, classica e orientale. VI (1965). 1050-1060 (P. Romanelli)

Frank. *ESAR*. IV pp. 107 (use of the Carthaginian language under Roman rule); 69, 111 (trade); (R. M. Haywood)

Garzetti. *TA*. 753 (bibl.)

*Haynes, D. E. L. *An Archaeological and Historical Guide to the Antiquities of Tripolitania*[2]. London 1959. 107-134

KP. IV (1972). 1485 (M. Leglay)

Mathews, K. D. *Cities in the Sand: Leptis Magna and Sabratha*. Ann Arbor 1957

OCD. 942 (O. Brogan)

PECS. 779-780 (J. B. Ward-Perkins)

(Charles-)Picard. *Roman Architecture*. 148-149, plates 159-162 (theater); 171 (plan of theater)

Piganiol. *HR*. 593 (bibl.)

Raven. *Rome in Africa*. 189 (index)

Rostovtzeff. *SEHRE*. 335, 338 (trade)

Snider, G., and Woloch, G. M. *The Byzantine Period: Slide Lecture on the Art and Architecture of the Byzantine Period*. Montreal 1977. slide 34 (floor-mosaic from the Basilica [church] of Justinian, c. A.D. 550)

Ward, P. *Sabratha*. Stoughton, Wisconsin, 1970

Ward-Perkins. *RA*. 352 (index)

Wheeler. *RAA*. 230 (oriental influence on a sculpture)

Wheeler and Wood. *Roman Africa*. 82-91; plates 21-23 (the theater); 24 (the Temple of Liber Pater); 25 (mosaic from the baths, now in the site-museum)

St. Albans: listed under LONDON

ST.-BERTRAND-DE-COMMINGES (Haute-Garonne, France) = *Lugdunum Convenarum, Aquitania*

pp. 43 (forum); 50-51 (?Capitol)

The *oppidum* of the Convenae was a hill-settlement which commanded the upper Garonne valley from the left bank. It was just below the magnificent Pyrenees, and it controlled access through a pass in the center of this east-west mountain range (Ebel). At the *oppidum*, in 72 B.C., Pompey settled survivors of the civil war against

Sertorius, a Roman general in Spain. An orthogonal town was built at a lower altitude from about 25 B.C. (Labrousse in *PECS*). The geographer Strabo (q.v.) tells us that the inhabitants had Latin rights and that there were some Roman citizens in the town (4.2.2), which was the tribal capital of the Convenae.

The size of this town is quite surprising—137 hectares or 338 acres lie inside its walls (see cities [Roman], comparison in area, below). Our knowledge of it is mainly due to Bertrand Sapène, a local schoolmaster, who excavated from 1920 to 1966. Roman structures include the forum (see *fora*, comparison in size), temples (not necessarily a Capitol), an aqueduct and baths, a theater, a small amphitheater, and a market. The date of a victory monument in local marble (a trophy) is disputed (Piganiol, *HR* 360). The apogee of the town was the reign of Trajan (98-117).

Marble from St.-Béat, fifteen kilometers further south, is found not only in this *Lugdunum* but also in BORDEAUX; it was shipped down the Garonne (in Latin, *Garumna*) River in Roman times. Near SAINT-BERTRAND were Roman mines, farms, forests, and spas. The Gallo-Roman town was on the road from TOULOUSE to Bayonne *(Lapurdum)*, and the road north to PERIGUEUX began nearby.

A Late Roman wall was built around the old *oppidum*, which became the site of the Cathedral of St. Bertrand (compare the migrations at VAISON-LA-ROMAINE). *Lugdunum Convenarum* was sacked by the Vandals (q.v.) in A.D. 409 and never recovered from this raid. There is a museum on the site of the ancient town.

Bailhache, M. "Contribution à l'étude de l'aqueduc gallo-romain de St.-Bertrand-de-Comminges," *Gallia* 30 (1972): 167-198 (on p. 171, they are compared with those at Rome)

Besnier. *Lexique*. 443

Brogan. *Roman Gaul*. 9-10, 97; 139 (on the marble)

Calmette, J. *Bulletin de la Société des Antiquaires de France* (1928). 253 ff.

Ebel. *TG*. 100

Eydoux, H.-P. "La résurrection de Lugdunum Convenarum," *Lumières sur la Gaule*. Paris 1960. 157-189

Grenier. *Manuel*. II 674-676; III 327-341 (forum), 327, n. 2 (bibliography); 496-505 (the basilica); 537-541 (the church); 648-649 (amphitheater); 808-814 (theater); IV 276-288 (the baths)

Lavedan, P. et al. *Les fouilles de Saint-Bertrand-de-Comminges (1920-1929)*. Mémoires de la Société archéologique du Midi. Toulouse 1929

—— and Rey, R. *Luchon, St.-Bertrand-de-Comminges et la région, Promenades archéologiques.* Toulouse/Paris 1931

Lizop, R. *Les Convenae et les Consoranni.* Toulouse/Paris 1931 (bibl. pp. xvii-xxix)

MacKendrick. *RF.* 36, 92-98; 259-260 (bibl.)

Maistre, L. *Revue archéologique* (1926). 25 ff. (on the iron and the mines of Aquitania)

McKay. *Houses.* 170

OCD. 625 (A. L. F. Rivet)

PECS. 531 (M. Labrousse)

Picard, C. "Observations sur les statues de prisonniers et les trophées de St.-Bertrand-de-Comminges," *Comptes rendus de l'Académie des inscriptions et belles-lettres* (1933): 138-159 (dates the trophy to the first century A.D., but rebuilt in the second)

(Charles-)Picard, G. "Sur la composition et la date des trophées de St.-Bertrand-de-Comminges," *Comptes rendus de l'Académie des incriptions et belles-lettres* (1942): 8-17

Piganiol. *HR.* 360 (bibl.)

RE. XIII (1927). 1723 (Cramer)

Sapène, B. *Au forum de Lugdunum Convenarum, Inscriptions du début du règne de Trajan.* Toulouse 1939 (see fig. 10B above and bibl. in *PECS*)

—— St.-Bertrand-de-Comminges (Lugdunum Convenarum), centre touristique d'art et d'histoire. Toulouse 1954. 2nd edition, 1962

Ward-Perkins. *RA.* 210, pl. 223 (plan of forum)

—— "Republic to Empire." figs. 1B, 7

SAINTES (Charente-Maritime, France) = *Mediolanum Santonum, Aquitania*

pp. 65 (amphitheater), 79 (Late Roman wall), 82 (arch)

Under Roman rule, SAINTES was the tribal capital of the Celtic Santones (compare PARIS, PERIGUEUX). It is on the left bank of the Charente River (in Latin, *Carantonus*), which flows north at this point and later northwest into the Bay of Biscay, an arm of the Atlantic Ocean.

The triumphal arch, of A.D. 19, is at the eastern end of the Roman *decumanus*, where the Roman bridge across the Charente began. The relative location of the bridge and the arch is similar to that at St.-Chamas (p. 82 above). The Roman highway from SAINTES and the Charente went east to LYONS, by way of Limoges. Another Roman road led north from BORDEAUX to SAINTES and then turned northeast to Poitiers.

In Roman times, as today, SAINTES was noted for its oysters. The present-day city of Cognac, famous for its brandy, is twenty-five kilometers up the Charente, to the east of SAINTES.

Besnier. *Lexique*. 475

Brogan. *Roman Gaul*. 136 (the oyster trade)

Chevallier. *Roman Roads*. 160-162 (the Romanization of SAINTES)

Dangibeaud, C. *Saintes, Mediolanum Santonum*. Saintes 1933

Grenier. *Manuel*. I pp. 568-569 (bridge); III pp. 651-657 (amphitheater), 656 (plan), 994-996 (the *circus*, for chariot races)

KP. IV (1972). 1544 (M. Leglay; see "Santoni")

MacKendrick. *RF*. 115-118

*Maurin, L. *Saintes antique*. Bordeaux 1978

Michaud, J. "Le développement topographique de Saintes au Moyen-Age," *Bulletin philologique et historique du Comité* (1961): 23-29

Millar. *REN*. pl. 8 (the arch)

PECS. 563 (L. Maurin)

RE. IA (1920). 2289-2301 (Keune; see "Santoni")

Triou, A. *Gallia* 26 (1968): 119 ff.

ST.-REMY-DE-PROVENCE (Bouches-du-Rhône, France), one kilometer north of *Glanum Livii* (the Greek name was *Glanon*), *Gallia Narbonensis*

p. 3 (Greek influence on the native *oppidum*)

The ancient site is just north of the picturesque Alpilles hills. The native *oppidum* underwent more Greek influence than that at ENSERUNE; Greeks, mainly from MARSEILLES, settled there in the third century B.C. This Hellenistic (q.v.) town was destroyed by Germanic invaders around 100 B.C. *Glanum* was rebuilt under Roman rule.

The town received Latin rights (q.v., Pliny, *Natural History* 3.37). A Roman road went southwest, skirting the Alpilles, and joined the ARLES-LYONS highway not far north of ARLES. A triumphal arch and the Mausoleum of the Julii (?a local family) remain, north of the site. Rivet dates these monuments, called Les Antiques, c. 48 B.C. The ruins of the town include Hellenistic houses, like those at Delos, Greece (see p. 86 and Chapter IV, n. 5 above), as well as a Roman forum (?), baths and sewer.

Glanum was destroyed by the Alamans (q.v.) and other invaders about A.D. 270, never to be reconstructed.

Balty, J.-C. "Basilique et curie du forum de Glanum," *Latomus* 21 (1962): 279-319

Barbet, A. *Recueil général des peintures murales de la Gaule (Narbonnaise)*. *Gallia*. Suppl. 27 (1974)

Benoît, F. "Le barrage et l'aqueduc romain de St.-Rémy-de-Prov-
ence," *Revue des études anciennes* (1935): 332-340
Boëthius and Ward-Perkins. *ERA*. plates 180 (house), 187 (mauso-
leum and arch)
Brogan. *Roman Gaul*. 97-99
Bruchet, J. *Les Antiques...de Glanum...* La Provence archéologique
et médiévale 1. Paris 1969
Chevallier. *ANRW*. II.3 pp. 692-696, 756-758 (plans); 769; 811-812
(list of figures and plates; bibl.)
Clébert. *Provence antique*. 207-218
Crema. *Arch*. 667 (index)
Desjardins. *Géogr.* III p. 427
Ebel. *TG*. 36 (Greek period)
Février. "CSG." 13, 17
—— *Dév. urbain en Provence*. 221 (index, see "Glanum"); fig. 29
Finley. *Atlas*. 59-60 (P. MacKendrick)
Greece and Rome. 2nd ser. 2 (1955). plates 160c, 161-164
Grenier. *Manuel*. III pp. 481-482 (*bouleuterion*, or Greek council
house, third century B.C. in the ?forum area), IV 245-251 (the
baths)
Grimal. *Civ. Rome*. 494; ill. 144
Gros, P. "Pour une chronologie des arcs de triomphe de Gaule Nar-
bonnaise (à propos de l'arc de *Glanum*)," *Gallia* 37 (1979): 55-83
KP. II (1967). 806 (M. Leglay)
Lavedan. *HU*. 491 (index, see Glanum)
MacKendrick. *RF*. 21-25; 255-256 (bibliography)
McKay. *Houses*. 159-161; 251, n. 292 (bibliography)
OCD. 467 (A. L. F. Rivet)
PECS. 356-357 (C. Goudineau)
Rolland, H. *L'Arc de Glanum. Gallia*. Suppl. 31 (1977)
*——— *Fouilles de Glanum. Gallia*. Suppl. 1 (1946). Suppl. 11 (1958)
—— "Les fouilles de Glanum...de 1945 à 1947," *Gallia* 6 (1948): 141-
169
—— *Glanum....* Paris 1960
—— *Glanum, notice archéologique*. Saint-Rémy-de-Provence 1977
—— *Le Mausolée de Glanum. Gallia*. Suppl. 21 (1969)
—— "Le pavement des maisons de Glanum," *Comptes rendus de
l'Académie des inscriptions et belles-lettres* (1949): 342, 346-351;
354-355 (baths); 619 (index)
—— *St.-Rémy-de-Provence*. Bergerac 1934
Salviat, F. *Glanum*. ECNMHS. Paris n.d.

Ward-Perkins. *RA*. 349 (index)

+ St.-Romain-en-Gal (Rhône, France): see VIENNE

Salpensa, charter of: see OSUNA

SANTA MARIA CAPUA VETERE: see CAPUA VETERE

Santiponce: see ITALICA

SANXAY (Vienne, France); in Roman *Aquitania*
pp. 55 (the Gallo-Roman shrine); 66-67 (the demi-amphitheater)
This site is comparable to CHASSENON for its location *(Aquitania)* and its monuments. Water was important at SANXAY also; there were baths for the pilgrims near the shrine. SANXAY is thirty kilometers southwest of Poitiers.
Crema. *Arch*. 667 (index)
Eggers, H., ed. *Kelten und Germanen*. Baden-Baden 1964. 101-102, figs. 3 and 4 (plans of SANXAY); (E. Will)
Formigé, J. "Le sanctuaire de Sanxay (Vienne)," *Gallia* 2 (1944): 43-120
Grenier. *Manuel* III pp. 54-55; 939-943 (the demi-amphitheater); IV 553-567 (baths)
Koethe, H. *Die keltischen Rund- und Vielecktempel*. Bericht der roemisch-germanischen Kommission 23. Frankfurt am Main 1934. 68-174
MacKendrick. *RF*. 167-171
PECS. 806-807 (G. Nicolini)

Segesta (Sicily, Italy; *Segesta* is the Latin name, *Egesta* the Greek)
p. 61 (theater)
The deserted site is in northwest Sicily, on and below Monte Varvaro, seventeen kilometers by road from the modern Castellammare de Golfo (on an arm of the Tyrrhenian Sea). Little is known about the origins of *Segesta*, a city of the native Elymi. By 416 B.C., the residents of the city seem to have become quite Hellenized, and they obtained Athens' help against their constant enemy, *Selinus* (q.v.); the story is told by Thucydides in his *History of the Peloponnesian War* (Books VI and VII). Athens and *Segesta* lost to *Selinus*, Syracuse, and Sparta, and *Segesta* next became an ally of CARTHAGE, whose army, as a result, destroyed *Selinus* in 409. Then, like *Seli-*

nus, Segesta became a dependency of CARTHAGE (with brief respite in the fourth century). In 262 B.C., during the First Punic War, *Segesta* surrendered to Rome and became an allied city (q.v.) of the highest rank (Cicero, *Against Verres* 3.6.13). The city's decline began in the first century B.C. There are two major monuments on the site, an unfinished Doric temple (of 416 B.C.?) and the Hellenistic (q.v.) theater, modified in Roman times.

Besnier. *Lexique*. 684-685

Blue Guide, Sicily. 74-75

Burford, A. "Temple Building at Segesta," *Classical Quarterly* N.S. 11 (1961): 87-93 (bibl.)

Crema. *Arch*. 76 (theater)

EB. XXIV p. 582 (T. Ashby)

Enciclopedia dell'arte antica, classica e orientale. VII (1966). 151-154 (V. Tusa)

Finley. *Ancient Sicily*. 200 (bibl.); 223 (index)

—— *Atlas*. 91-92 (M. I. Finley)

KP. V (1975). 71-72 (K. Abel)

McKay, A. G. *Vergil's Italy*. Greenwich, Conn., 1970. 306-310; plate 72

Natoli, L. "Segesta," *Kokalos* 22/23 (Palermo 1976/1977): 779-788

OCD. 970 (A. G. Woodhead)

PECS. 817-818 (V. Tusa)

Randall-MacIver, D. *Greek Cities in Italy and Sicily*. Oxford 1931; rpt. Amsterdam 1968. 220-222

RE. IIA.1 (1923). 1055-1069 (K. Ziegler)

Van Compernolle, R. "Ségeste et l'Hellénisme," *Phoibos* 5 (Brussels 1950/1951): 183-228

Woodhead. *Greeks in the West*. plate 65

Selinus (in Italian, Selinunte; Sicily, Italy)

p. 25 (no Etruscan influence when rebuilt, soon after 409 B.C.)

Selinus was founded on the southwest coast of Sicily in the second half of the seventh century B.C. by Greek colonists from nearby *Megara Hyblaea*. Destroyed by CARTHAGE in 409 B.C. (cf. Diodorus Siculus 13.54 and *Segesta* above), *Selinus* was quickly rebuilt under Carthaginian control. A rectangular grid of streets, discovered by aerial photography, north of the rebuilt city antedates 409 (Ward-Perkins). The new *Selinus* was definitively destroyed by CARTHAGE in 250 B.C. The site remained deserted, given over to malarial swamps. Four Greek temples on the acropolis (in the southeast part of the city) and of the sixth century B.C. are among the finest examples of archaic Greek architecture.

Bejor, G. "Problemi di localizzazione di culti a Selinunte," *Annali della Scuola Normale Superiore di Pisa, Cl. di Lettere e Filosofia* 7 (1977): 439-457 (To which gods were the various temples dedicated?)

Besnier. *Lexique*. 688

Blue Guide, Sicily. 76-78; finds at the Museo Nazionale Archeologico in Palermo, 55-57

Boëthius. *Golden House*. 35, n. 22; 42

Castagnoli. *Orthogonal Town Planning*. 10-12; fig. 1

Crema. *Arch*. 667 (index)

Di Vita, A. "Per l'architettura e la urbanistica di età greca arcaica," *Palladio* 17 (1967): 3-60

Dunbabin, T. J. *The Western Greeks*. Oxford 1948. 301 ff.

EB. XXIV pp. 607-608 (T. Ashby)

Enciclopedia dell'arte antica, classica e orientale. VII (1966). 175-188 (I. Marconi Bovio)

Finley. *Ancient Sicily*. 200 (bibl.); 223 (index)

—— *Atlas*. 86-87 (M. I. Finley)

Gábrici, E. "Studi archeologici selinunti," *Monumenti antichi* 43 (1956): 205-407

Grimal. *Search*. 216-221

Gutkind. *IHCD*. IV (1969). 603-609 (with good overall photographs); 634 (bibl.)

Hammond. *The City*. 222 (orthogonal plan c. 500 B.C.)

Hulot, J., and Fougères, G. *Sélinonte*. Paris 1910

KP. V (1975). 90-91 (K. Abel)

MacKendrick. *Greek Stones*. 199-201; 428 (index)

McKay, A. G. *Vergil's Italy*. Greenwich, Conn., 1970. 302-303; plate 70

OCD. 972 (A. G. Woodhead)

PECS. 823-825 (V. Tusa)

Randall-MacIver, D. *Greek Cities in Italy and Sicily*. Oxford 1931. 212-220

RE. IIA.2 (1923). 1266-1308 (K. Ziegler)

Robertson. *GRA*. 193 (plan); 368 (bibl.); 405 (index)

Rykwert. *Idea*. 42

Santangelo, M. *Selinunte*. Rome 1961

Vallet, G., and Villard, F. "La date de fondation de Sélinonte...," *Bulletin de correspondance hellénique* 82 (1958): 16-26

Ward-Perkins. *Cities*. 23-24; 119 (including bibl.); fig. 31 (plan)
Woodhead. *Greeks in the West*. 48-50, fig. 6 (plan); 242 (index)
Wycherley, R. E. "Hellenic Cities," *Town Planning Review* 22 (1951/ 1952). fig. 6 (plan)

SETIF (wilaya of Sétif, Algeria) = *Colonia Nerviana Augusta Martialis Veteranorum Sitifensium (CIL* VIII 8473 and others) or *Sitifis, Mauretania Caesariensis*
pp. 48, 83 (location of DJEMILA on the Roman highway)
      This Roman colony for veterans was founded in A.D. 96/98 in the limestone hills which dominate the high plateau (1,070 meters) lying between the Petite Kabylie Mountains (near the Mediterranean) on the north and the Hodna Mountains inland. In spite of the extreme climate, an agricultural economy (livestock and cereals) was and is possible. By the present road, which runs well to the south of DJEMILA, SETIF is 131 kilometers west of CONSTANTINE.
      According to J. Carcopino, the region of *Sitifis* became one large imperial estate c. A.D. 200. The farmers, who were then unprotected by Roman troops but near the Empire's southern frontier, manned a series of fortresses (Rostovtzeff). When Diocletian (284-305) subdivided the Roman provinces, *Sitifis* became the capital of *Mauretania Sitifensis*. This region was subsequently conquered by the Vandals (q.v), Byzantines (see Byzantine) and Arabs. A Byzantine fort of the mid-sixth century covered the center of the Roman city. It was partially rebuilt and used by French troops from the midnineteenth century for about 100 years.
      The present Algerian city and departmental capital of SETIF was founded by the French, who located a major crossroads (east-west and north-south) there. Only a small part of the Roman city has been uncovered (Février in *PECS*). There are some good Roman mosaics in the local museum.

Broughton. *RAP*. 130 (founded along with *Cuicul* [DJEMILA])
Carcopino, J. "Les Castella de la plaine de Sétif," *Revue africaine* 294 (1918)
Février, P.-A. *Fouilles de Sétif, les basiliques du quartier nord-ouest*. Paris 1965
────── "Notes sur le développement urbain en Afrique du Nord, les exemples comparés de Djemila et de Sétif," *Cahiers archéologiques* 14 (1964): 1-47
────── et al. *Fouilles de Sétif 1959-1966—Le quartier nord-ouest*. *Rempart et cirque*. Algiers 1970

Frank. *ESAR*. IV p. 38 (R. M. Haywood; evidence for the colony of
　veterans)
Gsell. *AAA*. fasc. 16 ("Sétif")
KP. V (1975). 216 (H. Cueppers)
Nagel's Guide, Algeria. 281-283
PECS. 844-845 (P.-A. Février)
Raven. *Rome in Africa*. 190 (index)
Rostovtzeff. *SEHRE*. 425-426, 724, n. 48
Soyer, J. "Centuriations en Algérie orientale," *Antiquités africaines*
　10 (1976): 137-139

+ Seville: listed under ITALICA

SILCHESTER (Hampshire, England, U.K.) = *Calleva Atrebatum,
Britannia*
pp. 55-56 (Romano-British temple); 91 (houses)
　The site is in the Thames valley but is fifteen kilometers south of
that river. *Calleva* was the tribal capital of the British Atrebates; the
continental Atrebates gave their name to Arras (Pas de Calais, France)
and the region of Artois. The British Atrebates were ruled by a client-
king (q.v.) named Tiberius Claudius Cogidubnus A.D. 43/52-75/80
(Tacitus, *Agricola* 14; the Romans invaded Britain in 43). The kingdom of Cogidubnus also included Chichester (now in West Sussex)
and Winchester (Hampshire). Upon his death, his former territory
was "split into three divisions: the *civitas Regnensium, civitas Atrebatum*, and *civitas Belgarum*, with capitals respectively at Chichester (Noviomagus Regnensium), Silchester (Calleva Atrebatum), and
Winchester (Venta Belgarum)" (Scullard, *RB* 50; also see Ogilvie and
Richmond, *Agricola* 189-190, Barrett, and *civitas* below).
　SILCHESTER probably did not become a *municipium*, but an inscription found at WROXETER (q.v.) shows that, under Rome, *civitates* and *municipia* had analogous magistrates.
　The orthogonal street plan of *Calleva* was superimposed on the
previous *oppidum* and was laid out later than the forum, which Ward-
Perkins dates to about A.D. 70 (p. 120) and Wacher to A.D. 83/100
(p. 260). Located in the center of town, the forum is slightly out of
alignment with the grid of streets (see *fora*, comparison in size, below).
　There were three fortifications around the town: an inner earthwork of about A.D. 43, an outer earthwork of the late first century
enclosing 93 hectares (230 acres) and a town wall, an octagon of earth

with unequal sides, of about A.D. 200 just inside the then useless inner earthwork. In the third century, the wall was faced with flint, the local stone (Wacher 265).

The wall surrounded an area of 42.5 hectares (105 acres [Ward-Perkins]), similar in size to but not quite the same as the section with *insulae* (see city blocks). These blocks varied in size from 70 by 82 meters to 119 meters square (Collingwood and Richmond, *ARB* 96). Because little has been built on the site since it was abandoned (? in about A.D. 500; see Saxons), the outline of the streets may be seen clearly in an aerial photograph (Margary 88, key to plate i; compare WROXETER). The inhabited area of *Calleva* was relatively large, but estimates for the population range from a low of 1,000 (Wilkes in Finley, *Atlas*) to only 7,500 (the upper figure given by Rivet, 89).

Under a grove of trees in the farm at present-day SILCHESTER lies an amphitheater (of ? c. A.D. 100). Like all the amphitheaters found in Britain, it was made of earth, but a flint revetment was reported as late as the eighteenth century (Wacher 264; see Chapter III, n. 25 above). The amphitheater was located between the town wall and the outer earthwork, to the north of the wall's east gate. There are also burials in this intermediate area (see *pomerium*).

Roman roads from SILCHESTER led east to LONDON (seventy kilometers or forty-four English miles), north to Towcester (Northamptonshire) and Watling Street, northwest to Gloucester (see colonies in *Britannia*), southwest to Old Sarum (in Wiltshire, near Salisbury) and south to Winchester (also in Hampshire; see Liversidge, 394 for a map based on the *Antonine Itinerary*, q.v.; also see Margary, map 11). *Calleva* was linked with even more Roman roads, and it is tempting to identify the largest house in town (just inside the south gate) as a *mansio* or inn for travelers on government business (Wacher 263-264; also see Rivet 84). Similar in shape to the house in fig. 28 above, it contained more rooms and had its own bathhouse. Besides the bathhouse, some of the rooms of the house itself were heated by hypocausts (furnaces; see pp. 70-71 above).

SILCHESTER was almost completely excavated by 1909, but scholars have continued to reinterpret the archaeological finds. Few writers of the present day, however, would disagree with Collingwood's description of it, "the head-quarters of a tribal canton, the seat of justice and administration as well as commerce and trade for the tribe of Atrebates, Silchester may be called a county town" *(RB* 46). There is a small museum on the site, and the Silchester collection of the Reading Museum (fifteen kilometers to the northeast in the county town of Berkshire) uniquely illustrates the daily life and work of a Romano-British town such as *Calleva Atrebatum*.

Archaeologia (1891-)

Archaeology. 30 (1977). 425 (an advertisement by Lilyheath Properties Ltd. to sell Silchester in 800 1/8 acre lots, one-third of the price to go to the Calleva [Silchester] Trust "to ensure the full and professional excavation, preservation and documentation of the site by Dr. Michael Fulford of Reading University, assisted by Professors Cunliffe and Frere [Oxford University] and Boon [National Museum of Wales]")

Barrett, A. A. "The Career of Tiberius Claudius Cogidubnus," *Britannia* 10 (1979): 227-242

Besnier. *Lexique.* 162

Blue Guide, England. 168

*Boon, G. C. *Roman Silchester.* London 1957

—— "Sarapis and Tutela: A Silchester Coincidence," *Britannia* 4 (1973): 107-114

—— *Silchester: The Roman Town of Calleva.* Newton Abbot, Devon/ North Pomfret, Vermont, 1974

Collingwood. *RB.* 46-50

—— and Richmond. *ARB.* 109 (plan of the forum); 347 (index)

Crema. *Arch.* 668 (index)

Finley. *Atlas.* 23-24 (J. J. Wilkes)

Frere, S. S. *ANRW.* II.3 (1975). 297, fig. 3 (the forum)

—— *Britannia.* 429 (index); an excellent map follows p. 432; plate 17 (air view); 401 (bibl.)

Haverfield, F. *The Romanization of Roman Britain*[4]. Oxford 1923

—— *Town Planning.* 127-132

Hawkes, C., and Dunning, G. C. "The Belgae of Gaul and Britain," *Archaeological Journal* 87 (1930): 150-335

KP. I (1964). 1017 (H. Cueppers)

Lavedan. *HU.* 414 (map); 494 (index)

Liversidge. *BRE.* 522 (index); plate 11 (the baths)

Margary. *RRB.* 88, 96, 166; map 11

McKay. *Houses.* 199-200 (on heating with hypocausts); 287 (index)

Morris. *Urban Form.* 58-59, fig. 3.28

OCD. 144 (A. L. F. Rivet on the continental Atrebates; S. S. Frere on the British Atrebates); 193-194 (C. E. Stevens)

O'Neil, B. H. St. J. "The Silchester Region in the Fifth and Sixth Centuries A.D.," *Antiquity* 18 (1944): 113-122

OSMRB

PECS. 186-187 (G. C. Boon)
Richmond. *RB*. 106 (aqueduct); 230 (index; see "Calleva")
Rivet. *TCRB*. 139-140 (on the Atrebates); 164 (bibl.); 191 (index)
Rostovtzeff. *SEHRE*. 229
Rykwert. *Idea*. 42
Wacher. *TRB*. 48-49 (on the baths); 255-277; 457 (index)
Ward-Perkins. *Cities*. 120; figs. 71, 72

+ *Spina:* listed under RAVENNA

SUBIACO (Latium, Italy) = *Sublaqueum, Samnium, Italia*
p. 73 (*Aqua Marcia* aqueduct; see Chapter III, n. 31 above on aqueducts)
   This site, on the western slopes of Monte Livata in the Apennines (q.v.), is at the confluence of the Acquaviva and the upper Anio Rivers, about fifty air or seventy-five road kilometers east of Rome. It was about five kilometers above the place where the *Anio Novus* aqueduct took in water from the Anio River (see p. 74 above) and about twenty kilometers above the purer sources of the *Aquae Claudia* and *Marcia*.
   One reaches SUBIACO by road on the *Via Sublacensis*, a beautiful, wooded byway of the *Via Valeria* (see TIVOLI). The town arose to serve the villa built by the Emperor Nero (A.D. 54-68; see Tacitus, *Annals* 14.22), and it remains today as a small industrial center (paper and optical equipment). Nero had the Anio dammed to form lakes, and his "state villa was mirrored in those artifical waters" (Hodgkin).
   About A.D. 495, St. Benedict retreated to SUBIACO, where he founded twelve monasteries by 528, when he left for even greater accomplishments at Monte Cassino. Two of St. Benedict's monasteries still exist at SUBIACO, and traces of Nero's villa may be seen there. (For an eighth-century Benedictine abbey, see + *Verulamium*, under LONDON.)
Ashby, T. *The Aqueducts of Ancient Rome*. Oxford 1935
Bagnani. *Rom. Cam*. 250-257
Besnier. *Lexique*. 721
Blue Guide, Rome. 357
Enciclopedia dell'arte antica, classica e orientale. VII (1966). 537-538 (M. Torelli)

*Guida d'Italia del Touring Club Italiano, Lazio*³. Milan 1964. 373-382

Hodgkin, T. *Italy and her Invaders*. IV. Oxford 1896; rpt. New York 1967. map next to p. 152; 468 (the aqueduct); 469-475 (St. Benedict)

Jones, H. Stuart. *Companion*. 144

KP. V (1975). 403 (G. Radke)

MacKendrick. *Mute Stones*. 317 (discovery by Ashby and Van Deman of the courses of the aqueducts named above); 359-360 (bibl.)

Nissen. *IL*. I p. 314; II p. 618

PECS. 864 (M. Torelli)

Radke. *Viae*. fig. 26

RE. IVA (1932). 480 (H. Philipp)

Smith, N. "The Roman Dams of Subiaco," *Technology and Culture* 11 (1970): 56-68

Van Deman, E. B. *The Building of the Roman Aqueducts*. Washington, D.C., 1934

+ Susa: listed under TURIN

Syracuse (Sicily, Italy): mentioned under TAORMINA

+ Tangier: listed under *Volubilis*

TAORMINA (Sicily, Italy) = *Tauromenium* (in Latin; *Tauromenion* in Greek), *Sicilia*
p. 61 (the theater)

   TAORMINA is in eastern Sicily at the foot of the volcano, Mount Etna; it overlooks the Ionian Sea. A colony of CARTHAGE (396 B.C.), it was captured by the tyrant (q.v.) Dionysius I of Syracuse, who refounded it as a Greek city (392; Diodorus Siculus 14.96.4). In 358, Andromachus gathered together refugees from Sicilian Naxos (a nearby city which Dionysius I had destroyed) and took over TAORMINA (Diodorus Siculus 16.7.1). The city came under the control of Hieron II, tyrant of Syracuse, but when he died in 215, it became an allied city (q.v.) of Rome (Cicero, *Against Verres* 3.13; see Finley, *Ancient Sicily* 124). (On Syracuse see Bengtson, *Atlas* 23d and *Erlaeuterungen*.)

   Julius Caesar granted all of Sicily Latin rights (q.v.). In 36 B.C., Octavian (to become Augustus in 27 B.C.) founded at *Tauromenium* one of the six veteran-colonies which he placed in the province of

Sicily. (For *Tauromenium*, see Diodorus 16.7.1, Pliny, *Natural History* 3.88.) Syracuse, the provincial capital, received a similar colony. These Roman colonies contributed to the spread of the Latin language in Greek-speaking Sicily (see Finley, *Ancient Sicily* 152, 165-166).

A Roman road ran south from the Strait of Messina to TAORMINA and on to Syracuse, also on the Ionian Sea. Sicily produced mainly wheat and wool, but marble and wine were also exported (Rostovtzeff and Scramuzza).

TAORMINA's theater, cut into a rocky hill, dates from the second century A.D. and is well preserved today (Besnier and Bell). Taken by the Arabs in the early tenth century A.D. and the Normans (q.v.) late in the eleventh, TAORMINA is today a winter resort of exceptional beauty.

Bérard. *Bibl. topogr.* 111 ff.

Besnier. *Lexique.* 745

Blue Guide, Sicily. 105-108

Crema. *Arch.* 668 (index)

EB. XXVI p. 402 (T. Ashby)

Enciclopedia dell'arte antica, classica e orientale. VII (1966). 598-599 (G. V. Gentili)

Finley. *Ancient Sicily.* 209 (bibl.); 224-225 (index)

Frank. *ESAR.* III pp. 235, 255 (allied city); 270 (wine), 271 (olive oil); 310 (city finances 150/100 B.C.); 346 (Roman colony); 355 (limestone and marble); (V. M. Scramuzza)

Guida d'Italia del Touring Club Italiano, Sicilia[4]. Milan 1953. 466-475

KP. V (1975). 544-545 (K. Meister)

Manganaro, G. "Tauromenitana," *Archeologia classica* 15 (1963): 13-31 (on language)

OCD. 1040 (A. G. Woodhead)

PECS. 886-887 (M. Bell)

Randall-MacIver, D. *Greek Cities of Italy and Sicily.* Oxford 1931. 80-81

RE. VA.1 (1934). 27-32 (K. Ziegler)

Rizzo, P. *Tauromenion.* 1928

Rostovtzeff. *SEHRE.* 566, n. 28 (wine and grain)

Salmon. *RC.* 164 (date of the colony)

Santangelo, M. *Taormine et ses environs.* Rome 1953. transl. from the Italian

Vittinghoff. *Roemische Kolonisation.* 120

TARQUINIA (until 1922, CORNETO, modern Latium, Italy), near
Tarquinii; ancient Roman region of *Etruria, Italia*
p. 15 (tomb paintings)
One of the twelve Etrurian cities of the Etruscan League, *Tarquinii* was located on a rocky plateau, five kilometers from the Tyrrhenian Sea (compare *Vetulonia*). Perhaps the chief of these cities from
the seventh century B.C., *Tarquinii* lost its independence to Rome
in the third century B.C. The tombs here date from the sixth to the
third centuries B.C. Chambers cut into the rock, they are decorated
with splendid frescoes which illustrate Etruscan life. Bits of the city
wall (c. 400 B.C.) remain. Sacked by the Arabs in the eighth century
A.D., the town of *Tarquinii* was later deserted and replaced by nearby
CORNETO, now called TARQUINIA. Finds may be seen at the National Museum in TARQUINIA and the National Archaeological Museum at FLORENCE.

Alfoeldi. *Early Rome*. 206-209
Banti, L. *The Etruscan Cities and their Culture*. Berkeley 1973. 70-
84
Besnier. *Lexique*. 740-741
Boëthius and Ward-Perkins. *ERA*. 621 (index); pl. 46
Coarelli. *Le città etrusche*. 180-213; 322-323 (bibl.)
Dennis. *CCE*. I pp. 314-410
Finley. *Atlas*. 120-121 (G. D. B. Jones)
Grimal. *Search*. 197-198
*Guida d'Italia del Touring Club Italiano, Lazio*³. Milan 1964. 114-
134
Harris. *REU*. 29-30 (early history); 42-48 (conflicts with Rome); 86-
89, 105 (allied city); 211-212 (continuity in second century B.C.)
Hencken, H. *Tarquinia and Etruscan Origins*. London/New York
1968
KP. V (1975). 523-524 (A. Pfiffig)
MacKendrick. *Mute Stones*. 38-60
OCD. 1038 (D. W. R. Ridgway)
Ogilvie. *Early Rome*. 163 (the walls)
Pallottino, M. *Etruscan Painting*. New York 1952
—— "Tarquinia," *Monumenti antichi* 36 (1937): 1-620; rpt. Mainz
1970
PECS. 880-881 (E. Richardson)
Piganiol. *HR*. 21, 534 (bibl.)
RE. IVA (1932). 2343-2348 (H. Philipp)
Romanelli, P. *Tarquinia: la necropoli e il museo*. Rome 1954

Scullard. *Etruscan Cities*. 84-92, 274; 294, n. 70 (bibliography)
Weeber, K.-W. "Tarquinia—Portraet einer etruskischen Metropole," *Antike Welt* 11.2 (1980): 15-24

Tarragona (Spain): mentioned under ITALICA above and *Hispania* in the glossary

Thugga: see DOUGGA

Thurii (in the modern region of Calabria, Italy; the Roman region was *Bruttium*)
p. 22 (orthogonal plan of Hippodamus)
 This colony was founded in 443 B.C. by several Greek cities, under the leadership of Athens (Diodorus Siculus 12.10). The plan is known not from excavations, but from Diodorus 12.10.7 (Ward-Perkins 119). The site, on the Gulf of Taranto and the right bank of the Crati River, was near the Greek colony of *Sybaris*, which had been destroyed in 510 B.C. Among the colonists of *Thurioi* (the Greek name) were the city planner Hippodamus and the historian Herodotus. *Thurii* was devastated by Hannibal in 204 (Appian, *Hannibalica* 57); a Latin colony, *Copia Thurii*, was founded on the site in 193 B.C. (Livy 34.53; 35.9), but it was unsuccessful.
Aletti, E. *Sibari, Turio, Copia*. Rome 1960
Besnier. *Lexique*. 767
Bullitt, O. H. *Search for Sybaris*. London 1971. 37, 89, 117-130, 158, 186
Castagnoli. *Orthogonal Town Planning*. 18-19, 131-132
—— "Sull'urbanistica di Thurii," *Parola del Passato* 139 (1971): 301-307
EB. XXVI p. 901 (T. Ashby)
Ehrenberg, V. "The Foundation of Thurioi," *Polis und Imperium* (Zurich 1965): 298 ff.
Gutkind. *IHCD*. IV (1969). 601-602
Hammond. *The City*. 222
KP. V (1975). 802-803 (K.-D. Fabian)
Martin, R. *L'urbanisme dans la Grèce antique*. Paris 1956. 40-41
Morton, H. V. *A Traveller in Southern Italy*. New York 1969. 320 (the probable site today)
Nissen. *IL*. II pp. 921-923
OCD. 1070 (E. T. Salmon)
PECS. 919 (W. D. E. Coulson)

Randall-MacIver, D. *Greek Cities in Italy and Sicily*. Oxford 1931.
70-71 (Sybaris)
RE. VIA.1 (1936). 646-652 (H. Philipp)
Salmon. *RC*. 68, 99-100
Ward-Perkins. *Cities*. 16, 119 (with bibl.); 127 (index)
Whatmough, J. *The Foundations of Roman Italy*. London 1937. 336
(The native inhabitants of the site were the Messapii.)
Wheeler. *RAA*. 26 (Hippodamus)

TIMGAD (wilaya or département of Batna, Algeria) = *Colonia Ulpia Marciana Traiana Thamugadi, Africa Proconsularis* (ancient region of *Numidia*, q.v.); Ulpius was the family name of Trajan and Marciana was his older sister.
pp. 12 (ideal plan), 41 (the forum), 45 (the basilica), 50 (location of the Capitol), 55 (native temple), 70-71 (the Large North Baths)
Founded in A.D. 100 by order of the Emperor Trajan, this colony was about thirty kilometers east of the camp at *Lambaesis* (q.v.), occupied by the Third Augustan Legion, of which the colonists were veterans. (For the inscription recording the founding of TIMGAD, see Salmon, *RC* 195, n. 290.) The two sites were connected by an excellent highway, which also led east to Tébessa, the legion's (q.v.) camp until the late first century A.D. Other Roman roads went from TIMGAD north to Skikda via CONSTANTINE and southwest over the Aurès Mountains.

TIMGAD should be compared with two veteran-colonies in northern Italy of 125 years before, AOSTA and TURIN. These were similar to TIMGAD in purpose (Romanization of the natives) and plan (strongly influenced by those of the contemporary military camp). At TIMGAD, there were twelve *cardines* and thirteen *decumani* (qq.v.). The city blocks (q.v.) were about seventy Roman feet square and the streets fifteen wide (Stuart Jones 28). In the approximate center of the colony, the forum filled nearly the equivalent of nine city blocks; the north-south axis was a bit short. This shape becomes more oblong if we add to it the basilica and public lavoratories on the east. The colony's housing was of high quality (Rostovtzeff, *Rome* 256; he compared it with Pompeii's).

Rostovtzeff estimated that ancient TIMGAD's population rapidly grew to at least 6,000 (*SEHRE* 375-376; cf. Grimal's 15,000, p. 71 above), and the area immediately beyond the walls was soon built on. According to Duncan-Jones, the city's built-up area was about fifty hectares (*ERE* 265, n. 4; also see cities [Roman], comparison in area, below). Irrigation made agriculture possible in the surrounding land, and the city served as a market for a large district. One would suppose that the local (Berber, q.v.) nomads, who turned to settled agriculture (Hammond), were not as easily assimilated as the Celts of northern Italy. After the Arab conquest and the breakdown of the irrigation system, the city was abandoned.

The extensive ruins were brought to the notice of Europeans when James Bruce, a Scottish traveler, discovered them in 1765. Excavation began in 1880, under French rule, and is nearly completed. In the words of Pierre Grimal, here we have "the most perfect specimen" of "the ideal rectangular plan" for a Roman city (*Civ. Rome* 355). Most of the cities in this catalogue deviate from this ideal plan in one way or another.

Ballu, A. *Les ruines de Timgad*. Paris 1911

Besnier. *Lexique*. 412 (see Lambaesis)

Boeswillwald, E., Cagnat, R., and Ballu, A. *Timgad, une cité africaine sous l'Empire romain*. Paris 1892-1905

Boëthius. "RGTA." 17 (lack of apartment blocks)

—— and Ward-Perkins. *ERA*. 479-482, 486; 599 (bibl.); plates 251 (air view), 252 (arch)

Broughton. *RAP*. 119, 128 (founding); 121 (*territorium*, q.v.); 233 (index)

Cagnat. *Armée romaine*. 590

Cagnat, R. "Les bibliothèques municipales dans l'"Empire romain," *Mémoires présentés par divers savants à l'Académie des inscriptions et belles-lettres* 38 (1909): 1-26

—— *Carthage, Timgad, Tébessa et les villes antiques de l'Afrique du Nord*. Paris 1909; 3rd ed. Paris 1927

Caprino. *MAR, Bibl*. 378

Chevallier. *ANRW*. II.1 plates lxxxiv-lxxxvi

Clavel and Lévêque. *Villes*. 150-155

*Courtois, C. *Timgad, antique Thamugadi*. Algiers 1951

Crema. *Arch*. 668-669 (index)

Cunliffe. *Rome*. 206-207 (excellent air view, in color); other air views on 101 and 231

EB. XXVI pp. 988-989

Finley. *Atlas*. 73-75 (C. R. Whittaker)

Frank. *ESAR*. IV pp. 38, 104 (founding); 60 (trade), 67 (roads), 109 (property); (R. M. Haywood)

Germain, S. *Les mosaïques de Timgad*². Paris 1973

Grimal. *Civ. Rome*. 355, 357, 506; illustrations 122, 128 (air views), 126

Gsell. *AAA*. fasc. 27 ("Batna")

Gsell, S. *Les monuments antiques de l'Algérie*. I. Paris 1901. 112, n. 2 (bibl.)

Hammond. *The City*. 295

Haverfield. *Town Planning*. 109-113

Jones, H. Stuart. *Companion*. 28-30 (orthogonal plan); 139-141 (the public library); 461 (index)

KP. V (1975). 647-648 (M. Leglay)

Lassus, J. "Adaptation à l'Afrique de l'urbanisme romain," *Actes du VIIe Congrès int. d'archéologie*. Paris 1965. 245-259

—— "Une opération immobilière à Timgad," *Mélanges Piganiol*. III. Paris 1966

——— Visite à Timgad. Algiers 1969

Lavedan. *HU*. 432-433 (maps); 475 (plan of forum); 495 (index)

McKay. *Houses*. 231-232

Menen, A. *Cities in the Sand*. New York 1972. 173-191

Monceaux, P. *Timgad chrétien*. Paris 1911

Morris. *Urban Form*. 54-55, fig. 3.21; 258 (comparative plans)

Nagel's Guide, Algeria. 352-358 (with 1 plan)

Nash-Williams, V. E. "Roman Africa," *Bulletin of the Board of Celtic Studies* 16 (University of Wales, Cardiff, 1956): 135-164

OCD. 1050 (?W.N.W.)

PECS. 899-902 (J. Lassus)

Pfeiffer, H. "The Roman Library at Timgad," *Memoirs of the American Academy in Rome* 9 (1931): 157-165

(Charles-) Picard. *Roman Architecture*. 175-177 and plan 17, plates 24-25 (the Arch of Trajan at TIMGAD)

Piganiol. *HR*. 356 (bibl.)

Raven. *Rome in Africa*. 56 *(colonia)*; 57 (aerial photograph); 79, 81 (orthogonal plan); 84 (market); 84, 87 (library); 88, 92 (baths); 183 (bibl. for North Africa)

Robertson. *GRA*. 192-193 with fig. 86 (plan); 356 (bibl.); 406 (index)

Rostovtzeff. *SEHRE*. 322, 375-376; 594 (bibl.)

Salmon. *RC*. 208 (index)

Ward-Perkins. *Cities*. 29, 31, 33, 35, 122, figs. 65-66

Wheeler. *RAA*. 46-52

—— and Wood. *Roman Africa*. 120-125; plates 40-42 (plate 42 the "Triumphal Arch" and the theater)

On the *Album* or list of decurions (q.v.) of c. A.D. 367:

Abbott and Johnson. *Municipal Administration*. 464-465, no. 136 (Latin text and commentary)

Chastagnol, A. *L'album municipal de Timgad*. Antiquitas Reihe III, 21, 22. Bonn 1976, 1978
Jones. *LRE*. II pp. 730-731, III p. 230, n. 40
Leschi, L. *Revue des Etudes anciennes* 50 (1948): 71-100 = *Etudes d'épigraphie, d'archéologie et d'histoire africaines*. Paris 1957. 246 ff. (text of the inscription)
Piganiol. *HR*. 495, 627-628 (bibl.)

TIPASA (wilaya of Algiers, Algeria) = *Tipasa, Mauretania Caesariensis;* from A.D. 138/161 *Colonia Aelia Augusta Tipasensium*
p. 78 (the city walls)

Originally a Carthaginian settlement, *Tipasa* was made a *municipium* (q.v.) with Latin rights (q.v.; Pliny, *Natural History* 5.2.20) by the Emperor Claudius, who annexed and organized the two Roman provinces of Mauretania A.D. 42/44. It was raised to the rank of Roman colony by the Emperor (Aelius) Antoninus Pius (Baradez, *Libyca* 4).

The settlement was located at a harbor on the Mediterranean thirty kilometers east of CHERCHELL, to which the Roman coastal road ran. The city's decline began with a revolt led by Donatists, a Christian sect (A.D. 361/363, Raven, p. 140) and was hastened by the Vandal (q.v.) conquest.

The Roman ruins visible today include the main features of a Roman city, Christianized in the fourth century: forum, amphitheater, temples, theater, and fortifications. (The walls date from A.D. 42/54—Février.) Just outside the walls to the east are the remains of a large Catholic basilica of the fourth or fifth century. Under French rule (1845-1962), part of the ancient city was occupied by colonists.

Today one can stay at one of two nearby holiday complexes. The ruins are contained in an "archaeological park" at the sea's edge, surrounded by grass and trees. There is an open-air site-museum. In the words of Stéphane Gsell, "No ancient remains are in a more attractive setting" *(Nagel's Guide;* compare Février's remarks in *PECS)*.

Baradez, J. "Les nouvelles fouilles de Tipasa et les opérations d'Antonin le Pieux en Maurétanie," *Libyca* 2 (1954): 89 (on the date of the city's walls)
—— *Libyca* 4 (1956): 271 ff. (on the colony)
—— *Tipasa, ville antique de Maurétanie²*. Algiers 1957
Besnier. *Lexique*. 773
Crema. *Arch*. 669 (index)

Duval, P.-M. Cherchel et Tipasa, Recherches sur deux villes fortes de l'Afrique romaine. Institut français de Beyrouth, Bibliothèque archéologique et historique 43. Paris 1946
Frank. *ESAR.* IV p. 106 (R. M. Haywood, evidence for settlers who were Roman citizens)
Frézouls, E. "Le théâtre romain de Tipasa," *Mélanges d'archéologie et d'histoire de l'Ecole française de Rome* 64 (1952): 110-177
Gsell. *AAA.* fasc. 4 ("Cherchel")
Gsell, S. *Guide archéologique des environs d'Alger.* Algiers 1896. 103-144
——— *Mélanges d'archéologie et d'histoire, publiés par l'Ecole française de Rome* 14 (1894): 322-408
KP. V (1975). 859 (M. Leglay)
Lancel, S. *Tipasa de Maurétanie.* Algiers 1966
——— "Tipasitana IV," *Bulletin d'archéologie algérienne* 4 (1970)
——— and Bouchenaki, M. *Tipasa de Maurétanie.* Algiers 1971
McKay. *Houses.* 231; 258, n. 410
Nagel's Guide, Algeria. 165-171 (with 2 maps)
OCD. 1078 (B. H. Warmington)
PECS. 925-926 (P.-A. Février)
Piganiol. *HR.* 594 (bibl.)
Raven. *Rome in Africa.* 190 (index)
Wheeler and Wood. *Roman Africa.* 144; plate 52 (the theater)

TIVOLI (Latium, Italy) = *Tibur, Samnium, Italia*
p. 20 (early, nonorthogonal hill-town)
   TIVOLI overlooks Rome, thirty kilometers away to the west-southwest. *Tibur* was an early city of the Latins (q.v.), older than Rome, on the Anio River in the lower slopes of the Sabine Hills. The two cities were connected by the *Via Valeria*, also called the *Via Tiburtina* up to this point. It was an allied city (q.v.) of Rome from the fourth century B.C. (Livy 7-8.14). *Tibur* received Roman citizenship c. 90 B.C. and thus became a *municipium* (Pliny, *Natural History* 3.107; Appian, *Civil Wars* 1.65).
   For the Romans, it was both a source of travertine stone (Frank; see Chapter III, n. 23 above) and a fashionable resort. The ruins of several villas are nearby, including the elaborate complex built by the Emperor Hadrian (A.D. 117-138). The well-preserved "Temple of Vesta" (early first century B.C.) is now a church.
Alfoeldi. *Early Rome.* 387-391
Ashby. *Rom. Cam.* 110-120

Aurigemma, S. *Villa Adriana*. Rome 1961

Bagnani. *Rom. Cam*. 205-242

Besnier. *Lexique*. 770

Blue Guide, Rome. 348-356

Boëthius and Ward-Perkins. *ERA*. plates 74 (Temple of Hercules Victor); 80; 83 ("Temple of Vesta"); 134-137, 174 (Hadrian's Villa)

Bourne, E. *A Study of Tibur*. Menasha, Wis., 1916

Brown. *RA*. 41-43, plates 86-90 (Hadrian's Villa); 20, pl. 17 (Round Temple, i.e. "Temple of Vesta")

Carducci, C. *Tibur*. Rome 1940

Chevallier. *ANRW*. II.1 p. 698 (bibl.)

Crema. *ANRW*. I.4 "Arch rep."

—— *Arch*. 669 (index)

EB. XXVI pp. 931-932 (T. Ashby), 1033-1034

Finley. *Atlas*. 111 (map of the environs of Rome), 114-115 (on Hadrian's Villa) (G. B. D. Jones)

Frank. *ESAR*. V p. 127 (travertine quarries)

Giuliani, C. F. *Forma Italiae, Tibur*. 2 vols. Rome 1966, 1970

Grimal. *Rome*. 201-210

—— *Search*. 110-118 (on the villas)

Guida d'Italia del Touring Club Italiano, Roma e Dintorni[6]. Milan 1962. 614-631

Helbig, W. *Fuehrer durch die oeffentlichen Sammlungen klassischer Altertuemer in Rom*[4]. IV. Tuebingen 1972. 153-172 (Hadrian's Villa)

Highet, G. *Poets in a Landscape*. London 1957. 122-126 (Horace)

Jones, H. Stuart. *Companion*. 461 (index; see Tibur)

Kaehler. *Art of Rome*. 146-151

Kaehler, H. *Hadrian und seine Villa bei Tivoli*. Berlin 1950

KP. V pp. 820-822 (G. Radke)

MacDonald. *Arch*. 6-7; plates 4-5 (Sanctuary of Hercules)

MacKendrick. *Mute Stones*. 134, 136 (on the Temple of Hercules Victor); 369 (index)

McKay. *Houses*. 131-132, 135; 249, n. 231 (bibliography); plate 52

McKay, A. G. *Vergil's Italy*. Greenwich, Conn., 1970. 176; 193

Millar. *REN*. pl. 4 (air view of Hadrian's Villa)

Nissen. *IL*. I p. 314; II pp. 610-615

OCD. 1073 (E. T. Salmon)

Paget. *Central Italy*. 190-195

PECS. 921-922 (W. L. MacDonald)

Radke. *Viae*. 65; fig. 25

RE. VIA.1 (1936). 816-841 (S. Weinstock)

Robertson. *GRA*. 406 (index)

Salmon. *RC*. 46-47 (map of *Latium*); 50

Salza Prina Ricotti, E. "Criptoportici e Gallerie sotterranee di Villa Adriana nella loro tipologia e nelle loro funzioni," *Les cryptoportiques dans l'architecture romaine*. Collection de l'Ecole française de Rome 14. Rome 1973. 219-259

Taylor. *Voting Districts*. 81, 111, 271

Ward-Perkins. *RA*. plates 36, 44 (Temple of Hercules); 61-63 ("Temple of Vesta"); 172-196 (Hadrian's Villa)

Wheeler. *RAA*. 100 and ill. 79 ("Temple of Vesta")

TOULOUSE (Haute-Garonne, France) = *Tolosa, Gallia Narbonensis*

p. 8 (Roman street plan visible today)

TOULOUSE is on the right bank of the Garonne River, about 250 kilometers upstream and southeast from BORDEAUX. Ancient *Tolosa* was the tribal capital of the Volcae Tectosages under Roman rule (from 118 B.C.). By A.D. 77, it had gained Latin rights (q.v.; Pliny, *Natural History* 3.37).

Besides shipping on the Garonne, trade on the Roman highway from NARBONNE to BORDEAUX ensured the ancient city's prosperity. Another Roman road led west from TOULOUSE to Bayonne. The land of the Volcae Tectosages was rich in gold (Strabo 4.1.13, cited by Grenier in *ESAR* 457-458 and others).

The city of Gallo-Roman times contained ninety hectares, and its orthogonal street plan is still visible in present-day TOULOUSE. The theater has been located, and remains of the amphitheater, two public baths, and part of the ancient walls may be seen (Labrousse in *PECS*). *Tolosa* was praised by the poet Martial as the city of Minerva (goddess of wisdom), and its schools were mentioned by Ausonius (q.v.) in the fourth century (Brogan).

The city continued to flourish in Late Roman times, and the conquering Visigoths made it their capital in 418. Defeated by the Franks in 507, the Visigoths retreated to Spain (Gregory of Tours, *History of the Franks*. 2.37). Continuously inhabited, TOULOUSE is now the fourth largest city in France, following LYONS.

Baccrabère, G. *L'enceinte gallo-romaine de Toulouse*. Paris 1973 (the wall)

—— *Etude de Toulouse romaine*. Toulouse 1977

Bannert. "Volcae"

Besnier. *Lexique*. 776

Broëns, M. "Essai de topographie antique de Toulouse," *Mémoires présentés...à l'Académie des inscriptions et belles-lettres* 14.2 (1952): 287-314 (also printed separately)

Brogan. *Roman Gaul*. 53, 227

Bruehl. *PC*. 189-200

Chevallier. *ANRW*. II.1 plate xlvii (plan); *ANRW*. II.3 p. 737 (plan of a bath), 812 (bibl.)

Clavel and Lévêque. *Villes*. 77-82

Coppolani, J. *Toulouse, étude de géographie urbaine*. Toulouse 1954

EB. XXVII pp. 99-101

Février. "CSG." 15, 27

Frank. *ESAR*. III pp. 457-458 (gold); 467, 482 (roads); (A. Grenier)

Grenier. *Manuel*. I p. 289; III 271-272 (the ?Capitol)

Gutkind. *IHCD*. V (1970). 216-220, 479 (bibl.)

KP. V (1975). 883 (M. Leglay)

*Labrousse, M. *Toulouse antique, des origines à l'établissement des Wisigoths*. Bibliothèque des Ecoles françaises d'Athènes et de Rome 212. Paris 1968

—— "Une ville et un fleuve: Toulouse et la Garonne," in *Thèmes* by Duval. 325-328 (geographic importance of the river)

OCD. 1081 (C. E. Stevens)

PECS. 928 (M. Labrousse)

Ramet, H. *Histoire de Toulouse*. Toulouse 1935

Schreiber, H. *Auf den Spuren der Goten*. Munich 1977. plate 40 (air view)

Stier. *Atlas*. 88-89 (archbishopric)

Thompson, E. A. "The Settlement of Barbarians in Southern Gaul," *Journal of Roman Studies* 46 (1956): 65-75

Wolff, P. *Histoire de Toulouse*². Toulouse 1961

——, ed. *Histoire de Toulouse*. Toulouse 1974 (see especially pp. 7-47 by M. Labrousse)

TRIER (in English, sometimes called Trèves, the French name); Rhineland-Palatinate, Federal Republic of Germany) = from A.D. 41/54, *Colonia Augusta Treverorum, Gallia Belgica;* mint of the Later Roman Empire (q.v.)

p. 80 (on the *Porta Nigra*)

The site is on the right bank of the Moselle River (Latin *Mosella*), which is navigable and flows northeast about 100 kilometers to join the Rhine *(Rhenus)* at Koblenz *(Confluentes)*, between Bonn and

MAINZ. The lands of the tribe or *civitas* (q.v.) of the Germano-Celtic Treveri covered a large area, which falls within the borders of present-day France, Germany, Belgium, and Luxembourg. Under Augustus (27 B.C.-A.D. 14), when *Augusta Treverorum* was named, an auxiliary (q.v.) or noncitizen Roman army unit was stationed here. An inscription of the first century points to the Emperor Claudius as the founder of the colony, but it is not certain what kind of colony it was (see *colonia*). Since Treveri served in the noncitizen auxiliary forces, it probably had either Latin or honorary status (Wightman 40-42). Salmon favors the latter possibility, which, he says, began under Claudius *(RC* 158, 161; also see Vittinghoff 101 and Hammond 294).

Unlike the lands of the *civitas*, the *territorium* (q.v.) of the colony may have been quite small, just the environs of the city (Wightman 42). This would be in contrast with SILCHESTER and WROXETER (qq.v., *civitates* and not colonies or *municipia*) as well as VIENNE (a colony with a very large *territorium*). One would then suppose that the magistrates and the council of the colony of TRIER and of the *civitas* of the Treveri were different. Inscriptions recording the officers of the *civitas* have been found, but none for the city's (Wightman 41).

The orthogonal city was most likely laid out under Claudius; it covered about 81 hectares (cf. Reusch in *PECS* 119). The inhabited area grew to 280 hectares by A.D. 200. The *decumanus* led west from the colony's amphitheater (first century, restored 293/306) across the Moselle to meet the road to Rheims. This road was joined by the highway north to +Cologne. TRIER 's *cardo* led south to Metz and LYONS; the Porta Nigra, the north gate, was set east of the *cardo* and spanned the road which went northeast along the Moselle and then east to MAINZ. The northwest quadrant made by the crossing of the *decumanus* and the *cardo* was filled by the immense forum (see *fora,* comparison . . . below); it contained a cryptoporticus (q.v.). Some of TRIER 's Roman streets may still be recognized today in an aerial photograph (Wheeler, p. 70, fig. 49).

From the first century, the imperial *procurator* or chief financial officer for *Gallia Belgica* and the two provinces of Roman Germany served at *Augusta Treverorum* (cf. LYONS, LONDON). The capital of *Belgica* was Rheims *(Durocortorum),* and the governor's headquarters was there (Brogan 24-25), although TRIER, the supply-post for the Roman army in Germany, was economically more important.

Rostovtzeff compared TRIER to LYONS as a place for merchants (p.

166) and went on to say, "Trèves was not only a great centre of commerce; it became, as it was bound to become, the economic centre of the whole surrounding country. The merchants of the city, who acquired great wealth by selling goods to the army, invested their money, as might be expected, in profitable undertakings in the vicinity" (p. 223). Clothes and weapons were made at TRIER, and, as today, it was the market for the Moselle wine trade (on the wine, Grenier in *ESAR* 583).

From A.D. 285, TRIER was the capital of the new province of *Belgica Prima* and after 337, the seat of the Praetorian Prefect of the Gauls, the chief legal officer of a large part of the Late Roman Empire. About 400, TRIER lost this honor to ARLES (q.v.); the Rhine frontier was becoming too dangerous, for invaders threatened.

TRIER prospered most during the late third and fourth centuries, when it was one of the residences of the western Roman emperor (the division of the Empire goes back to 285). Existing structures from this imperial period are, besides the Porta Nigra, a second complex of baths (the Kaiserthermen) and the emperor's audience chamber (the Aula Palatina or so-called Basilica).

St. Jerome tells us that (?some of) the Treveri still spoke Celtic in the late fourth century (questioned by Wightman 19-20), while Latin schools, such as that attended by the saint, flourished at TRIER in the Late Roman period. Mommsen cited a law of A.D. 376 from the Theodosian Code to show that the state paid the professors of TRIER more than any others in Gaul; hence, they were the most respected (*Provinces*, Chapter III; *Cod. Theod.* 13.3.11). Ausonius (q.v.) summarized the prosperity of the imperial residence as follows: ". . . that royal city of the Treveri, which, though near the Rhine, reposes unalarmed . . . because she feeds, she clothes and arms the forces of the Empire. Widely her walls stretch forward over a spreading hill; beside her the bounteous Moselle glides past . . . carrying the far-brought merchandise of all races of the earth *(Ordo* 6, transl. Evelyn-White).

Early in the fifth century, TRIER was conquered by the Franks (q.v.). But life, nevertheless, went on (Salvian of Marseilles [probably born at TRIER, c. 400], *On the Government of God* 6.15; cf. Wightman 70). During the Middle Ages, the city was ruled by its archbishops. Occupied by France in 1797, it was awarded to Prussia in 1815, after the defeat of Napoleon. Prussia became part of Germany, founded in 1871.

Among the fine local museums in Germany is the Rheinisches

Landesmuseum of TRIER, with significant Roman material. Furthermore, it may well be true that there are more important Roman structures at TRIER than at any other place in northern Europe (cf. A. B. Gough in *EB* [1911] XXVII p. 268).

Artemis Lexikon. 399-400 (bibliography)

Bengtson, H., and Milojčić, V. *Grosser historischer Weltatlas*. I⁵. Munich 1972. 45 (the roads)

Besnier. *Lexique*. 107

Bianchi Bandinelli. *Rome*. II pp. 175-178

Boëthius and Ward-Perkins. *ERA*. 350-351 (native shrines); 517-522; 601 (bibl.); plates 268-271

Brogan. *Roman Gaul*. 111-116; 242 (bibl.); 249 (index)

Brown. *RA*. 37-38, plates 74-75 (the Kaiserthermen)

Castagnoli. *Orthogonal Town Planning*. 110, n. 53 (bibliography)

Crema. *Arch*. 669 (index; see "Treveri")

Cueppers, H. *Das Spaetroemische Trier*. Trier 1978

—— "Die Stadt Trier und die verschiedenen Phasen ihres Ausbaues von der Gruendung bis zum Bau der mittelalterlichen Stadtbefestigung," in *Thèmes* by Duval. 223-228 (historical outline)

Ewig, E. *Trier in Merowingerreich*. Trier 1954 (on Trier under the Franks, from the fifth to eighth centuries)

Finley. *Atlas*. 42-44 (J. J. Wilkes)

Frank. *ESAR*. III (see index); (A. Grenier)

Gose, E. *Die Porta Nigra in Trier*. Berlin 1969

Grenier. *Manuel*. I 541-546 (the gates); 546-548 (the amphitheater); III 257-262; 541-551 (the so-called Basilica); 552-557 (the Cathedral; part of it dates from the fourth century); 705-711 (the amphitheater); 997-998 (the *circus*, for chariot races); IV 362-383 (the baths), 857-875 (native shrines)

Grenier, A. *Quatre villes romaines de la Rhénanie*. Paris 1925 (on TRIER, MAINZ, Bonn, + Cologne)

Gutkind. *IHCD*. I (1964). 265-267

Hammond. *The City*. 294-295

Haverfield. *Town Planning*. 124-127

Kaehler. *Art of Rome*. 192-202; 223 (bibl.)

Koethe, H. "Neue Daten zur Geschichte des roem. Trier," *Germania* 20 (1936): 27-35 (foundation; economic prosperity)

KP. V (1975). 939-943 (H. Cueppers; see "Treveri")

Krencker, D. *Das roemische Trier*. Berlin 1926

—— et al. *Die Trierer Kaiserthermen = Trierer Grabungen und Forschungen* 1. Augsburg 1929

Laufner, R., ed. *Geschichte des Trierer Landes*. I. Trier 1964. 98-221 (J. Steinhausen)

Lavedan. *HU*. 495 (index)

MacKendrick. *RoR*. 215-247; 257-258 (bibl.)

Mommsen. *Provinces*. Chapter III

Morris. *Urban Form*. 56, fig. 3.22

OCD. 148 (O. Brogan and P. Salway)

PECS. 119-121 (W. Reusch)

Piganiol. *HR*. 362, 623 (bibliography)

Raepset-Charlier, M.-T., and Raepset-Charlier, G. "*Gallia Belgica et Germania Inferior*," *ANRW*. II.4 (1975). 181-185 (bibl. on 185)

RE. VIA.2 (1937). 2301-2353 (Rau; see "Treveri")

RE. Supplement 3 (1918). see "Augusta (Treverorum)"; addition to *RE*. II (1896)

Reusch, W. *Augusta Treverorum Guide*. 11th ed. Trier 1978

—— "Die Aula Palatina in Trier," *Germania* 33 (1955): 180-210

—— "Die spaetantike Kaiserresidenz im Lichte neuer Ausgrabungen," *Archaeologischer Anzeiger* (1962): 875-903

—— *Treveris: A Guide through Roman Trier*[5]. Trier 1977

Richmond. *RAA*. 276-279 (the "Basilica")

Robertson. *GRA*. 361 (bibl.); 396 (index)

Rostovtzeff. *SEHRE*. 166-167; 762 (index)

Rykwert. *Idea*. 42

Schindler, R. "Augusta Treverorum," *Bonner Jahrbuecher* 172 (1972): 258-270

Signon, H. *Die Roemer zwischen Koeln, Bonn und Trier*. Frankfurt am Main 1977

Stier. *Atlas*. 80; 88-89 (archbishopric)

Ternes, C.-M. "Die roemerzeitliche Civitas Treverorum im Bild der Nachkriegsforschung, I. Von der Gruendung bis zum Ende des dritten Jahrhunderts," *ANRW*. II.4 (1975). 320-424

Trierer Grabungen und Forschungen (1929-)

Trierer Zeitschrift fuer Geschichte Und Kunst.... (1926-)

Vittinghoff. *Roemische Kolonisation*. 101 (The author believes that Claudius made *Augusta Treverorum* a Latin colony.)

*von Elbe, J. *Roman Germany*. Mainz 1975. 388-439

von Hagen, V. W. *The Roads that Led to Rome*. London 1967. 176 (photograph of Roman bridge on the Moselle)

Ward-Perkins. *Cities*. 31; fig. 64 (plan)

—— *RA*. plates 403-409, 411; p. 347 (index)

Wheeler. *RAA*. 70-76; 233 (bibl.)
*Wightman, E. M. *Roman Trier and the Treveri*. New York 1971
   (bibl. on pp. 257-302)
Woloch, G. M. *American Classical Review* 1 (1971): 254 (review of
   Wightman)
Zahn, E. "Die Porta Nigra in Trier," *Antike Welt* 2.1 (1971): 21-32

TURIN (Piedmont, Italy; capital of the region; in Italian, Torino) =
Colonia Iulia Augusta Taurinorum (CIL V 7047), region of *Transpadana, Italia*
p. 8 (Roman street plan visible in modern city)

+ Susa

Augustus founded this Roman colony in 27 B.C.; mainly for veterans, it helped with the Romanization of north Italy (compare AOSTA). G. D. B. Jones compares TURIN with VERONA, to the east; both guarded the approaches to strategic Alpine passes. TURIN is on the left bank of the Po River, where navigation ends (Pliny, *Natural History* 3.123). The Dora Riparia River joins the Po above the site of the colony's walls.

The city's nearly square walls enclosed 48 hectares or 119 acres—about the size of a camp for two legions. The inhabited area grew to 51 hectares (see cities [Roman], comparison in area, below). Inside the walls, there were eight *cardines* by seven *decumani* (qq.v.); the main *cardo* was displaced two streets to the east (compare AOSTA). Also as at AOSTA, the Roman city blocks were seventy to eighty meters on a side (see city blocks below). Augustan remains include a theater, part of the city walls and the Palatine Gate on the north; part of the Roman east gate is contained in the thirteenth to eighteenth century Palazzo Madama.

After the end of the Western Roman Empire late in the fifth century A.D., TURIN was occupied by the Ostrogoths (q.v.) and Lombards (q.v.). Late in the thirteenth century, it passed to the House of Savoy (an Alpine region now in eastern France; see Aix-les-Bains). The head of this family became a duke in the fifteenth century and a king at TURIN in the eighteenth. In 1861, Victor Emmanuel II of Savoy became king of Italy. Nine years later, the capital of Italy was moved to Rome.

Turin today is the fourth largest city in Italy, after NAPLES. It is an industrial center, especially for building automobiles.

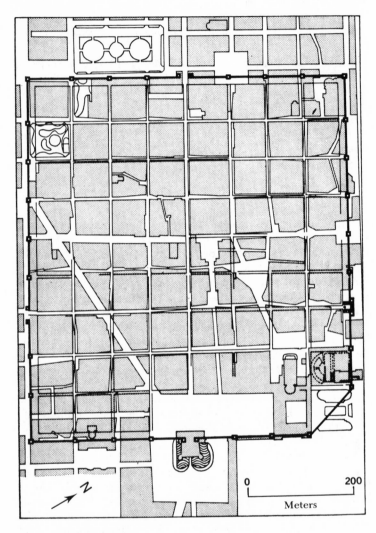

Figure 33. Plan of Turin
From Salmon, *Roman Colonization*, fig. 10

TURIN:
Bendinelli, G. *Torino romana*. Turin 1929
Besnier. *Lexique*. 106-107
Boëthius and Ward-Perkins. *ERA*. 304-305, fig. 117 (the Porta Palatina)
Caprino. *MAR*, *Bibl*. 263, 333
Castagnoli. *Orthogonal Town Planning*. 110-112; fig. 48
Chevallier. *ANRW*. II.1 p. 700 (bibl.); plates xvii and xviii (aerial photograph and maps)
Chilver. *Cisalpine Gaul*. 20-21 (the *colonia*); 42-43 (the highways); 51 (area of the city)
Cognasso, F. *Storia di Torino*². Milan 1974
Crema. *Arch*. 222, figs. 234-236 (the Porta Palatina); 669 (index)
Earl. *AA*. plate 21 (the Porta Palatina)
EB. XXVII pp. 418-419 (T. Ashby)
Finley. *Atlas*. 103 (G. D. B. Jones)
Frank. *ESAR*. V p. 119 (bibl.)
Frothingham. *RCID*. 209-225 (with Susa)
(Gec-) Gianeri, E. *Storia di Torino*. Turin 1975
Gribaudi, D. *Il Piemonte nell'antichità classica*. Turin 1928
Grimal. *Civ*. *Rome*. 348-349, 509
*Guida d'Italia del Touring Club Italiano, Torino e Valle d'Aosta*⁷. Milan 1959
Gutkind. *IHCD*. IV (1969). 249-256; 629 (bibl.)
Haverfield. *Town Planning*. 86-89
Jones, H. Stuart. *Companion*. 15 (The square blocks here, about 240 Roman feet square, are compared with those at ORANGE and TIMGAD.)
KP. I (1964). 738 (G. Radke)
Lavedan. *HU*. 383 (map); 495 (index)
MacKendrick. *Mute Stones*. 112
Nissen. *IL*. II pp. 163-167
OCD. 148 (E. T. Salmon)
Patriossi, L. "Studi su Augusta Taurinorum," *Istituto Lombardo di Scienze e Lettere, Rendiconti* 105 (1971): 281-319
PECS. 118-119 (C. Carducci)
Promis, C. *Storia dell'antica Torino*. Turin 1869
Radke. *Viae*. fig. 20
Richmond, I. A. "The Roman Gates at Torino and Spello," *Papers of the British School at Rome* 12 (1932): 52-62

Rondolino, F. *Storia di Torino antica*. Atti della Società Piemontese
   di Archeologia e Belle Arti 12 (1930)
Rykwert. *Idea*. 42
Salmon. *RC*. 140 (plan), 144
Savoja, U. "Turin, the 'Regular' Town," *Town Planning Review* 12
   (1926): 191-198, and pl. 43
Toesca, P. *Torino*. Bergamo 1911
Ward-Perkins. "ERTI." fig. 23 (plan)
Wheeler. *RAA*. 43-44, 46
Zucker. *Town and Square*. 48 (comparison with Roman AOSTA and
   VERONA)

+ Susa:
   Thirty kilometers west of TURIN is + Susa (ancient *Segusio*), fa-
mous for its arch to Augustus (8 B.C.) and ancient capital of the minor
province of the Cottian Alps. The Roman road from TURIN to VIENNE
passed through Susa, which is now in the region of Piedmont, Italy.
Besnier. *Lexique*. 686
Brown. *RA*. 30, plate 55 (the arch)
Earl. *AA*. plate 32 (the arch)
EB. XXIV p. 585 (T. Ashby), XXVI p. 162
Ferrero, E. *L'arc d'Auguste à Suse*. Turin 1901
Hatt, J. J. *Histoire de la Gaule romaine*. Paris 1959. 88
Kaehler. *Art of Rome*. 59-61 (on the arch), with a plate on p. 64; 219
   (bibl.)
KP. V (1975). 75-76 (G. Radke)
Nissen. *IL*. II pp. 150-151
PECS. 819-820 (S. Finocchi)
Radke. *Viae*. 263; fig. 27

On the minor province of the Cottian Alps:
Prieur, J. "L'histoire des régions alpestres (Alpes Maritimes, Cot-
   tiennes, Graies et Pennines) sous le haut-empire romain," *ANRW*
   II.5.2 (1976): 630-656
—— *La province romaine des alpes cottiennes*. Villeurbanne (Rhône,
   France) 1968. 142-145 (There was an auxiliary unit [q.v.] at + Susa;
   indigenous troops were also used; compare *Volubilis*.)

Tusculum (Italy), near modern Frascati
p. 20 (early, nonorthogonal hill-cities)

Tusculum was at the north end of the Alban Hills of *Latium*, twenty-five kilometers southeast of Rome and near the *Via Latina*. It was the first city of the Latins (q.v.) on which Rome conferred its citizenship (381 B.C.; Livy 6.25-26); it then became a Roman *municipium*. Like *Tibur* (TIVOLI), *Tusculum* was famous for its country villas nearby, one of which belonged to Cicero.

The city was thus described by Strabo (q.v.): "It is on [the Alban Hills] that Tusculum is situated, a city with no mean equipment of buildings; and it is adorned by the plantings and villas encircling it" (5.3.12, cited by Frank 127-128; on the garden products, see Frank 129). The town was permanently destroyed in a battle of A.D. 1191 (Ashby in *EB*). Remains of the theater, the city walls, and villas may be seen today.

Frascati (five kilometers to the west) is known for its Renaissance villas, including the Villa Aldobrandini, and its white wine.

Alfoeldi. *Early Rome*. 380-385

Ashby, T. "The Classical Topography of the Roman Campagna," *Papers of the British School at Rome* 5 (1910): 339-347

—— *Rom. Cam*. 167-173

Bagnani. *Rom. Cam*. 104-126

Besnier. *Lexique*. 792

Blue Guide, Rome. 332-333

Borda, M. *Tuscolo*. Rome 1958

EB. XXVII pp. 486-487 (T. Ashby)

Frank. *ESAR*. V pp. 127-129

*Guida d'Italia del Touring Club Italiano, Roma e Dintorni*⁶. Milan 1962. 653-654

KP. V (1975). 1011-1012 (G. Radke)

McCracken, G. *A Short History of Ancient Tusculum*. Washington, D.C., 1939

Nissen. *IL*. II pp. 597-600

OCD. 1100 (E. T. Salmon)

Ogilvie. *Early Rome*. 77, 111, 113 (history of the sixth and fifth centuries B.C., based on Livy)

Paget. *Central Italy*. 217

PECS. 941-942 (B. Goss)

RE. VIIA.2 (1948). 1463-1491 (G. McCracken)

Salmon. *RC*. 49-50

Urso: see OSUNA

VAISON-LA-ROMAINE (Vaucluse, France) = *Vasio Vocontiorum,
Gallia Narbonensis*
pp. 89-90 (houses, apartments)

+ Die (Drôme)

Vasio was the tribal capital of the Celtic Vocontii under Roman
rule (Goudineau). This *civitas* (q.v.) had another town which was a
religious center, farther north, *Dea Augusta Vocontiorum;* today it
is + Die, Drôme département. (On Die, see Grenier, *Manuel* I pp.
557-560.) The Vocontii had the Roman status of allied city (q.v.),
with Latin rights (Pliny, *Natural History* 3.37). *Vasio* had its own
local government, with a prefect and aediles *(CIL* XII 1357).

The original *oppidum* (q.v.) at *Vasio* was probably on the hill above
the left bank of the Ouvèze *(Ouas)* River, which flows west at this
point and soon turns south to join the Rhône. The Gallo-Roman town,
on the opposite bank of the Ouvèze, was founded perhaps in 20/19
B.C., when Agrippa, Augustus' son-in-law, was in Gaul. VAISON is
twenty-five kilometers northeast of ORANGE, to which a Roman road
ran. The region of VAISON, in the western foothills of the Maritime
Alps, has a favorable climate and abundant vegetation.

Finds of coins tell us that the Gallo-Roman town flourished until
the fourth century A.D., but even afterwards a cathedral, now dis-
used, was built under Frankish rule (sixth and seventh centuries).
Later, in the turbulence of the Middle Ages, the townspeople retreated to settle on the heights of the left bank. A bridge, whose
construction is still mainly Roman, joins the two banks of VAISON
today.

The Gallo-Roman site was excavated from 1907 to 1955 by Canon
J. Sautel. His role was comparable to that of the schoolmaster B.
Sapène at ST.-BERTRAND-DE-COMMINGES. The forum at *Vasio* has not
yet been found, nor has any city wall. Grenier is of the opinion that
the plan of the Gallo-Roman town was not regular. The resettlement
of part of the right or north bank in the eighteenth century has prevented digging south of the Puymin Hill and west of the district of
La Villasse. The outstanding discoveries at VAISON — private houses—
took place in both of these sections. As at *Pompeii*, we can form a
better idea of this town's social structure than we can at a place which
was continuously occupied. The good site-museum at VAISON is a
further help.

Shops and a commercial basilica have been found in La Villasse.

Buildings brought to light on the Puymin Hill include the theater (now restored; it contained several statues, now in the site-museum), a public garden surrounded by porticoes and containing a fish-pool (compare + St.-Romain-en-Gal under VIENNE), and a so-called praetorium (that it was one of the governor's law-courts is not likely).

Vasio is a noteworthy example of a town which realized the full potentialities of an agreeable location. In MacKendrick's words, "The sunlit terraces, green gardens, cool colonnades are typical of Roman urbanism in Provence, 'urban' connoting pleasant living conditions and a sense of community. This civilized urbanity was one of the benefits of Roman rule." And here it was attained by an indigenous people.

Besnier. *Lexique*. 805-806
Boëthius and Ward-Perkins. *ERA*. fig. 136 (house); plate 181 (street)
Brogan. *Roman Gaul*. 99
Chevallier. *ANRW*. II.3 p. 813 (list of figures and bibl.)
Clébert. *Provence antique*. 234-239
Crema. *Arch*. 228; fig. 242 (House of the Silver Bust); 191, 192; fig. 193 (theater)
Desjardins. *Géogr*. 180 ff.; 237; 430-431; map x
Dumoulin, A. *Guide archéologique de Vaison-la-Romaine*. Vaison-la-Romaine 1976
EB. XXVII pp. 838-839
Février. "CSG." 24-26
—— *Dév. urbain en Provence*. 226 (index)
Finley. *Atlas*. 58 (P. MacKendrick)
Ginouvès, R. "Remarques sur l'architecture domestique à Vaison," *Revue archéologique* 34 (1949): 58-65
Goudineau, C. *Les fouilles de la Maison au Dauphin*. *Gallia*. Suppl. 37 (1979)
Grenier. *Manuel*. II 676-679; III 194-210; 766-772 (the theater); IV 263-265 (the baths—five have been found)
KP. V (1975). 1145-1146 (M. Leglay)
Lassus, J. "Remarques sur les mosaïques de Vaison-la-Romaine," *Gallia* 29 (1971): 45-72
Lavedan. *HU*. 387 (map)
Liou, B. "La maison au dauphin à Vaison-la-Romaine," *Comptes rendus de l'Académie des inscriptions et belles-lettres* (1971): 286-301
MacKendrick. *RF*. 105-115

McKay. *Houses*. 161-164; 251, n. 293 (bibl.)

Mommsen. *Provinces*. Chapter III (tribal government)

OCD. 1130 (A. L. F. Rivet; see "Vocontii")

PECS. 955-957 (C. Goudineau)

Pellerin, P. *En ressuscitant Vaison-la-Romaine*. Paris 1962

RE. VIIIA.1 (1955). 440-453 (P. Goessler and P. Wuilleumier), IXA.1 (1961). 704-716 (H. Rolland, see "Vocontii")

Sautel, J. *CAGR*. VII, *Vaucluse* (1939)

—— "Remarques sur les vestiges d'un grand édifice romain," *Comptes rendus de l'Académie des inscriptions et belles-lettres* (1955): 427-432

—— *Revue des études anciennes* (1940): 600-670

——— Sites, histoire et monuments de Vaison-la-Romaine. Lyons 1955

—— *Vaison dans l'antiquité*. 3 vols. Avignon 1926

—— *Vaison dans l'antiquité*. 2 vols. and 1 album. Avignon 1941/1942

VERONA (Veneto, Italy) = *Verona*, ancient region of *Venetia, Italia;* for a while after A.D. 265 *Colonia Augusta Nova Gallieniana*

p. 8 (Roman street plan still visible)

The Roman city was bounded on three sides (all but south) by the Adige River, which flows south from Merano to VERONA and then east to the Adriatic Sea. The poet Catullus (died 54 B.C.) called his home town a Latin colony (17.1), but this is most probably incorrect (Forlati Tamaro in *PECS*). *Verona* was a Roman *municipium* from 49 B.C. (Pliny, *Natural History* 3.130; see *Gallia Cisalpina* below).

The orthogonal Roman street plan probably dates from 28/15 B.C. (G. D. B. Jones); it is comparable to TURIN and AOSTA not only in date but also in the size of the city blocks (c. seventy-two meters square; see city blocks below). Because of VERONA's position on the right bank of the river, its Roman streets are not in accord with the cardinal points of the compass. Two Roman arches of the bridge now called the Ponte della Pietra remain (Forlati Tamaro in *PECS*).

A Roman road ran from the Alpine province of Raetia (western Austria, also Bavaria) through VERONA to join the *Via Aemilia* at MODENA. Tacitus tells us that in A.D. 69, VERONA was a rich city surrounded by extensive plains; it held a central strategic position blocking the Raetian Alps (*Histories* 3.8.1). The Emperor Gallienus built a new wall and made *Verona* an honorary colony in A.D. 265 (*CIL* V 3329).

Theodoric, Ostrogothic king of Italy 493-526, improved the city walls and renovated the aqueduct *(Excerpta Valesiana* 71). Because of his extended residence at Verona (compare RAVENNA), he is called Dietrich von Bern in German legend and the *Nibelungenlied*. The Roman city produced wine and woolen blankets, although the main source of its prosperity was probably trade through the Brenner Pass (Frank). Valpolicella, whose wine has a good reputation nowadays, is eight kilometers northwest of the modern city. Roman monuments of continuously inhabited VERONA are well preserved: gates, walls, and the theater, within whose walls stands a medieval church. The reconstructed amphitheater is once again used for shows (Ward-Perkins, *Cities* 29, 35).

Bengtson, H., and Milojčić, V. *Grosser historischer Weltatlas*. I⁵. Munich 1972. 40-41 (roads)

Besnier. *Lexique*. 812

Boëthius and Ward-Perkins. *ERA*. pl. 166 (gate)

Bradford. *Ancient Landscapes*. 256-261

Brown. *RA*. 29, pl. 46 (The amphitheater, difficult to date, is considered very early.)

Castagnoli. *Orthogonal Town Planning*. 108

Chevallier. *ANRW*. II.1 p. 698 (bibl.); plates xxviii-xxx (map and photographs)

Chilver. *Cisalpine Gaul*. 21, 25, 46-47, 51, 55, 80

Coarelli, C. *Arena di Verona*. Verona 1973 (the amphitheater)

Crema. *Arch*. 669 (index)

Dudley. *RS*. ill. 6 (air view)

EB. XXVII pp. 1033-1036 (J. H. Middleton and T. Ashby)

Finley. *Atlas*. 103 (G. D. B. Jones)

Frank. *ESAR*. V p. 109

Frothingham, A. "Discovery of the Capitolium and Forum of Verona," *American Journal of Archaeology* 18 (1914): 129-145

—— *RCID*. 244-263

Gazzola, P. *Ponti romani*. I, *Ponte Pietra a Verona*. Florence 1963

Grancelli, U. *Il piano di fondazione di Verona romana*. Verona 1964

Gutkind. *IHCD*. V (1970). 187, 239-243

Highet, G. *Poets in a Landscape*. New York 1957. 52-55 (Catullus)

Kaehler. *Art of Rome*. 96, 98-100

Kaehler, H. "Die roemischen stadttore von Verona," *Jahrbuch des Deutschen Archaeologischen Instituts* 50 (1935): 138-197

KP. V (1975). 1206-1207 (G. Radke)

Lavedan. *HU*. 379 (map)

Marconi, P. *Verona romana*. Bergamo 1938

McKay, A.G. *Vergil's Italy*. Greenwich, Conn., 1970. 68 (comparison with MANTUA); plate 6
Nissen. *IL*. II pp. 204-208
OCD. 1114 (E. T. Salmon)
PECS. 968-969 (B. Forlati Tamaro)
Radke. *Viae*. 179 (bibl.)
RE. VIIIA.2 (1958). 2426, 2429-2433 (G. Radke)
Richmond, I. A., and Holford, W. G. "Roman Verona," *Papers of the British School at Rome* (1935): 69-76
Salmon. *RC*. 163 (date of colony)
Taylor. *Voting Districts*. 273
(Il) territorio veronese in età romana. Accademia di agricoltura, scienze e lettere di Verona, Atti (1973)
Ward-Perkins. *Cities*. 123; figs. 58, 59 (aerial photograph and plan)
—— *RA*. pl. 227 (air view); 353 (index)
Whatmough, J. *Harvard Studies in Classical Philology* (1937): 181
Wheeler. *RAA*. 46; ill. 25 (air view)
Zarpellon, A. *Verona e l'agro veronese in età romana*. Nova Historia. Verona 1954
Zorzi, F. et al. *Verona e il suo Territorio*. I. 1961

+ *Verulamium:* listed under LONDON

Vesunna Petrucoriorum: see PERIGUEUX

Vetulonia (Italy)
p. 18 (nonorthogonal Etruscan city)
    One of the twelve Etruscan (q.v.) cities of ancient *Etruria*, *Vetulonia* was, like *Tarquinii*, located on a height near the Tyrrhenian Sea. Surrounded by a wall, *Vetulonia* is about 100 kilometers northwest of *Tarquinii* (see TARQUINIA). Both became unimportant *municipia* under the Roman Empire.
    It is thought that the insignia of Roman magistrates and senators had their origin at *Vetulonia*. Since 1898, the Etruscan tombs there have yielded valuable artifacts and such symbols as iron *fasces* (a bundle of rods). These finds are now in the Archaeological Museum at Florence.
Besnier. *Lexique*. 814-815
Boëthius and Ward-Perkins. *ERA*. 622 (index); fig. 31 (map)
Coarelli. *Le città etrusche*. 102-109; 321 (bibl.)
Curri, C. B. *Forma Italiae, Vetulonia*. I. Florence 1978

Dennis. *CCE*. II pp. 256-267
EB. XXVIII p. 15 (T. Ashby)
Enciclopedia dell'arte antica, classica e orientale. VII (1966). 1157-1161 (A. Talocchini)
KP. V (1975). 1239-1240 (G. Radke)
Levi, D. "Carta archeologica di Vetulonia," *Studi etruschi* 5 (1931): 13-40
Nissen. *IL*. II pp. 306-307
OCD. 1117 (D. W. R. Ridgway)
Ogilvie. *Early Rome*. 49 (the *fasces*)
Paget. *Central Italy*. 129-131
Patroni, G. "Vetulonia, Pompei e la sua storia," *Studi etruschi* 15 (1941)
PECS. 973-974 (A. Talocchini)
Piganiol. *HR*. 21, 24 (bibl.)
RE. VIIIA.2 (1958). 1874-1880 (G. Radke)
Scullard. *Etruscan Cities*. 134-141
Taylor. *Voting Districts*. 275

VIENNE (Isère, France) = (under Augustus) *Colonia Iulia Augusta Florentia Vienna, Gallia Narbonensis;* this city is to be distinguished from Vienna, Austria *(Vindobona* in Upper Pannonia to the Romans) and the River Vienne, which gives its name to a French départe-ment (see SANXAY); cf. colonies in *Gallia Narbonensis* below.
pp. 51 (Temple of Augustus and Livia); 87 (on the founding of LYONS)

+ Geneva (Geneva Canton, Switzerland), + St.-Colombe and + St.-Romain-en-Gal (Rhône)

VIENNE began as a Celtic *oppidum* on the left bank of the Rhône, thirty kilometers south of LYONS. The date of the colony's foundation there is debated (see Vittinghoff, *Roemische Kolonisation* 29, n. 3). Leglay believes that Julius Caesar made *Vienna* a Latin colony dur-ing the Gallic War (58-52 B.C.; *KP* 1268). The local tribe, the Allo-broges, were already Romanized at this time.

It was probably under Caligula or Claudius (emperors A.D. 37-54) that *Vienna* obtained the status of Roman colony (Salmon, *RC* 161; see Pliny, *Natural History* 3.36). On the growth of *Vienna*, we can look at Strabo 4.1.11: "Most of the Allobroges live scattered in vil-lages, but the most noble live in Vienne. At first, it was a village although it was called their capital, but [now] they have made a city out of it" (cited by Grenier, *ESAR* 486-487). By A.D. 48, as Claudius tells us in his speech to the Senate (see LYONS above), a number of important Romans had ancestors who were Allobroges.

The *territorium* (q.v.) covered all the lands of the Allobroges, unlike a possible arrangement at TRIER (q.v.). It included, as Mommsen pointed out, "Dauphiné and Western Savoy and . . . the equally old and almost equally considerable townships of Cularo (Grenoble) and Genava (Geneva) . . ." *(Provinces,* Chapter III). This territory was carefully farmed (Strabo 4.1.11, Rostovtzeff, *SEHRE* 218, Chevallier, ". . . trois centuriations . . ." [q.v.]; also see Aix-les-Bains). The population of Gallo-Roman +Geneva was never larger than 2,500.

Vienna's walls were built under Augustus (27 B.C.-A.D. 14). The large area enclosed was similar to that of NIMES or AUTUN, but its inhabited area was in fact much smaller (see cities [Roman], comparison in area, and cities [Roman], population of, below). The Augustan wall is no longer extant, but bits of the much smaller Late Roman wall (third/fourth centuries) are (Leglay in *PECS* 978).

Several indications of the city's *decumani* and *cardines* have been recognized (cf. Pelletier, "La structure urbaine de...Vienne"); unlike *Lugdunum*'s, *Vienna*'s *groma* (q.v.) was *not* placed on a hill.

Noteworthy among the Roman buildings visible today are the Temple of Augustus and Livia, the theater, and the portico which belongs to the Theater and Baths of Cybele. The odeum was excavated in 1960 (Senay); the only other one in Gaul was at LYONS. Of the *circus* for chariot races, a pyramid from its center remains. (In the Middle Ages, the Pyramid was thought to be the tomb of Pontius Pilate.) The colony's Capitol may have been atop Mont Pipet, just east of the theater's back. The hill now supports the nineteenth-century Church of Notre-Dame de la Salette (compare Fourvière Hill at LYONS).

Roman VIENNE was joined to a suburb across the Rhône (now +St.-Romain-en-Gal, Rhône département) by a stone bridge. Excavations there, begun in 1967, have disclosed warehouses, workshops, markets, and residences decorated with mosaics. At the Baths was a basin containing live fish, for decoration (Leglay and Tourenc [1970] 26).

VIENNE was on the highway (along the east bank of the Rhône) from LYONS to ARLES. While Roman roads from LYONS led west, those from VIENNE went east, one to Lausanne or AOSTA and one to Grenoble, +Susa, and TURIN. By the early third century, *Vienna* was honored with the *ius Italicum* (q.v., Paulus, [Legal] *Digest* 50.15.8.1). When Diocletian (284-305) subdivided the Roman provinces, VIENNE became the capital of both *Gallia Viennensis* and the seven provinces of southern Gaul. We learn from the *Notitia Dignitatum* (q.v.) that the Rhône fleet's command was located there c. A.D. 400 (*Oc.* [West] 42.14). Like LYONS, *Vienna* and its old *territorium* were controlled by the Burgundians (q.v.) from c. A.D. 460 to 534, when the Franks (q.v.) conquered (Boehm 60-61, 71).

Especially recommended now are visits to St.-Romain-en-Gal, where the buildings are very well marked, and the Roman exhibit in Geneva's Musée d'art et d'histoire.

VIENNE:

Bazin, H. *Villes antiques: Lyon et Vienne gallo-romaines*. Paris 1891

Besnier. *Lexique*. 819

Boehm, L. *Geschichte Burgonds*. Urban Taschenbuecher 134. Stuttgart 1971. 60-61, 71-72 (see reference to this entry under LYONS above)

Brogan. *Roman Gaul*. 100-101

Bruehl. *PC*. 223-233

Centre de recherches archéologiques de Vienne. *A la découverte de Vienne gallo-romaine*. 1965

Charlesworth. *Trade-Routes*. 191, 192 (wine; river-trade)

Chevallier. *ANRW*. II.1 plate xlix (plan); II.3 pp. 813 (list of figures and plates); 813-814 (bibl.)

Chevallier, R. "Notes sur trois centuriations romaines: Bononia, Ammaedara, Vienna," in *Hommages à A. Grenier*. Edit. M. Renard. Collection Latomus 58. Brussels 1962. 403-418

Crema. *Arch*. 670 (index)

Desjardins. *Géogr*. 422-425

Desjardins, T. "Le temple romain de Vienne," *Congrès archéologique de France* 46 (1879; publ. 1880): 422-435

EB. XXVIII p. 56 (history after A.D. 534; W. A. B. Coolidge)

Février. "CSG." 14

Formigé, J. "Remarques sur les dates de construction des théâtres d'Arles, d'Orange et de Vienne," *Revue archéologique* 29/30 (publ. 1949): 382-386

—— *Le théâtre romain de Vienne*. Paris 1931

—— "Vienne," *Congrès archéologique de France* 86 (1923; publ. 1925): 7-94, 121-127

Fournier, see ARLES

Frank. *ESAR*. III (A. Grenier; see index)

Grenier. *Manuel*. I pp. 323-329; III 211-220; 393-396 (Temple of Augustus and Livia); 773-780 (theater); 989-993 (*circus*); IV 111-117 (aqueduct)

KP. V (1975). 1268-1269 (M. Leglay)

Leglay, M. "Le Rhône dans la genèse et le développement de Vienne," in *Thèmes*, by Duval. 307-317 (trade-routes by road and river; comparison with LYONS)

—— "Vienne-la-Romaine, 'Vienna colonia ornatissima ac valentissima,'" *Archéologia* 88 (1975): 8-11 (The quote about the beautiful and powerful colony of *Vienna* is inspired by words in Claudius' speech of A.D. 48.)

MacKendrick. *RF*. 81-83; 257-258 (bibl.)

OCD. 1120 (C. E. Stevens)

PECS. 978-980 (M. Leglay)

Pelletier, A. "Centre de recherches et d'études archéologiques de Vienne, un nouveau départ," *Archéologia* 67 (1974): 71

—— *Le sanctuaire métroaque de Vienne (France)*. Etudes préliminaires aux religions orientales dans l'empire romain 83. Leiden 1980 (the shrine of Cybele)

—— "La structure urbaine d'une cité gallo-romaine au Haut-Empire: Vienne," *Actes du 95e Congrès national des Sociétés Savantes, 1970*. Paris 1974. 49-54

—— Vienne gallo-romaine au Bas-Empire, 275-468 après J.-C. Lyons 1974

Picard, C. "Le théâtre des mystères de Cybèle-Attis à Vienne...," *Comptes rendus de l'Académie des inscriptions et belles-lettres* (1955): 229-248

RE. VIIIA.2 (1958). 2113-2128 (A. Bruhl; see "Vienna 2")

Senay, P. "Odéon romain de Vienne. Rapport préliminaire des fouilles archéologiques 1970 et 1971," *Cahier des études anciennes* 1 (1972): 165-196

Stier. *Atlas*. 88-89 (archbishopric)

von Hagen, V. W. *The Roads that Led to Rome*. London 1967. 209 (color plate of the Pyramid)

On Claudius' speech of A.D. 48:

(see bibliography for LYONS above)

Frank. *ESAR*. III pp. 524-526 (A. Grenier); (on VIENNE)

+ Geneva (= *Genava, Gallia Narbonensis*):

Besnier. *Lexique*. 335

Blondel, L. "Le développement urbain de Genève à travers les siècles," *Cahiers de préhistoire et d'archéologie* 3 (1946): 16-30

—— "Le pont romain de Genève," *Genava* N.S. 2 (1954): 205-209
(the Gallo-Roman bridge across the Rhône)

Bonnet, C. "Genève, capitale Burgonde," *Archéologia* 56 (1974): 12

Broise, P. *Genève et son territoire dans l'Antiquité*. Brussels 1974

Bulletin de la société d'histoire et d'archéologie de Genève. 1892/
1897- (ref. provided by A. Hurst)

Caprino. *MAR, Bibl*. 242

Frei-Stolba, R. *ANRW*. II.5.1 pp. 318-324 (cf. AUGST)

Genava. 1923- (publ. by the Musée d'art et d'histoire)

Grenier. *Manuel*. III pp. 506-507 (commercial basilica)

Gutkind. *IHCD*. II (1965). 226-227; 490 (bibl.)

Helvetia archaeologica 14 (1973); (an issue devoted to Geneva)

Howald, E., and Meyer, E. *Die roemische Schweiz*. Zurich 1940.
219 ff.

KP. II (1967). 738-739 (E. Meyer)

Maier, J.-L. *Genève romaine*. Geneva 1976 (bibl. on 32)

—— and Mottier, Y. "Les fortifications antiques de Genève," *Genava* 24 (1976): 239-257

PECS. 347-348 (V. von Gonzenbach)

Staehelin, F. *Die Schweiz in roemischer Zeit*[3]. Basle 1948. 614-615

+Ste.-Colombe (just south of +St.-Romain-en-Gal):

Grenier. *Manuel*. IV pp. 265-276 (opulent houses and the baths called
"Palais du Miroir"—Palace of the Mirror)

+St.-Romain-en-Gal:

Chevallier. *ANRW*. II.3 p. 758 (house plan)

Février. "CSG." 26-27; pl. iv (air view)

Leglay, M. "Découvertes archéologiques à St.-Romain-en-Gal," *Revue archéologique* (1970-1971): 173-183

—— and Tourenc, S. "A St.-Romain-en-Gal Vienne gallo-romaine
retrouve un de ses quartiers urbains," *Archéologia* 26 (1969): 18-
29 (bibl. on 29)

—— *Comptes rendus de l'Académie des inscriptions et belles-lettres*
(1971): 764-774

—— *Saint-Romain-en-Gal, quartier urbain de Vienne gallo-romaine*. Lyons 1970 (bibl. on 32, also on VIENNE)

PECS. 979-980 (M. Leglay; see "Vienna")

Viroconium Cornoviorum: see WROXETER

Volsinii (Italy); one of the twelve cities of the Etruscan League, c. 600 B.C.

pp. 18 (nonorthogonal Etruscan city); 30 (fortifications compared to Rome's Servian Wall); (see Chapter I, n. 11 above on the city blocks)

+ Bolsena *(= Volsinii Novi)*

The location of the Etruscan city of *Volsinii* is debated by scholars. Grimal places it overlooking Bolsena (a city in modern Latium) following R. Bloch. Zonaras, a Byzantine (q.v.) historian of the twelfth century A.D., mentioned a wall (8.7) at *Volsinii.* Such a wall has been found above Bolsena. On the other hand, O. Muller, T. Ashby, Tenney Frank, D. W. R. Ridgway, and L. Richardson, Jr., place *Volsinii* at present-day Orvieto (in modern Umbria). Procopius, a Byzantine historian of the sixth century, commented on the lack of a wall at Orvieto (Hodgkin), and none has been found.

The problem about Orvieto is that it neither needed nor had an ancient wall. Even so, the rich archaeological finds there (of the sixth century B.C., the height of Etruscan power) would indicate that Orvieto is the more probable location. Both sites were in the Roman region of Etruria and are only fourteen air-kilometers apart. Bolsena is on the northeast side of the Lake of Bolsena, and Orvieto is northeast of Bolsena.

According to Pliny, *Natural History* 34.34, *Volsinii* was destroyed by the Romans in 265 B.C. A new city, *Volsinii Novi,* was built nearby, and it is underneath present-day Bolsena. The city blocks of orthogonal *Volsinii Novi* varied—some 240 by 480 Roman feet and some slightly more than 360 by 240 (Castagnoli). + Bolsena was on the *Via Cassia* from Rome to FLORENCE (begun c. 225 B.C.).

The name of Orvieto is derived from the Latin *urbs vetus* or "old city." It is first mentioned by Procopius in connection with the Byzantine reconquest of Italy (Radke; see Ostrogoths below). Today it is famous for its white Umbrian wine.

The Etruscan city:
Alfoeldi. *Early Rome.* 205 (the common shrine, near *Volsinii,* of the twelve Etruscan cities in *Etruria)*
Besnier. *Lexique.* 824
Bloch, R. *Comptes rendus de l'Académie des inscriptions et belles-lettres* (1951)

—— *Recherches archéologiques en territoire volsinien de la préhistoire à la civilisation étrusque*. Paris 1972
—— "Volsinies étrusque, étude historique et topographique," *Mélanges d'archéologie et d'histoire de l'Ecole française de Rome* 59 (1947): 9-39
—— "Volsinies étrusque et romaine," *Mélanges... Ecole française de Rome* 62 (1950): 53-119
Boëthius and Ward-Perkins. *ERA*. 30-32; pl. 27 (cemetery at Orvieto)
Coarelli. *Le città etrusche*. 267-274; 324 (bibl.)
Dennis. *CCE*. I pp. 530-535 (Orvieto)
EB. XXVIII p. 198 (T. Ashby)
Enciclopedia dell'arte antica, classica e orientale. V (1963). 773 (M. Bizzarri)
Frank. *ESAR*. I pp. 69-71 (Zonaras 8.7, on the Roman conquest)
Grenier, A. *Mélanges . . . Ecole française de Rome* 62 (1950): 119-122
Grimal. *Search*. 196-197
Harris. *REU*. 75-78, 115-118 (conflicts with Rome); 43, n. 7 (Orvieto as the site); 85, n. 3 (allied city); 313-317 (under Augustus)
Hodgkin, T. "Note C. On the Topography of Orvieto," *Italy and her Invaders*. IV (A.D. 535-553). Oxford 1896; rpt. New York 1967. 336-337 (following Procopius, *Gothic Wars* 6.20.5-11)
Klakowicz, B. *La necropoli anulare di Orvieto*. I-II. Rome 1972, 1974
KP. V (1975). 1324-1325 (G. Radke)
Lavedan. *HU*. 303 (bibl.)
OCD. 1131 (D. W. R. Ridgway)
Paget. *Central Italy*. 144-146
PECS. 657 (L. Richardson, Jr., see Orvieto)
RE. IXA.1 (1961). 998-999 (G. Radke on "Urbs Vetus")
Robertson. *GRA*. 337 (temple with triple *cella*, fifth/third centuries B.C., at Orvieto = Volsinii); 366 (bibl.)
Scullard. *Etruscan Cities*. 126-132

+ Bolsena (= *Volsinii Novi*, the Roman city):
Besnier. *Lexique*. 824
Castagnoli. *Orthogonal Town Planning*. 137 (with bibl.)
Dennis. *CCE*. I pp. 510-521
Frank. *ESAR*. V p. 102 (public library)
Harris, W. V. "The Via Cassia and the Via Traiana Nova between

Bolsena and Chiusi," *Papers of the British School at Rome* 33 (1965): 112-133

Nissen. *IL*. II pp. 339-340

RE. IXA.1 (1961). 830-847 (G. Radke)

Taylor. *Voting Districts*. 115, 274

Volubilis, Mauretania Tingitana (in present-day Morocco; thirty-one road kilometers north of Meknès, a city founded in the tenth century A.D.); the Roman province is to be distinguished from present-day Mauretania, a country south of Morocco.

p. 50 (the Capitol, q.v.)

+ Tangier

Volubilis is on a fertile plateau, between two streams (compare DJEMILA); to the south is the massif (peaks) of Zerhoun, which is watered by springs. The name of the city is Berber (q.v.) in origin and means "winding" (?like the streams). The site had long been occupied when Juba II, the client-king (q.v.) of *Mauretania* (25 B.C. - c. A.D. 23), and his wife, Cleopatra Selene (the daughter of Cleopatra and Mark Anthony), built a city on it, as they did at CHER-CHELL (q.v.). The royal couple's son and successor, Ptolemy, was murdered at Rome in A.D. 40 by the Emperor Gaius (Caligula), his cousin. As a result, the people of Mauretania revolted, and the kingdom was pacified by the Romans. By 44, it had been divided into two minor provinces. It is debated whether *Volubilis* or Tangier was the capital of *Mauretania Tingitana*.

Perhaps it is preferable to place the capital at + Tangier (Woloch; on Tangier see Vittinghoff, *Roemische Kolonisation* 117-118), with the governor traveling to *Volubilis* to preside over court cases. + Tangier was made a *municipium* eighty years before *Volubilis* (then it was part of Roman Spain; Gascou, *Ants. afrs.*), and Claudius gave it colonial rank (Pliny, *Natural History* 5.2). Roman roads connected it to *Sala* (near present-day Rabat) and *Volubilis*. Since the eleventh century, Roman + Tangier has been hidden beneath the Arab-Berber city (Euzennat in *PECS*).

We learn from the honorary inscription, translated below, that *Volubilis* favored Rome in the revolt and was rewarded by Claudius (41-54) with Roman citizenship and the status of *municipium* (q.v.). It would seem that Claudius thought that this client-king's city was sufficiently Romanized and built up to merit this rank. From their *nomina* or Roman family names (taken from those of their sponsors), we see that his supporter Valerius Severus and his wife did not get their Roman citizenship as a direct result of Claudius' grant. Their fathers' names, though, are Carthaginian (Bostar) and Berber (Izelta; Liversidge 66). In addition to casting light on civic status and citizenship, this inscription shows the happier side of a marriage among the local aristocracy in the Empire.

HONORARY INSCRIPTION OF AFTER A.D. 54

Latin texts: R. Cagnat, A. Merlin, L. Chatelain, *Inscriptions latines d'Afrique* (Paris 1923) no. 634 = Abbott and Johnson, *Municipal Administration* 356-358, no. 53 (with commentary and bibl.) = Chatelain, *Inscriptions latines du Maroc* (Paris 1942) no. 116 = E. M. Smallwood, *Documents Illustrating the Principates of Gaius, Claudius and Nero* (Cambridge 1967) no. 407b = Riccobono, *FIRA²*. I no. 70; transl. by G. M. Woloch.

To the son of Bostar, Marcus Valerius Severus, enrolled in the Galerian tribe for elections at Rome[a]; (at Volubilis), he was aedile (q.v.), suffes (of the pre-Roman town; compare *Lepcis Magna*), duovir (q.v.), chief priest (of the imperial cult) in the *municipium*, and he was commander of the auxiliary unit (q.v.) against Aedemon, who was defeated in the war. The Council of the *Municipium* honors him because of his services to the city and a well-conducted embassy, by which he obtained (for *Volubilis)* from the deified Claudius[b] Roman citizenship, the right to marry non-Roman women, immunity from taxes for ten years, (inclusion of) residents not citizens of *Volubilis*, and the goods of citizens killed in the war if they were without heirs. His wife, Fabia Bira, the daughter of Izelta, had been treated honorably by her husband, a most generous man; having returned the money (to the Council), she paid for and set up (this inscription) with her own money.

Little can be said as yet of the city's public buildings before 193, when Septimius Severus became emperor (see *Lepcis Magna)*. The forum and its adjoining basilica, built of stone from the Djebel Zerhoun, date from the early third century, as does the Capitol. They

[a] Such elections were meaningless after about A.D. 14.

[b] This reference dates the inscription, after the death of the Emperor Claudius.

were constructed on the foundations of earlier structures. The Arch of Caracalla (Severus' son and successor, 211-217) was embellished with two water-spouts, facing the city's colonnaded main street (Wheeler and Wood 150). An aqueduct, running parallel to this so-called *decumanus*, brought in water from a mountain spring one kilometer away (Liversidge 67). Although the excavations, begun by the French in 1915, are far from complete, it is clear that the plan of *Volubilis* was not orthogonal.

A number of second- and third-century houses have been found, both inside the city's walls and outside, along the streams. They range, in McKay's words, from "rich men's mansions to more modest workmen's housing—two-room mud-brick affairs,…a plain style of living which still abides throughout North Africa and the Near East" (225-226). Those along the Colonnaded Street, with their mosaic-covered floors (as at +*Verulamium*, listed under LONDON, and +St.-Romain-en-Gal, listed under VIENNE) and piped-in water (compare pp. 72-73 above), were both elegant and comfortable. The mosaics and fine bronze statues found at *Volubilis* may be seen at the site-museum and the Musée des Antiquités at Rabat.

The economy of *Volubilis* was based on agriculture, olives and wheat. The population grew to 10,000/12,000 (Whittaker) in over forty hectares. Granted colonial status at an uncertan date *(Antonine Itinerary*, q.v.; Salmon, *RC* 163), the city was nevertheless abandoned by the Empire in 284/5, when Diocletian located the frontier behind it. City life continued there for quite some time, perhaps until the Arab conquest (early eighth century). Stones from it were used in the new city of Meknès.

Volubilis:

Besnier. *Lexique*. 825

Bulletin d'archéologie marocaine. 1- (1956-)

CAH. X² (1952). 976 (bibl.)

Carcopino, J. *Le Maroc antique*. Paris 1943 (Ptolemy was killed at Lyons, not Rome, pp. 191-199.)

Chatelain, L. *Comptes rendus de l'Académie des inscriptions et belles-lettres* (1922): 28 ff.

—— *Le Maroc des romains*. Bibliothèque des Ecoles françaises d'Athènes et de Rome 160 (Paris 1944): 139-250; 294-297 bibl.; the inscription for M. Valerius Severus is reproduced, translated into French and discussed on pp. 143-150, with bibliography in the footnotes

—— illustrations for *Le Maroc des romains.* Paris 1949

Chevallier. *ANRW.* II.1 p. 721 (bibl.); plates lxxxi-lxxxiii

—— *Roman Roads.* 152

Clavel and Lévêque. *Villes.* 161-166 (a house)

Crema. *Arch.* 371, 517 (basilica); 513; fig. 671 (colonnades on the *"decumanus maximus"*)

Etienne, R. "Maisons et hydraulique dans le quartier nord-est à Volubilis," *Publications du Service des Antiquités du Maroc* 10 (1954): 25-211

—— *Le quartier nord-est de Volubilis.* Paris 1960

Euzennat, M. "Les Voies romaines du Maroc dans l'Itinéraire antonin," *Hommages à A. Grenier.* Edit. M. Renard. Collection Latomus 58. Brussels 1962. 595-610

Finley. *Atlas.* 71 (C.R. Whittaker)

Fishwick, D. "The Annexation of Mauretania," *Historia* 20 (1971): 467-487 (The inscription for M. Valerius Severus is quoted in Latin on p. 473.)

Frank. *ESAR.* IV (R. M. Haywood); (see index)

Garzetti. *TA.* 592-593 (bibl. on the M. Valerius Severus inscription)

Gascou, J. *Latomus* 30 (1971): 133-141 (the Roman *municipium*)

—— "La succession des bona vacantia et les tribus romaines de Volubilis," *Antiquités africaines* 12 (1978): 109-124 (on the inscription for M. Valerius Severus)

Grimal. *Civ. Rome.* 348 (urbanization by Juba II); 357 (on the houses; compare pp. 86-87 above); 513; illustration 123 (air view)

Gsell, S. *Histoire ancienne de l'Afrique du Nord.* VIII². Paris 1929

KP. V (1975). 1328-1329 (M. Leglay)

Lavedan. *HU.* 430 (map and air view)

Liversidge. *Everyday Life.* 65-70

Luquet, A. "La basilique judiciaire de Volubilis," *Bulletin d'archéologie marocaine* 7 (1967): 407-445

—— *Volubilis.* Tangier 1972

Marion, J. "Les trésors monétaires de Volubilis et de Banasa," *Antiquités africaines* 12 (1978): 179-215 (on finds of coins and the Roman abandonment)

McKay. *Houses.* 208, 225-226

Millar, F. *The Emperor in the Roman World.* Ithaca, N.Y., 1977. 160, 404 (on the honorary inscription for M. Valerius Severus)

Millar. *REN.* 171-172

Momigliano, A. *Claudius . . .*². Cambridge 1961. 54-55, 64-67; 114, 139-140 (bibl.)

Nagel's Guide, Morocco. 105-109 (1 plan)

OCD. 1131-1132 (B. H. Warmington); 566 (A. Momigliano and J. T. C. on Juba II)

PECS. 988-989 (M. Euzennat)

Piganiol. *HR*. 358, 556, 594 (bibl.)

Piganiol, A. "Note sur l'inscription de l'arc de triomphe de Volubilis," *Revue archéologique* (1924): 114-116 = *Scripta Varia*, Collection Latomus 133, vol. III. Brussels 1973. 165-166, plate xii (Roman citizenship for the surrounding tribesmen, A.D. 212)

Ponsich, M. *Volubilis*. Zurich 1974

—— "Volubilis," *Antike Welt* 1.2 (1970): 2-21

Raven. *Rome in Africa*. 191 (index)

RE. IXA.1 (1960). 864-873 (M. Euzennat)

Rebuffat, R. "Le développement urbain de Volubilis au IIe siècle de notre ère," *Bulletin archéologique du Comité des travaux historiques et archéologiques* N.S. 1/2 (1965/1966): 231-240

Romanelli. *Storia*. 257-271; 716 (index)

Rostovtzeff. *SEHRE*. 572, n. 5, 594 (bibl.); 822 (index)

Scullard. *Gracchi to Nero*. 308; 467 (bibl.)

Sherwin-White. *RC*. 241-243; 341-343

Sigman, M. C. "The Romans and the Indigenous Tribes of Mauretania Tingitana," *Historia* 26 (1977): 415-439, especially 419-420; 439 (A contrary view—the highways were not paved, and the towns were small and undistinguished.)

Thouvenot, R. "L'area et les thermes du Capitole de Volubilis," *Bulletin d'archéologie marocaine* 8 (1968-1972): 179-195 (The Capitol was in the open space south of the basilica.)

—— *Les maisons de Volubilis: le palais dit de Gordien et la maison à la mosaïque de Vénus*. Publications du Service des Antiquités du Maroc 12. Rabat 1958

—— *Volubilis*. Paris 1949

Vittinghoff. *Roemische Kolonisation*. 33-34, 37, 40, 48

Wheeler and Wood. *Roman Africa*. 148-155; plates 54-57 (plate 54, a handsome bronze bust of Juba II; 55-56, the Arch of Caracalla)

+Tangier (= *Tingis* or *Tingi*):

Besnier. *Lexique*. 773

Cagnat. *Armée romaine*

Chatelain. *Le Maroc des romains*. 33-39

Chevallier. *ANRW*. II.1 p. 722 (bibl.)

Gascou, J. "Notes sur l'évolution du statut juridique de Tanger entre 38 av. J.-C. et le règne de Claude," *Antiquités africaines* 8 (1974): 67-71

KP. V (1975). 855 (M. Leglay)

Michaux-Bellaire, E. *Tanger et sa zone.* 1921

Millar. *REN.* 172 (sea route to *Mauretania Caesariensis*)

Mommsen. *Provinces.* Chapter II (auxiliary units [q.v.] posted at Tangier also protected *Baetica*; see ITALICA)

OCD. 1078 (B. H. Warmington and W. N. W.)

PECS. 923 (M. Euzennat)

Ponsich, M. *Recherches archéologiques à Tanger et dans sa région.* Paris 1970

RE. VIA.2 (1937). 2517-2520 (Windberg)

Teutsch, L. *Das roemische Staedtewesen in Nordafrika.* Berlin 1962. 191 ff., 205 ff.

The Roman Army and the Frontier (cf. *Lambaesis*):
Cagnat. *Armée romaine.* 669-670 (description)

Euzennat, M. "Le limes de Volubilis," *Studien zu den Militaergrenzen Roms.* Cologne 1967. 194-199

Frézouls, E. "Les Baquates et la province romaine de Tingitane," *Bulletin d'archéologie marocaine* 2 (1957): 65 ff.

Mann. *ANRW.* II.1 p. 529

Nesselhauf, H. "Zur Militaergeschichte der Provinz Mauretania Tingitana," *Epigraphica* 12 (1950): 34-48

Roxan, M. "The Auxilia of Mauretania Tingitana," *Latomus* 32 (1973): 838-855

Speidel, M. P. "A Thousand Thracian Recruits for Mauretania Tingitana," *Antiquités africaines* 11 (1977): 167-174 (stationed at *Volubilis* c. A.D. 200; on the road to *Mauretania Caesariensis*, see p. 170)

+ Wiesbaden: listed under MAINZ

WROXETER (Shropshire; since 1974, officially Salop, England, U.K.)
= *Viroconium Cornoviorum, Britannia*
p. 44 (the forum)

+ Caerleon (Gwent, Wales), + Chester (Cheshire), + Gloucester (Gloucestershire)

The River Severn (in Latin, *Sabrina*) originates in central Wales, flows northeast, turns southeast at the English border, and travels southeast and then southwest in a kind of half-oval to the Bristol Channel, an arm of the Atlantic Ocean. WROXETER is on the left bank of the upper river, about twenty-five kilometers from Wales. In A.D. 48/49, a fort manned by an auxiliary unit (q.v.) of Roman cavalry was placed about 400 meters south of the site, which from A.D. 52/58 to 66 was the camp of the Fourteenth Legion; the Twentieth Legion was located there from 66 to 87/90, when it moved to + Chester (Cheshire), two kilometers from northern Wales. Timber buildings from the legionary camp at WROXETER have been discovered, but since they are two and a half meters (eight feet) below the level of *Viroconium,* the camp cannot be studied without difficulty (Webster, *Army* 182). G. Webster is in fact doing this now.

In addition to + Chester, there were two permanent legionary camps (each had one legion, q.v.) in *Britannia* from A.D. 90: + Caerleon (Gwent, Wales; note the similarity in name with León, Spain— see ITALICA) and York (Yorkshire; see colonies in *Britannia* and compare MAINZ for the distribution of Roman legions in Upper and Lower Germany).

While a legion resided at WROXETER, camp followers stayed nearby, but when the Twentieth left, the town was organized. *Viroconium* was the capital of the *civitas* (q.v.) or tribe of the Cornovii; we do not know if it was ever recognized as a *municipium* (q.v.). An inscription found at WROXETER shows that the local government of the town was the same as that of the Celtic tribe (Rostovtzeff, *SEHRE* 635, n. 51; Collingwood and Taylor; compare Rivet 65-66, 132). The same held true for the other tribal capitals of Britain, as well as most of *Gallia Comata* (but compare TRIER).

Excavation at WROXETER is still in progress, but the site has been completely studied by means of aerial photography. The roughly oval walls (built of earth late in the second century and surrounded by stone during the next century) contained an area of 69 hectares (170 acres), but only 28 (70 acres) seem to have been built on. The outline of the town's streets was, in Wacher's words, "reasonably regular" (p. 366). There are blocks of 94.5 by 116 meters (Collingwood and Richmond, *ARB* 96-97). The principal remains visible are the south wall of the basilica (which the council-hall adjoined), the forum (all A.D. 129/130, *RIB* 288; see Collingwood and Wright under "Ancient Sources" below), public baths (about A.D. 150, just east of the forum in the center of town) and an aqueduct.

WROXETER was the terminus of the Roman highway northwest from LONDON; it is called Watling Street, and the distance is more than 230 kilometers (144 English miles). An extension ran north to + Chester and continued on to Carlisle (county of Cumbria) on Hadrian's Wall (see p. 79 above). Other roads led south to + Caerleon and west to a fort, manned by auxiliary troops, at Caersws, also in modern Wales; the latter route followed the River Severn for part of the way. The importance of *Viroconium* as a junction on mainly military roads is clear.

The Romans abandoned the fort at + Chester late in the fourth century, and then Celts from Ireland seem to have invaded *Viroconium*, whose population probably left for nearby hilltops, such as what is now Shrewsbury (on the Severn seven kilometers to the northwest), the county town of Shropshire. Collingwood remarked, "WROXETER, like SILCHESTER, is a Roman site which has never had upon it a post-Roman town" *(RB 52)*. There is, however, at WROXETER a church, containing many stones from the Romano-British town.

WROXETER:

Barker, P. "Excavations on the Site of the Baths at Wroxeter 1966-1974, An Interim Report," *Britannia* 6 (1975): 106-117 (also fourth/fifth century buildings on the site of the basilica)
Besnier. *Lexique*. 821
Blue Guide, England. 382
Collingwood. *RB*. 52, 54
—— and Richmond. *ARB*. 350 (index); plates ix (air view), xvi (inscription dating the forum)
Collingwood, R. G., and Taylor, M. V. *Journal of Roman Studies* 14 (1924): 244 (inscription on the tribal government)
Frere. *Britannia*. 393, 401 (bibl.); 432 (index); plates 10, 19, 20 (aerial photographs)
Haverfield, F. *The Romanization of Roman Britain*[4]. Rev. by G. MacDonald. Oxford 1923. 58
Lavedan. *HU*. 415 (map)
Liversidge. *BRE*. 526 (index)
Margary. *RRB*. 292-299, 318, 344; for maps: 278, 316
McKay. *Houses*. 181, 200
OCD. 1128; also see p. 292 ("Cornovii"; both by S. S. Frere)
OSMRB
PECS. 984-985 (G. Webster)
Richmond, I. A. "The Cornovii," in *Culture and Environment*. Edit.

Figure 34. Legions in Britannia

Legions	A.D. 15	//	50	60	70	80	90	100	110	120	130
Second *Adiutrix*				RAVENNA where raised	Lincoln	Chester	——— Danube Frontier ——— Belgrade (Yugoslavia)				Budapest (Hungary) →
Second Augustan*	Strasbourg (France) Rhine Frontier				Gloucester	Caerleon ————————————————————————————— →					
Fourteenth*	MAINZ Rhine Frontier			WROXETER →		MAINZ Rhine	——— Danube Frontier ——— Budapest		Vienna (Austria)	Carnuntum (Austria) →	
Twentieth*	Cologne Neuss Rhine Frontier			Gloucester ———	WROXETER →		Scotland ——— Chester →				
Sixth	Spain					Neuss = *Novaesium*	Birten (see MAINZ)				York →
Ninth*	Sisak ? (Yugoslavia)			Lincoln			York				Nijmegen (Netherlands) (see *Noviomagus Batavorum*)

*The four legions which invaded Britain in A.D. 43.
Cf. A. R. Birley, *The Fasti of Roman Britain* (Oxford 1981) 219–222.

I. L. Foster and L. Alcock. London 1963. 251 ff.
—— *RB*. 240 (index)
Rivet. *TCRB*. 150-151 (on the Cornovii), 171 (bibl.), 192 (index)
Wacher. *TRB*. 50 (plan of the baths); 55 (plan of the market); 358-374; 459 (index)
Webster, G. *Army*. 330 (index)
—— *The Cornovii*. London 1975
—— "Excavations at Roman Viroconium," *Archaeology* 31 (1978): 50-52 (on the Training School, Birmingham University)
—— "The Roman Advance under Ostorius Scapula," *Archaeological Journal* 115 (1958): 49 ff. (Ostorius was governor of *Britannia* A.D. 47-52.)
—— "Viroconium, A Study of the Problems," *Transactions of the Shropshire Archaeological Society* 57 (1962/63)
—— and Barker, P. *Viroconium . . . Roman City*[3]. London 1978 ("The Baths," 16-24; bibl. 25-26; 2 maps)

+ Caerleon *(= Isca Silurum):*
From about A.D. 75, it was garrisoned by the Second Augustan Legion, which had been stationed at Strasbourg sixty years before. "Isca" meant "water" in Celtic.

Besnier. *Lexique*. 399
Boon, G. C. *Isca: The Roman Legionary Fortress At Caerleon, Monmouthshire*. Cardiff 1972
—— and Williams, C. *Plan of Caerleon*. Cardiff 1967 (with bibl.)
Collingwood and Richmond. *ARB*. plate iv (air view of the *ludus*, or training ground, similar to an amphitheater)
Houlder, C. H. *Wales, An Archaeological Guide*. Park Ridge, N.J., 1975. 140-142
Mommsen. *Provinces*. Chapter V
Nash-Williams, V. E. *The Roman Frontier in Wales*[2]. Cardiff 1969. 18 ff.
OCD. 552 (C. E. Stevens)
PECS. 415-416 (G. C. Boon)
Rivet. *TCRB*. 160 (the local tribe, the Silures)
Webster. *Army*. 306-307 (index)
Wheeler. *RAA*. 76 (mainly on Caerwent = *Venta Silurum*, eleven kilometers away, the tribal capital)

+ Chester *(= Deva):*

The Grosvenor Museum in present-day Chester houses many of the Roman finds.

+ Chester is to be distinguished from Chesters on Hadrian's Wall (see p. 79 above). Hammond remarks that after the Angles and Saxons (qq.v.) invaded Britain, "Latin therefore vanished as a language except words which the invaders adopted for things not familiar in their primitive culture, as in terminations of place names -chester, from Latin *castra* or camp; street from *via strata*, a paved road, and the like" *(The City* 333).

+ Chester was garrisoned by the Second Legion, *Adiutrix*, from A.D. 74/8 to 87 and by the Twentieth from 87/90. The Second Legion was stationed at Lincoln (see colonies in *Britannia)* from about A.D. 71 until it was moved to + Chester. The adjective *adiutrix* (helping) refers to the fact that this legion was raised from the fleet at RA-VENNA in A.D. 69, and its original members did not have to be Roman citizens.

Besnier. *Lexique.* 267-268
Collingwood and Richmond. *ARB.* plate iv (the North Wall)
Frere. *Britannia.* 393 (bibl.)
Gutkind. *IHCD.* VI (1971). 350-355; 499 (bibl.)
Liversidge. *BRE.* plate lxviii (the Roman quay)
Nash-Williams. *The Roman Frontier in Wales* (see + Caerleon above)
OCD. 292 (S. S. Frere, see "Cornovii"), 333 (C. E. Stevens)
PECS. 270-271 (D. F. Petch)
Thompson, F. H. *Roman Chester.* Chester 1959
Watkin, W. Thompson. *Roman Cheshire.* Liverpool 1886; rpt. 1974
Webster. *Army.* 308 (index)

+ Gloucester, Gloucestershire *(= Glevum):*
See colonies in *Britannia.* This was the site of the first bridge over the River Severn (compare ARLES); here was the camp of the Twentieth Legion, A.D. 49-66, and of the Second Augustan Legion from 66 to about 75, when it moved to + Caerleon. In 96/98, *Glevum* became a Roman colony (compare + Cologne, under MAINZ).
Besnier. *Lexique.* 341
Frank. *ESAR.* III pp. 1-118 (R. G. Collingwood)
Fullbrook-Leggatt, L.E.W.O. *Roman Gloucester.* Stroud, Gloucestershire, 1968
Green, C. "Glevum and the Second Legion," *Journal of Roman Studies* 32 (1942): 39-52; 33 (1943): 15-28

Heighway, C. et al. "Excavations at Nos. 1 and 30 Westgate Street, Gloucester: The Roman Levels," *Britannia* 11 (1980): 73-114

Hurst, H. "Excavations at Gloucester, 1968-1971, First Interim Report," *Antiquaries Journal* 52 (1972): 24-69

—— "Glouchester (Glevum): A Colonia in the West Country," in *The Roman West Country.* Edit. K. Branigan and P. J. Fowler. Newton Abbot, Devon/North Pomfret, Vermont, 1976. 63-80

KP. II (1967). 813 (F. M. Heichelheim)

McWhirr, A. *Roman Gloucestershire.* London 1981

OCD. 468 (S. S. Frere)

PECS. 357 (J. F. Rhodes)

The Roman Army in Britain:

Birley, E. *Roman Britain and the Roman Army.* Kendal, Cumbria, 1961

Bonser, W. *A Romano-British Bibliography.* Oxford 1964

Chapot. *MR.* 388-411

Christ. *Bibl.* 349-352, 396-397

Frere. *Britannia* (bibl. on pp. 399-400)

Harmand. *Occ. rom.*

Holder, P. A. *The Roman Army in Britain.* London 1982

Mann. *ANRW.* II.1 pp. 529-531, 533

Piganiol. *HR.* 241 (index)

Richmond. *RAA*

St. Joseph, J. K. "Air Reconnaissance in Roman Britain, 1969-72," *Journal of Roman Studies* 63 (1973): 214-246

Simpson, G. *Britons and the Roman Army.* London 1964 (mainly about Wales)

Webster. *Army.* 282-286 (bibl.)

Bibliographies

Master List

ANRW. See *Aufstieg und Niedergang.* . . .

Albertini, E. *L'Afrique romaine*[2]. Algiers 1950.

Alfoeldi, A. *Early Rome and the Romans*. Ann Arbor 1963.
  = *Early Rome*

Allais, G. *Le Alpi occidentali nell' antichità*. Turin 1891.

Andreae, B. *The Art of Rome*. New York 1977. (transl. from the German; on the Roman Empire, see Part III pp. 481-586, "Descriptions of Archaeological Sites," which has plans of cities; general bibl. on pp. 631-645)

Andresen, C. et al., eds. *Lexikon der alten Welt*. Zurich and Stuttgart 1965.
  = *Artemis Lexikon*

Argan, G. C. *The Renaissance City*. New York 1969. (bibl. on pp. 122-124)

Arnold, W. T. *The Roman System of Provincial Administration*...[3]. Oxford 1914.
  = *RSPA*

Artemis Lexikon. See Andresen, C.

Ashby, T. *The Roman Campagna in Classical Times*. London 1927; rpt. with an introduction by J. B. Ward-Perkins, London 1970.
  = *Rom. Cam.*

Atlante aerofotografico delle sedi umane in Italia. 2 vols. Florence 1970.

Aufstieg und Niedergang der roemischen Welt. Edit. H. Temporini. Berlin 1972- .
  = *ANRW*

Articles often cited are:

Chevallier, R. "Cité et territoire. Solutions romaines aux problèmes de l'organisation de l'espace. Problématique 1948-1973," *ANRW.* II.1 (1974): 649-788. (with 106 plates)

Chevallier, R. "Gallia Lugdunensis. Bilan de 25 ans de recherches historiques et archéologiques," *ANRW.* II.3 (1975): 860-1060.

Chevallier, R. "Gallia Narbonensis. Bilan de 25 ans de recherches historiques et archéologiques," *ANRW.* II.3 (1975): 686-828.

Crema, L. "L'architettura romana nell'età della repubblica," *ANRW.*

I.4 (1973): 633-660 + 46 plates.
= "Arch. rep."
Dilke, O. A. W. "Archaeological and Epigraphic Evidence for Roman Land Surveys," *ANRW*. II.1 (1974): 564-592.
Mann, J. C. "The Frontiers of the Principate," *ANRW*. II.1 (1974): 508-533.
Bagnani, G. *The Roman Campagna and its Treasures*. London 1929.
= *Rom. Cam.*
Bailey, C., ed. *The Legacy of Rome*. Oxford 1923.
= *Legacy*
(see 385-428 "Architecture and Art" by G. M. Rushforth and 429-474 "Building and Engineering" by G. Giovannoni)
Balsdon, J. P. V. D., ed. *Roman Civilization*. Harmondsworth, Middlesex, 1969. (see: M. W. Frederiksen, "Towns and Houses," 151-168 [bibl. 167-168] and I. A. Richmond, "Architecture and Engineering," 127-150 [bibl. 150])
Bannert, H. "Volcae (Arecomici and Tectosages)," *RE*. Supplement 15 (1978): 937-960.
= "Volcae"
(for southern France)
Banti, L. *Etruscan Cities and their Culture*. Berkeley 1973.
Baratier, E. *Histoire de la Provence*. Toulouse 1969.
——, ed. *Documents de l'histoire de la Provence*. Paris 1971.
Barley, M. W., ed. *European Towns, their Archaeology and Early History*. London 1977. (papers on early medieval cities, with plans and bibliographies)
——, ed. *The Plans and Topography of Medieval Towns in England and Wales*. London 1976.
Bénabou, M. *La résistance africaine à la romanisation*. Paris 1976. ("the best account of Roman expansion into Africa that has been written"—- C. R. Whittaker, *Journal of Roman Studies* 68 [1978]: 190)
Bengtson, H. *Introduction to Ancient History*. Transl. R. I. Frank and F. D. Gilliard. Berkeley 1970. (130-135, bibl. for archaeology)
—— and Milojčić, V. *Grosser historischer Weltatlas*. I⁵. Munich 1972.
= *Atlas*
(The numbers I cite refer to maps; I was unable to use the sixth edition 1978, which differs little; there is a separate volume of *Elaeuterungen*, a commentary, with good bibliographies; its fourth edition [1976] accompanies the fifth edition of the *Atlas*.)
Bérard, J. *Bibliographie topographique des principales cités grec-*

ques de l'Italie mériodionale et de la Sicile dans l'antiquité. Paris 1941.

= *Bibl. topogr.*

—— *La colonisation grecque de l'Italie mériodionale et de la Sicile . . .².* Paris 1957.

Bérenguier, R. *La Provence romaine...villes et monuments.* Paris 1976.

Bertrand, L. *Les villes d'or, Algérie et Tunisie romaines.* Paris 1921.

*Besnier, M. *Lexique de géographie ancienne.* Paris 1914.

= *Lexique*

(citations of ancient authors, lists of monuments; on pp. 833-893 a useful table of modern names, giving the classical names)

Bianchi Bandinelli, R. *Rome, le centre du pouvoir.* Paris 1969.

= *Rome* I

(transl. from the Italian; Roman art to A.D. 200; English transl. London 1970)

—— *Rome, la fin de l'art antique.* Paris 1970.

= *Rome* II

(transl. from the Italian; Roman art from A.D. 193-395; English transl. London 1971)

Birley, A. *The People of Roman Britain.* London 1979. (mostly on the officials; has bibliographical footnotes)

Blackwell's Book Catalogue 1130(1): Greek and Latin Classics. Oxford 1979. (see 95-112 history, geography, law; 112-123 archaeology, art)

Blake, M. E. *Ancient Roman Construction in Italy....* Washington, D.C., 1947. (to Augustus)

—— *Roman Construction in Italy from Nerva through the Antonines.* Philadelphia 1973.

—— *Roman Construction in Italy from Tiberius through the Flavians.* Washington, D.C., 1959.

Blue Guide, England. See Rossiter, S.

Blue Guide, Northern Italy. See Macadam, A.

Blue Guide, Rome. See Rossiter, S.

Blue Guide, Sicily. See Macadam, A.

Blue Guide, Spain. See Robertson, I.

Boëthius, A. *Etruscan and Early Roman Architecture.* New York 1978. (a second edition of his part of *ERA*; not used)

—— *The Golden House of Nero: Some Aspects of Roman Architecture.* Ann Arbor 1960.

= *Golden House*

(also on city planning; has bibliographical footnotes)

306 **Part II**

—— "Roman and Greek Town Architecture," *Goeteborgs Hoegsko-las Aarsskrift* 54 (1948). printed separately.
= "RGTA"
—— and Ward-Perkins, J. B. *Etruscan and Roman Architecture.* Harmondsworth, Middlesex, 1970.
= ERA
(275 plates and 204 figures, explained in the text; bibl. on pp. 587-601; pp. 3-180 are by Boëthius, 183-536 by Ward-Perkins)
Boissier, G. *Roman Africa.* New York 1899. (archaeology, geography and history)
Bonnard, L. *La navigation intérieure de la Gaule à l'époque gallo-romaine.* Paris 1908.
Bosi, R. *Le città greche d'Occidente.* Milan 1980. (a catalogue of Greek cities from Albania to Spain; 280 color photographs; useful bibl. on pp. 311-312)
Bouchier, E. S. *Life and Letters in Roman Africa.* Oxford 1913.
= LLRA
Bradford, J. S. P. *Ancient Landscapes.* London 1957.
= Ancient Landscapes
("L'Erma" di) Bretschneider. *Bibliografia d'archeologia classica.* Rome 1969.
—— *Bibliografia di storia antica e diritto romano.* Rome 1971. (see 9-171, on ancient history)
Brogan, O. *Roman Gaul.* London 1953.
= Roman Gaul
Broughton, T. R. S. *The Romanization of Africa Proconsularis.* Baltimore 1929; rpt. Westport, Conn., 1972.
= RAP
(political development; see esp. 51-87, 130-156 on *coloniae* and *municipia*)
Brown, F. E. *Roman Architecture.* New York 1961.
= RA
*Bruehl, C. *Palatium und Civitas.* I. *Gallien.* Cologne/Vienna 1975.
= PC
(in German; topography of Late Roman cities, 3rd to 13th centuries; bibl. and plans with each article on a city; excellent general bibl. 258-269; index to authors cited 270-273; French transl. by M. Fleury of Vol. I, on Gaul, forthcoming; Vol. II, Germany, forthcoming)
Brunt, P. A. *Italian Manpower, 225 B.C.-A.D. 14.* Oxford 1971.
= Italian Manpower
(ancient sources usually cited; helpful on colonies and *municipia;*

especially good on *Gallia Cisalpina*)

Bunbury, E. H. *A History of Ancient Geography*[2]. 2 vols. London 1883; rpt. New York 1959, with an introduction by W. H. Stahl.

= *HAG*

CAH = *Cambridge Ancient History*.

Cagnat, R. *L'armée romaine d'Afrique et l'occupation militaire d'Afrique sous les empereurs*[2]. Paris 1913; rpt. New York 1975.

= *Armée romaine*

—— and Chapot, V. *Manuel d'archéologie romaine*. 2 vols. Paris 1916, 1920.

Cambridge Ancient History. 12 vols. Edit. J. B. Bury et al. Cambridge 1923-1939. (2nd edition has minor corrections. 3rd edition in progress)

= *CAH*

(bibliography with each chapter; bibls. are "fundamental" up to 1939—-Garzetti, *TA* 775, n. 1)

Cambridge Medieval History. 8 vols. Edit. J. B. Bury et al. Cambridge 1911-1936. (2nd edition in progress)

Caprino, C. et al. *Mostra Augustea della Romanità, Appendice bibliografica al Catalogo*. Rome 1938; rpt. Rome 1968.

= *MAR, Bibl.*

(see especially "Città romane dell'Impero" 241-243 and "Città romane d'Italia" 263-264)

Carcopino, J. *Daily Life in Ancient Rome*. Transl. E. O. Lorimer. Edit. with bibl. and notes by H. T. Rowell. New Haven 1941; rpt. Harmondsworth, Middlesex, 1978.

= *Daily Life*

Carte Archéologique de la Gaule Romaine.

= *CAGR*

(15 sections have appeared to date, each one on a département of France; the series is under the patronage of the Académie des inscriptions et belles-lettres and, since 1957, the Centre National de la Recherche Scientifique. Until 1959, the sections were also called *Forma Orbis Romani*.)

(= *FOR*)

Cary, M. *The Geographic Background of Greek and Roman History*. Oxford 1949.

= *Geogr. Backgr.*

Castagnoli, F. *Orthogonal Town Planning in Antiquity*. Cambridge, Mass., 1972.

= *Orthogonal Town Planning*

(translated from the Italian; bibliography is found in the footnotes)

Chapot, V. *Le monde romain*[2]. Evolution de l'humanité no. 22. Paris 1951. (extensive bibl. mainly on the Roman provinces, including Africa 485-496)
= *MR*
(English transl. of 1st edition by E. A. Parker. London 1928; provincial and municipal administration; [compare Mommsen, *Provinces* and Reid, *Municipalities*])

Charlesworth, M. P. *Trade-Routes and Commerce of the Roman Empire*[2]. Cambridge 1926; rpt. Hildesheim 1961.
= *Trade-Routes*
(French transl. by G. Blumberg and P. Grimal. Paris 1938)

Chevallier, R. *La cité romaine à travers la littérature latine*. Paris 1948.
—— *Roman Roads*. Transl. N. H. Field. London 1976.
= *Roman Roads*
(maps of the roads, incl. pp. 156, Spain and 161, Gaul)
—— *Villes et monuments de l'Italie antique*. Paris 1974.
—— also see under *Aufstieg und Niedergang*....

Chilver, G. E. F. *Cisalpine Gaul*. Oxford 1941.
= *Cisalpine Gaul*

Christ, K., ed. *Roemische Geschichte: Eine Bibliographie*. Darmstadt 1976.
= *Bibl.*

Clavel, M., and Lévêque, P. *Villes et structures urbaines dans l'occident romain*. Paris 1971.
= *Villes*
(source-book; bibl. on pp. 227-257)

Clébert, J. -P. *Provence antique*. II. Paris 1970.
= *Provence antique*
(an introduction based on Grenier, *Manuel*)

Clemente, G. *I Romani nella Gallia meridionale, II-I sec. a. C*. Bologna 1974. (bibl. on 185-207; 93 ff. text of and commentary on Cicero's *For M. Fonteius*)

Coarelli, F., ed. *Le città etrusche*[2]. Milan 1974. (good plates; bibl. on pp. 317-326; English translation 1975)

Cole, J. P. *Italy, An Introductory Geography*. New York 1966.

Collingwood, R. G. *Roman Britain*. London 1923.
= *RB*
—— and Myres, J. N. L. *Roman Britain and the English Settlements*[2]. Oxford 1937; rpt. Oxford 1975.
= *RBES*
(two separate works of history in one volume)

—— and Richmond, I. *The Archaeology of Roman Britain*[2]. London 1969.
= *ARB*

Coulson, W. D. E. *An Annotated Bibliography of Greek and Roman Art, Architecture and Archaeology*. New York 1975.

Courtois, C., and Julien, C. *Histoire de l'Afrique du Nord*. I[3]. Paris 1964.

Crema, L. "Arch. rep." See under *Aufstieg und Niedergang*....
—— *Architettura romana* = Enciclopedia classica. III. xii. 1. Turin 1959.
= *Arch*.
(bibliography on each major monument)

Cunliffe, B. *Rome and her Empire*. London 1978.
= *Rome*
(an expensive popularization; excellent color photographs by B. Brake and L. von Matt; good bibl. on p. 310)

Dal Maso, L. B., and Vighi, R. *Lazio archeologico*. Florence 1975.
(guidebook to the Italian region)

Daremberg, C., Saglio, E. et al., eds. *Dictionnaire des antiquités grecques et romaines*. 10 vols. Paris 1877-1919.
= *Dar Sag*
(use to find out *what* a tangible thing was: many illustrations)

D'Arms, J. H., and Kopff, E. C., eds. *Roman Seaborne Commerce*. *MAAR* 36 (1980).

de la Croix, H. *Military Considerations in City Planning*. New York 1972. (bibl. on pp. 121-122)

Dennis, G. *Cities and Cemeteries of Etruria*[4]. 2 vols. London 1907.
= *CCE*

de Ruggiero, E. *Le colonie dei romani*. Spoleto 1896; rpt. Rome 1977. (extract from his *Dizionario epigrafico*...)
—— et al. *Dizionario epigrafico di antichità romane*. Rome 1895-; part rpt. Rome 1961-1967.
= *Diz. ep*.
(citations of ancient authors; references to inscriptions by subjects and locations; bibliographies)

Desjardins, E. *Géographie...de la Gaule romaine*. Paris, I, 1876; II, 1878; III, 1885; IV, 1893; all vols. rpt. Brussels 1968.
= *Géogr*.

De Witt, N. J. *Urbanization and the Franchise in Roman Gaul*. Lancaster, Pa., 1940.

Dilke, O. A. W. *Roman Land Surveyors*[2]. London 1980.

Dion, R. *Histoire de la vigne et du vin en France*. Paris 1959.

Dizionario Garzanti della lingua italiana[19]. Milan 1978. (963-978;
   bibl. on 946; Italian cities' names)
Dollinger, P. et al. *Bibliographie d'histoire des villes de France*. Paris
   1967.
Dudley, D. R. *Roman Society*. Harmondsworth, Middlesex, 1975.
   = *RS*
   (bibl. on 295-307)
—— *Urbs Roma*. London 1967.
   = *Urbs Roma*
   (a source-book with good historical comments)
Duncan-Jones, R. *The Economy of the Roman Empire*. Cambridge
   1974.
   = *ERE*
   (bibliography on pp. xii-xvi; 370-378)
Duval, P. -M. *La Gaule jusqu'au milieu du Ve siècle*. Paris 1971. Vol.
   I of series, *Les sources de l'histoire de France* . . . , edit. A. Mol-
   inier and R. Fawtier.
—— *La vie quotidienne en Gaule pendant la paix romaine (Ier-IIIe
   siècles)*[3]. Paris 1961. 4th edition, Paris 1976.
*—— and Frézouls, E., eds. *Thèmes de recherches sur les villes
   antiques d'Occident*. Colloques internat. du Centre National de la
   Recherche Scientifique 542, Strasbourg 1971. Paris 1977.
   = *Thèmes*
   (conference on continuity of cities and river-trade in Roman times)
EB = *Encyclopaedia Britannica*.
ECNMHS = Editions de la Caisse nationale des monuments histo-
   riques et des sites.
ESAR. See Frank, T.
Earl, D. *The Age of Augustus*. New York 1968. (2nd edition, 1980,
   not used)
   = *AA*
   (good plates)
Ebel, C. *Transalpine Gaul*. Studies of the Dutch Archaeological and
   Historical Society 4. Leiden 1976.
   = *TG*
   (history down to 59 B.C.; bibl. on pp. 106-109)
Enciclopedia dell'arte antica, classica e orientale. I-VII. Rome 1958-
   1966. (especially good on Italy; has maps, plans, and plates; there
   is a bibliography with each article)
Enciclopedia Italiana. 35 vols. Milan/Rome 1937-1969.
Encyclopaedia Britannica[11]. New York 1911. 29 vols.

= *EB*
(usually good for history)

Ennen, E. *Die europaeische Stadt des Mittelalters*[2]. Goettingen 1975.

Evans, E. E. *France, An Introductory Geography*[2]. New York 1959.

Eydoux, H.-P. *Les grandes heures du Languedoc*. Paris 1973.

Février, P. -A. *Le développement urbain en Provence de l'époque romaine à la fin du XIVe siècle (Archéologie et histoire urbaine)*. Paris 1964.
= *Dév. urbain en Provence*
(bibliography on pp. 7-22)

—— "The Origin and Growth of the Cities of Southern Gaul to the Third Century A.D.," *Journal of Roman Studies* 63 (1973): 1-28.
= "CSG"

Finley, M. I. "The Ancient City: From Fustel de Coulanges to Max Weber and Beyond," *Comparative Studies in Society and History* 19 (1977): 305-327.

—— *The Ancient Economy*. Berkeley/Los Angeles 1973. (see Chapter V, "Town and Country" 123-149)

—— *Ancient Sicily to the Arab Conquest*. New York 1968.
= *Ancient Sicily*
(new edition 1979 could not be used)

*——, ed. *Atlas of Classical Archaeology*. New York 1977.
= *Atlas*
(Eleven authors discuss about 100 sites, mainly cities; very concise but excellent bibliographies in each article, along with plans and pictures; the book is divided into 14 regions, each with a useful bibliography.)

Formigé, J. *Monuments romains de Provence*. Paris 1924.

Frank, T., ed. *An Economic Survey of Ancient Rome*. I, Baltimore 1933 (on Italy); III, 1937 (on Britain, Spain, Sicily and Gaul); IV, 1938 (on Africa and the East); V, 1940 (on Italy); Index 1940.
= *ESAR*
(good for ancient sources; bibliographies in vol. I pp. 409-421; V pp. 423-433)

Frere, S. S. *Britannia: A History of Roman Britain*. London 1967. (2nd edition, 1974 and 3rd, 1978, not used)
= *Britannia*

Frothingham, A. L. *Roman Cities in Italy and Dalmatia*. New York 1910.
= *RCID*

Frova, A. *L'arte di Roma e del mondo romano*. Turin 1961.

Fustel de Coulanges, N. D. *The Ancient City*. Transl. W. Small.
Garden City, New York, 1956; rpt. with a new introduction by A.
Momigliano and S. C. Humphreys, Baltimore, 1980. (I cite the
1956 edition.) French text Paris 1864; rpt. 1978.
= *Ancient City*
García y Bellido, A. *Urbanistica de las grandes ciudades del mundo
antiguo*. Madrid 1960. (especially good on Spain)
Garzetti, A. *From Tiberius to the Antonines*. . . . Transl. J. R. Fos-
ter. London 1974.
= *TA*
(Roman history A.D. 14-192; excellent bibliographies 775-822; see
especially: "on the [ancient] sources" 775-795, "general works of
reference" [*RE, Dar Sag* et al.] 795-796, "atlases" 796, "provincial
and municipal administration" 801, "economy, society, culture" 803-
806, "building technology" 814)
Gascou, J. *La politique municipale de l'Empire romain en Afrique
Proconsulaire de Trajan à Septime-Sévère*. Collection de l'Ecole
française de Rome 8. 1972.
George, P. *France, A Geographical Study*. New York 1974. (transl.
from the French)
—— *Géographie de l'Italie*³. "Que sais-je?" no. 1125. Paris 1973.
(bibl. on 125-126)
—— *Précis de géographie urbaine*². Paris 1964.
Graham, A. *The Roman Provinces of Africa*. London 1905.
Grand Larousse encyclopédique. I-X. Paris 1960-1964. (with bibli-
ography)
*Grenier, A. *Manuel d'archéologie gallo-romaine*. I, Paris 1931; II,
1934; III, 1958; IV, 1960.
= *Manuel*
("irreplaceable," Chevallier. *Roman Roads* p. ix; "essential but with
some limitations," *HFU*. Vol. I p. 583); (II pp. 402-458, bibliogra-
phy on the Roman roads.) Some writers number the volumes of
Grenier's *Manuel* as if they were Volumes V and following of J.
Déchelette, *Manuel d'archéologie préhistorique, celtique et gallo-
romaine*². 4 vols. Paris 1924-1927.
Grimal, P. *The Civilization of Rome*. Transl. W. S. Maguinness. New
York 1963.
= *Civ. Rome*
—— *Guide de l'étudiant latiniste*. Paris 1971.
= *Guide*
(bibliographies on many fields; see especially 212-213 construction

of buildings, 214-215 navigation, 238-243 economics, 274-275 geography, 275-277 archaeology, 277-279 architecture)
—— *In Search of Ancient Italy*. Transl. P. D. Cummins. London 1964.
= *Search*
—— *Nous partons pour Rome*[3]. Paris 1977.
= *Rome*
(a guide, including the Renaissance and Baroque periods; bibl. on pp. 25-26)
Gsell, S. *Atlas archéologique de l'Algérie*. Algiers/Paris 1911; rpt. Osnabrueck 1973.
= *AAA*
(bibliography on pp. ix-xii)
Guido, M. *Southern Italy: An Archaeological Guide*. London 1972.
= *Southern Italy*
Gutkind, E. A. *International History of City Development*. 8 vols. New York 1964-1972.
= *IHCD*
(Vols. I-VI are on Western and Central Europe; descriptions of each city from antiquity to the present; good photographs and bibliographies; recommended general bibliographies: Vol. II, 1965, 487-488, Switzerland; III, 1967, 522-524, Spain; IV, 1969, 620-624, Italy; V, 1970, 471-475, France; VI, 1971, 492-497, Great Britain)
HFU. See *Histoire de la France urbaine*.
Hammond, M. *The City in the Ancient World*. Cambridge, Mass., 1972.
= *The City*
(on Roman cities, see 249-345; bibliographies on pp. 495-594; general bibliography on 487-493)
Hammond, N. G. L., ed. *Atlas of the Greek and Roman World in Antiquity*. Park Ridge, New Jersey, forthcoming as of 1981. (thirty-five contributors; gazetteer, listing over 10,000 sites)
—— and Scullard, H. H., eds. See *Oxford Classical Dictionary*[2].
Harmand, L. *L'Occident romain*. Paris 1969.
= *Occ. rom.*
(see chapter XII, "L'urbanisation . . ." pp. 291-353; bibl. on pp. 477-492)
Harris, W. V. *Rome in Etruria and Umbria*. Oxford 1971.
= *REU*
Harvey, P. *The Oxford Companion to Classical Literature*. Oxford

1966. (classical civilization; proper names, technical terms explained)

Hatt, J. J. *Celts and Gallo-Romans*. London 1970. (transl. from the French)

Haverfield, F. *Ancient Town Planning*. Oxford 1913.
= *Town Planning*

Healy, J. F. *Mining and Metallurgy in the Greek and Roman World*. London 1978. (see Chapter III, "Sources of Ore Minerals" pp. 45-67 with maps I and II)

Heurgon, J. *The Rise of Rome to 264 B.C*. Berkeley 1973. (translated from the French)

Histoire de la France urbaine. Edit. G. Duby. Paris 1980- .
= *HFU*
(Two volumes of this five volume series were published in 1980: Vol. I, *La ville antique, des origines au IXe Siècle*, and Vol. II, *La ville médiévale, des Carolingiens à la Renaissance*. Both volumes contain several sections, most of which are devoted to a period of time, and general topics are discussed within each section. Vol. I was written by four scholars and Vol. II by three. The illustrations and plans are excellent.
In Vol. I, there is a bibliography on pp. 581-589, a useful summary of ancient sources on 576-577, a glossary on 566-575, and a geographical index [for finding individual cities] on 593-601.
I was unable to cite *HFU* in the *Descriptive Catalogue* above. It should be consulted for cities in France and neighboring regions.)

Historic City Plans and Views. Ithaca, New York, 1979. (Catalogue 22 of facsimiles available from Historic Urban Plans, Box 276, Ithaca, N.Y. 14850)

Homo, L. *Rome impériale et l'urbanisme dans l'antiquité*. Evolution de l'humanité no. 18 bis. Paris 1951.
= *Rome impériale* = Evolution de l'humanité no. 33. Paris 1971. (on Rome only)

House, J. W. *France: An Applied Geography*. London 1978.

Hugo-Brunt, M. *The History of City Planning: A Survey*. Montreal 1972.

Huguenin-Gonon, N. et al., eds. *Nagel's Encyclopedia- Guide, Algeria*. Geneva 1973.

Hugues, L. *Dizionario di geografia antica*. Turin 1897.

Humbert, M. *Municipium et civitas sine suffragio. L'organisation de la conquête jusqu'à la guerre sociale*. Collection de l'Ecole française de Rome. Rome/Paris 1978.

Jackson, K. *Language and History in Early Britain*. Edinburgh 1953.

(I could not use the 2nd edition, 1963.)
= *LHEB*
Jenison, E. S. *The History of the Province of Sicily*. Boston 1919.
Jones, A. H. M. "The Cities of the Roman Empire," *Recueils de la Société Jean-Bodin pour l'histoire comparative des institutions* (Brussels) 6 (1954): 135-164.
——— "The Economic Life of the Towns of the Roman Empire," *Recueils de la Société Jean-Bodin* . . . 7 (1955): 161-192.
——— *The Greek City from Alexander to Justinian*. Oxford 1940.
——— *A History of Rome Through the Fifth Century*. I. *The Republic*; II. *The Empire*. London and New York 1968.
= *HR*
(a source-book)
——— *The Later Roman Empire*, (*A.D.*) *284-602*. 3 vols. + maps. Oxford 1964.
= *LRE*
(see Vol. I pp. 11-13, Vol. II pp. 712-767, "The Cities," and map V, "Distribution of Cities in the Middle of the Fifth Century" — the concentration is heaviest in North Africa.)
——— *The Roman Economy*. Edit. P. A. Brunt. Oxford 1974. (see "The Cities of the Roman Empire; Political, Administrative and Judicial Functions" 1-34 and "The Economic Life of the Towns of the Roman Empire" 35-60)
Jones, E. *Towns and Cities*. New York 1966. (bibl. 143-145)
——— and Van Zandt, E. *The City: Yesterday, Today and Tomorrow*. New York 1974. (a popularization of the book above)
Jones, H. Stuart. *Companion to Roman History*. Oxford 1912.
= *Companion*
Julien, C. -A. *Histoire de l'Afrique du Nord des origines à la conquête arabe*[2]. Paris 1951.
Jullian, C. *Histoire de la Gaule*. 8 vols. Paris 1920-1925; rpt. Brussels 1964; abridged rpt. ed. by P.-M. Duval. Paris 1971.
Jung, J. *Grundriss der Geographie von Italien und dem Orbis Romanus*[2]. Handbuch der klassischen Altertumswissenschaft. III. 3.1. Munich 1897. (outline of the geography of Italy and the Roman world)
KP. Kleine Pauly, Lexikon der Antike. See Ziegler, K.
Kaehler, H. *The Art of Rome and her Empire*. New York 1963.
= *Art of Rome*
(transl. from the German; bibl. on 216-224)
Kiepert, H. *Atlas Antiquus*. Berlin 1902. (The index is useful, giving modern names after the ancient ones.)

Kirsten, E. *Sueditalienkunde: Ein Fuehrer zu klassischen Staetten*. I. *Campanien und seine Nachtbarschaften*. Heidelberg 1975.

Kotula, T. ". . . Recherches sur le statut des villes nord-africaines sous le Bas-Empire romain," *Antiquités africaines* 8 (1974): 111-132.

Landels, J. G. *Engineering in the Ancient World*. London 1978.

Lassère, J. -M. *Ubique populus*. Peuplement et mouvement de la population dans l'Afrique romaine de la chute de Carthage à la fin de la dynastie des Sèveres. Paris 1977.

Laurand, L., and Lauras, A. *Manuel des Etudes grecques et latines* [13]. II.4. Paris 1960.

= *Manuel*

(see 1-22 geography, 87-88 art and architecture)

Lavedan, P. *Les villes françaises*. Paris 1960.

—— and Hugueney, J. *Histoire de l'urbanisme*. I[2] *(Antiquité)*. Paris 1966.

= Lavedan, *HU*

Lehmann-Hartleben, K. *Die antiken Hafenanlagen des Mittelmeeres*. *Klio*. Suppl. 14, New Series 1. 1923; rpt. 1963.

Lelièvre, P. *La vie des cités de l'antiquité à nos jours*. Paris 1950.

Lepelley, C. *Les cités de l'Afrique romaine au Bas-Empire*. I, Paris 1979; II, 1980.

Lézine, A. *Architecture romaine d'Afrique*. Paris/Tunis ?1964.

Liebenam, W. *Staedteverwaltung im roemischen Kaiserreiche*. Leipzig 1900.

Liversidge, J. *Britain in the Roman Empire*. London 1968.

= *BRE*

—— *Everyday Life in the Roman Empire*. London and New York 1976.

= *Everyday Life*

(see 23-70 on Roman cities; 223-224 list of Roman emperors; 225-226 Roman provinces compared with modern countries; 228-231 bibliography of the Roman provinces)

L'Orange, H. P. *Art Forms and Civic Life in the Late Roman Empire*. Princeton 1965. (transl. from the Norwegian; see chapter II, "Architectural Forms" pp. 9-18)

Louis, P. *Ancient Rome at Work: An Economic History of Rome from the Origins to the Empire*. New York 1927; rpt. 1965.

Lugli, G. *La tecnica edilizia romana*. Rome 1957; rpt. New York/London 1968.

= *Tecnica edilizia*

MAAR = *Memoirs of the American Academy in Rome*.

MAR, Bibl. See Caprino, C.

Macadam, A., ed. *The Blue Guides, Northern Italy*[7]. London 1978.

—— *The Blue Guides, Sicily.* London 1975.

MacDonald, W. L. *The Architecture of the Roman Empire.* I, *An Introductory Study.* New Haven 1965.

= *Arch.*

(bibl. on pp. xix-xxi, 189-198)

MacKendrick, P. *The Greek Stones Speak.* New York 1962; rpt. New York 1966.

= *Greek Stones*

—— *The Iberian Stones Speak.* New York 1969.

= *Iberian Stones*

—— *The Mute Stones Speak.* New York 1960.

= *Mute Stones*

*—— *The North African Stones Speak.* Chapel Hill, North Carolina, 1980. (I saw the excellent bibliography in typescript but was unable to cite the final page numbers. This book should be consulted for every North African city above.)

—— "Roman Colonization and the Frontier Hypothesis." In *The Frontier in Perspective.* Edit. W. D. Wyman and C. B. Kroeber, pp. 3-19. Madison, Wisconsin, 1965.

—— *Roman France.* London 1971.

= *RF*

—— *Romans on the Rhine.* New York 1970.

= *RoR*

MacMullen, R. "Roman Imperial Building in the Provinces," *Harvard Studies in Classical Philology* 64 (1959): 207-235.

—— *Roman Social Relations, 50 B.C. to A.D. 284.* New Haven 1974.

= *Social Relations*

(daily life; town-country relations)

Mahjoubi, A. *Les cités romaines de (la) Tunisie.* Tunis n.d. ?1970.

= *CRT*

(bibl. for North Africa 154-155; for Tunisia 155-156)

Mansuelli, G. A. et al. *Geografia e topografia storica.* Enciclopedia classica. III. x. 4. Turin 1957.

—— *Urbanistica e architettura della Cisalpina romana fino al III sec. e. n.* Collection Latomus 111. Brussels 1971.

Margary, I. D. *Roman Roads in Britain*[3]. London 1973.

= *RRB*

Mattingly, H. *Roman Imperial Civilisation.* London 1957. (see Chapter III, "Cities and Citizenship" 81-100 for a political analysis)

McKay, A. G. *Ancient Campania.* II: *Naples and Coastal Campania.* Hamilton, Ontario, 1972.

= *Naples*

—— *Houses, Villas and Palaces in the Roman World.* Ithaca, N.Y., 1975.

= *Houses*

(see 264-268, an excellent bibliography of the Roman provinces; review by J. Russel, *Phoenix* 30 [1976]: 306-308, with additional bibliography)

Millar, F. *The Emperor in the Roman World.* Ithaca, N.Y., 1977. (see pp. 410-447 on the emperors' relations with individual cities, mainly in the East; ancient sources are cited)

—— *The Roman Empire and its Neighbours.* London 1967.

= *REN*

(carefully selected plates; also see chapters V, "State and Subject: The Cities" 81-103; VI, "The Army and the Frontiers" 104-126; VII, "Italy" 127-145; VIII, "The Western Provinces; Gaul, Spain and Britain" 146-168; IX, "Africa" 169-181; bibl. on 338-340)

Miller, M. *The Sicilian Colony Dates.* Albany, N.Y., 1970.

Mommsen, T. *History of Rome.* IX: *The Provinces of the Roman Empire.* 2 vols. Transl. W. P. Dickson. New York 1909; rpt. edit. T. R. S. Broughton. Chicago 1968.

= *Provinces*

(cited by chapter and not by page, because there are two editions in English)

Moreau, J. *Dictionnaire de géographie historique de la Gaule et de la France.* Paris 1972.

Morestin, H., ed. *Nagel's Encyclopedia-Guide, Morocco*². Geneva 1969.

Morini, M. *Atlante di storia dell'urbanistica.* Milan 1963.

Morris, A. E. J. *History of Urban Form, Prehistory to the Renaissance.* London 1972.

= *Urban Form*

Murphy, J. P. *Index to the Supplements and Suppl. Volumes of Pauly-Wissowa's R.E.* Chicago 1976. (unauthorized but useful)

Nagel's Guide, Algeria. See Huguenin-Gonan, N.

Nagel's Guide, Morocco. See Morestin, H.

Nash, E. *Pictorial Dictionary of Ancient Rome.* 2 vols. London and New York 1968.

= *PD*

(bibliographical articles; general bibliography on pp. 9-12)

Nencie, G., and Vallet, G., eds. *Bibliografia topografica della colon-*

izzazione greca in Italia e nelle isole Tirreniche. Vol. I. *Opere di carattere generale* by G. G. Panessa. Rome/Bonn 1976.

Nissen, H. *Italische Landeskunde*. 2 vols. Berlin 1883-1902; rpt. Amsterdam 1967.

= *IL*

(good for primary sources)

OCD. See *Oxford Classical Dictionary*.

OSMRB. See *Ordnance Survey Map of Roman Britain*[4].

Oberschelp, R. *Die Bibliographien zur deutschen Landesgeschichte und Landeskunde, Zeitschrift fuer Bibliothekswesen*. Suppl. 7 (1977). (a bibliography of bibliographies)

Ogilvie, R. M. *Early Rome and the Etruscans*. Atlantic Highlands, N.J., 1976.

= *Early Rome*

(bibliography on pp. 177-184)

—— and Richmond, I. A. *Commentary on Tacitus' biography of Agricola, De Vita Agricolae*. Oxford 1967, pp. 1-90, 125-344.

= *Agricola*

(useful for Roman Britain)

Ordnance Survey Map of Roman Britain[4]. Southampton 1978.

= *OSMRB*

(Since the third edition, Chessington [London] 1956, contains complementary information and is easier to consult, it is also recommended.)

Oxford Classical Dictionary[2]. Edit. N. G. L. Hammond and H. H. Scullard. Oxford 1970.

= *OCD*

PECS. See *Princeton Encyclopedia of Classical Sites*.

Pace, B. *Arte e civiltà della Sicilia antica*. 4 vols. Milan 1935-1949; Vol. I rpt. 1958.

Paget, R. F. *Central Italy: An Archaeological Guide*. London 1973.

= *Central Italy*

Pais, E. *Italia antica; Ricerche di storia e di geografia storica*. Bologna 1922.

—— *Storia della colonizzazione di Roma antica*. Rome 1923.

Petit, P. *Guide de l'étudiant en histoire ancienne*[3]. Paris 1969. (bibliographies; see especially 49-53 economic and social history; 152-158 archaeology, including that of cities; 197-198 geography)

—— *Pax Romana*. Berkeley 1976. (transl. into English from the French. Roman history, civilization; bibl.)

Pevsner, N. *An Outline of European Architecture*[7]. Harmondsworth, Middlesex, 1963.

(Charles-) Picard, G. *La civilisation de l'Afrique romaine*. Paris 1959.
—— *Living Architecture: Roman*. New York 1965.
  = *Roman Architecture*
  (bibliography, relating to cities, pp. 189-190)
—— *Rome et les villes d'Italie....* Paris 1978. (history, 133 B.C.-A.D. 14)
Piganiol, A. *Histoire de Rome*[6]. Paris 1977.
  = *HR*
  (bibliography for cities, pp. 353-368, 590-601)
Pippidi, D. M., ed. *Assimilation et résistance à la culture gréco-romaine dans le monde ancien. Travaux du VIe Congrès international de la Fédération internationale des Associations d'études classiques, Madrid septembre 1974*. Bucharest/Paris 1976.
  = *Assimilation*
Pounds, N. J. G. *An Historical Geography of Europe 450 B.C.-A.D. 1330*. Cambridge 1973.
Prag, A. J. N. W., ed. *Archaeological Reports* 26 (for 1979-1980). London 1980.
  = *AR*
  (with no year or volume stated; publ. by the Council of the Society for the Promotion of Hellenic Studies and the Managing Committee of the British School at Athens; may be obtained from the secretary of the Hellenic Society, 31-34 Gordon Sq., London WC1 H OPP)
The Princeton Encyclopedia of Classical Sites. Edit. R. Stillwell. Princeton 1976.
  = *PECS*
  (about 3,000 sites discussed by 375 scholars; no plans, but where to find them is indicated in each article's bibliography)
Quirin, H. *Einfuehrung in das Studium der mittelalterlichen Geschichte*[3]. Brunswick 1964. (307-309, historical atlases and indexes of places; 334-335, historical geography and cartography)
RE. Paulys Real-Encyclopedie. See Wissowa, G.
Radke, G. *Viae Publicae Romanae*. Stuttgart 1971. = *RE* Suppl. 13. Munich 1973, pp. 1417-1686.
  = *Viae*
Ramin, J. *La technique minière et métallurgique des anciens*. Collection Latomus 153. Brussels 1977.
Raven, S. *Rome in Africa*. London 1969.
  = *Rome in Africa*
Reid, J. S. *The Municipalities of the Roman Empire*. Cambridge 1913.

= *Municipalities*

(lectures, dependent on Mommsen, *Provinces*)

Richmond, I. A. *Roman Britain²*. The Pelican History of England, 1. Harmondsworth, Middlesex, 1963.

= *RB*

(see "Towns and Urban Centres" 66-108, bibl. on 218-220)

—— and Salway, P., eds. *Roman Archaeology and Art*. London 1969.

= *RAA*

Ritter, J. *Le Rhin*. "Que sais-je?" no. 1065. Paris 1968. (geography; bibl. on 126)

—— *Le Rhône*. "Que sais-je?" no. 1507. Paris 1973. (geography; bibl. on 127)

Rivet, A. L. F. *Town and Country in Roman Britain²*. London 1964.

= *TCRB*

—— and Smith, C. *The Place-Names of Roman Britain*. London and Princeton 1979.

= *PNRB*

(basic; also useful for the Continent; bibl. on pp. xiii-xvi)

Robertson, D. S. *Greek and Roman Architecture²*. Cambridge 1945.

= *GRA*

(chronological list of buildings, pp. 322-346; bibliography pp. 349-354, 354-378)

Robertson, I., ed. *The Blue Guides, Spain, The Mainland³*. London 1975.

Romanelli, P. *Storia delle provincie romane dell'Africa*. Rome 1959.

= *Storia*

—— *Topografia e archeologia dell'Africa romana*. Enciclopedia classica. III.x.7. Turin 1970.

Rossiter, S., ed. *The Blue Guides, England⁸*. London 1976.

—— *The Blue Guides, Rome and Environs²*. London 1975.

Rostovtzeff, M. *Rome*. Oxford 1960. Transl. from the Russian by J. D. Duff, edit. by E. J. Bickerman; rpt. from *A History of the Roman World*. II². Oxford 1927.

—— *The Social and Economic History of the Roman Empire²*. 2 vols. Oxford 1957. Garzetti recommends 3rd edition, in Italian, Florence 1933 (*TA* 797).

= *SEHRE*

(on cities, see 130-150 [especially 142-143], 192-343; on the urbanization of native tribes see 83-85; on interprovincial trade, 157-183; bibliography 593-597; list of emperors 752-753)

Rougé, J. *Recherches sur l'organisation du commerce maritime en Méditerranée sous l'Empire romain*. Paris 1966.

= *Recherches*

Rounds, D. *Articles on Antiquity in Festschriften*. Cambridge, Mass., 1962.

= *AAF*

(This index, to 1954, lists recipients, authors and key-words, including technical terms, and ancient or modern names of cities; a festschrift is a volume of articles by different authors presented as a tribute to a scholar.)

Rudolf, H. *Stadt und Staat im roemischen Italien*. Leipzig 1935.

Ruggini, L. *Economia e società nell'Italia annonaria*. Milan 1961. (4th and 5th centuries A.D.)

Rykwert, J. *The Idea of a Town, The Anthropology of Urban Form in Rome, Italy and the Ancient World*. Princeton 1976.

= *Idea*

("Psychology" would have been a better word in the title than "Anthropology"; cf. A. Jaffé, "Symbolism in the Visual Arts" in C. G. Jung et al., *Man and his Symbols*. New York 1968, pp. 255-322. Rykwert has good control of his ancient sources and provides excellent illustrations, but there are problems with his belief that the ritual in founding all Roman cities was unvarying; see Ward-Perkins, "Rykwert" [listed below] and the review by R. R. Holloway in *American Journal of Archaeology* 81 [1977]: 254-255.)

Saalman, H. *Medieval Architecture*. New York 1962.

—— *Medieval Cities*. New York 1968. (bibl. on pp. 116-118)

Salama, P. *Les voies romaines de l'Afrique de Nord*. Algiers 1951.

= *Voies*

(Roman roads in North Africa)

Salmon, E. T. *Roman Colonization under the Republic*. London 1969.

= *RC*

Salway, P. *Roman Britain*. Oxford 1981. (brings the first part of Collingwood and Myres, *RBES*, up to date)

Sandys, J. E. *A Companion to Latin Studies*³. Cambridge 1921; rpt. Cambridge 1938.

Scullard, H. H. *The Etruscan Cities and Rome*. London 1967.

= *Etruscan Cities*

—— *From the Gracchi to Nero*⁴. London 1976.

= *Gracchi to Nero*

—— *Roman Britain, Outpost of the Empire*. London 1979.

= *RB*

(for the layman; see "Life in the Towns" 93-111 and bibl. 182)

Semple, E. C. *The Geography of the Mediterranean Region; Its Re-*

lation to Ancient History. London 1932.

Sherwin-White, A. N. "Geographical Factors in Roman Algeria," *Journal of Roman Studies* 34 (1944): 1-10.

—— *The Roman Citizenship*[2]. Oxford 1973.

= *RC*

Smith, William, ed. *Dictionary of Greek and Roman Geography*. 2 vols. London 1878.

Sorrell, A. *Roman Towns in Britain*. London 1976. (short introduction; shows reconstructions, plans)

Stevens, V., and Stevens, J. *Algeria and the Sahara, A Handbook for Travellers*. London 1977.

= *Algeria*

Stevenson, G. H. *Roman Provincial Administration*. . .[2]. Oxford 1949; 1st ed. 1939; rpt. Westport, Conn., 1975.

Stier, H. E. et al., eds. *Westermanns grosser Atlas zur Weltgeschichte*. Brunswick 1968.

= *Atlas*

(tenth edition 1978 could not be used)

Storoni Mazzolani, L. *The Idea of the City in Roman Thought*. Bloomington, Indiana, 1970. (transl. from the Italian)

Studi di urbanistica antica. Quaderni dell'Istituto di Topografia Antica dell'Università di Roma 2. Rome 1966.

Taylor, L. R. *The Voting Districts of the Roman Republic*. Papers and Monographs of the American Academy in Rome 20 (1960).

= *Voting Districts*

(with 2 maps)

Thomsen, R. *The Italic Regions*. Copenhagen 1947; rpt. Rome 1966.

Thouvenot, R. *Essai sur la province romaine de Bétique*. Bibliothèque des Ecoles françaises d'Athènes et de Rome 149. Paris 1940.

= *Essai*

(bibliography on pp. 693-701). Supplement (1973).

Tissot, C. *Géographie comparée de la province romaine d'Afrique*. 2 vols. Paris 1884, 1888.

Tomasetti, G. *La Campagna romana*. 4 vols. Rome 1910-1926.

Tout, T. F. *Mediaeval Town Planning*. Manchester, England, 1968.

Toutain, J. *The Economic Life of the Ancient World*. New York 1968. (bibl. on 331-335)

—— "Les progrès de la vie urbaine dans l'Afrique du Nord, sous la domination romaine." In *Mélanges (R.) Cagnat*. Paris 1912, pp. 319-347.

Van Buren, A. W. *A Bibliographical Guide to Latium and Southern*

Etruria[4]. Rome 1938.
= *Bibl.*

Vermeule, C. G. *A Bibliography of Applied Numismatics*. London 1956. (see especially 115-131, "Geography, Topography and Architecture")

Vittinghoff, F. *Roemische Kolonisation und Buergerrechtspolitik unter Caesar und Augustus*. Wiesbaden 1952.
= *Roemische Kolonisation*

Wacher, J., ed. *Conference on Romano-British Cantonal Capitals, Leicester University, 1963*. Leicester 1975.

—— *Roman Britain*. London 1978. (see especially "Cities, Towns and Minor Settlements" 62-105)

—— *The Towns of Roman Britain*. Berkeley/Los Angeles 1974.
= *TRB*

*Ward-Perkins, J. B. *Cities of Ancient Greece and Italy*. New York 1974.
= *Cities*
(bibl. on pp. 113-114)

*—— "Early Roman Towns in Italy," *Town Planning Review* 26 (1955/1956): 126-154; bibl. on 153-154.
= "ERTI"
(basic; in time, from MARZABOTTO to AOSTA)

*—— "From Republic to Empire: Reflections on the Early Provincial Architecture of the Roman West," *Journal of Roman Studies* 60 (1970): 1-19.
= "Republic to Empire"

—— *Roman Architecture*. New York 1977.
= *RA*
(416 excellent plates; bibl. on pp. 344-346; chronological table on pp. 326-343)

—— review of Rykwert, *Idea,* in (London) *Times Literary Supplement* (1977): 265.
= "Rykwert"

Warmington, B. H. *The North African Provinces from Diocletian to the Vandal Conquest*. Cambridge 1954.

Webster, G. *The Roman Army*[2]. Chester 1973.

—— *The Roman Imperial Army*. New York 1969.
= *Army*
(expansion of the work listed above; revised edition, London 1979, not used)

West, L. C. *Imperial Roman Spain, The Objects of Trade*. Oxford 1929.

—— *Roman Britain, The Objects of Trade*. Oxford 1931.

—— *Roman Gaul, The Objects of Trade*. Oxford 1935.

Wheeler, R. E. M. *Roman Art and Architecture*. London 1964.
= *RAA*
(pp. 25-88 on cities)

—— and Wood, R. *Roman Africa in Color*. New York 1966.
= *Roman Africa*
(good plates)

Williams, P. F. de C. "Roman Harbours," *International Journal of Nautical Archaeology...* 5 (1976): 73-79.

Wilson, R. J. A. *A Guide to the Roman Remains in Britain²*. London 1980.

—— *Sicily under the Roman Empire*. London 1981.

Wissowa, G. et al. *Paulys Real-Encyclopedie der classischen Altertumswissenschaft*. Stuttgart 1894- .
= *RE*

Woodhead, A. G. *The Greeks in the West*. London 1962.
= *Greeks in the West*

Wycherley, R. E. *How the Greeks Built Cities²*. London 1962; rpt. New York 1976.

Ziegler, K. et al., eds. *Der Kleine Pauly, Lexikon der Antike*. I-V. Stuttgart 1964-1970.
= *KP*
(based on *RE* but more recent; bibliographies; very good for finding ancient sources)

Zucker, P. *Town and Square, From the Agora to the Village Green*. New York 1959.
= *Town and Square*
(a survey of city planning from Greece in 500 B.C. to Europe and the Americas in the 19th century; bibl. on 256-275; bibl. for Roman planning 261-263)

Ancient Sources

Historians from antiquity, other than Ammianus Marcellinus, are not listed below, nor are well-known authors such as Caesar and Cicero.

Abbott, F. F., and Johnson, A. C. *Municipal Administration in the Roman Empire*. Princeton 1926; rpt. New York 1968.

= *Municipal Administration*
(documents in Greek and Latin)

Ammianus Marcellinus: (late 4th century A.D.); the geographical digressions of this soldier-historian are worth looking at—see *Gallia Transalpina* in the glossary below and Rome above; although he came from Antioch, he wrote in Latin. Text and translation by J. C. Rolfe, 3 vols. Cambridge, Mass., and London 1935; rpt. 1956. See Bunbury, *HAG* II pp. 679-683.

The Antonine Itinerary: a list in Latin of stopping places (mainly towns and cities) along the highways of the Roman Empire; it was compiled for travelers on government business and probably dates from c. A.D. 200; the section for Britain is given, with a translation, in Margary, *RRB* pp. 522-533; cf. A. L. F. Rivet, "The British Section of the Antonine Itinerary," *Britannia* 1 (1970): 34-82, Rivet, *PNRB* pp. 150 ff., and *OSMRB* pp. 12; 14, 16 (map of Britain according to the *Itinerary*); also see Bunbury, *HAG* II pp. 694-695; Desjardins, *Géogr.* IV pp. 36-71; Jackson, *LHEB* 32-33; Ziegler, *KP* II (1967): 1488-1490 (G. Radke); and K. Miller, below, in this bibliography.

(Decimus Magnus) Ausonius: (died A.D. 395), from BORDEAUX, both a teacher of oratory and a poet; his poems include *Ordo Nobilium Urbium* or *Order of the Famous Cities* (a list of the 20 major Late Roman cities) and *Mosella* (on the river of TRIER); Latin text and translation by H. G. Evelyn-White, 2 vols. Cambridge, Mass., and London 1919-1921.

Burn, A. R. *The Romans in Britain, An Anthology of Inscriptions*[2]. Oxford, England, and Columbia, South Carolina, 1969. (translations and commentaries)

Collingwood, R. G., and Wright, R. P. *The Roman Inscriptions of Britain*. I. Oxford 1965.
= *RIB*

Corpus of Latin Inscriptions. 16 vols. Berlin 1863-
= *CIL*
(Supplementary fascicles to the various volumes have been and will be published.)

Dessau, H. *Inscriptiones Latinae Selectae*. 3 vols. Berlin 1892-1916; rpt. 1954-1955.
= *ILS*
(selections from the *Corpus of Latin Inscriptions;* Volume III of *ILS* has very good indexes)

(Sextus Julius) Frontinus: governor of Britain (A.D. 74-77/78), placed in charge of Rome's aqueducts in 97; his *De aquis urbis Romae (The Aqueducts of Rome)* provides evidence about them; it was translated into French and edited by P. Grimal, Paris 1944; another work in Latin by Frontinus, his *Strategemata (On Military Science)*, is useful for research about the frontiers; on Frontinus' writings and career, see Frere, *Britannia:* 101-103; G. C. Whittick in the *OCD*, p. 448; Ogilvie and Richmond, *Agricola*, pp. 206-207; A. R. Birley, *The* Fasti *of Roman Britain*, Oxford 1981, 69-72.

Miller, K. *Itineraria Romana.* Stuttgart 1916; rpt. 1964.
(a synthesis of Roman sources; e.g. itineraries, histories, milestones; thus more complete than the *Antonine Itinerary*)

Notitia Dignitatum: a semiofficial handbook of the Roman government, dating from c. A.D. 400; edited by O. Seeck, Berlin 1876; rpt. Frankfurt am Main 1962. See H. von Petrikovits, review of *Aspects of the Notitia Dignitatum, Britannia* 11 (1980): 423-427, Rivet, *PNRB* pp. 216-225, *OSMRB* 12 and A. H. M. Jones, *LRE* III pp. 347-380, "Appendix II: The Notitia Dignitatum" with map II; on the date, also see T. D. Barnes, *Phoenix* 32 (1978): 82; the *Notitia Galliarum* was also included by Seeck in his edition, pp. 261-274; see A. H. M. Jones, *LRE* III p. 225 n. 2 and J. Harris, *Journal of Roman Studies* 68 (1978): 26-43; n. 8 cites an edition by T. Mommsen in *Monumenta Germaniae Historica, Auct. Ant.* IX, Berlin 1892.

Pliny (the Elder): A.D. 23/24-79, wrote a "scientific encyclopedia" called the *Natural History*, Latin text with translation by H. Rackham et al., 10 vols. Cambridge, Mass., and London, 1942-1963; see Bunbury, *HAG* II pp. 371-438. Pliny was the commander of the Roman fleet at Misenum (near Pompeii); he was killed in the eruption of Mt. Vesuvius; he is to be distinguished from his nephew and adopted son, Pliny the Younger, also from Como in northern Italy.

Ptolemy: (wrote A.D. 127-148); he is not to be confused with the Hellenistic kings of Egypt with the same name; despite its faults, his *Geography* in Greek was the most accurate and complete of the ancient treatises (E. H. Warmington in the *OCD*). English translation by E. L. Stevenson, New York 1932; see Bunbury, *HAG* II pp. 546-643; Jackson, *LHEB* pp. 31-32; Rivet, *PNRB* pp. 103-147; I. A. Richmond, "Ancient Geographical Sources" in I. A. Richmond, ed., *Roman and Native in North Britain*, London 1958 and *OSMRB* 12; 14-15 (map of Britain according to Ptolemy).

Riccobono, S. et al. *Fontes Iuris Romani Anteiustiniani*². I. Florence
   1968.
   = *FIRA*². I
   (Roman laws in Latin and Greek; bibliographies; cites *CIL* and
   ILS when possible)
Sherk, R. K. *The Municipal Decrees of the Roman West*. Buffalo,
   New York, 1970.
Strabo: (64/63 B.C.-A.D. 21+); *Geography*, Greek text with transla-
   tion by H. L. Jones, 8 vols. Cambridge, Mass., and London 1917-
   1932, rev. 1931-1949; see Bunbury, *HAG* II pp. 209-337 and G.
   Aujac, *Strabon et la science de son temps*, Paris 1966.
Tabula Peutingeriana: a 12/13th-century copy of a Late Roman (q.v.)
   road map of the Eastern and Western Empires; cf. Rivet, *PNRB*
   pp. 149-150; there are two recent reproductions of the map with
   accompanying commentaries, one by E. Weber, Graz, Austria,
   1976, and the other by A. and M. Levi, Bologna 1978.
Vitruvius: (c. A.D. 5); *Architecture;* the only such work which we
   have; translated from the Latin by M. H. Morgan, Cambridge,
   Mass., 1914; rpt. New York 1960.

Glossary

acropolis: the elevated, walled part or citadel of a Greek city

aedile: at Rome and in Roman cities, a magistrate in charge of the streets, public buildings and shows; the office was costly to the holder

Alamans or *Alamanni:* a loose confederation, starting in the third century A.D., of Germanic tribes; about A.D. 260 they crossed the Main River and occupied the right bank of the upper Rhine; at that time, they raided Roman Upper Germany and sacked AUGST and AVENCHES; their forays across the Roman frontier continued, and in the fifth century, they settled permanently in Alsace and northern Switzerland; here they were conquered by the Franks (q.v.) in the sixth century; they gave their name to Germany in the French and Spanish languages, as well as German-speaking Switzerland in French ("Suisse alémanique"); J. Hoops, ed., *Reallexikon der germanischen Altertumskunde* (Berlin 1973), I: 137-163 (H. Steuer).

allied city (= *civitas foederata;* also see *civitas*): until the late third century A.D., the Roman Empire consisted essentially of cities, each of which had a territory (see *territorium*) attached to it; Egypt, the private property of the emperor from the time of Augustus, was a special case with only one city, Alexandria; the cities were grouped into provinces and Italy, which had a particular tax-free status; other than *coloniae* and *municipia*, all cities were related to Rome by a treaty *(foedus)*, and this treaty did not necessarily change the constitution of the allied city; still, the nearby *coloniae* and *municipia*, as well as Rome itself, usually influenced these constitutions; the highest rank of allied city was the *civitas foederata libera et immunis* ("free and exempt" from taxes and from intervention by the provincial governor); this status was held by

329

Athens, Rhodes, *Massilia* (MARSEILLES) and *Segesta* (see Abbott
and Johnson, *Municipal Administration* pp. 39-54 and E. G. Hardy,
Roman Laws and Charters [Oxford 1912], Part I, pp. 94-101).

Angles or *Angli:* a Germanic tribe which originated in the southern
part of Jutland (the Cimbric peninsula now shared by Denmark
and the Federal Republic of Germany); they invaded Britain in
about A.D. 480 and gave their name both to East Anglia (the modern
counties of Norfolk and Suffolk) and to England as a whole; they
entered Britain at the same time as the Saxons (q.v.); the Angles
and Saxons were the least Romanized of the Germanic invaders
(after about A.D. 250, except for the 10th-century Normans); for
the later conquest of England by speakers of French, see Normans
below.

Apennines (in Italian, Appennini): the chain of mountains running
from north to south throughout the Italian peninsula; see Nissen,
IL I pp. 217-247

Aquitania: the southwest part of *Gallia Comata* (q.v.); named after
the Aquitani, an Iberian, not a Basque, people; Augustus enlarged
the province's boundaries so as to include many Celts.

arch, surbased: an arch having its curve-center below the springing
line of its imposts (the blocks on top of the supporting pillars); a
low-springing arch

atrium: entrance hall of a Roman/Etruscan-style house between the
fauces (entrance passage) and *tablinum* (originally the master
bedroom, later a room for the family archives and receptions), in
the middle of the far end; the central part of the roof sloped inwards
so that rain would flow to a central catch basin and then to cisterns
(McKay, *Houses* 269).

attributed persons: natives without Roman or full local citizenship
and legally within the jurisdiction of the nearest city; examples are
Alpine tribes in *Gallia Cisalpina* (q.v.), the Salassi at AOSTA, and
the Spaniards mentioned in section CIII of the charter of *Urso*,
printed above under OSUNA.

auspices (in Latin, *auspicia):* signs from heaven (especially Jupiter)
indicating approval or disapproval of a proposed action; an idea of
how the founder's auspices worked may be gathered from the legend
in Livy 1.6; Remus standing on the Aventine Hill saw six vultures,
while Romulus on the Palatine (where Rome was supposedly
founded) saw twelve; in fact, the height, speed and direction of
the birds were more important than the number; for observing
their flight, the sky was "marked out" into a square (compare the

city), called a *templum;* the *templum* (q.v.) was divided into four squares, as was the city by the *cardo* and *decumanus;* the founder faced east to take the auspices; see Boëthius, "RGTA" 20, n. 16 (bibl.); eagles and vultures were favored birds for this rite, but others would do.

auxiliary army unit: a Roman squad of cavalry or infantry which usually comprised men who were not Roman citizens, and they received the citizenship on discharge; see *CAH* X^2 (1952) 228-232 (G. H. Stevenson), G. L. Cheesman, *The Auxilia of the Roman Imperial Army* (Oxford 1914; rpt. Chicago 1975), D. B. Saddington, *ANRW* II.3 (1975) 176-201, and P. A. Holder, British Archaeological Reports International Series 70 (Oxford 1980); auxiliary units were *not* part of a legion (q.v.), the emperor's Praetorian Guard (stationed mainly at Rome but see AOSTA) or the city police of Rome (see LYONS, CARTHAGE).

basilica: a courthouse or market; see Robertson, *GRA* 267-269, Crema, *Arch.* 61-68, Grimal, *Civ. Rome* 427, Wheeler, *RAA* 110-115; to be distinguished from a Christian basilica, see pp. 45-46 above

battlement: a second low wall with open spaces atop an ancient wall or fortification; they were sometimes built projecting outwards.

Berbers: an aboriginal Caucasoid people of North Africa; they inhabit the land between the Sahara Desert and the Mediterranean Sea from Egypt to the Atlantic Ocean; mostly small farmers, they live in villages; their trades include metal-working, pottery and weaving; see p. 83 above and M. Rachet, *Rome et les Berbères,* Collection Latomus 110 (Brussels 1970).

building methods, Roman, in brick, stone, and concrete (q.v.): see Vitruvius 2.8; H. Stuart Jones, *Companion* 52-58; Boëthius, "RGTA" 12-13; Grimal, *Civ. Rome,* p. 448 and illustrations 194-199; Boëthius and Ward-Perkins, *ERA* 116-118; McKay, *Houses* 270 (under *"opus");* F. Coarelli, *Guida archeologica di Roma* (Milan 1974) 340-342

Burgundians: a people who originated in central Germany; they conquered LYONS, VIENNE and +Geneva about A.D. 460 but this land was in turn taken by the Franks (q.v.) about 75 years later; the Burgundians' main capital was LYONS; they gave their name to the medieval region of France north of LYONS and around Dijon, where Burgundy wine is now grown (see AUTUN).

Byzantine (adj.): pertaining to the art and culture of Constantinople (founded by Constantine the Great at Byzantium in Thrace, A.D. 330); pertaining to the Empire of which Constantinople was the capital (A.D. 330 to the capture of Constantinople by the Turks in 1453 except for a brief period in the 13th century); also see Later Roman below

canabae: well described by Rostovtzeff, *Rome* 223: "Round (the military camps) grew up settlements known as *canabae,* inhabited by innkeepers and winesellers and dealers in spoils of war. There were women also, some married, regularly or irregularly, to soldiers, with their children; for army marriages, though illegal [till 193/ 211—Woloch], were winked at by the authorities. When a man had served in the same place for a number of years and formed ties there, it was natural that he should . . . prefer, when he received his discharge, to migrate from the camp to the *canabae* where his wife and children were. There he could open a shop in the town, or farm a piece of land in the neighbourhood. . . . Thus the *canabae* grew into a village, and village into a town; and such was the origin of the great cities that now stand on the Rhine and Danube—Cologne, Mainz, Strasbourg, Vienna, Budapest"; see MAINZ above, as well as *Lambaesis;* however, the origin of + Cologne, listed under MAINZ, was different; also compare the *canabae* at LYONS, where there were no legions (p. 87 above).

capital: in architecture, the uppermost member of a column or pillar (see orders of architecture, Greek, below)

Capitol (an English word from the French "Capitole," which comes from the Latin *"Capitolium"*): one of the hills of Rome, the Capitoline Hill (in Latin *mons Capitolinus);* on the Roman hill, see Dudley, *Urbs Roma* 51-72; in *coloniae* and, later, in many cities of the Roman West, the Capitol was the chief temple, dedicated to Jupiter, Juno, and Minerva; we call these local temples the Capitol or *Capitolium* (q.v.); see pp. 5, 14-15, 29, 36, 50-53 above; the word "Capitol" is sometimes used for the Temple of Jupiter Optimus Maximus at Rome; in the United States today it is used for the meeting-house of Congress in Washington and buildings of the various state legislatures.

Capitolium: the south summit of the Capitol (q.v.) in Rome; on it was the Temple of Jupiter Optimus Maximus (also called the Temple of Jupiter Capitolinus), inside of which were three *cellae* (q.v.), in a row, to Jupiter (the middle one), Juno and Minerva (see pp. 36 and 14-15 above and Nash, *PD* II pp. 530-533); sometimes the word for the whole Capitoline Hill in Rome and also for the Capitols of other Roman cities.

cardo: see p. 11 above and city blocks below, as well as Wheeler, *RAA* 35; the main *cardo* was the *cardo* or the *cardo maximus;* on

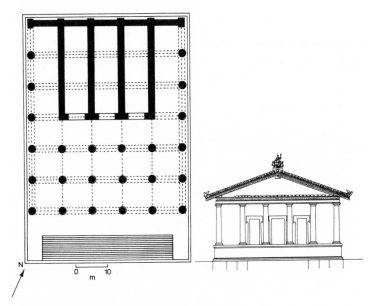

Figure 35. Temple of Jupiter Capitolinus at Rome
Left: plan; *right:* restored front elevation. From F. Coarelli, *Guida archeo-logica di Roma³* (Milan 1980) p. 45

the relation of the streets with centuriation around the city, see Ward-Perkins, *Cities* 28 and "ERTI" 150-151; Ward-Perkins considers *"cardo"* and *"decumanus"* to have been surveying terms rather than streets, but this distinction is usually ignored today; on it, cf. Rykwert, *Idea* 218, n. 22a.

Carthaginian (adj.): pertaining to the civilization of CARTHAGE (q.v.) and its colonies; "Punic" is a synonym; (noun): the Semitic language of the Carthaginians

cella: the main body of a classical temple, excluding the portico (q.v.); the cult statue was kept in this walled room.

Celtic names of cities: under Roman rule, they were used from Yugoslavia to Britain; the components were rather limited and included:

-bona ground	*-briga* mountain
-dunum fort	*-durum* gate
-magus field or market	*-nemetum* shrine
-ritum ford (of a river)	

(F. Staehelin, *Die Schweiz in roemischer Zeit³* [Basle 1948] p. 128;

also see A. L. F. Rivet, "Celtic and Roman Places," *Britannia* 11 [1980]: 1-19, Chevallier, *Roman Roads* 127-130 and S. Piggott, *Ancient Europe* [Chicago 1968] figs. 95-97 [maps]); cf. Gauls below centuriation: the Roman chessboard system of city planning (see city blocks) was extended to the surrounding countryside and accompanied Roman cities; the farm-owners usually lived inside the city until about A.D. 250 (compare Rostovtzeff, *SEHRE* 554, n. 31 and, on Britain, R. G. Collingwood in Frank, *ESAR* III p. 72); ideally, the cardinal points of the compass were used to draw the baselines; the standard unit of land was the *centuria*, a square 2,400 Roman feet on each side, which contained 200 Roman *iugera* (a total area of 51.9 hectares or 128 acres); when the procedure originated, perhaps the *centuria* was divided equally among 100 colonists (in Latin, one hundred is *centum);* roads usually marked the four sides of the *centuria* and the Roman plan can often be seen today by means of aerial photography; no examples of centuriation, however, have been found in Britain (on the debate, see Frank, *ESAR* III p. 72); the Romans began centuriation in the late 3rd century B.C. and continued the practice, when possible, from then on; see E. H. Warmington, *The Remains of Classical Latin* IV, *Archaic Inscriptions* (London/Cambridge, Mass., 1940) plate opp. p. 174; H. Stuart Jones, *Companion* 16-20, Salmon, *RC* 19-24, Ward-Perkins, "ERTI" fig. 12, MacKendrick, *Mute Stones* 109-115, Ziegler, *KP* III (1969) 666-667 (H. Chantraine) and O. A. W. Dilke in *ANRW* II.1 (1974) 564-592, an article with extensive bibliography; for a recent bibliography, also see Piganiol, *HR* p. 586; one might compare the American system, begun west of the Alleghany Mountains in 1785; it was originally based on "hundreds" (contrast the meaning of *centuria)* of 10 miles square (= 100 square miles), but the standard unit was soon reduced to townships of 6 miles square, of 36 mile-square plots of 640 acres each.

Cisalpine Gaul: see *Gallia Cisalpina*

cities (Roman), comparison in area (from Lavedan, *HU* p. 353 and Grenier, *Manuel* I—based on wall length):

	length of 1st century A.D. wall	area
AUTUN	6,000 m.	200 ha.
NIMES	6,000 m.	220 ha.
LYONS	5,000 m.	140 ha.
VIENNE	6,000 m.	200 ha.
+ Cologne	4,000 m.	100 ha.

Compare early Rome (inside the Servian Wall) 450 ha. and Nissen, *IL* pp. 37-39 (a list); also see Collingwood and Richmond, *ARB* 96 (estimates of occupied area):

LYONS	127 ha. (314 acres)
Milan	133 ha. (329 acres)
NIMES	320 ha. (790 acres)
AUTUN	200 ha. (494 acres)
VIENNE	87 ha. (214 acres)
TURIN	51 ha. (127 acres)

Note the divergence for NIMES and VIENNE; cf. Bruehl, *PC* 245-247 on the size of the city walls in France from Roman times to the 16th century; there are 3 tables. For the inhabited areas of cities in North Africa, see Duncan-Jones, *ERE* p. 265, n. 4:

TIMGAD	50 ha.
DOUGGA	20 ha.
DJEMILA	12 ha.

cities (Roman), population of: citing C. Jullian, *Histoire de la Gaule* (Paris 1908/1926), A. Grenier gives the following estimates: 200,000: LYONS; 80,000 to 100,000: NARBONNE, NIMES, ARLES, VIENNE, AUTUN, TRIER, + Cologne, MAINZ; 40,000 to 60,000: TOULOUSE, ORANGE, FREJUS, BORDEAUX, SAINTES, Poitiers (in Frank, *ESAR* III 530, n. 65); *warning:* these figures are too large, that for LYONS (q.v.) by four times (Audin); but the relative ranking is correct, c. A.D. 100 (Woloch); later, c. A.D 325, the population of AUTUN was 50,000 (R. Duncan-Jones, *Journal of Roman Studies* 53 [1963] p. 90 in "City Population in Roman Africa" pp. 85-90); also see F. Lot, *Recherches sur la population et la superficie des cités remontant à la période gallo-romaine*, 3 vols. Bibliothèque de l'Ecole des Hautes Etudes . . . 287, 296, 301 (Paris 1945-1953); on Rome see Chapter III, n. 38 above.

city blocks: the size of blocks formed by the *cardines* and *decumani* (see *cardo* and *decumanus*) varied from city to city and sometimes within a city (e.g. *Cosa* [q.v.], BOLOGNA and FLORENCE); however, the blocks at AOSTA, TURIN, and VERONA were about 240 Roman feet (72 meters or 233 English feet) square, an area of 2 Roman *iugera* (see centuriation); those at Roman CARTHAGE were 480 by 120 Roman feet and those at ORANGE may have been 240 by 120 feet; at TIMGAD, they were 70 Roman feet square (all these measurements are approximate); for blocks in Romano-Celtic towns, see SILCHESTER and WROXETER; the Latin word *insula* (meaning "island") was used both for "city block" and for the apartment buildings contained in a city block (see OSTIA ANTICA; Homo, *Rome impériale* 552-579; Grimal, *Civ. Rome* 302-305, illustration 202; and Carcopino, *Daily Life* 351 [index, under *"insulae"*]).

city walls, comparison in length: see cities, comparison in area

civitas: the Latin word for a local government, used for Greek "poleis" (or cities) and Celtic tribes; used for cities other than *coloniae* or *municipia;* in late Latin, *civitas* may mean *municipium* (see MAINZ) or colony (see the *Notitia Galliarum* in Seeck's edition of the *Notitia Dignitatum,* q.v.); the English word "city" is derived from it through the French word "cité"; in Latin, *civitas* also meant "citizenship."

client-kings (of Rome): they administered border areas both inside and outside the Roman Empire; since such kingdoms were often incorporated into Roman provinces, these served as an intermediate stage in this process; see CHERCHELL, SILCHESTER, *Volubilis;* P. C. Sands, *The Client Princes of the Roman Empire* (Cambridge 1908; rpt. New York 1975).

colonia (or colony): originally a military colony of Roman citizens or those with Latin rights (q.v.); also see "Latins"; next, they were settled by veterans who had completed their term of service; in the late Republic, some were settled by the poor of Rome (see OSUNA); veteran-colonies were still the most common sort in the 1st century A.D., but, as the Roman Empire matured, most colonies were honorary, yet with full rights, Latin or Roman, as stated; *municipia* (q.v.) asked the emperor to be promoted to colonial status purely for the sake of prestige; for a tax-privilege, see *ius Italicum;* for lists of colonies, see Nissen, *IL* II 27-29, 31-33; Frank, *ESAR* I 40-41, 59-60, 122-123, 220; Vittinghoff, *Roemische Kolonisation* 148-150; Brunt, *Italian Manpower* 589-602 (list of colonies by provinces); Salmon, *RC* 110-111 (Latin colonies), 158-164; also see *RE* IV (1901) 511-588 (E. Kornemann); Abbott and Johnson, *Municipal Administration* 3-8; Bengtson, *Atlas* 31c (colonies up to 133 B.C.), with *Erlaeuterungen; Cambridge Ancient History* VII[2] (1954) map 12, with a list up to 241 B.C.; note that *colonia* refers to a city with its *territorium* (q.v.).

colonies in *Britannia: Camulodunum* (Colchester, Essex), 41/54; *Glevum* 96/98 (+Gloucester, Gloucestershire); *Lindum* (Lincoln, Lincolnshire) and *Eboracum* (York, Yorkshire) dates unknown; all were Roman colonies for veterans; see I. A. Richmond, "The Four Coloniae of Roman Britain," *Archaeological Journal* 103 (1946): 57-84, Rivet, *TCRB* p. 63 and recent issues of the periodical *Bri-*

tannia: 8 (1977): 65-105 (Colchester), 10 (1979): 383-385 (York), 11 (1980): 73-114 (Gloucester), 61-72 (Lincoln); for their roles as provincial cities, Mommsen unfavorably compared Colchester to LYONS and York to MAINZ, *Provinces,* Chapter V.

colonies in *Gallia Narbonensis* (q.v.): the first Roman colony was NARBONNE in 118 B.C.; there were five colonies for legionary veterans; NARBONNE in 46 B.C., ARLES in 45 B.C. (both founded for Julius Caesar by Tiberius Claudius Nero, the father of the Emperor Tiberius); NARBONNE was settled by veterans of the Tenth Legion and ARLES by those of the Sixth; + Béziers was founded 36/27 B.C. for veterans of the Seventh Legion, ORANGE 35/33 B.C. for the Second Legion and FREJUS in 30 for the Eighth; Cavaillon (q.v.) was an honorary Roman colony of 41 B.C.-A.D. 14; Latin colonies included Carpentras 58/44 B.C., VIENNE in 58/52, NIMES in 28 and Aix-en-Provence 27 B.C.-A.D. 14; see *CAH* IX² (1951) 957 (bibl.), Vittinghoff, *Romische Kolonisation* 100-101, Salmon, *RC* 160-161, Février, "CSG" 19-20 and Brunt, *Italian Manpower* 589-590.

concrete: a material for building invented by the Romans; it was made of mortar (lime and sand), mixed with crushed rock or bricks; see building methods, Roman.

cornice: any projecting ornamental molding along the top of a building, entablature, wall or arch, finishing or crowning it

cryptoporticus or cryptoportico: see p. 43 above; also see AOSTA, ARLES, NARBONNE, TRIER; an enclosed gallery having walls with openings instead of columns; a covered or subterranean passage; see *Les cryptoportiques dans l'architecture romaine,* Collection de l'Ecole française de Rome 14 (Rome 1973), esp. R. A. Staccioli, "Sulla destinazione e l'uso dei cryptoportici," pp. 57-66; he thinks that both public and private ones (such as at the House of the Cryptoporticus at *Pompeii)* were areas for strolling out of the sun or bad weather; in Late Roman times, they were turned into storehouses; in their original function, cryptoporticoes were precursors of Montreal's underground shopping areas.

curia: see pp. 46-48 above; the Senate-House in Rome and the meeting-house of the local orders of decurions

decumanus: see p. 11 and city blocks above; the main *decumanus* was often called the *decumanus maximus,* but we sometimes say just the *decumanus.*

decurion: see pp. 6, 46-48 above; a member of the City Council (Order of Decurions) of a Latin-speaking city; the decurions usually served for life in a body of 100 men; new members were chosen by the Council itself; they met in the *curia* (q.v.) of their city; see OSUNA (text of charter) and Abbott and Johnson, *Municipal Administration* 64-68.

duoviri, duumviri or duovirs: see p. 49 above; the two chief magistrates of a *colonia* or *municipium* were usually called the *duoviri;* the model was that of the two consuls of Rome, at the same time a city and the capital of an Empire; elected by the citizens of their city (see *forum*), the *duoviri* served for one year; see OSUNA (text of charter) and Abbott and Johnson, *Municipal Administration* 59-63; also see Latin rights below; the order of holding these offices was quaestor (q.v.), then aedile (q.v.), then *duovir*.

Etruscans: a non-Indo-European people of ancient Italy; their origin is still an unsolved problem; see J. B. Ward-Perkins, "The Problem of Etruscan Origins," *Harvard Studies in Classical Philology* 64 (1959): 1-26; *OCD* 410-411; Finley, *Atlas* 116-117 and Ogilvie, *Early Rome* 11-14; on them, also see R. Bloch, *The Etruscans* (New York 1958), Christ, *Bibl.* 106-112 and D. Ridgway in Prag, *AR* p. 62; expanding south out of *Etruria* but around Rome, the Etruscans took control of Campania in the 7th century B.C. (see CAPUA VETERE); they seized Rome c. 600 B.C., and during the 6th century their power spread as far north as Emilia (see MARZA-BOTTO, BOLOGNA and Ogilvie, *Early Rome* 160); the Etruscans (a small number) were cast out of Rome c. 455 B.C.; their power in Italy declined after the Samnite conquest of Campania c. 450-420 and the Gallic invasion of the early 4th century; the disunited Etruscan cities were conquered by the Romans in the 4th and 3rd centuries B.C.; the Etruscans gave their name to the region of *Etruria* (Tuscany today) and the Tyrrhenian Sea; on Etruscan art see: M. Sprenger and G. Bartolini, *Die Etrusker: Kunst und Geschichte* (Munich 1977, photogr. M. and A. Hirmer); L. von Matt et al., *The Art of the Etruscans* (New York 1970), transl. from the Italian; O.J. Brendel and E. Richardson, *Etruscan Art* (Harmondsworth, Middlesex, 1978).

finances, city: taxes were paid on real estate and sales, as well as local imports and exports; cities earned income by renting out shops and land (as at ORANGE); in addition, all local magistrates and decurions (q.v.) served unpaid and usually paid subsidies to the city; on city finances, see Frank, *ESAR* V 94-106 and Rostovtzeff, *SEHRE* 143, 145-150; on exemption from "federal" taxes to Rome, see *ius Italicum* below.

fora, comparison in size: from S. Frere in *ANRW* II.3 (1975) 322:

LONDON	29,392 m²
+ *Verulamium*	18,415 m²
SILCHESTER	8,455 m²
TRIER	37,400 m²
ST.-BERTRAND-DE-COMMINGES	13,200 m²
PARIS	16,000 m²
AUGST	10,439 m²
ALISE-STE.-REINE (*Alesia*)	4,800 m²

see Wacher, *TRB* 42, 46, 60 on British *fora;* Harmand, *Occ. rom.* p. 323 (seven *fora* from North Africa to Britain), Lavedan, *HU* p. 473 (PARIS, AUGST and ST.-BERTRAND-DE-COMMINGES); also see Ward-Perkins, "Republic to Empire"

forum: see pp. 7, 41-43 above; the buildings mentioned on p. 7 and porticoes (p. 41) surrounded the *forum*, which could be entered only on foot; it was the center literally and figuratively of the Roman city, usually at the junction of the *cardo* with the *decumanus,* and it was used for assemblies of the city's citizens; one was at the same time a Roman citizen and the citizen of a city or *civitas* (q.v.); see: H. Stuart Jones, *Companion* 95-109; Caprino, *MAR, Bibl.* 236-240; R. G. Goodchild, "The Origins of the Romano-British Forum," *Antiquity* 20 (1946): 70-77; Wheeler, *RAA* 100-115; Castagnoli, *Orthogonal Town Planning* p. 121; R. Martin, "Agora and Forum," *Mélanges de l'Ecole française de Rome, Antiquité* 84 (1972): 903-933 (includes PARIS).

Franks: a group or groups of Germanic tribes, living on the east bank of the middle and lower Rhine; by the 3rd century A.D., they had achieved some sort of unity; invading Gaul under King Clovis, they defeated the remnants of the Romans in 486 at Soissons (in *Gallia Belgica* and the present-day département of Aisne, France); Clovis made PARIS his capital and converted from paganism to Roman Catholicism; the Franks gave their name to France (formerly *Gallia Transalpina,* q.v.) and to Franconia in northern Bavaria, a state of the Federal Republic of Germany (also see Lombards).

Gallia Belgica: the northeast part of *Gallia Comata* (q.v.); also see TRIER

Gallia Cisalpina (Cisalpine Gaul): for a general survey, see Chilver, *Cisalpine Gaul;* in 89 B.C., its inhabitants north of the Po received Latin rights and those to the south, Roman citizenship; the former received Roman citizenship in 49 B.C. (except for the Alpine tribes); the province was incorporated into Italy (becoming its northern part) in 42 B.C.; see the *Lex Rubria de* (Law of Rubrius on) *Gallia Cisalpina* (= Riccobono, *FIRA*² I no. 19) and the Edict of Claudius *De Civitate Anaunorum* (Roman citizenship of a tribe near Trent = *FIRA*² I no. 71); both are also in E. G. Hardy, *Roman Laws and Charters* (Oxford 1912): translations and commentaries; there is a translation of Claudius' edict in A. H. M. Jones, *HR* II 287-288; cf. U. Ewins, "The Enfranchisement of Cisalpine Gaul," *Papers of the British School at Rome* 23 (1955): 73-98 and Taylor, *Voting Districts* 129 as well.

Gallia Comata ("Long-Haired Gaul"): the part of Gaul conquered by Julius Caesar (58-49 B.C.); it was divided into three provinces by Augustus, c. 27 B.C., *Aquitania* (q.v.), *Gallia Lugdunensis* and *Gallia Belgica;* on administration, see LYONS; on the cities Rostovtzeff remarks that, generally in late antiquity, their proper name was replaced by the name of the local tribe (e.g. Parisii for Lutetia) and that their wealth usually came from the land and not urban commerce *(SEHRE* 219); the three provinces were subdivided by the Emperor Diocletian (284-305 A.D.); see S. J. de Laet, "La Gaule septentrionale à l'époque romaine . . .," *Bulletin de l'Institut historique belge de Rome* 26 (1950).

Gallia Narbonensis: lying between *Gallia Cisalpina* (q.v.) and Spain, it was annexed by Rome in 121 B.C.; it became the medieval French region of Languedoc, west of the Rhône River, and Provence, east of it; see Février, "CSG" and J. Koenig, *Die Meilensteine der Gallia Narbonensis,* Itinera Romana 3 (Berne 1970) 9-27, 291-298 (bibl.).

Gallia Transalpina (in English, Transalpine Gaul or Gaul) = *Gallia Comata* and *Gallia Narbonensis* (qq.v.); see especially *HFU;* on the history down to 59 B.C., see J. J. Hatt, *Histoire de la Gaule romaine...* (Paris 1959) and Ebel, *TG;* the geographical survey by the historian Ammianus Marcellinus (15.11, late 4th century, q.v.) and the *Notitia Galliarum* in Seeck's edition of the *Notitia Dignitatum* (q.v.) are worth looking at, as the Gallic cities of the Late Empire are catalogued; on the economic geography of the present-day towns and cities, see *Grand Larousse encyclopédique* I (Paris 1960) and *Le petit Robert* 2 (Paris 1977); (they cover other regions as well).

Gaul = *Gallia Transalpina* (q.v.)

Gauls: the Celts residing in *Gallia Cisalpina* and *Gallia Transalpina* (qq.v.); the history of the Celtic migrations is quite difficult to discern.

gens: a Roman clan, or group of families, linked together by a common *nomen* (family name) and their belief in a common ancestor; see Fustel de Coulanges, *Ancient City* 100-116

groma: see pp. 11, 15 above and Rykwert, *Idea* 50-51; the Latin word very probably came from the Greek word, "gnomon" (with the same meaning), by way of Etruscan; hence, the junction of the main *decumanus* and *cardo.*

headers and stretchers: the former are bricks or stones laid with their ends towards the face of a wall; the latter are laid with the lengths parallel to the face of the wall.

Hellenistic (adj.): pertaining to Greek art and culture after 323 B.C. (the death of Alexander the Great, who had spread them as far as western India; some dilution of Greek culture by native elements was inevitable); pertaining to the kingdoms ruled by the successors of Alexander (323 B.C. to the various dates of Roman conquest; the latest was Egypt in 31 B.C.); a number of urban centers were established in Asia during the Hellenistic period.

Hispania: under Augustus in 16/13 B.C., Roman *Hispania* (= modern Spain and Portugal) was divided into three provinces: *Tarraconensis* (capital Tarragona on the Mediterranean, cf. AMPURIAS; on Tarragona see *RE*. Supplement 15 [1978]); *Baetica* (capital Cordova; see ITALICA and OSUNA) and *Lusitania* (capital + Mérida); in A.D. 69/79, all of *Hispania* received Latin rights (q.v.); for *Hispania* under the Germanic invaders (fifth-eighth centuries), see Vandals and Visigoths below; for the three provinces, see the map in A. Tovar and J. M. Blázquez Martínez, "Geschichte des roemischen Hispanien" in *ANRW* II.3 (1975), between pp. 432 and 433; also see Boëthius and Ward-Perkins, *ERA* 340-341; J. M. Blázquez, "Ciudades hispanas de la época de Augusto," *Simposio de ciudades augusteas de Hispania, Bimilenario de Zaragoza, 29 sept.- 2 oct. 1976* (Saragossa 1976) 79-136; E. Albertini, *Les divisions administratives de l'Espagne romaine* (Paris 1923); A. García y Bellido, "Die Latinisierung Hispaniens" in *ANRW* I.1 (1972) 462-500 (with bibl. by M. Koch); J. M. Blázquez, "The Rejection and Assimilation of Roman Culture in Hispania during the Fourth and Fifth Centuries," *Classical Folia* 32 (1978): 217-242; R. Etienne, *Le culte impérial dans la peninsule ibérique d'Auguste à Dioclétien,* BEFAR 191 (Paris 1958); H. Galsterer, *Untersuchungen zum roemischen Staedtewesen auf dem iberischen Halbinsel,* Madrider Forschungen 8 (Berlin 1971); F. Wattenberg, *Carta arqueológica de España* (Valladolid 1974); references in P. O. Spann, *Transactions of the American Philological Association* 111 (1981): 229 n. 1.

insulae: see city blocks above

Ionia: the central section of the west coast of Anatolia, the peninsula which forms the main part of present-day Turkey in Asia; Ionia became a part of the Roman province of *Asia,* whose capital was Ephesus.

Italic (adj.): pertaining to the languages or peoples of ancient Italy, especially those of Indo-European descent (not the Etruscans, q.v.)

ius Italicum: freedom from land and poll (head) taxes to the government at Rome; the privilege of Italy, it was gradually spread to privileged cities beyond.

Late, or Later, Roman (adj.): c. A.D. 284-565, both in the East and the West of the Roman world; the term can overlap with Byzantine (q.v.); see *EB* XXIII pp. 510-525 (J. B. Bury), A. H. M. Jones, *LRE* and G. Downey, *The Late Roman Empire* (New York 1969).

Latin rights *(ius Latii):* the holder had a status somewhat below that of a Roman citizen; until c. 150 B.C., he could obtain Roman citizenship simply by moving to Rome; after 150, the magistrates of Latin cities received Roman citizenship; from 89 B.C., when those with Latin rights in Italy received Roman citizenship, the status continued to have legal validity, since it was accorded to cities or individuals, not ethnically Latins (q.v.), as an intermediate step towards Roman citizenship; cf. C. Saumagne, *Le droit latin et les cités romaines sous l'Empire, essais critiques* (Paris 1965) and Sherwin-White, *RC* 360-379; in A.D. 212, the Emperor Caracalla granted Roman citizenship to all in the Empire except slaves and criminals.

Latins: the inhabitants of *Latium* (a region of Italy); they spoke Latin, an Italic language; on Etruscan (q.v.) lines of communication through *Latium* in the 7th and 6th centuries B.C., see Alfoeldi, *Early Rome* 185-192; Rome's power over the other Latin cities was firmly established by 338 B.C.; legally speaking, the terms "Roman" and "Latin" then became distinct; under Roman rule, the Latins had a special legal status (see Latin rights); Latin colonies (see *colonia)* were founded by Romans and/or Latins; their inhabitants had Latin rights but not Roman citizenship; from late in the 4th century B.C., Latin colonies were founded outside of *Latium;* in 89 B.C. the Latins in Italy were granted Roman citizenship.

legion (in Latin, *legio):* an infantry unit of Roman citizens, of 4,000 to 6,000 men; in A.D. 14, there were 25 such legions; later the number was slightly increased; c. A.D. 290, Diocletian reduced the size and greatly increased the number of legions; cf. *CAH* X^2 (1952) 222-228 (G. H. Stevenson), as well as *KP* and *OCD.*

legions in the Roman West: in *Britannia* — for a chart and bibl., see WROXETER; in *Germania* — for a list and bibl., see MAINZ; also see ITALICA (for *Hispania*) and *Lambaesis* (North Africa); on the towns near these camps, see *canabae* above

limes: a Roman frontier, fortified or not; the precise meaning depends on the context; on fortified frontiers cf. Mommsen's note in *Provinces,* chapter IV and Ziegler, *KP* III (1969) 652-665 (H. Volkmann et al.).

Lombards: a central-Germanic people, perhaps originating in the valley of the upper Elbe; they invaded Italy in A.D. 568 and gave their name to Lombardy, now a region of northern Italy whose capital is Milan (see MANTUA); the Frankish king Charlemagne was crowned king of the Lombards (as well as the Franks, q.v.) in A.D. 774 (see RAVENNA) at Monza in Lombardy.

measurements of distance, Roman: 1 Roman mile = .919 (preferred) or .935 English mile = 5,000 Roman feet; 1 Roman foot *(pes)* = 11.62 English inches

metric measurements, converted to English ones: 1 hectare (ha.) = 2.471 acres; 1 kilometer (km.) = .621 mile (There are 640 acres in a square English mile, and one square km. equals 100 ha.)

mint of the Later Roman Empire: even some years before, but mainly as a result of Diocletian's (A.D. 284-305) coinage reforms, continued by Constantine I (306-337), imperial mints were established at a few major cities besides Rome: LONDON, TRIER, LYONS, ARLES, Milan, Pavia, RAVENNA and CARTHAGE; this step is indicative of the importance of these cities in the Later Roman period and of their status as imperial residences; cf. *Notitia Dignitatum* (q.v.) *Oc.* (West) 11 (the Minister of Finance), P. V. Hill, J. P. C. Kent and R. A. G. Carson, *Late Roman Bronze Coinage* (London 1965) and A. H. M. Jones, *LRE* I pp. 435-437.

mints of the Roman Empire: Rome and LYONS (q.v.); some cities had local coinages, for example NIMES (q.v.).

mundus: see p. 14 above, Castagnoli, *Orthogonal Town Planning* 79 and Rykwert, *Idea* 59; for a psychological view, see A. Jaffé in C.G. Jung et al., *Man and his Symbols* (New York 1968) 269 (ref. provided by L. Baryluk); the mundus at *Cosa* (q.v.) has been found.

municipium: a city with either Latin rights (q.v.) or Roman citizenship; similar in this way to *coloniae, municipia* ranked below them in prestige; see Abbott and Johnson, *Municipal Administration* 8-9, *RE* XVI.1 (1933) 570-638 (E. Kornemann), E. Schoenbauer, "Municipia und coloniae in der Prinzipatzeit," *Oesterr. Akad. d.*

Wiss., Phil.-Hist. Klasse, Anzeiger 91 (1954): 13-49, A. H. M. Jones, *HR* I pp. 247-249 (transl. of Festus' definition), J. Gascou, "Municipia civium Romanorum," *Latomus* 30 (1971) 132-141 and Brunt, *Italian Manpower* 602-607, "Appendix 16, List of Provincial *Municipia* down to A.D. 14."

Normans: a Germanic people from Scandinavia; in the tenth century they conquered and gave their name to the region of Normandy in northwest France; coming from Normandy in the eleventh century, a group of them took southern Italy with Sicily (see TAORMINA), while others conquered England.

Numidia: roughly, the eastern part of present-day Algeria; a Roman client-kingdom (q.v.) from 203 B.C., it was merged into the province of *Africa Proconsularis* (see CARTHAGE) in the 1st century A.D.; in 197/198 Septimius Severus made it a separate Roman province, with its capital at *Lambaesis;* the capital was moved to CONSTANTINE 313/337; see C. R. Whittaker, *Journal of Roman Studies* 68 (1978): 191 for bibl.

odeum (Latin; in Greek "odeion"): a small roofed theater for musical performances

oppidum: in Latin, "town"; used by the Romans for native settlements in the West; they were usually within the territory of a tribe or *civitas;* sometimes the word was used for any town or city.

orders of architecture, Greek: see fig. 36A below

Oscans: the prehistoric inhabitants of Campania, Italy; conquered by the Samnites (q.v.) c. 450-420 B.C., the Oscans were absorbed by them; the Italic language imposed on the new group then is called "Oscan."

Ostrogoths: a Germanic people, closely related to the Visigoths and Vandals (qq.v.), who had similar histories; they probably migrated from Scandinavia to the Ukraine early in the Christian era; in the 5th century, they went to *Pannonia* (modern Hungary) as so-called allies of the Byzantine (q.v.) Empire; under King Theodoric, the Ostrogoths invaded Italy in A.D. 489 and conquered it; they were defeated by the Byzantines in A.D. 552 near Mount Vesuvius and disappeared from history; see RAVENNA (their main capital), VERONA, ARLES, *Volsinii,* as well as G. M. Woloch, "A Survey of Scholarship on Ostrogothic Italy . . .," *Classical Folia* 25 (1971): 320-331; 350-356 (bibl.) and H. Wolfram, *Geschichte der Goten* (Munich 1979).

paganus: the inhabitant of a *pagus,* an area of land used for mining, lumbering, hunting or farming; such *pagi* were usually legally at-

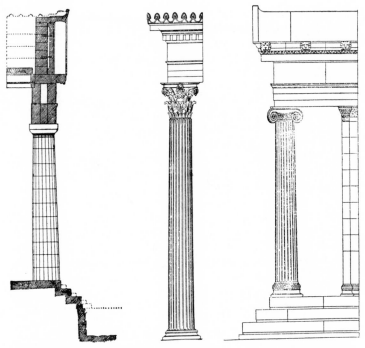

Figure 36A. Orders of Greek Architecture
From *EB* XX pp. 177-179
Doric Order   Corinthian Order   Ionic Order

tached to the nearest municipality (see Abbott and Johnson, *Mu-nicipal Administration* 14-15; on *pagus*, see Grenier, *Manuel* I pp. 145-146); the Latin word, *"paganus,"* carries the meaning of "un-cultured" (for cities were the centers of civilization) and, later, "non-Christian" (see J. J. O'Donnel, *Classical Folia* 31 [1977] 163-170).

peristyle: inner, colonnaded garden court of Pompeian and Hellen-istic homes (McKay, *Houses* 271)

pomerium: a religious boundary around Rome and her colonies; it was marked by *cippi* (stones) and was ideally quadrangular in out-line; it was often distinct from the city wall and limit of settlement; corpses had to be cremated and buried *outside* all *pomeria;* ac-cording to legend, the original *pomerium* at Rome enclosed the Palatine Hill and was extended by King Servius Tullius (mid 6th century B.C.); later, it was enlarged by the dictators Sulla (c. 80

Figure 36B. The Arcade Order
The Greek orders were modified by the Romans for use as semi-detached columns between arches (compare Figure 17). From *EB* XX p. 182

B.C.) and Caesar (45 B.C.), as well as the emperors Claudius (A.D. 47) and Vespasian (A.D. 73); revealed by finds of *cippi,* the imperial *pomerium* followed the Servian Wall on the east and included the Aventine Hill, the *Emporium,* the southern half of the Campus Martius and all of the Pincian Hill (see fig. 6 and pp. 5, 28, 30 above); see Tacitus, *Annals* 12.24; T. Mommsen, "Der Begriff des Pomerium," *Hermes* 10 (1876): 40-50 = *Roemische Forschungen* II (Berlin 1879), rpt. Hildesheim 1962 pp. 23-41; H. Stuart Jones, *Companion* 30-36; J. H. Oliver, *Memoirs of the American Academy in Rome* 10 (1932); M. Labrousse, "Le pomerium de la Rome impériale," *Mélanges...Ecole française de Rome* 54 (1937): 165-199; Homo, *Rome impériale* 93-97; J. Le Gall, "A propos de la muraille servienne et du pomerium," *Etudes d'archéologie classique* 2 (1959); Grimal, *Civ. Rome* 135, 147, 253-254, 487; R. M. Ogilvie, *A Commentary on Livy, Books 1-5* (Oxford 1965) 179-180; *OCD* 856 (I. A. Richmond and J. North); Ziegler, *KP* IV (1972) 1015-1017 (B. R. Voss); Carcopino, *Daily Life* 316, n. 17 (bibl. note by H. T. Rowell); Rykwert, *Idea* 239 (index).

portico: a roofed space, outlined by columns at least on the front; usually it formed the entrance to a temple or house.

Punic: pertaining to CARTHAGE (see Carthaginian above)

quaestors: the financial officers of a *municipium* or *colonia;* the number varied from three to seven (see Abbott and Johnson, *Municipal Administration* 59, 64); in the government of Rome, there were twenty quaestors a year under Sulla and under Augustus and following; during the Empire, no quaestors (except for a brief period) were in charge of the Senate's treasury, but some of them served as the financial officers of certain provinces.

Sabines: an Italic people, probably Oscan-speaking and of whom the Samnites (q.v.) are thought to have been a branch; the Sabines' hill-top towns were located in the northern part (now in Latium) of the ancient region of *Samnium,* northeast of *Tibur* (see TIVOLI); the legends connecting primitive Rome with the Sabines probably have some basis in fact—some of the Sabines migrated to Rome; Rome conquered the Sabine country in 290 B.C., and they became Roman citizens in 268 (well before the Samnites); the link to Rome was the *Via Nomentana.*

Samnites: a people who spoke Oscan, an Italic language related to Latin; coming from and keeping the Apennine (q.v.) region of *Samnium* in central Italy, they conquered Campania c. 450-420 B.C.; the Romans won control of northern Campania by 341 and conquered all the Samnites by 201 B.C.; see Oscans above, CAPUA VETERE, *Pompeii* and E. T. Salmon, *Samnium and the Samnites* (Cambridge 1967).

Saxons: a Germanic tribe which originated in the southern part of Jutland (the Cimbric peninsula now shared by Denmark and the Federal Republic of Germany); these lands lay south of those belonging to the Angles (q.v.); some of the Saxons invaded Britain about A.D. 480 and settled mainly in the south of the island in Wessex (that is, the upper Thames valley and the lower Severn), Essex, Middlesex and Sussex; others remained behind on the Continent; in 531 these conquered Thuringia (now a region in the southwest corner of the German Democratic Republic); in 566, they were conquered by the Franks (q.v.); the continental Saxons gave their name to the state of Lower Saxony in the north of the F.R.G. and to the region of Saxony in the southeast G.D.R.

siphon, inverted: for aqueducts, see fig. 37 below

templum: 1) a consecrated area in the sky; see auspices above; 2) a consecrated area on the ground for omens or sacrifices (see Castagnoli, *Orthogonal Town Planning* 75-79 and Rykwert, *Idea* 45-48 on 1 and 2); 3) a place consecrated to a particular deity; a temple

terramara (or terremare, pl.): a bronze-age culture of Emilia, a region in Italy; see pp. 20-21 above

territorium: all the land in the Roman Empire had to belong to some city or other; the *territorium* was the land outside the city limits "attributed" or belonging to the city; for the Roman, "the country was an adjunct of the town (city), not the town of the country" (Rivet, *TCRB* 65); see p. 6 above.

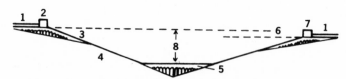

Figure 37. Inverted Siphon on the Garon (5 km southwest of Lyons)
Following J. Burdy, *Promenades gallo-romaines* I (Lyons 1977) p. 84

1. Channel	5. Siphon bridge
2. Header tank	6. Difference in height
3. Masonry ramp	7. Receiving tank
4. Pipe system	8. Depth

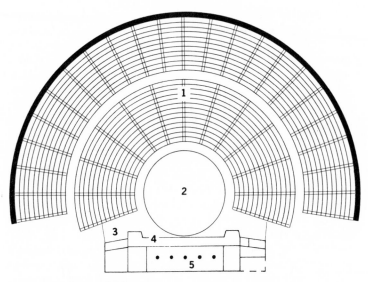

Figure 38. The Greek Theater

1. Cavea
2. Orchestra
3. Parados

4. Proskenion
5. Skene

theater, Greek: see fig. 38

Tripolitania: the region which we call Tripolitania (from "three cities" in Greek) takes its name from three ancient cities and is part of the present-day country of Libya; *Sabratha* and *Lepcis Magna* (qq.v.) are no more than archaeological sites today, while *Oea* continues to exist as the capital of Libya under the name of Tarabulus (in Arabic; Tripoli in Italian); founded by the Carthaginians (q.v.), the cities came under Roman rule in the 1st century B.C., compare p. 8 above; *Tripolitania* was organized as a separate Roman province A.D. 284/305 with its capital at *Lepcis Magna;* the three cities were conquered by the Vandals (q.v.) in the 5th century A.D., by the Byzantines (q.v.) in the 6th and the Arabs in the 7th; more recently, Tripolitania was taken by the Turks in 1511 and the Italians in 1911; Libya became independent in 1951.

tyrant: one-man ruler of a Greek city-state; his rule was obtained by force or by inheritance from someone who had; the institution of tyranny died out in Greece by 480 B.C. but continued in Sicily through the Hellenistic (q.v.) period.

Umbrian: an Italic language closely related to Oscan (see Oscans, Samnites); it was spoken in the central Italian region of *Umbria*.

Vandals: a Germanic people, closely related to the Ostrogoths and Visigoths; they crossed into the Roman Empire at MAINZ in A.D. 406 and conquered southern *Hispania* (q.v.) in 409 (also see IT-ALICA); they were pushed into North Africa by the Visigoths in 429; their capital there was CARTHAGE, till the Byzantine (q.v.) conquest of 533; the Vandals may have given their name to southern Spain: Andalusia (= Roman *Baetica*).

Visigoths: a Germanic people, closely related to the Ostrogoths and Vandals (qq.v.), who had similar histories; they crossed the lower Danube into the Byzantine (q.v.) or Later Roman (q.v.) Empire in A.D. 376; next, they migrated westward, sacking Rome in 410; in 412, they settled in southern Gaul and northern Spain; they took southern *Hispania* (q.v.) from the Vandals in 429; their capital at this time was TOULOUSE; defeated by the Franks (q.v.) in Gaul in 507, they left most of their Gallic possessions but kept NAR-BONNE (and NIMES); the next capital of the Visigoths was Toledo; in 6th century Spain, the Visigoths were attacked by the Byzantines; they were defeated there by the Arabs in 711.

Maps

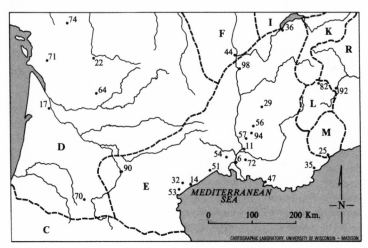

Map 1. Southern Gaul

Roman Provinces

A. Baetica	I. Germania Superior	Q. Illyricum
B. Lusitania	J. Britannia	R. Italia
C. Hispania	K. Alpes Graiae et	S. Sicilia
Tarraconensis	Poeninae	T. Africa
D. Aquitania	L. Alpes Cottiae	U. Numidia
E. Gallia Narbonensis	M. Alpes Maritimae	V. Mauretania
F. Gallia Lugdunensis	N. Raetia	Caesariensis
G. Gallia Belgica	O. Noricum	W. Mauretania
H. Germania Inferior	P. Pannonia	Tingitana

Roman Sites

Italics indicate a site for which the modern name is used because the ancient name is unknown.

1. Alba Fucens	40. Lambaesis	75. Segesta
2. Alba Longa	41. Legio	76. Selinunte
3. Alesia	42. Lepcis Magna	77. Sitifis
4. Emporiae	43. Londinium	78. Hispalis
5. Augusta Praetoria	44. Lugdunum	79. Calleva Atrebatum
6. Arelate	45. Mogontiacum	80. Spina
7. Asisium	46. Mantua	81. Sublaqueum
8. Augusta Raurica	47. Massilia	82. Segusio
9. Augustodunum	48. *Marzabotto*	83. Tingis
10. Aventicum	49. Augusta Emerita	84. Tauromenium
11. Avenio	50. Mutina	85. Tarquinii
12. Valentia Banasa	51. *Montpellier*	86. Thurii
13. Basilia	52. Neapolis	87. Thamugadi
14. Baeterrae	53. Narbo	88. Tipasa
15. Bononia	54. Nemausus	89. Tibur
16. Volsinii Novi	55. Norba	90. Tolosa
17. Burdigala	56. Noviomagus	91. Augusta
18. Isca Silurum	Tricastinorum	Treverorum
19. Casilinum	57. Arausio	92. Augusta
20. Capua	58. Ostia	Taurinorum
21. Carthago	59. Urso	93. Tusculum
22. Cassinomagus	60. Paestum	94. Vasio Vocontiorum
23. Caesarea	61. Praeneste	95. Verona
24. Deva	62. Lutetia Parisiorum	96. Verulamium
25. Cemenelum	63. Parma	97. Vetulonia
26. Colonia Agrippina	64. Vesunna	98. Vienna
27. Cirta	Petrucoriorum	99. *Orvieto*
28. Cosa	65. Pompeii	100. Volubilis
29. Dea	66. Ravenna	101. Aquae Mattiacae
30. Cuicul	67. Durocortorum	102. Viroconium
31. Thugga	68. Roma	Cornoviorum
32. *Ensérune*	69. Sabratha	
33. Faesulae	70. Lugdunum	
34. Florentia	Convenarum	
35. Forum Iulii	71. Mediolanum	
36. Genava	Santonum	
37. Glevum	72. Glanum	
38. Italica	73. *St-Romain-en-Gal*	
39. Igilgili	74. *Sanxay*	

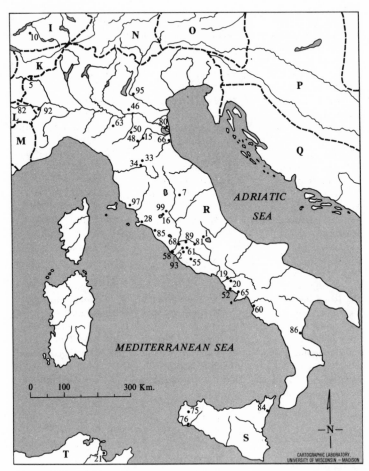

Map 2. Roman Italy

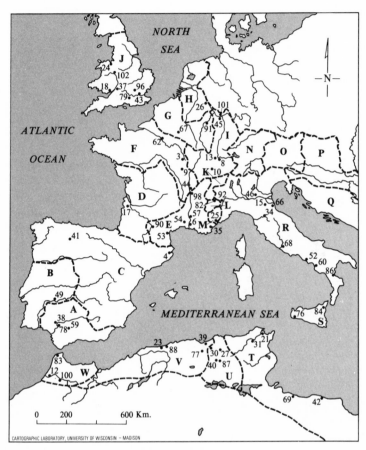

Map 3. Western Provinces of the Roman Empire